BUSINESS MAGNETISM

BUSINESS MAGNETISM

The power of partnership

Lars Thinggaard

Published by Milestone Systems A/S
Banemarksvej 50, 2605 Brøndby, Copenhagen, Denmark

milestonesys.com

ISBN: 978-0-615-89214-6

*Dedicated to my wife, Mette,
and our children Jens Christian,
Carl Emil and Helena.
Thank you for your unconditional
support over the years.*

Lars Thinggaard

President and CEO
Milestone Systems A/S

CONTENTS

BUSINESS MAGNETISM

Over 17 years, Milestone Systems has grown from a fledgling start-up to a major player in the world of video surveillance, driving the industry's move into the digital era, and now redefining industry expectations about what a video surveillance system can be – and do. When co-founders John Blem and Henrik Friborg Jacobsen established the business, they saw an opportunity: for software that could monitor, record, and retrieve video images in digital format.

Lars Thinggaard, now Milestone's president and CEO, came on board in 2003, bringing with him an entrepreneurial background and spirit of distinct Scandinavian leadership which has guided the company to the top of its market. This is Lars' story, and the story of Milestone. It's about uniting a fragmented industry around a unique vision. It's about the leadership required to bring together a business ecosystem, and the courage needed to adapt and change in the face of a turbulent economy. It's about looking to the future, learning from the past, and being open to new ideas. This is the story of a small, ambitious business, flourishing at the start of the 21st century, through leadership, openness, and partnership.

PRAISE FOR BUSINESS MAGNETISM

It has been a privilege... *to witness Lars' unique and highly effective management style. In this book he shares some of his secrets and it has become obligatory reading for all the entrepreneurs I am working with!"*

Tony Zappala, Highland Capital Partners Europe

I appreciated reading... *this great book and Lars Thinggaard's insightful views on IP video, partnership and how to build a business ecosystem. Open platforms are certainly in their DNA and something I really believe in. This book describes how the industry has benefited from the open approach driving the shift from analog to IP."*

Martin Gren, Founder, Director new Projects, AXIS

This book demonstrates... *how unlimited imagination can lead to a big change in the physical security industry. Lars and the co-founders' insight drove toward a unique vision for the future that was not achieved by others. You will be amazed at how they bring the players together to grow a successful business in the ecosystem."*

Cheolkyo Kim, CEO of Samsung Techwin

I think the highlight... *of the book was the leadership compass. You have defined measurable behaviors of leaders. I'm not sure I have seen anyone else that has done this to the extent you have. I will use this at our next leadership meeting."*

Phil Aronson, President, ASG

While telling the Milestone story... *Lars shares his first-hand experience in leading a self-funded startup, which grew from its Danish roots to become a global leader in its sector. This is interesting and valuable reading for entrepreneurs and anyone interested in startups."*

Giuseppe Zocco, Co-founder and Partner, Index Ventures

ABOUT THE AUTHOR

Lars Thinggaard is President and CEO of Milestone Systems A/S. Lars is a dynamic manager with years of entrepreneurial experience. He was Co-founder and CFO at Mondosoft, COO and CFO at Beologic (acquired by Baan), CFO at In2itive (acquired by SPSS), Auditor at Arthur Andersen and at Price Waterhouse, now Price Waterhouse Coopers. He holds a Bachelor's degree in Corporate Finance and Accounting from the Copenhagen Business School.

Lars has been CEO of Milestone Systems A/S since 2003, steering the Danish-headquartered company to be the global industry leader in open platform Internet Protocol (IP) video management software.

Under his leadership, Milestone Systems has followed a unique vision to bring the physical security industry together as a business eco-system. During his thirteen years as CEO, Milestone Systems' revenue has increased more than fifteenfold. Today, Milestone is one of the most valuable companies in the video management software industry.

PREFACE

A great deal of my career has been dedicated to the critical importance of leadership, and I am always looking for refreshing and novel approaches to this subject. Business Magnetism details the drive needed to lead a company that is innovative and independent.

Throughout the book I have tried to offer crucial insights for any manager or budding entrepreneur. I explain my, at times, unconventional techniques for enhancing meeting dynamics, and demonstrate the value of being open to new ideas.

Milestone's commitment to openness is at its very core and has helped pry open the traditionally conservative physical security industry. Users are now beginning to ask about new ways to apply technology and how they can optimize their business using video surveillance. The result has been to redefine industry expectations as to what a video surveillance system can be – and do.

This is the story of a small Danish software start-up with global ambitions. It's about having the courage to create the trends and let others follow. It's about the power of shared knowledge and partnership. And most of all, it's about leading in a way that instills a sense of trust in your co-workers, and in the industry as a whole.

Lars Thinggaard, June 2015

ACKNOWLEDGMENTS

This book has been a collaborative effort. I have had significant help in creating its content from the Milestone organization, their ideas and contributions have added great value to the book. Thanks to everyone who has helped me with the project.

Throughout the project, Jakob Wedel has worked closely with me in developing the message and refining the content. His illustrations have made my ideas clear and easy to understand. Thanks Jakob for raising the level of the book.

Writing the book reminded me of all the help I have had along the way. To Milestone's former chairman, Ole Stangegaard and our current chairman Jesper Balser, I would like to say thanks for the guidance and support I received throughout the journey.

Milestone System's leadership team and Anette Bisgaard have been my long-term sparring partners. Together we have refined many ideas and notions into the solid business plans I describe in the book.

Damian Arguimbau and Michael Madsen Sjö were my sounding boards on which I tested my thinking. Their constructive questioning and criticism have helped me attain the level of quality I wanted for the book.

Good writing is not easy. A big thank you to Courtney Dillon Pederson for her help in editing this book and making my ideas flow well, easy to understand and as brief as possible.

Every project needs a driver. For this I would like to thank Mark S. Wilson for pushing me when needed and doing the "sheep dogging" as he would call it.

It has been a long process, and I would like to thank Birgitte Lilmose for her constant support along the way and for reminding me to take my own advice and laugh once in a while.

Finally, during my upbringing my parents taught me "evnen til at ville, giver evnen til at kunne" or, "where there's a will there's a way." The principles I learned from you early in life have guided me through my business career. Thanks to you both for this invaluable gift.

BUSINESS MAGNETISM

The power of partnership

1

The End of the Beginning

A workshop. Two Danish engineers. A coffee machine. They're beavering away on ideas for products that will change our approach to conventional physical security and surveillance systems. Pioneering a new way for users to interface with their building controls.

Taking existing ideas, and seeing if there's a way they can tweak them, adjust them, or redefine them in ways no one has ever thought of before. It's hard work, because they don't know precisely what they are working towards. But that's also what makes it exciting.

The potential is limitless, only tempered by their understanding that what they are aiming towards should be useful. Should work for people. Help them. Make them more efficient.

These two Danish engineers are bolstered by the fact that they have a sound financial base from which to let their creativity loose. They realize the rarity of this opportunity, and feel the pressure to succeed, but delving into this unchartered territory is also liberating.

Thanks to their company's Scandinavian management model, which promotes collectiveness and inclusiveness, as well as a flat organizational hierarchy, they have the freedom to develop these new product concepts without burdening layers of management bearing down on them.

They are free to innovate and find that one idea. That one killer concept, that grows from a distant dream, to a business success. It's just a matter of time, thinking, testing, and taking risks.

These two Danish engineers work for Milestone Systems. The year is 2012. The location is Silicon Valley, the beating heart of the world's technology industry.

But for the year and the location, this could be an almost exact description of the very first days of Milestone, when co-founders John Blem and Henrik Friborg Jacobsen set out to start a new business venture with not much more than an opportunity and a belief – that they could devise a software product to take to market.

> The difference is that it's 17 years later, and Milestone has grown into an internationally successful company, with offices in 18 countries, and generates over 50 percent of its revenue in the notoriously competitive United States physical security market.

This is a significant achievement for Milestone as a Scandinavian company, especially when considering its choice not to take outside financing within its first ten years. In his book, Illusions of Entrepreneurship: The Costly Myths that Entrepreneurs, Investors, and Policy Makers Live By, Scott Shane, Professor of Entrepreneurial Studies at Case Western Reserve University, shows that less than 30 percent of businesses survive the initial 10-year period when launching in the U.S.

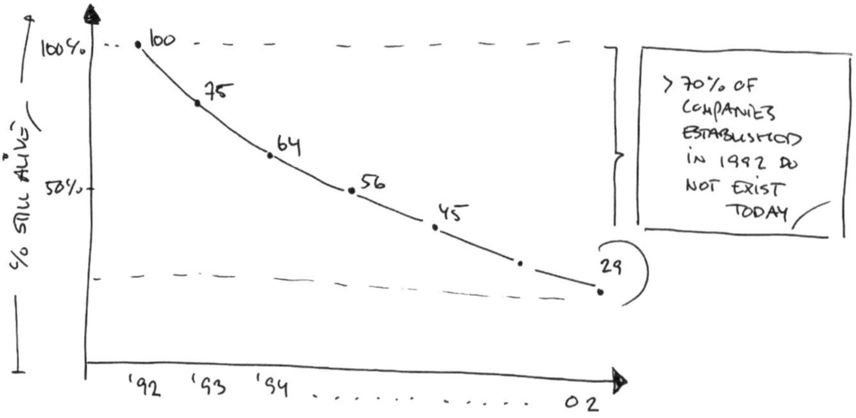

Proportion of new businesses founded in 1992 still alive by year — from a special tabulation by the Bureau of the Census produced for the Office of Advocacy of the U.S. Small Business Administration

Part of sustaining a successful business is keeping close to your customers and the market, while constantly watching for signs of change. Once you see change coming, you need to act quickly. You must adapt the company to take advantage of opportunities the change could bring, and to avoid potential concerns. This is how I have always run Milestone.

In late 2012, we underwent an update of our corporate strategy and the way we operate the company, guided by the management team, which I head up. This involved refocusing into three business units. One of these was the newly established Incubation and Ventures unit, which includes a small team in Milestone's Copenhagen Headquarters – and an initial operation in Silicon Valley.

I believe this unit is crucial to the future of our business. We have created the means to act like an entrepreneurial technology company without impacting the growth and well-being of our main products, partners, and their customers. It's designed to recreate the conditions required for creative, entrepreneurial thinking, but with advantages our founders never had. The Silicon Valley office will increase the possibilities for partnership and inspiration, drawing on that region's wealth of technical brilliance to enhance our existing products and drive new ones. It lets our engineers do what they do best, amid the brightest minds the digital world has to offer. As I write this, just a few months after its establishment, the numbers of dedicated team members involved in the Incubation unit are growing, and the first very promising new products have already been released to the market.

The update to Milestone's corporate strategy was a response to the way we saw our market evolving. It was achieved in large part thanks to the agility of our company structure – a relatively flat hierarchy – which allowed us the flexibility and buy-in to make the change quickly and dynamically. Allied to our flat hierarchy are our 'ROIFI' values: Reliability, Openness, Innovation, Flexibility and Independence, which are embraced throughout the entire organization. These are real values, which have an impact on every aspect of our business, and combining them with our flat management model allows us to act quickly and decisively.

So Milestone has come a long way in 17 years, and in the thirteen since I joined the company. It hasn't always been a smooth journey and there have been a number of lessons learned along the way. Lessons about leadership, management, and about changing the way an industry thinks while giving employees and partners the freedom to create value. Milestone's story is about the power of openness: to new ideas, to technical brilliance, and to partnership. It's a story about being open to making new connections, and to having the foresight – and the luck – to make the most of them.

A Scandinavian story

Denmark and the entire Scandinavian region have enjoyed something of resurgence in the last decade or so. Danish restaurants are now considered to be some of the best in the world, offering adventurous, experimental takes on traditional Nordic fare. For example, the famous restaurant Noma was named the world's best restaurant for many years. Scandinavian design has also long been accepted as the template for a streamlined, modern lifestyle.

The success of Stieg Larsson's 'Millennium' trilogy, including the international success of The Girl with the Dragon Tattoo book, film, and Hollywood remake, has shone a spotlight on the vibrant – and now incredibly popular – Scandinavian crime writing scene.

At the same time, Danish television has crossed from domestic to worldwide appeal, with programs such as Borgen (The Castle) and Broen (The Bridge) reaching global audiences, and Forbrydelsen (The Killing) spawning a highly rated American remake. In 2011, the Danish film In A Better World, directed by Susanne Bier, won the Best Foreign Film Oscar, and the directors involved in the 'Dogme' movement of the 1990s, most prominently Lars von Trier, have continued to make a sizable impact on the world stage, along with auteurs like Nicolas Winding Refn of Drive fame. Our actors take leading roles in major films and TV shows such as Game of Thrones and Hannibal.

We lead the world in green eco-living and design initiatives. In Copenhagen, you'll see stylishly dressed women cycling to work every morning. The Scandinavian technology sector is booming with big names like Skype, MySQL, Spotify, Candy Crush and Angry Birds.

Residents of the region are consistently reported to be among the happiest in the world, despite paying some of the highest tax rates. Why is that the case? What are we doing right?

In February 2013 The Economist dedicated a special supplement to the region, with a front-page image of a Viking and the headline 'The Next Supermodel – why the world should look at the Nordic countries.'

In the supplement, writer Adrian Wooldridge describes the burgeoning economies in the region, and suggests an important element of their success is the way they have been able to balance welfare-state 'tax and spend' policies with a flexible approach to employment law.

> "In the workplace, Denmark is a pioneer of flexicurity: companies can sack employees with almost American ease, but the government provides displaced workers with generous benefits and helps them get new jobs," he writes. It's a safety net that allows employers to take risks they might otherwise shy away from.

Education has also been a Scandinavian priority, and a key area of government spending. If you're an American reader, for instance, you might find it unusual that Danish students, who attend university for free, also receive a monthly stipend to do so! As a result, education levels are high, and highly skilled workers are numerous – particularly in the IT sector.

The Danish approach is working. Despite the economic downturn of the past half-decade severely affecting the rest of Europe, and most of the world, the Scandinavian economies have not just survived – they have thrived. The Viking warriors seem to be winning in a dynamic world of competition, combining innovation, work/life balance, and a welfare safety net to create an environment in which its citizens are well-paid, happy, and eager to make their mark on the world.

A different approach

I believe one of the biggest contributing factors to the success of Scandinavian companies, particularly in the technology field, is the Scandinavian approach to management. It is borne out of a mindset of fairness and pragmatism typical of most people here and has emerged as a particular strength in the technology industry, marshaling the creative energies of a highly educated and innovative workforce.

So what do I mean by 'Scandinavian management?'

It's an approach to managing an organization similar to what we have implemented at Milestone. Structurally, we're talking about companies with flat hierarchies. This means a lack of layers in middle management, and generally more responsibility is delegated to those managers, along with more employees reporting directly to them. All employees are actively encouraged to take a participatory role in the business, by contributing ideas and making their voices heard on issues affecting the company. This is in contrast to the more top-down, authoritarian management structures seen elsewhere. Our approach also encourages innovation; without layers of bureaucracy to navigate, employees are able to suggest creative solutions to problems from almost anywhere in the organization.

There's an emphasis on equality seemingly ingrained in the Scandinavian psyche that cannot help but transfer to the workplace. Sometimes this can be expressed as a healthy distrust of authority, but it can also find form as a questioning of the status quo, or as a desire to ask why things can't be changed.

Scandinavian management (and government) has sometimes been described as a 'consensus' model, but I don't think that's accurate, at least not any more. Consensus implies that all parties involved or affected need to be in agreement before a decision is made – whereas the modern Scandinavian model actively seeks input from those affected, while being dynamic enough to trust its ultimate decision-making to strong leaders.

> The key here is trust, and it ties directly to Milestone's philosophy of openness

We don't believe that withholding information from employees and partners is a useful way to build a business or a relationship. Sharing knowledge empowers all stakeholders, and builds a strong sense of unity and purpose.

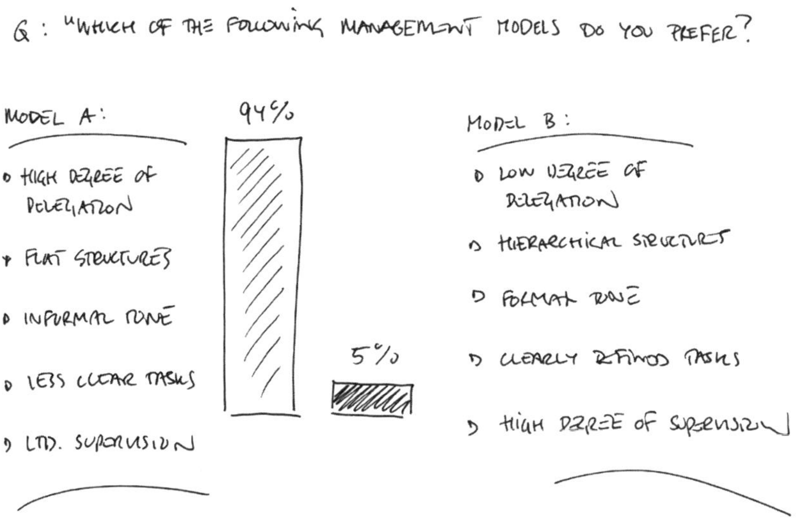

This graph from the independent Danish think tank 'Monday Morning' shows that the vast majority of Danish managers like the Scandinavian management style. When presented with the more autocratic, American style, just five percent said they would prefer it.

The Scandinavian approach has been criticized as lacking a 'killer instinct' in the mold of American corporations, and historically speaking, there has been some truth in that. Milestone managed to thrive in the U.S., however, through adapting in both directions. We appointed the Danish-American, Eric Fullerton, to head up our efforts there because he understood how to employ the strengths of the Scandinavian model and protect it from threats posed by the American model. Thanks to the adapted style of management, more than half of our revenue now comes from the competitive U.S. market.

We also understood, early on, that as a small company from a small nation, we would not be able to take on the world alone. This is why we embraced the 'ecosystem' approach, working closely with partners – camera, software, and other physical security equipment manufacturers; physical security installers and integrators; consultants and physical security product distributors – to approach the market jointly.

The Scandinavian style, based on trust and mutual respect, is uniquely suited for success with the ecosystem model. Milestone's video management software acts as the core of the ecosystem. We work alongside our partners to provide the best possible system for customers, both in terms of value and effectiveness.

In a Harvard Business Review article entitled 'Predators and Prey: A new ecology of competition,' JF Moore says: "A business ecosystem, like its biological counterpart, gradually moves from a random collection of elements to a more structured community."

Milestone has seen this progression within our own ecosystem. We introduced training and certification requirements as part of the partnership success structure, ensuring knowledge is shared and also used in a way that is most mutually beneficial for all involved.

Moore also writes: "Every business ecosystem develops in four distinct stages: birth, expansion, leadership and self-renewal."

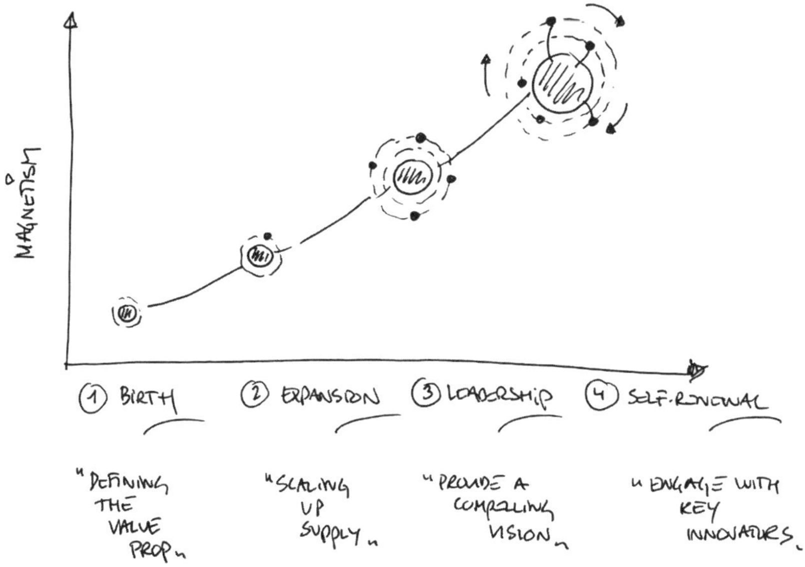

At present, Milestone and our partners are entering into the 'leadership' stage, where video enabling – which we'll look at more later on – is creating opportunities beyond those offered by a traditional video surveillance system, and into areas that provide additional business benefits to our customers.

"A leader must emerge in the ecosystem," Moore says, "to initiate a process of rapid, ongoing improvement that draws the entire community toward a grander future." This is the role Milestone has played in leading the industry towards the video enabling phase and redefining the industry's expectations of what a surveillance system is capable of.

In the article, Moore underlines that "executives whose horizons are bounded by the traditional industry perspectives will find themselves missing the real challenges and opportunities that face their companies."

We have found that listening to our partners, employees, and end customers, and acting on what they have to say, has been a key to our success.

The Scandinavian management model, is therefore more likely to succeed in a business ecosystem structure as it is based on the very concepts which strengthen the ecosystem: communication, trust, knowledge sharing and dynamic leadership.

Getting connected

In his massively successful book The Tipping Point, Malcolm Gladwell describes what he calls 'The Law of the Few,' which says: "The success of any kind of social epidemic is heavily dependent on the involvement of people with a particular and rare set of social gifts." This is based on the 80/20 principal, "which is the idea that in any situation roughly 80 percent of the 'work' will be done by 20 percent of the participants."

He goes on to identify three types of people with these gifts: Salesmen, who are skilled in persuasion and negotiation, Mavens, who collect and disseminate useful information, and Connectors.

Connectors, Gladwell says, are those people with a wide range of contacts across different social circles who can make introductions and create links between otherwise disparate individuals.

> I would identify myself as a 'Connector'.

I think that this is one of my greatest strengths in business. Being able to reach out to people at the right time for help, advice, or to fill an important role, can be a distinct competitive advantage.

I have an enormous number of contacts, for example via my LinkedIn profile, and I'm not shy about putting them in touch with each other when opportunities arise.

In the wider scheme of things, Milestone effectively acts as a 'Connector' in our business ecosystem and in the overall physical security industry. We bring together companies who are brilliant in their respective fields, and make it easy for them to work together to create a valuable solution for the customer. We provide the environment for that to occur, and work closely with them to ensure the end result is useful and effective.

In a sense, Milestone shares this trait with another iconic Danish company: Lego. Their success has been about making connections. Providing the building blocks to create something bigger and better than the individual parts on their own. I'm a big fan of Lego. While Milestone and Lego might address slightly different users (other than me), the end result we are aiming for is the same: a customer excited by the possibilities in front of them, and happy with what they have paid for. And our ecosystem model, guided by the principals and thinking behind modern Scandinavian management, proves that we play well with others.

Milestone is a small, ambitious company, which has grown to become an industry leader. But that journey was not without bumps along the way. We came from an IT background, and in some respects we were a little naïve. We learned the hard way that we would need to make significant investments in education and training to create the demand for our products that the conservative physical security industry required. We learned the value of partnership and took the 'open' approach, which was a central part of the thinking behind our software. We extended this approach to our entire business model, creating the ecosystem that has been the driving force of our success. And while we embraced the best of the Scandinavian management model, its inclusiveness and encouragement of creativity, we needed to have the courage to make changes to the business, changes which would ensure that we were in the best possible position to take on the challenges that the future had in store for us.

2

All the Way Back

I was born in 1965, and grew up in a small town in northwestern Jutland, far away from the Danish capital of Copenhagen. My hometown is made up of just 5,000 residents, and it's windy. Man, is it windy. I grew up on the coast, so I put the wind to good use and spent a lot of time sailing, wind surfing, flying kites, and the like.

It's the sort of town where there's no around-the-clock police force, so we were driving cars around town and on the fields from the age of 14. It's a bit like the rural U.S. in that sense. I didn't own a car, though – I'd zip around on my moped.

I have two sisters, and my parents ran the local bookshop. They'd always been involved in independent retailing, and they were really good at it. Looking back, I'd say that's where my interest in business stems from – seeing them lead a successful, contented life, running their own enterprise.

So I started working early. I helped in the bookshop, of course – no choice there! I also had jobs delivering mail, making roof tiles, and working as a projectionist in the local cinema.

I enjoyed high school, and did pretty well academically. But as the end of my school years approached, I wasn't sure what I wanted to do with my life.

My great passion then was music. I played drums and guitar, and I really threw myself into it, playing rock and pop music with a number of different bands. It's something I still like to do every now and then – there's a focus and intensity that's simultaneously draining and relaxing. Even now at Milestone we have a band that I occasionally play with at our parties.

So at the time, I was seriously contemplating pursuing a career as a musician. And who knows – maybe if I had, I'd be rich and famous, hobnobbing with glamorous stars! Though statistically speaking... Let's just say the choice of my career perhaps was for the better.

My father always told me "evnen til at ville, giver evnen til at kunne" or, "where there's a will there's a way." And this has formed the root of much of my business thinking. In fact, we recently released a business tool at Milestone that we call the Leadership Compass – we'll talk more about this later – and at the center of this Compass it says "Think like a Købmand." In Danish, a Købmand is a shop owner or a small businessman, renowned for their knowledge and acumen, and this links directly back to what I learned in my parents' bookshop.

I didn't have to decide on a career path immediately. My thoughts were much more short term. I would head to Greenland, work, and save. Then I would use that money to head to the U.S. and travel. See the world. Or a small, but influential part of it.

I chose Greenland because I wanted to see nature at its wildest – to experience one of the last great frontiers. Also, at the time the tax rate was extremely low compared to Denmark, just 23 percent. Greenland had been a Danish province until 1979, when it became a dependent territory with its own limited government and parliament. At the time there was still a kind of frontier vibe about the place. And plenty of opportunities for someone like me, who was prepared to work hard.

> So I worked. And I worked, and worked!

I had three jobs at the same time and worked up to 20 hours a day. I'd start off working in a laundry, then doing a cleaning job, and in the evenings I'd work in a bakery past midnight. It was exhausting. But I was young and had the energy. Plus, during those six months, I was making relatively good money. The time I spent in Greenland included the summer months, where I experienced perpetual daylight – when the sun never sets, and it's daylight for 24 hours. I had very little time to sleep between jobs, and it was never dark. Which was a bit of a problem for me! I remember this as a period with little rest, but great reward.

In a way, perpetual daylight serves as a fitting metaphor for Scandinavia as a whole. It's a region where we are used to these conditions – they're weird, certainly, but not unrecognizable. To those from elsewhere, though, 24-hour daylight seems alien.

> We've had to develop our own methods of coping with endless days (and nights in winter) in the same way as we have developed our own style of management and approach to business.

It's not completely foreign to those from other countries, but it is a reflection of the Scandinavian mindset.

After Greenland I took all the money I'd saved and flew to the U.S. I was there from 1985 – 86 and during that time I visited 32 states and made a lot of new friends, some of whom I'm still close to. It was a fantastic time and one of the best experiences of my life.

I ended up in New York helping some of my parents' friends renovate a barn they'd bought. I still hadn't lost the music bug entirely and purchased the quintessential eighties musical instrument, a saxophone. But despite my love of music, I finally decided that I wanted to get into business. I just wasn't sure where to begin.

I knew a guy in New York who was involved in real estate, which I thought was interesting and if nothing else, a good place to start. So I learned about the business, and seriously considered staying in the U.S. and working in property. I even went as far as passing the exams to become a real estate agent in the state of New York. But after a while, I decided against it.

I was 20, and genuinely wanted to learn about the business of business. I wanted a more rounded business education than simply taking a real estate exam. It appealed because it was easy and straightforward, but it didn't feel right. I wanted to go to business school, and there was a place at Copenhagen Business School (CBS) waiting for me.

While I was in the U.S. I'd also applied for two jobs back in Denmark. One was at Maersk, the international shipping company and the other was for Arthur Andersen, the then accounting and consulting firm.

I ended up being offered both jobs, and chose Arthur Andersen. Maersk would also have been great, but Arthur Andersen had a very tough, immersive entry-level program, bringing on board young talent with a will to win and a motto at the time of 'there is no substitute for action.' They also had very tight connections with American culture, which appealed to me. And apart from what we have developed at Milestone, I have to say that their company culture was the strongest I have come across during my career.

I made immediate connections by starting off in a team of extremely smart, motivated young people, who worked together in a tight knit group. It was one of the strongest networks I have ever experienced, and I maintain many of those contacts to this day.

What Arthur Andersen offered was, essentially, on-the-job training. Which was great. Except that I was also a full-time student at CBS. And that meant I was working 75 to 80 hours a week for several years. Thankfully my stint in Greenland had prepared me for that sort of intensity – and it turned out to be a very useful experience for the years to come.

I worked at Arthur Andersen for four years, in accountancy initially. Then I moved to Price Waterhouse, where I focused more on business consultancy. Clients served during these years included Schlumberger, Alfa Romeo, Fiat and Fiat Agri, Arrow Exatech, Tandy, Grid, Victor Micronic, and Bose loudspeakers. Those seven or eight years were invaluable, and taught me about business in practice and the importance of strong leadership in any organization.

It built up my business know-how as a whole, which is imperative for success in the corporate world: understanding the needs and demands of all parts of the business cycle, internally in company systems and employee relationships, and externally in dealing with customers. It's an area I have emphasized at Milestone. I believe that an executive truly needs a thorough understanding of not only business theory, but the way companies operate in practice: the nuances and subtleties that may not be immediately obvious to the outside observer.

Understanding the complex interplay between competitive and cooperative business strategies in an industry would become an essential ingredient for future success when we started to build Milestone's ecosystem.

Meanwhile, my determination and hard work took me through my bachelor degree at the Copenhagen Business School as well as a master's program. Though I didn't end up finishing my thesis, as a new venture seemed far more intriguing: my first software start-up.

Taking the plunge

With a bit of experience behind me, I decided the time was right to dip my toes in the waters of entrepreneurship. On April 24, 1993, I co-founded a company called In2itive Technologies.

Back then, market and data analysis companies gathered all of their information on paper. Which seems almost unthinkable now! But together with a few colleagues, one of my Price Waterhouse customer contacts (and later close friend) had the idea that it might be possible to gather all of this data on a portable handheld device – novel thinking in the days before Personal Digital Assistants (PDAs). Users could gather the data, upload it via cable to a server, then publish and analyze it.

The idea was a big hit and quickly became successful. It was used, for example, in the new field of exit polls at elections. We were young, we executed the business idea well, and we made money. We had some venture capital supporting us as well – but more on that later.

In fact, the business did so well that we were able to sell the company to a U.S. firm called SPSS in 1997, which was later acquired by IBM. I was invited to join SPSS at their headquarters in Chicago, but I decided to stay where I was.

Instead, I took another offer, from the venture capital guy who had backed In2itive. The company was called Beologic – a spin-off from the famous Danish home entertainment and multimedia products business, Bang & Olufsen.

They were producing an excellent product. Bang & Olufsen had established an internal innovation department that developed a sales configuration tool. The tool enabled you to tell a customer exactly which configurations of a loudspeaker system they were able to buy – combinations of components like woofers, tweeters, and amplifiers, some of which wouldn't work with each other, or which had conditions attached, so if you used one component, it meant you wouldn't be able to use another.

All of this could get quite complicated in terms of pricing, especially when telling customers what the impact of making changes to their system would be. But the sales configuration tool solved this problem. It worked like a decision tree – quickly calculating the price and impact of different choices. It was a novel idea, and was originally built for internal purposes.

As a Scandinavian company, Bang & Olufsen had a management style that was looking for ways to mobilize employees' ideas and creativity in the development of new solutions. I would later draw on this experience as we started to grow Milestone.

We thought the idea had a lot of potential, so we used Beologic as a way to find external markets where the product could be successful. And successful it was, particularly in the automotive industry. You can imagine why – a salesman being able to easily let his customer know whether certain configurations of options are possible, and what they'd cost, is very useful in a showroom. He'd be able to say, if you go for the convertible, you won't be able to have a sunroof. Or perhaps, if you're having a mid-life crisis, you can have a red sports car, but you can't necessarily have a 21-year old girlfriend. That sort of thing. Well, almost.

Within its first few years of existence, we received a number of offers for Beologic, and in 1997 one came along that we decided to accept. It was a big deal. At that point, it was one of the largest exits (preparation for the exit of an entrepreneur from their company) of a technology company in Denmark. But it turned out that the acquirer wasn't a good fit for the business.

We sold Beologic to Baan, a Dutch ERP vendor. ERP stands for Enterprise Resource Planning – it's software that integrates information management across an organization, from financial management, to procurement, and beyond. At the time, Baan was an extremely successful company, run by the Baan brothers. Rather importantly, this was before the Sarbanes-Oxley Act and many of the other accounting regulations which were to come.

The management of Baan began buying a lot of weird stuff with company cash, and of course, that wasn't sustainable. It was a horrible situation – their shares, which had been trading at around 55 Dutch guilders, were worth only 2 guilders within a few months. Astonishing, really.

I was lucky though. When Baan bought Beologic it was via what the Americans call a 'pooling of interests' transaction, which is more like a merger than an acquisition. This meant that we received shares in their publicly traded company, rather than cash. But I got out early. Sold my shares before it went bad.

Foresight, or fortune? I think it was probably a little of both. And to put it ridiculously simply, that's perhaps the secret to business success. But you can't plan for fortune – all you can do is encourage the right conditions for things to fall your way, while securing as much as possible against things going bad.

> In reality, though, this was a lesson I had yet to learn.

Addicted to the needle: the entrepreneur's conundrum

By this time I'd been through two very successful exits from tech companies. I couldn't quite retire, but things were looking good. Still, I was eager to prove myself again.

So I started looking for a new opportunity. I got in touch with my previous neighbor, a guy called Henrik Friborg Jacobsen, who had just started an interesting new business with his colleague, John. They were developing software to manage the viewing of surveillance cameras, and it looked like an excellent business idea. They called their company Milestone Systems.

But we agreed that the timing wasn't yet right for me to join them. They hadn't got to the stage where having a CEO on board would make sense. I said I'd help them where I could, and we'd keep our options open for working together in the future. I did, however, join the board of Milestone and helped form the first external board of directors.

I decided the time was right to play venture capitalist myself, and invest my own money into a company which had exciting prospects and vast potential. The company was called Mondosoft. They had developed some of the earliest algorithms for searching corporate websites.

It was late 1998, early 1999, the same time period that Google was founded, but back then, we were way ahead on the technology. At Mondosoft, we had great patents and great ideas. The dotcom business was booming, and I invested a lot of my own cash and effort in the business.

Unfortunately, it turned out to be a bad idea by the end of the venture. It didn't seem that way at the start, though. Between 1998 and 2000, as CFO I grew the company to 250 employees. But we weren't making a profit, which wasn't uncommon for tech start-ups in those days. So we turned to venture capital (VC).

As an entrepreneur – as someone with an interest in the welfare of start-up businesses – I have to say a VC deal structured in the right way is a major advantage, it gives you the value of speed. This can be the difference between fast growth and being left on the sidelines. I stress: the deal has to be structured in the right way – more about this later.

The value of speed

This is where VC can make a difference to your company. If you can continue growing your company on a steady path – bootstrapping your company – you may not need to raise money. This may be the case if you are working in a more conservative than disruptive sector. But it is likely to take longer and who knows what is going to happen in your market during the time it takes you to grow. For most companies, opportunities require fast action, otherwise they are gone. In these situations you need the freedom and flexibility to act quickly – the value of speed – this is the advantage of having capital readily available.

> When an opportunity arises, it's not the time to start looking around for funding. You need to act now!

With the right type of VC backing, you can take advantage of these opportunities to accelerate your company's growth. As a result, you are in a stronger position for future opportunities: if you happen to need additional funding, you will be raising money as a market leader. It's a trade-off between raising money, how much and at what risk, and the pressure the industry places on your company to become a market leader quickly. I would say that you cannot put too high a price on the value of speed. It's like a catalyst for your company when getting noticed and growing fast is crucial to your success.

Think about video game companies: they usually grow very fast, 0 – 100 million in a couple of years. However, you have a well-defined window in which you can be successful, if you miss that window there may not be another opportunity. It's critical to accelerate growth and build market share fast.

In this situation, a VC deal is a balancing act, on the one side you have valuation and on the other you have terms. Structuring a deal is a trade-off between these two. You might get a very high valuation, but at the cost of strict terms, preferred stock, anti- dilution and liquidation preferences. If you realize the upside, the complex terms in a deal may not matter. But you need to be sure: a complex deal may come back to bite you. In these circumstances a dollar is not really a dollar, deals can get so tangled that it may be almost impossible for you to get any return out of your hard work. If you are not sure you'll make the upside, I think it's better to have a cleaner deal with less complex terms at a lower price.

Over the years, I have experienced both sides of VC: excellent VC partners as you will see with Milestone, and the not so good, as I will describe for you next. I have learned at my own cost that a clean deal with transparent terms is easier for everyone to work with.

The deal we did for Milestone was a deal structured in the right way. Unfortunately, the receivers of VC often do not understand the real impact the structure of their deal can have on their business.

Let me explain why.

Say you have a couple of guys with a good idea for a business. Let's call them Statler and Waldorf[1]. They each own 50 percent of the company. This is share class A. Sounds nice, right? They can go home at night and say to their wives: "I have 50 percent of a great company."

At a certain point, Statler and Waldorf decide they want to raise money to take the company further – to accelerate growth. So they approach a venture fund.

A venture fund is often backed by a number of pension funds, often referred to as Limited Partners (LPs) – it's one of the ways that pension funds look to make money, so it's your pension and my pension involved. Quite rightly, their aim is to make as much money as possible so we can all live well into our old age. But that means they have a list of conditions that apply to all their investments. Therefore, the venture capital firm can only invest according to these stipulated conditions. Which can be OK, but doesn't necessarily address the issues that the target company's shareholders want.

That is a valid problem. Because when Statler and Waldorf come knocking on the VC firm's door, they're told that one of the conditions attached to the venture fund's investment is that it has to be in what is called 'preferred' stock.

That preferred stock is a second share class – class B. And let's say this first venture fund raises US $10 million or 10 percent of the company.

1) Statler and Waldorf are registered trademarks of ITC Entertainment and Henson Associates.

That dilutes the ownership of Statler and Waldorf by 5 percent each, leaving them with 45 percent apiece. OK.

But there's a problem: the preferred stock has some disturbing conditions attached to it. For instance, the preferred stock includes terms for a 'liquidation preference.' Not only does this ensure the venture fund gets paid first in the event of the sale of the company, it may also specify how much they get paid.

During the internet bubble it was not uncommon to see VC deals with 'multiple liquidation preference' terms, in which the sum could be between two to three times what an investment was worth. Today, these types of terms are rarely seen.

There are some cases where this has worked well. However, if you do not thoroughly understand both the up- and down-side of your situation, I would stay away from this type of deal. The problem is that multiple liquidation preferences may push the sales price for your company very high, maybe to unachievable levels.

Going back to our example, if the company was sold for US $30 to $50 million – and nothing more – then the only people to get paid would be the venture fund.

> Statler and Waldorf would get nothing, despite owning 90 percent of the company between them.

Another term I remember, and one to be careful with is an 'anti-dilution' clause. This helps protect the venture fund from the dilution that would occur if further stocks were issued at a lower price than they paid. So the venture fund still owns 10 percent of the company, while Statler and Waldorf's share is reduced.

And, of course, the guy from the venture fund will be skeptical. It's natural – he's likely to be seeing a lot of graphs with steeply inclined up-curves on them – the so-called 'hockey sticks.' So instead of paying the $10 million in one sum, he would say: "We believe your projected growth is possible, but we want you to prove your case until we fund this fully."

Consequently, they only provide a certain portion of the investment funds at the beginning, with the remainder to follow over a set period of time if the projections are achieved.

Inevitably, the situation arises where Statler and Waldorf need more money. Typically, a second venture fund is called in, and another share class is created – share class C. If this has similar conditions attached: preferred stock, liquidation preference, and an anti-dilution clause, the outlook for our two entrepreneurs starts to look bleak.

I've seen instances where this has gone all the way to share class K, and that's a lot of investors. Each of these classes is regulated by their own shareholders' agreement, which means that each class along the line has to agree on what can happen with the company, all the way back to the founders, our old pals Statler and Waldorf. They have no money for follow-up investments, so their ownership gets progressively diluted. And with all of the liquidation preferences and other constricting conditions, the company would need to be sold for an unrealistically high price – before Statler and Waldorf would see any real return.

Looking at this from the venture fund's point of view, they typically talk about three stages of investment:

- **Seed capital**
  The initial stage for companies where investors may be friends, family and angel investors.

- **Early-stage investment**
  This is where most venture funds operate. Companies are growing slowly and profits are often less than zero. The business model is yet unproven and terms such as preferred stock, liquidation preference

may be acceptable at this stage because they compensate for the greater risk the investor is taking.

- **Growth-stage investment**
  Investments in this stage usually come from growth equity funds. Companies are established and growing faster, profits are greater than zero. Preferred stock, liquidation preference terms are not usually needed here which means you can get a cleaner deal.

Venture funds would see Statler and Waldorf as an 'early-stage.' Their risk is high because of the failure rate – typically one success for every ten investments – and this is built into their model. They can afford to take this risk because it is spread across a number of investments, and that one success will pay for the other failures. The entrepreneur, on the other hand, can't spread their risk in the same way, making their gamble far greater.

This is what I call the entrepreneur's conundrum: you don't understand what you don't understand until it's too late.

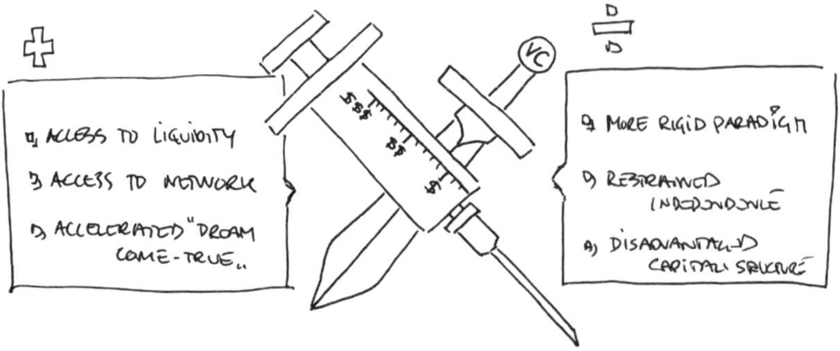

As I explained, aggressive terms in the early stage are not as common today, however, there are lessons to be learned from the past. During the business frenzy around the internet bubble, I saw many entrepreneurs caught in this web of 'preferred preferences.' The conditions you're forced to accept under the first round of funding – which is, by definition, too little cash for what the company needs to survive – means you get addicted to further funding. It's like a hypodermic needle, and the capital is the drug. As soon as you've got the needle in your arm, you're hooked!

What entrepreneurs should always be asking is how much would the company need to be worth in order for them to receive, say, $10 million?

I won't argue with anyone who says the above is a simplified way of looking at the dilemma, but I would say it is a fair assessment. I know many venture capital fund executives who are great people, and I respect that they have to protect their assets.

Ultimately it comes down to whether the entrepreneur has the stamina to stick with his idea, using his business acumen to guide the company. If external funding is needed to accelerate growth he needs to be in a strong position to negotiate a VC deal as much in their favor as possible. My preference would always be funding a case using common stock.

Common stock means that the entrepreneur and the investors have the same share class, and that 'a percentage' really is a percentage of ownership. Not many "ordinary" venture funds can offer this kind of flexibility on terms, as – again – they have obligations to their limited partners.

Falling off my chair

Back at Mondosoft, we had 250 employees but no profit. We started hanging about in the back streets of venture capital, getting a little bit of funding here, another hit there.

This happened in the spring of 2000, when the internet bubble burst. You may have heard about it: the war for money had begun.

It was a sleepless period. I thought: I've worked hard for all these years, going to school and working for Arthur Andersen and Price Waterhouse, and now my money is at stake, and I have a new house, a new baby, and all of that could go down the drain (not the baby, of course – but how would I support him?) – all of a sudden, everything stood on shaky ground.

In situations like these, I become extremely decisive. A survival instinct kicks in. I began restructuring Mondosoft. We went from 250 employees to 20 people overnight. I was planning to take myself out of the equation as well, since we didn't need an executive taking home that level of salary, too.

When I did catch a few hours of troubled sleep, I dreamt fitfully of the situation I'd put my family in, stressing over tiny details, mistakes, and regrets. I'd wake feeling drained, more tired than I had when my head first hit the pillow. Then I'd drag myself to meeting after meeting in an effort to save the company, and to save my family's livelihood.

We were negotiating down to the next share class, and all the existing shareholders could see that this was likely to be mission impossible. Because you have the shareholder agreement for each class, but you also have a number of different shareholders in each class as well. And the task in front of me was to get everyone to agree, from the most recent investors all the way back to share class A. And that wasn't going to happen.

What we needed to do was to convert everything – all the shares in the company – to common stock, the same as share class A. This made it possible to understand what a percentage of the company really meant. For instance, if you had 20 percent of the company and you were part of the latest capital increase share class, that 20 percent had a lot more power than if you were on a previous share class and had 40 percent of the company. We had to decide what the conversion rate for all the shares was. What was the common denominator? That was an incredibly tough question to answer.

I'd gone to a meeting at an investment house in Stockholm to push on with the negotiations. We were all gathered around the boardroom table, hammering out details. Lots of coffee. Lots of thick binders. Paperwork. Laptops.

And I fainted.
I fell off my chair in the meeting room. And as I was falling, I remember thinking: this is it. I'm dying. This is where it leads. The inevitable end.

> I hit the room's carpeted floor, out cold. I'm not sure for how long, but when I came around, all I could think was: I'm quitting. I cannot do this anymore.

To prove to myself I wasn't dead, I turned to the investors, and said: "You know what? I don't want to do this. You can do whatever you want. I'm out of here. Don't call me. Call someone else."

I flew home to my wife and told her what had happened. We went to a friend's house in the French countryside to de-stress. Time slowed down, and we talked about the future. I went running, which energizes me and helps me not to think about anything else. My focus was on the activity. And nothing else...

I said to myself, OK. My pulse, my heart, my brain. They're OK. I was alive, and felt rejuvenated.

We came back to Copenhagen, where I was still on the board of Milestone Systems, the little video surveillance software company. I met again with John and Henrik, the company founders. They'd progressed a long way in a short time. I told them I didn't want to be involved in a company funded by venture capital. I'd learned my lesson there. I said if this is a good time for you, I think it's a good time for me to come on board. They agreed, and we began to build the company together.

So, with the last of my money I bought some shares in Milestone, and came on board as Chief Executive Officer. It was January 1, 2003.

coffee 2 go
Frellsen
SIDEN 1897

3

Early Days

Back in the early nineties, a British company called Tenfore operated a Copenhagen office. Tenfore was a software company that delivered real-time, high-end financial information, such as changing stock market prices, to banks and brokers throughout Europe. This was before the widespread availability of internet access, so it was broadcast via satellite – the only available means of providing real time data.

Tenfore's Copenhagen staff included two talented software engineers working with their research and development, support and operations teams. These two were John Blem and Henrik Friborg Jacobsen.

As I mentioned, Henrik had been my neighbor when we met in the mid-nineties. Parents of young kids have a good excuse to become friendly with others, so Henrik and I would chat while our sons played together. He'd tell me about his work, and as an entrepreneurial type, interested in technology, I'd listen attentively. Henrik is a very clever guy. He's quiet, but when he has something to say it's considered and insightful.

John was both his colleague and friend. He was also a fairly quiet guy, but intense in the way engineers can sometimes be. Both he and Henrik have Masters Degrees – John's in electronics, and Henrik's in computer science and mathematics. So we're talking about two very intelligent, focused individuals. Both brilliant in their own way.

Tenfore decided to close their Copenhagen subsidiary, which specialized in R&D and employed around 30 people. Both John and Henrik were invited to move to Germany, to work at another R&D hub. After some discussion and consideration, they decided against it.

The timing was actually good because both John and Henrik had been looking for an opportunity to become independent and begin their own venture. So, they negotiated with Tenfore and came to agreement: taking some of their staff, they would form a new company, a consultancy, and deliver software research and development services back to Tenfore. Essentially, they'd be running the development department as a separate entity.

First, their new company needed a name. Henrik had already registered a company called Milestone Systems, so they decided to go with that.

When describing the name choice, John says: "It was deliberately generic. And it could be understood internationally, instead of being a Danish name, perhaps with strange Danish characters. We weren't entirely sure what we wanted to do in the long term, what sort of product we wanted to create with our expertise. We wanted to leave our options open and that name allowed us to do that."

With the name decided, John and Henrik shifted their focus to coming up with a logo. Bear in mind that these were two pragmatic software engineers – they didn't really care too much about marketing. They settled on a light blue diamond shape with the word 'milestone' written simply across it. The inspiration, Henrik said, was the project planning program Microsoft® Project[2], which featured small diamond symbols to indicate when certain project 'milestones' had to be accomplished. And the blue came from the globally successful Danish shipping company

2) Microsoft Project is a licensed trademark of Microsoft Corporation. All rights reserved.

Maersk, which has a white star on a blue background as its logo. Henrik liked the color, and respected the company. So a blue diamond it was. Simple.

> That gives you an idea of how much time and effort was spent on marketing at the company's start! They took a couple of ideas from things they already liked, and said, that'll do. Instead of fussing over different hues of blue, they concentrated on their technology strengths.

The company's generic naming wasn't exactly a coincidence, but it wasn't deliberate or thought through either. Yet, it turned out to be a very good choice later on. What they created was a simple, iconic image. It's a big stamp and has huge recognition and branding power within our industry today. Fortune or foresight? Again, maybe a little of both.

One of the most important factors in the eventual success of Milestone Systems was John and Henrik's initial ability to negotiate favorable contracts. This was the case in their very first deal with Tenfore, which provided them with upfront payments.

The start-up money for Milestone was $25,000 – the only investment made in the company for 10 years. All the other money came from skillfully negotiated contracts. The skilled negotiations must be attributed to their business acumen, thinking like a 'købmand.'

The ongoing work for Tenfore meant that the newly formed Milestone Systems had a steady stream of income, while John and Henrik started brainstorming ideas for products they could apply their expertise to. "After three or four months, we could see that things were working," John said. "All the structures around the business, the procedures that needed to be in place – were effective. So we started looking for a potential product line, as opposed to simply providing our consultancy services."

That opportunity came from an unexpected source.

AxNet was a Danish distributor of products from a Swedish company called Axis Communications. At the time, Axis was well established in the network print server business, and John and Henrik were familiar with their products from their work at Tenfore.

Several months into their new consultancy venture, John was approached by technical engineer Mikael Jensen, who had worked for John at Tenfore, and was now working at AxNet. He and his boss Peter Biltsted had something interesting to show them, he said.

Axis had made a network video camera, designed to enable website owners to embed a live image into their site – but they had no software to control them. John and Henrik saw an opportunity for these types of network cameras to be used in physical security applications.

The security story

By its very nature, the physical security industry, is a conservative beast. It's concerned with protecting people and property – and sometimes that property is of massive importance to the way a country is run. Physical security systems help keep burglars and thieves out of homes, schools, and businesses. The industry helps to stop shoplifters, trace stolen cars, and safeguard sports stadiums. And as we've all seen in the past decade, it is of vital importance to law enforcement authorities in identifying those criminals responsible for terrorist atrocities, and bringing them to justice. Used most effectively, it can help to prevent these awful incidents from occurring in the first place, and to respond quickly if they do.

Those, of course, are just a few examples of the important work the physical security industry does. These days, the products involved in the business of physical security are capable of doing much more – extending into beneficial areas beyond their original physical security use. But we'll get to that later.

Because of the massively important role the industry plays protecting people and property, it can be relatively slow to accept change. That's understandable – if your job is to minimize risk, it makes sense to want to ensure that the products and systems you're using to do so, are tried, tested, and reliable.

That natural caution can also make it difficult for potentially advantageous new technologies to gain widespread acceptance within the industry. Such was the case when network, or IP-based surveillance cameras first emerged in the late 1990s. IP stands for Internet Protocol, and it refers to the addressing system that locates computers and other devices on a network – so each camera has its own IP address, for instance.

Television Rides Wires

THE television camera and receiver shown below work without radio waves. They were designed to keep an eye on dangerous industrial processes or bring a close-up of demonstrations and surgical operations to large groups of students. The system, called Vericon®, operates entirely on wires and requires no government permit.

Video surveillance – traditionally known as CCTV (for Closed Circuit Television) has a history that dates back to the 1940s. Its first reported use was by the Germans in World War II, for monitoring their V-2 rocket tests. In the U.S., the first commercial system became available in 1949 called Vericon. It appeared in a short article titled 'Television Rides Wires' in the February 1949 edition of Popular Science.

However its use didn't really take off until the 1960s. In the United Kingdom, police used temporary cameras in Trafalgar Square to monitor crowds during major events, and installed systems at rail stations, in city centers, and near government buildings. By the end of the decade, there were more than 60 permanent CCTV cameras operating nationwide.

In the U.S., police use of CCTV really began in the late 1960s and early 1970s, and escalated in the 1980s with the introduction of Video Home System (VHS) tapes as the storage media. Cameras were connected using coaxial cable – similar to that used for consumer analog television – and recorded to videotape.

This didn't really change until the late 1980s and early 1990s, when multiplexing recorders were introduced, allowing several cameras to record to the same videotape. However, the basics remained the same – standard image resolution for analog cameras is 480 x 640 pixels, or the equivalent of 0.3 megapixels, in today's language. Color images became slightly more common, though not that often, as monochrome cameras are much more effective at filming nighttime and darker scenes.

This period, from the beginning of the technology up until the early to mid-1990s, I'd call generation 1, in terms of video surveillance equipment and recording techniques.

Then, in the mid to late 90s, the first hard disk recorders began to emerge. These were able to convert standard analog camera images to digital signals and store them on a computer hard disk, allowing for space saving (no tapes) and simpler search ability.

Still, the basic camera technology remained the same – TV-style cameras, with coaxial cable linking them to a central control room, outfitted with Cathode Ray Tube (CRT), tube-based monitors. Flat-screens were still a few years away. This, I'd call generation 2 – but the 'form factor' is pretty much the same as generation 1, in terms of the way surveillance systems were designed and installed.

Things hadn't changed in a really major way since the inception of CCTV as a technology. Which meant that the major players in the video surveillance industry were comfortable with the status quo, making minor adjustments to existing products rather than being forced to deal with any significant, disruptive change.

John and Henrik weren't really aware of this background context, but this was the market they would profoundly alter in just a few years' time. Their introduction came in the form of the NetEye 200+ camera, developed by Axis Communications.

New opportunities emerge

The shift into physical security cameras was an interesting move for Axis. It was founded in 1984 by Martin Gren, Mikael Karlsson and Keith Bloodworth. Axis specialized in protocol converters and printer interfaces to connect PC printers to IBM mainframes, and later, in networking and the TCP/IP protocol for print servers.

In a 2011 interview with SDM magazine, Gren – the inventor of the network camera – reminisced about the origins of the NetEye 200: "In the early '90s while on a business trip to Tokyo, I met a customer with an inventory of unsellable analog cameras and he asked if we could network-attach them. I thought it was a cool idea, we saw an industry that was all analog and was bound to move into networking (funny enough, still a common problem today)."

"Coincidentally, one of our engineers named Carl-Axel Alm had been working on a network video conference system. When I got back from Tokyo and saw what he was working on, I said, "Let's scrap the use of it as a video conference system. I don't believe in that market and it doesn't fit the Axis way of doing business. But your hardware is great for creating a network camera, so let's do that instead."

So the Axis NetEye 200 was born.

At the time, it generated one frame a second – 24 frames per second is roughly 'real-time' – and took 17 seconds to generate an image. The camera had its own internal web server, allowing its images to be shown via an Internet browser. It had no dedicated software for viewing, and was actually designed more for viewing live images than for recording. By the time John and Henrik saw the camera, some additional features and developments had been included – they saw the Axis NetEye 200+.

John and Henrik looked at this camera, and thought – there's an opportunity here to design software that can be used to view and record the images it produces. They realized that with the speed of technological change, more powerful cameras would be just around the corner.

John says: "We were open to a product line where we could re-use our expertise on real-time data using the Microsoft Windows platform. Thanks to our work with Tenfore, we were very proficient at creating real time systems on a platform that wasn't really designed for that. Normally you'd run those sorts of real-time systems on a mainframe computer, not Windows."

> The secret to John and Henrik's successful development of the first Milestone video management product was how they treated the camera images as just another form of data.

This doesn't sound unusual, let alone revolutionary now, but at the time, it was a new way of thinking about surveillance video. One that allowed two software engineers with no experience in the physical security industry to create a useful, workable product.

These early network cameras produced Joint Photographic Experts Group (JPEG) images, the same way many still cameras do now. Today, video cameras typically use H.264 image compression, providing much higher quality pictures without taking up huge amounts of space on a hard disk or flash drive.

So instead of building a system to manage stock exchange data, they were now building a system to manage JPEG data. They built a database for video, which was highly unusual, even unique. As John says, it was the first step towards digitizing the video surveillance industry at a high level.

The outcome was Milestone's first software product, Surveillance PRO. It was able to monitor and record up to five independent digital camera streams and ran on Windows. The ability to run on Windows was crucial, as this opened up the software's use to the widest possible range of customers, thanks to the operating system's increasing corporate ubiquity.

The software controlled the storage of the camera images in a database, stamping them with a digital time code so they could be searched. Surveillance PRO incorporated motion detection – when an unauthorized person entered a scene, the software would generate an 'alarm,' and an alert could be sounded, or a text message, or an email could be sent to an operator to alert them which camera had detected the intrusion.

Early versions only allowed video to be viewed on the PC on which the software was installed, but later versions provided for live and recorded video viewing on other PCs through a built-in web server. This was pretty remarkable at the time. Digital video recorders had yet to become commonplace at this point, and most video was still recorded to tape.

Milestone soon released XXV – an expanded version of the software, which was capable of recording up to 25 cameras.

The knowledge gained from dealing with real-time financial information had proved extremely useful in the video management software sphere: both incorporated real-time data coming from different sources, and both necessitated fast processing and reliability at their core.

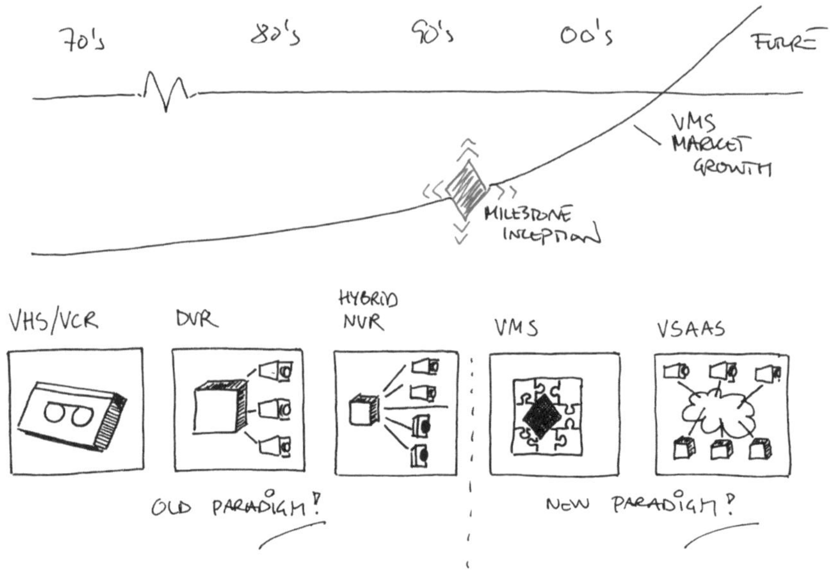

Into the market

The first version of Milestone's video management software was released in 1999, only a year after the company was established. By this time, there were a few more network, or IP, cameras on the market. A crucial aspect of IP video is its ability to be integrated with other areas of building and organization management systems that also reside on the network.

In 1999 this was all new. A few smaller, forward-thinking camera manufacturers had followed Axis' lead and had begun developing their own products. John and Henrik decided early on that they weren't going to limit their software to just working with Axis camera models. They wanted it to be as broad in its application as possible. It was a lesson they'd brought with them from their IT industry experience.

Henrik says: "The fundamental principle was that you should be able to add more cameras to it after the initial installation. And in the IT industry, that feels natural. You make a driver for integration, and you can supplement or replace drivers without replacing the core management product."

This concept of openness was built into Milestone's software from the very beginning.

The first Danish customer for Surveillance PRO was a telecommunications company called Sonofon. They needed to monitor a single camera in a new building. The first international customer was 3M in Canada. The international take up was fast, since there weren't any equivalent products available.

Later that year Axis came out with a new camera, the 2100 series, which had improved functionality, and was the most popular and successful IP surveillance camera for the next five years.

With these early sales under their belts, John and Henrik decided that the time was right to introduce their software to the physical security industry in general. Their first step would be the Skydd security exhibition in Sweden, held in the summer of 1999.

At this stage, Milestone was still a very small company, with less than 10 employees. So like many small businesses, people were forced to take on roles that they wouldn't, perhaps, have thought themselves best suited to.

> John says: "When you have a small company, you have to do more or less everything. So we had to start deciding who did what. And actually it was pretty natural, because Henrik and I are very different – we like to do different things, so splitting up the tasks was easy."

This meant that John became responsible for the more administrative side of things, while Henrik took on – for technical, engineering types – the onerous task of looking after sales and marketing. I have a lot of respect for him for doing that and for John taking on the administrative tasks, equally 'boring' for an engineer by trade.

The advantage of building a business from scratch is that you can offer employees the opportunity to move into roles that they enjoy, which is exactly what John and Henrik were able to do with the small group they'd gathered around them.

John says: "People do a better job if they enjoy what they're doing, rather than just doing what they're told to do. And sometimes we had people who could do the job, and other times we had to attract people with the right skillset. We're still doing that, I'd say!"

This is reflective of the thinking behind Milestone's Scandinavian management style – creating an organization and company culture that employees can respect and embrace. The relatively flat organizational structure means there are few barriers to communication between employees, allowing a direct and inclusive decision-making process to emerge.

As the newly minted head of sales and marketing, Henrik went to the Skydd security show in Sweden, where the reception for the Milestone product was positive, but muted. They quickly realized that to make a splash in the physical security industry, they had to have a presence beyond their local market. And there was no bigger market in the physical security business than the U.S.A., both in terms of sales possibilities and influence on other markets throughout the world.

Heading to the United States

At the dawn of the new millennium, Henrik and a couple of colleagues found themselves at ASIS International, one of the biggest physical security trade shows in the world. These are massive events, with tens of thousands of visitors taking in all the latest physical security products and technological innovations.

The halls are dominated by the booths of the major manufacturers, great towering temporary structures, sometimes on multiple levels, complete with giant signs emblazoned with their logos descending from the venue's vast ceiling. The best positions – those in the entrances and along the most obvious paths for visitors to take – tend to cost the most, or are reserved years in advance. They're usually occupied by large companies like Siemens, ADT, Tyco, and Pelco, and the big Asian technology manufacturers: Sony, Panasonic, and in recent years Samsung.

The new companies – the start-ups with a great idea, and those venturing into the physical security sphere for the first time – can usually be found on the perimeters, in the small, inexpensive, modular booths. With expressions of mixed hope and fatigue, the days of travel, client entertaining, and hours spent standing under the heat of thousands of electronic lights can dull the enthusiasm somewhat. These days, Milestone is in the large booth area, but I still like to circle around the perimeter and experience some of the up and coming tech trends.

It was in one of these perimeter booths that Henrik and his colleagues found themselves in on their first venture into the U.S. They were at the back of the hall, not far from the restrooms – visitors would hurry past quickly, and come back more slowly. If luck were on Milestone's side, they'd pause at the little booth staffed by the hopeful Danes, and check out the funny set up of a camera attached to a computer. It just didn't look the way a physical security system should, they thought.

Henrik recalls: "The guys from the security industry didn't really regard it as a physical security product. They didn't feel there was a tangible use for it. It was fun and interesting, but they couldn't see how it applied. It was a bit of a novelty."

"But the end customers had a different response. They could see what benefits it had compared to their existing systems. Suddenly they could re-use their network cabling, and they could scale the system much more easily, and of course it was more flexible, allowing them move cameras around.

> ...They had a very positive reaction and that really inspired us to move on, and continue to develop it. And over time, I believe that we helped the physical security industry change their perception, too."

John and Henrik could afford to wait for the industry to come around to their way of thinking. They'd ensured the company would be able to survive on the income from their consultancy business while they began making inroads to the world of physical security. Their decision not to rely on external investors meant that they were relatively immune to the vagaries of the dotcom bubble, which was soon to burst – and which would eventually bring me back to them, moving from the board room to the chief executive's position.

In fact, the consultancy business was doing rather well for itself. Tenfore had been through some difficult times, and sold off the rights to its services to an Italian company who decided to continue using Milestone's services for their future R&D needs. Thanks to John's Italian background and language skills, a close relationship developed. In fact, they were soon asking for additional consulting hours, so a team was put together specifically dedicated to this work. Despite the fact that the video software business might still have been cash flow negative, the consultancy business was thriving.

So they were prepared to wait. But the reality was, that they didn't need to wait too long. The video software business was growing organically and fast. By the end of 2002, Milestone had sold its software to more than 2,000 customers in over 40 countries. Not bad going for a four-year old company.

This was the position that Milestone Systems – with a staff of 20 – found itself in when I joined as CEO at the beginning of 2003. The time had come to take the business to the next level.

4

Building the Foundation

At Milestone's inception in 1998, the landscape of the physical security industry was evolving. Thanks to rapidly changing technology, computer networks and the web were becoming more powerful, and starting to be integrated across an increasing number of business areas. While this offered exciting, if untested, opportunities for business leaders, it also meant that gaps were emerging in the way that traditional physical security providers could cater to their needs.

A 'one size fits all' approach, where a single product was expected to be suitable for all physical security scenarios, was not always appropriate anymore. Some organizations had gone further down the integrated IT route than others, or were planning on moving in that direction. An expectation that the IT network could be harnessed for uses across the business – not just for word processing and spreadsheets – was becoming more prominent. These modernized businesses wanted physical security solutions that fit with the structure of their company, not the other way around. Traditional physical security products and systems, tied to a proprietary, 'closed' way of thinking, would not necessarily be flexible enough to meet the changing requirements of the new breed of physical security users.

In their 1995 book The Discipline of Market Leaders, Michael Treacy and Fred Wiersema identified "three fundamental strategies" which companies "must choose from if they are to build a workable organization." These were Operational Excellence (focusing on your business's procedures and ability to deliver in a cost-effective fashion); Product Leadership (creating the best products or services); and Customer Intimacy (delivering what specific customers want). A company was only able to focus on one of these strategies, they believed.

Yet, the thinking behind Milestone was different. John and Henrik's approach was to address all three strategies simultaneously. They created a highly efficient business based on the way they had run Tenfore's R&D operation. They created a product which was new, disruptive, and the best in its field. And the way they designed that product – making it

flexible and adaptable – meant that it could be tailored to the specific needs of individual customers.

By simultaneously focusing on all three of Treacy and Wiersema's disciplines, they had created a new, multi-faceted approach: a new market discipline. And the reason this discipline was achievable was that Milestone's software – and its approach to the market – was 'open.'

Opening up

> Openness. It's a simple word, but one that embodies the philosophy behind Milestone's success. And it's a concept that we have applied across the board, in all facets of the business. It's not just lip service – like a corporate idea that has no traction beyond the boardroom and marketing literature. We truly live it.

The idea was in place from the conception of Milestone's video management software. The gamble that John and Henrik took was to separate the software component from the hardware, and to concentrate on making that software as open as possible, in order for it to connect with as many products from as many different vendors as possible.

The aim was to provide as much flexibility as possible for users of the physical security systems – the end customers – and the integrators who design and install the systems. It's a concept that John and Henrik inherited from their time in the IT industry, where it was natural to build a platform, which other devices and systems could then plug into.

It was also part of their Scandinavian business heritage. Jette Schramm-Nielsen, former management researcher at the Copenhagen Business School (the second-largest business school in Europe) and co-author of the book Management in Scandinavia, puts it like this: "We do not keep knowledge to ourselves – knowledge is power. In many other countries it is used as a resource. If you've discovered something you keep it for yourself. We jump on the table and tell it to everyone because we trust each other – trust is the basis of sharing with others."

This made perfect sense to John and Henrik; indeed, they hadn't really thought too much about it as a 'revolutionary' concept. It was just business as usual.

In the physical security industry however, proprietary systems were the norm. This meant that generally, devices from one manufacturer could not work easily with those from another. Systems were designed to be entirely populated by products from one company. This made sense to the manufacturer, as it meant that the customer, by preferring, say, a certain camera, would then be obliged to use the camera manufacturer's other components if they wanted their system to work properly.

John and Henrik felt this was too restrictive. It meant that customers weren't able to select the components they felt best suited their system. Instead, John and Henrik viewed the role of video management software as the core of the solution, providing a central hub into which the widest possible variety of video products could be connected and controlled.

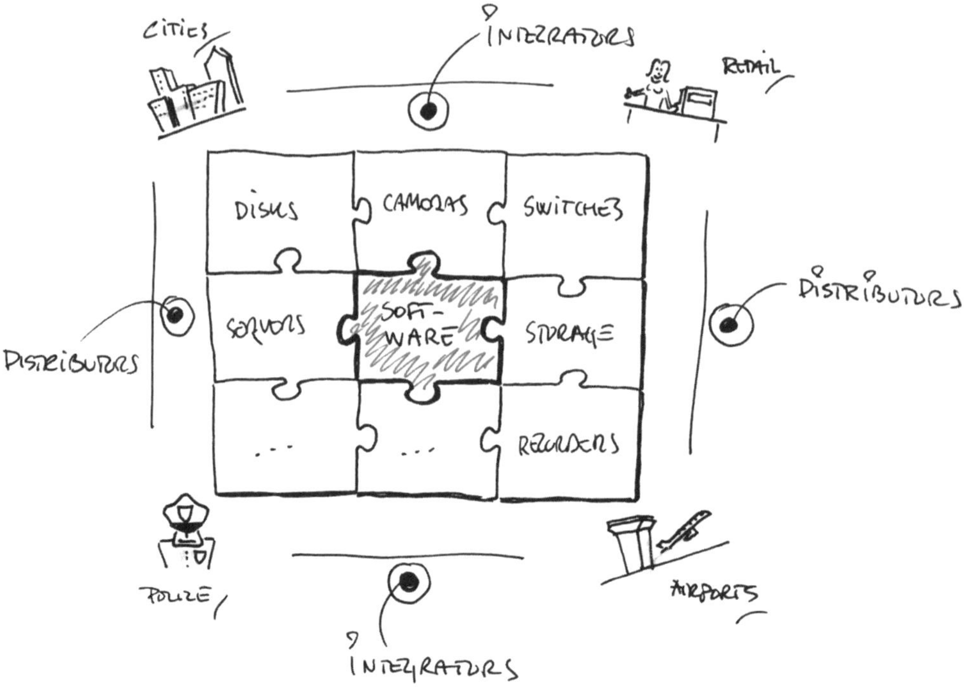

It's a concept, which Milestone refers to as 'escaping from proprietary jail.' It provides freedom for the user, allowing their choice of components and add-ons. Our aim is to provide the best possible video management software, and to work with companies who are specialists in their fields. Allowing customers this freedom, we have found, encourages loyalty to our product and to those of our partners. This might seem counter-intuitive, but we have found that being restricted by a proprietary system can eventually breed resentment.

In fact, this was the beginning of Milestone's business ecosystem, although we didn't know it at the time. The openness of the Milestone platform encouraged third parties to support it, dramatically accelerating the ecosystem's growth.

There are parallels here to the consumer computing market. I have huge respect for Apple as a company – the way they revolutionized the design and use of computers, phones, music devices, and tablets cannot be underestimated. However, they operate largely closed, proprietary systems – so, for instance, I'm forced to use iTunes to sync my music to my various Apple devices. But iTunes is an unwieldy piece of software: it's large, can be confusing at times, and seems to be constantly updated for reasons beyond my understanding and acceptance. Despite this, I am still forced to use it if I want to continue synching my music – if there's an alternative, it's not advertised, or easy to find. Apple firmly encourages consumers to use their products because it fits their business plan.

That works for them, but I sense a growing resentment among users who are not die-hard Apple fans. Most recently, I've seen this resentment in my children's generation, and heard it from their friends in their late teens – they are moving away from using Apple products for the same reasons as my own: the sense of being locked in proprietary jail.

The situation is similar for proprietary physical security systems – all may be well initially, but once an upgrade or change is required, the only choice is to use that manufacturer's products. John and Henrik's vision was to put the power back in the hands of the user – to provide them with openness, transparency, and flexibility. To unlock proprietary jail, and let their customers escape.

It was not uncommon for users to have to compromise their physical security solution design to accommodate proprietary solutions. Rather than creating the best solution for the job, they were forced to make do with the only solution that their supplier was capable of supporting. Milestone's open approach was a much appreciated way for them to build solutions that matched their business needs precisely, without technical compromises.

The end user of a physical security system does not know what he or she may need in the future, and which new technologies may become available. Milestone's openness accounts for this, and allows the user to leave their future options flexible. Our open platform allows them to upgrade, evolve, and replace components as needed.

Learning the ropes

When I joined Milestone at the start of 2003, the concept of openness was at the forefront of my mind. The first point of order was to start putting into place some processes and systems that would allow us to grow and become a bigger business. To create conditions that would enable the company to flourish.

So to get a handle on the day-to-day operation of the business, I shared an office with John Blem. We're quite different characters. I'm outgoing, social, and extroverted; John is technical, focused, and introverted, which formed a great complementary view of the business. I talk on the phone a lot; John likes to focus on his work onscreen. But we like each other, and get along well.

This meant that I was able to stay on top of almost everything that was going on at Milestone. People would stop by to talk to me about the commercial aspects of the business, and others would come to ask John questions on the technical and development side. It was a fantastic way to learn about Milestone, and to feel embedded in the culture that had already developed around John and Henrik's vision. The plan was always that I would move into my own office at some point – but I felt so comfortable sharing an office with John that we ended up in the same space for eight years!

Testing the waters

I was keen for us to leverage this guiding concept of openness as a way to strengthen our move into the American market. There is a history of European companies making disappointing attempts in the U.S. market, because they hadn't been prepared for what it took to be successful there. We wanted to avoid that fate for ourselves, obviously.

We'd built a strong connection with the Italian successors to Tenfore – helped in large part by John's Italian background and command of the language – so we felt that Italy would be an ideal test market for our first subsidiary. And it turns out, we were right.

We established an Italian sales subsidiary, and although they weren't too far away in terms of time difference, they were still operating a significant distance from our Copenhagen HQ. And they operated extremely successfully.

"We saw that it was working," John said. "Italy is still one of our biggest sales territories. It showed us that we were ready to expand."

> Next stop, the United States.

Position open

Our presence in the U.S. at the time was limited to an OEM relationship with a third party manufacturer, and a decent, but not impressive level of sales through a limited network of distributors and resellers, primarily built on Axis Communication's existing sales channel.

An OEM is an Original Equipment Manufacturer agreement, where a product built by one company is badged and marketed by another. It happens more than you might imagine – many cars, for example, use engines and other major components from a different original manufacturer. It's also common in the electronics industry.

After the initial industry trade shows, John and Henrik decided that there was a need for someone to be present in the U.S. to help support their product. So in 2001, we made an arrangement with a guy from the Danish foreign ministry who worked in an international trade role, to head up a phone support line in the U.S. He was based in Los Angeles and did an absolutely fantastic job because he was so enthusiastic about the product. He delivered our front line support for three years.

Things were going well, in the sense that those customers who were using our product were happy with it, and received quality support. But we could see future difficulties arising – Axis and other camera manufacturers began developing their own video management software, and when they brought that to market, their desire to sell our software alongside their cameras would be diminished. The time was right to look at expanding into more areas. However, considering the fate of many European companies new to the U.S. market, it was a big risk.

When confronted with difficult decisions like this, I always think of famed Danish philosopher Søren Kierkegaard. He believed that 'to dare is to lose one's footing momentarily, not to dare is to lose oneself.' The quote bears great significance for many Danes and it lies at the very core of my leadership philosophy.

> As I go about my daily life, I try to exemplify Kierkegaard's idea by never becoming complacent and always challenging the status quo. This thinking was the driver behind our decision to expand into the U.S. market.

At the time, I remember it felt very daring for the whole management team. During the early stages we lost our footing a few times, but recovered quickly. Looking back, had we not taken this step, Milestone would not be anything like the business success it is today.

We believed – as we do now – that our openness would be the key to our success. Our software was already able to interface with new cameras from Sony, Canon, Sanyo, JVC and others. Axis, of course, would build their software to work only with their own camera products. But we wanted to be brand 'agnostic,' as much as possible. We wanted to give the end customers, system integrators, and physical security managers the choice of which cameras to use in their systems, even to mix and match to suit any need. We wanted them to be able to create their own 'best-of-breed' physical security systems.

But we needed the right person in the U.S. to convey that message to the market. I didn't want to rush in and appoint someone who was a less than ideal fit simply for convenience's sake; if we had to wait to ensure we got the best person for the job, then we would.

There was another issue here too: Scandinavian management values are about equality and unity, because that is what we believe forms the basis for cooperation and coherency. This was working extremely well for Milestone in Denmark. However, from my earlier experience in the U.S., I understood that American business values are different; they are built on values such as individualism, and sometimes just raw authority, which both feel distant to Scandinavians.

Knowing this cultural difference could be a significant hurdle for us to overcome, I had a particular individual in mind to run our U.S. sales operation: Eric Fullerton.

The right man for the job

I'd met Eric a few years earlier when he was looking for someone to run the Danish arm of his company VigilantE. His depth of knowledge of the technology business, his experience, his enthusiasm, and his sheer tenacity impressed me.

That's not surprising, really – Eric has had a long and illustrious career as an executive in the high tech industry for three decades. He was born in California to an American father and Danish mother, and when his parents split up he moved to Copenhagen with his mother. He has a degree in chemical engineering and an MBA from the Swiss International Institute for Management Development (IMD).

He worked at Ericsson, where he helped restructure a division, then became a general manager for a subsidiary. From there, Eric moved to Nokia, where he was involved in mergers and acquisitions – dealing with efficiencies and redundancies – streamlining companies, essentially. After five years he moved to Cray Communications, a faltering data communications start-up.

After turning Cray's fortunes around, the company was sold to technology giant Intel, where it became the core of a new division. Based just outside Portland, Oregon, at Intel's Jones Farm campus, Eric ran the division for four years, before moving on to a start-up called VigilantE, an internet-based vulnerability assessment company that sold both technology and manual vulnerability assessment services. It was at this time that Eric and I first met.

We stayed in touch over the next few years, and I was convinced that Eric was the right person to represent us in the U.S. He had a wealth of experience in the technology business, working for large companies and small start-ups, spoke Danish, and understood the business cultures of both the U.S. and Scandinavia. I thought of him as a high-caliber Viking – one who would fit in perfectly with Milestone and help to drive us forward. So I called him regularly to arrange a visit where I could sell him on our prospects and plans. He wasn't taking the bait, though. He kept saying that he planned to retire soon, perhaps buy a golf course – do something different and relax.

Eventually, we did manage to organize a meeting! I was in the U.S. with John Blem – whom I had persuaded to travel overseas with me for the first time – and Milestone's sales and marketing VP at the time, visiting a customer. We arranged to meet with Eric for dinner at the Portland City Grill, a fine restaurant atop one of the tallest buildings in town.

I finally had the chance to explain to Eric what this opportunity was about. How big this could be, and what our vision was. By the end of the dinner, he was hooked.

What did I say to get Eric so interested? I told him:

> "Our vision is to change the world...

...this is an old-fashioned industry that has to change to digital over the years. And it's a huge opportunity, because we think we have a very good connection with the camera manufacturers, particularly Axis, with a lot more on the radar. We have a nice product that is already selling well in a number of countries, we have proven the first subsidiary sales model in Italy, and we're going to invest in the U.S. next. We want to empower the users of physical security systems, and we want you to lead that."

Eric had a number of insightful questions about the business, and about the physical security market's convergence to IP-based systems, which he addressed to both John and myself. The following day Eric went out and bought an IP surveillance camera, and using a Milestone software license, he installed it at his house and experimented with it.

Within a week he called me and said: "Okay, I'll join you for three months, helping to build your strategy for entering the U.S. After that, you can decide if you want to implement the strategy, and I'll move on to something else."

We had Eric for at least three months. It happened quickly: we had dinner early in August, signed our agreement a week later, and by September 2004, Eric was in Copenhagen undergoing some training.

This was great news for me. I knew Eric's guidance would help us avoid the problems, other small Danish companies had encountered when trying to break into the American market.

John, Henrik, Eric, and I attended the ASIS exhibition in Dallas later that month. We handled the set up ourselves, which we did most of the time in those days, as we didn't have too many support staff on hand. It was, as usual for us back then, a very small booth area, but we were enthusiastic and hopeful about potential customers visiting the stand and signing on with us.

Eric just stared at us. "Man, you're way too Danish," he said. "I'll show you how this works. I'm going to head out into the aisles and find people."

And he did. While we waited for people to come to us, he approached visitors, and told them that they looked like they needed software, and that we had the software to support their dreams. It worked: they placed orders. Here we were, two engineers and a business guy, and suddenly we had a genuine salesman among us. It was fantastic.

Eric recalls: "I was the guy in the hallway, grabbing people by the collar and asking if they knew about IP video and if they needed IP video. Being a sales guy by nature, I felt like a fish that'd been thrown back into the pond and was swimming happily. It felt like a huge injection of adrenaline into my system."

After the event, Eric put together a strategy to increase our presence in the U.S. He created an initial training and certification process – the beginning of a channel partner program that would prove crucial to the growth of Milestone's ecosystem.

The importance of perception

The three months flew by, and Eric agreed to continue with us, becoming a full-time employee and the face of Milestone in the United States. He offered us a process-oriented mentality gained from his years in the worlds of Intel and Nokia.

Eric said: "I would look at how I could build a process that could scale. I met a lot of people who told me afterwards that at the beginning they thought I had 10 or 15 people employed in the U.S., when it was actually just our first channel partners and I. Later on as we started employing people, and even when we were 5, they thought we were 25."

Making the market believe that you are a bigger organization than you actually are has the effect of generating trust – trust that you are an established business, and trust that you will deliver on your promises. An important aspect of this is the way you present your work to the wider industry media, and thus, to those who may not have come across your product before. Not long after, I became CEO, we put in place a PR and communications strategy, starting with a new website and quickly expanding to advertising, regular PR, and partner newsletters. We placed particular focus on customer case stories, and the credibility of these testimonials helped Milestone earn its first industry award, not to mention growing visibility in the trade press. This new focus also helped steer our management team through the process of defining our company mission, vision, and values that still motivate us today. It was also invaluable in translating the work we were doing in Copenhagen to our potential U.S. customers.

But there's no point in appearing bigger than you are if you don't have the product, and the level of service to back that up – if you don't, you'll be found out eventually. Since we were relatively small, but acting like we were much bigger, we had to ensure that we over-delivered on our promises to customers. We had to shower them with attention, and we had to provide the best post-sales support in the industry.

And, crucially, we needed to make sure our software evolved and developed according to not just the existing needs of our customers, but addressed their possible future needs as well.

> We had to be flexible, and the best way to ensure that flexibility was to take our philosophy of openness to the next logical phase: by becoming a truly open platform software solution.

Building the ecosystem foundation

At this point, we were at what J. F. Moore calls the 'birth stage' of our business ecosystem. Success at the birth stage, in the short term, often goes to companies who best define and implement their customer value proposition. For Milestone, this was our commitment to openness. It was the foundation on which we would build the ecosystem, and we realized that we needed to establish a mutually beneficial relationship between our partners and ourselves.

As a small company, not only did we have a typically Scandinavian flat hierarchy, we were actively looking for ways to work together with partners and customers with full participation from both sides. This gave people that met with us the feeling that they would be able to work happily with Milestone and, more importantly, trust us as a business partner.

In those early days of building our ecosystem, our Scandinavian style was one of our greatest strengths. Early partners soon understood that we were not trying to dominate; we were trying to work together with our partners. This was one of the elements that I believe enabled Milestone to build a sustainable business ecosystem – one that would continue to expand and deepen as we grew.

5

The Magnetic Center

Our American business started to pick up quickly. We were extremely successful at taking ideas which seemed like sound concepts and putting them into practice. The key was in doing it in a way that was scalable, without detrimental short-term effects – a more difficult task to pull off than it might seem at first.

Take, for example, the evolution of our software into a truly open platform product. This centered on the development of an API – an Application Programming Interface – and then an official software development kit, or SDK.

In the U.S., we began selling the concept of our software as an integration platform before either an API or an SDK existed. It was a bold move, but Eric knew our software engineers were up to the task. As we expanded, I continued John and Henrik's strategy of employing smart, creative people to strengthen the business.

Eric had been talking to Ken Gruber, the founder of Transact Payment Systems, based in St. Petersburg, Florida. Transact was involved with a payment system for scrap metal yards. In fact, Eric had met Ken during a technology conference. They got to talking about Transact's scrap yard business and issues, and from there, a partnership was born.

It's amazing how often a friendly chat – often at a hotel bar! – can lead to mutually beneficial business opportunities. It's one thing to talk about 'networking', but it's often more important to connect with people on a friendly, personal level – to be open to listening, learning, and helping them. Or vice versa.

Gruber recalls: "A scrap yard asked me to make a solution for their transactions using an Automated Teller Machine (ATM) machine to pay their peddlers rather than dealing with cash. We came up with a solution to encode the information on a card, encrypt it, and use the card in an ATM-type machine. The machine retains the one- time-use card, and pays their peddlers. Because of the proliferation of ATMs, it was very easy to get service and support, so it spread across the U.S."

But the scrap yards were regular victims of fraud. Sometimes people would come in with barrels on the back of their truck – barrels filled with water. They'd be weighed, then the water from the barrels would be emptied as they offloaded their metal, and weighed again on the way out to calculate the weight of scrap they had delivered to the yard. But of course, the calculation would be skewed in their favor as a result of the weight of the water, meaning they'd be paid more than they deserved at the ATM on the way out.

So the solution we developed was to integrate their ATM system with Milestone's video surveillance software, which by then was called XProtect®. Initially, this was used to link video footage of customers with their transaction records, so that any impropriety could be spotted. This wasn't a traditional 'physical security' use of surveillance cameras — monitoring potential intruders – it was a fully integrated part of a business system. This was then extended to include perimeter surveillance of scrap yard premises, so they could see if people were trying to steal the scrap to re-sell.

Those who ran the scrap yards were paying for the metal they actually received. As a result, the return on investment for the scrap yard was very high, and easily identifiable.

Transact went on to develop a product called Scrap Dragon, which is based on the Milestone Integration Platform™. Scrap Dragon was sold to scrap yards in every state of the U.S. It was a huge success, and obvious evidence of the benefits of working more on ways in which we could integrate our software with others.

Dynamic synergies

At the same time in Copenhagen, we were working with several end customers on major integration projects, including a couple of internationally renowned retailers. By making sure their business systems benefitted from the seamless way they worked with our software, we were able to demonstrate significant and rapid return on investment – the outlay for the integrated system was quickly recovered through the savings made, and thefts or mistakes prevented.

Demonstrating return on investment with purely a physical security system has been a stumbling block for the physical security industry. Convincing those who hold the purse strings to dedicate part of their budget to a defensive investment – one which does not show obvious contribution to business profit or growth – can be difficult. Because of this, physical security is often treated as a 'grudge purchase,' and those without a real understanding of the benefits of a sophisticated system would often prefer to go for the cheapest possible option that still meant they were meeting their obligations to their insurers.

In these integration cases, however, there was a clear financial benefit to the system user. And that benefit was a direct result of the way we were able to integrate our software with that of others. It was our philosophy of openness in action, and we wanted to explore it further.

Making the private public

We garnered significant coverage in the industry press on the projects we were allowed to publicize. We could feel the impetus growing.

Up to this point, we had really done the integration work ourselves. That is, our engineers in the consultancy department had worked on the programming jobs required to make our software work with the ATM or Point of Sale device, or whatever other software was required. We also integrated with access control systems – door entry with swipe cards, automated barriers, and that sort of thing.

The significant difference with the Transact scrap yard integration was that we allowed them to do the integration on the API. And they did all of it themselves. In this way we had indirectly enabled our first third-party vendor to sell this API.

Shortly after, we realized that if we really wanted the API we were developing to become widely distributed, we should just give it away for free with users signing a non-disclosure agreement, and start building the necessary business infrastructure around it.

We decided the future was in making integration to our software as widely available as possible. It meant that companies who were specialists in their fields could concentrate on their strengths, and use our software's centralized system position to enable them to broaden their customer base, and their appeal. We would train people in integrating their products with our software, and we would train users and installers of our software. In fact, we would make that training – certification – a requirement in our business model.

> Milestone would become an enabler.
> An educator. An innovator. A connector.

The power of partnership

This idea quickly gained traction. We may not have been the first to think of it – but in the physical security world we were the first to properly put it into practice, and to make it work. There's no point in having a wonderful concept if it doesn't make sound business sense in the real world. We believed that letting people work with our API would not only produce more innovative applications, it would allow our engineers to develop our core products further, and to provide specialized assistance to our partners.

In 2005, we decided to have a Milestone Developers Forum in the U.S. the following year. The idea was based on the Intel Developers' Forum, annual gatherings where there were presentations on Intel's work, on their architecture and interface, their APIs and SDKs, and their product road map. We planned to implement something similar for people who want to work with us.

And what today is called Milestone Integration Platform Symposium

(MIPS) – began life as the Milestone Developers' Forum. At the very first event, Ken Gruber of Transact Payment Systems presented the Scrap Dragon integration on stage. It was crucial to us that in this environment, in front of a wide variety of developers, Milestone software was presented as a viable and powerful integration platform.

The forum was a success right from the outset. We created a model, which saw attendees paying to come to our events – a rarity in the physical security industry, where manufacturers typically put on customer events for free. This demonstrated the value in the events. They weren't just a series of platitudes specifying how great our products were – they provided valuable information. Details on how we saw the industry and our products evolving, with guest speakers from outside Milestone offering updates on trends and future developments.

The MIPS events now attract hundreds of paying attendees, as well as many alliance partner exhibitors to demonstrate their complementary products and applications. We also run smaller partner events each year in around 20 countries throughout the world. These partner Open Platform days offer a more localized format, and a chance to talk in-depth with our national or regional teams, and in their native languages, too. Together, these partner events have a total attendance in the thousands.

We started to draw the industry together around our open platform through the power of partnerships. It was a business concept that a large number of customers valued and that we were able to scale up to reach a broader market through our partner events. Milestone was emerging as a leader in the industry. As the ecosystem expanded, our challenge was to make sure we could meet the market demand we were stimulating.

Truly open platform

When you see a third party make a profit by integrating their solution to your platform, it's tempting to get the feeling that we should do that ourselves and bring it to market. But by positioning Milestone as an open platform that does the video recording, it enables all the others to specialize in their own fields of expertise, and the overall solution becomes even stronger. The more we can empower our partners, the more profitable they will become, and the more profitable we become as a result.

We have stood by this thinking over the years that followed, introducing a full Software Developer Kit in 2007. This was an important landmark, providing any interested partners with the full set of tools to develop applications to work with our software – making it easier than ever for them to do the work. It showed a commitment to openness that was obvious to our entire industry.

Around 2008, many other companies in the physical security business had noticed the success we were achieving, and started describing themselves as being 'open platform' or 'open integration' companies. Some of our partners started asking if we would be looking at another way of differentiating ourselves to the industry.

But we held fast, because John, Eric, Henrik and I were united in our vision of what Milestone should be.

> We are a truly open platform. So much so, that we decided to define the essential aspects of being an open platform, and added a tagline to our logo that reads: Milestone Systems – the open platform company.

milestone

The open platform company

We released a white paper on what we believe are the five hallmarks of a truly open platform company. They are:

Use and availability of common external programming interfaces, such as APIs: Open platforms provide these and make them readily available to partners and end users.

Published documentation (such as an SDK): This is extremely important because it's one thing to offer APIs and quite another to go the extra mile and provide the tools, libraries, and documentation that make them easy to use.

Availability of training for programmers on how to use the API: This is often the ultimate differentiator between a true open platform and one with merely the aspects of an open platform. Providing training to third-party programmers enables other vendors to more efficiently and effectively use the SDK and write to the APIs to integrate their products to the platform and provide a truly seamless user experience.

Availability of project consulting: A manufacturer who is genuinely interested in providing an open platform will provide the engineering help to ensure quality integrations with other vendors' products.

Walking the talk: In an age where everyone is claiming to provide an open platform, it's important to do business only with the ones who really follow through on all the factors that make an open platform a solid foundation for integration. After all, you're making more than an investment in today. You're investing in the future. 'Walking the talk' means following through on all that is promised above, not just saying that you will.

Our software, the VMS, is at the core of the physical security system, and at the center of our ecosystem. That's our role. But because we're truly open, we can say to end users of our software: if you really want to, you can replace Milestone, just like you might replace cameras from a specific manufacturer or your access control provider. We don't think you'll want to, because we believe we provide the most effective video management system out there. But that's a risk we're willing to take.

The magnetic center

Alongside our unique approach to training and certification – which we'll take a detailed look at in Chapter 7 – Milestone began to function as what I would call the 'magnetic center' or core of a universe inhabited by all of our different partners. This is the inclusive ecosystem, which thrives with Milestone as its environment.

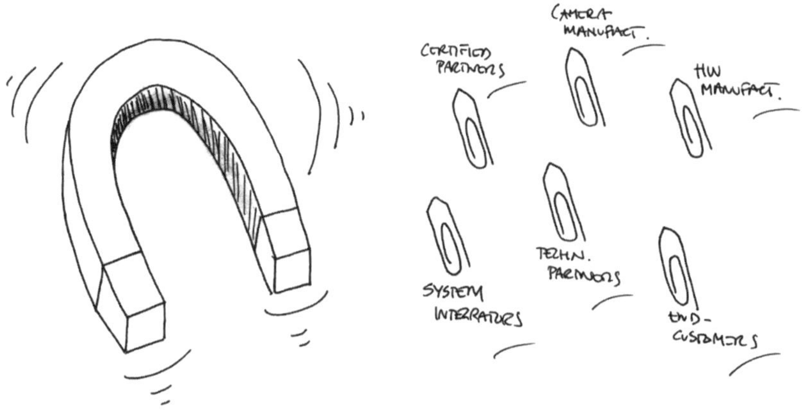

The real value of what we bring, in sheer monetary terms, is as an enabler – a multiplier. When you look at a video management system as part of a larger physical security system installation, the cost of Milestone software, including camera licenses, amounts to around 10 percent of the total. But we have an impact on a much larger scale.

In 2013, for instance, we had around US $75 million in revenue. But in terms of the combined value of all the other parts of a physical security system– cameras, servers, video analytics software – we are enabling 10 to 20 times more than our revenue, because much of the system is hardware, and therefore has a higher fixed price. We do not go direct to the market – our software, and all the other elements of the physical security system, is sold through distributors to integrators and installers, who then sell the final solutions to the end customers. So we calculate that from our US $75 million revenue, and the total real value we are enabling for the extended Milestone ecosystem – all of the manufacturers, distributors, installers and integrators involved in that chain – is somewhere in the region of US $1.2 billion. Which is hugely significant in a niche market.

Our ongoing success amounts to a 'win-win-win' scenario for all involved. Distributors of our software, who sell more products, and are involved in more projects. Manufacturer partners, who are able to integrate their products with ours and access an increased number of projects, and work seamlessly with products from other specialist manufacturers. Physical security systems integrators and installers, who are confident in our software, in its performance and its integration capabilities, and its ease of installation. And physical security system users, who benefit from the increased functionality that our partners offer, the power and ease of use of our video management interface, and our dedicated levels of service.

And of course, our partners' success is great news for us – it means we can continue to develop and evolve our existing products, and look for opportunities to develop innovative new offerings as well. We're able to create the conditions to make those innovations possible.

When you look at Milestone's universe, at all the people who benefit from our success, I no longer see us as a company employing 450 people. I see it as a 7,000- or 10,000-person organization, including all those who work with us and are affected by the decisions we make – this is what I call our 'virtual organization.' Because we're the magnetic center of this universe, our decisions can have a real impact on other companies and individuals. We need to ensure that our performance continues to benefit all those who work with us.

It's a way of looking at your business that I think is key to understanding the importance of leadership. It's all very well to say that you're looking out for the best interests of your business, and your shareholders or stakeholders. But to make sure that success has longevity, you need to step back and look at all the partners you can affect, and you need to take steps to ensure that your decision- making is focused on the sustainability of that success.

> You need to build for the future, and to do so, you have
> to take a strategic view of the market that you're in.

6

Redefining Industry Expectations

In any industry or, indeed, any aspect of life, it can be quite challenging to form an objective view when you're really close to your subject.

> Think about the cinematic close-up — you've got all the details of an actor's face, all the emotion that they are conveying, and the intense focus on what they're saying.

But if the camera pulls back to reveal the actor is actually being dangled feet first from the top of a building by menacing goons, their words take on a new meaning. The character is motivated by a threat to their life, so they're willing to say anything to get themselves out of such a situation. It's a matter of short-term survival, not of long-term objectivity and honesty.

That's understandable. Just like the poor guy hanging by his toes, business-owners, leaders, and executives often need to make the short-term decisions that will ensure they survive. It's what I had to do during the early 2000s in the dotcom war for money. In that case, the goons dangling you from the skyscraper are the market, and you do what you can to get out of that situation.

But once you're free of that – once your business is standing upright and the headache has lessened – one of the most important things any business leader can do is to take a step back and assess the true state of the market they are in. That way, they can understand the underlying dynamics at play, make informed predictions, and plan strategically.

In a sense, Milestone was at an advantage from the very beginning, as John and Henrik's vision for the company was borne of a desire to use their skills and talents to find a suitable market with a specific need and create a new product to meet that need. They didn't say to each other: we have developed a product, let's find a market to slot it into. They said: we have software engineering skills involving the handling and processing of real-time critical data on the (at the time) unwieldy Windows platform – how can we apply those skills?

It meant that there was a flexibility of mindset right from the outset, and an ability to look at the market from the outside in. And no matter how far we have gone in the physical security business, we haven't forgotten our roots, and the unique perspective they provided us with.

With that in mind, we set about looking at our video surveillance market, and identified three distinct phases – one historical, one current, and one that we feel the industry is moving towards, and that we want to lead.

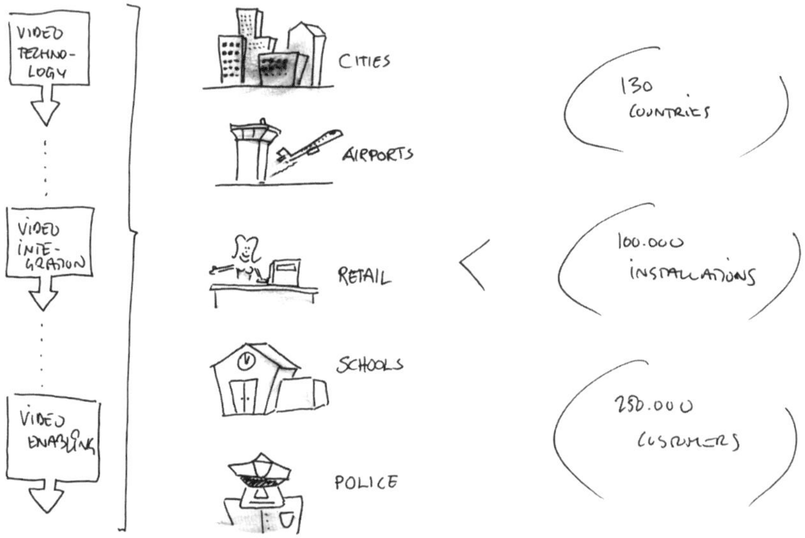

Phase One: Video technology

Video technology was what we called the early phase. As we've seen, when Milestone was formed in 1998, the physical security landscape was completely analog. The acronym CCTV was apt: the systems were closed circuits, putting severe restrictions on what could be done with the recorded images. They were physical security systems, but that's all they ever could be. Even though the concept has changed a lot since then, most people today still think of analog video when they think of video surveillance. Video surveillance is a tool to view and record video images, and the general public generally sees it as being used in physical security only.

But digital images were becoming clearer, storage media were getting smaller, and video compression improved dramatically. Digital files could be moved far easier, footage could be found much quicker – no more spooling of tapes backward and forward – and long-term storage no longer had an effect on image quality. Digital video was the future, we were convinced! For many there were clear advantages in purchasing a digital video solution, but in practical terms it was not much different from analog in the way it was used. It was still basically a physical security tool.

Part of our task was to help drive the industry towards the convergence of analog and IP technology, both because we could see the benefits it could provide, and, of course, because it was a means of creating new business for us.

At the same time Milestone was already thinking about the new possibilities that IP could bring and how we could enable people to use video for more than physical security. From the start, we aimed to enable using video as part of an IP-based business system and to break the stranglehold that analog technology had on the market.

End customers almost immediately saw the benefits of this enabling approach and we set out to be a driving force behind IP in the video surveillance industry. Our goal was to expand the possibilities of surveillance video beyond simply physical security.

At this stage, we also realized that developing our business beyond physical security was not something we could do on our own. To achieve this we would need to build a community of companies that cooperate in business with products and skills that reach far beyond our own – the Milestone ecosystem.

While working through an ecosystem was a huge advantage for Milestone, there were also competitive challenges. To maintain our lead we had to protect Milestone's innovative ideas from others who may be working toward defining similar offers.

Phase Two: Video integration

The current phase we see in the industry is video integration. The Internet brought with it a new electronic infrastructure that made IP applications like email, instant messaging, peer-to-peer file sharing, and Voice over IP (VoIP) widely available. Digital video was soon added to this list, and saw application in video conferencing and, of course, video surveillance. The main advantage of networked applications was that they were programmable, and this opened up a range of other benefits. These typically included better user experiences, network visibility and control, better access to data and development advantages, notably in the form of tailor-made video integrations.

One can program a simple IP network to give a building administrator an overview of controllable doors or gates in a building, so they can be locked and unlocked remotely. However, by integrating video surveillance with this existing network, access control can be given a higher level of sophistication and efficiency. By combining it with security-related evidence or by ultimately automating the access procedure through the use of video content analysis, or face recognition, the customer experience is elevated to a new level.

With Milestone's introduction of the open platform standard, it was soon evident that innovations in this area were going to be driven by the Milestone partner alliances. Our innovative partner ecosystem was the driving force in identifying customer requirements

and creating distinctive and revolutionary video integrations. And our focus on ease of use, at the forefront of our thinking since Milestone's inception, was paramount in IP video management software gaining widespread acceptance.

Phase Three: Video enabling

We are now entering the next phase in our industry, video enabling. While new video integrations were a natural result of a growing and diversifying partner ecosystem, we have recognized that there are new opportunities which networked video is beginning to offer to the world of video surveillance. Companies are starting to adapt their existing video solutions for other uses, notably for purposes that optimize and improve their business processes.

> This phase is really about the realization of our vision. Rather than just converging technology – digital and analog – we are now driving the convergence of video surveillance and IP-based business systems.

Video enabling is to video surveillance what the smartphone is to the telephone: it is an added set of functionalities that surpasses the original concept. We no longer use phones just to make calls; we use them to take photos, record video and audio, surf the internet, and play games – and third parties are constantly adding new applications to make the user's smartphone experience so much more rewarding.

Video enabling simply means that video surveillance has shifted into a new paradigm of usability. This is notably because of the unique combination of network programmability and the extensive partner ecosystem made possible by the open platform. For Milestone, the recognition of these new possibilities is not a passive one; it is a motivation to mobilize a greater awareness of video integration's scope. It is a call to action, to partners and customers alike that video enabling is the way forward. It is not a move away from physical security, but rather an addition of function to that of traditional asset protection and loss prevention.

We are helping to expand opportunities for the end user – providing them with the most value that a 'physical security' system can offer. And as an added incentive, the amount of revenue generating potential inherent in video enabling is a 'win-win-win' for all parties involved: vendors, partners and their customers.

There are a number of possible ways in which companies can video-enable their businesses. For example:

- **Compliance:** Workers can be monitored to enforce protective clothing and safety equipment procedures, preventing loss due to fire, chemicals, accidents, and injury.
- **Staffing optimization:** Prevent queuing at point-of-sale locations by notifying when extra personnel are needed.
- **Safety:** Alert maintenance crews to impending structural failures in buildings and vehicles.
- **Marketing and demographics:** Retailers are installing new products that use video to track traffic patterns, measure the effectiveness of displays and other merchandising strategies, as well as devise ways to increase sales or visits.

Through the open platform, Milestone has led the industry in a new direction, redefining the industry's expectations about how video surveillance is used. It has allowed them to think beyond traditional conceptions of the simple physical security role of video surveillance, and to explore the ways in which different parts of a business can work together to provide benefits for all. Importantly, in financially-straitened times like these, the 'multi-department' use of digital video means that the cost of installing a system can be shared across department budgets, making it a cost-effective tool for a business, and an appealing sales prospect for the smart integrator.

By identifying these phases, by stepping back and looking clearly at the way the industry is developing, we have been able to take the lead and help guide and educate our customers on the potential and benefits of video surveillance. And as with most new innovations, they have started to think of applications for our software that simply wouldn't have been possible had we not stayed true to our philosophy of openness and partnership.

Video enabling in action

Douglas Village, a high-end shopping mall in Cork, Ireland, has installed a video surveillance system which incorporated around 180 IP cameras and a state-of-the-art control room, all managed using Milestone XProtect® software.

The mall provides free parking, and using an automated license plate recognition system linked to the Milestone video platform and car parking management systems, they can allow people to park for up to three hours free of charge. The system records their registration numbers on the way in and out. If they stay more than three hours, a member of staff will leave a notice on their car to remind them of the limit, and repeat offenders could have their vehicles clamped. The center also employs a car parking guidance system, integrated with our software, which automatically detects empty spaces and shows drivers where to find them with color-coded lights.

This is an example of video enabling – but what makes it unusual, and inspiring, is what the management decided to do to extend their levels of customer service. They adapted the system to send an alert to the control room when someone parks in the disabled persons' bay. A mobility chair is then made immediately available, delivered by a member of staff to the disabled bay. That vehicle's license plate is then registered so that on future visits it is automatically recognized as it enters the parking lot, notifying the control room and enabling staff to ensure the mobility chair is already waiting for the customer when they reach the disabled parking bay. This both improves customer service, and helps to ensure that only those who need it use the disabled bay. It's a video enabling solution with benefits for everyone involved.

Iconic enabling

One of the most important aspects of the video enabling phase is that by its very nature it involves multiple contributors – a number of specialist product vendors, a skilled and creative integrator, and an imaginative, future-focused end user. It takes that imagination to see the opportunities available beyond purely providing physical security, and it takes creative thinking and cooperation from all the players involved to make these solutions happen.

Fortunately, that spirit of cooperation and innovation is fostered through Milestone's partner ecosystem. An example of this in action is the high profile re-opening of the Statue of Liberty.

The Statue of Liberty, Ellis Island, and Liberty Island reopened to the American public on Independence Day, July 4, 2013, following eight months of renovation and repairs due to the devastation caused by Hurricane Sandy. Technology provider and Milestone ecosystem partner Total Recall Corp. offered its services to the U.S. Park Police of the National Park Service, and the Department of Interior, providing a state-of-the-art digital surveillance solution designed to enhance public safety and improve operational efficiencies. Total Recall Corp. worked with nine technology vendors– including Milestone, of course – to deliver the project.

Our XProtect® software serves as the central hub of the solution, enabling first responders to quickly search for incidents while pushing video to mobile devices.

This is the first time an all-digital surveillance system has been installed at the monument. It will allow the National Park Service (NPS) to cover areas of the islands never reached before, thanks to a mix of fiber and wireless connections. The system will be used for the day-to-day safety and physical security of the park's visitors, while also helping the U.S. Park Police and NPS monitor traffic flow and expand people management to keep lines moving, assist ferry service operation, reconnect parents with lost children, and effectively respond to any medical emergencies on the islands or inside the Statue.

The surveillance solution goes well beyond the traditional physical security function, and was only possible because of the existing strong relationship between Milestone, Total Recall Corp, and the other technology partners.

That's not the only recent high-profile project we've been involved with. Over the course of a weekend in November 2012, the retired Space Shuttle Endeavour was moved from Los Angeles International Airport to its final home at the California Science Center, with hundreds of thousands of people lining the streets during its slow parade. An effective and flexible monitoring solution was a key tool for completing the two-day trip, which is obviously where our software played its part.

Along with XProtect® software, the Los Angeles Police Department relied on strategically placed high-definition cameras to ensure the safety of all concerned. The cameras were installed on a temporary basis. A critical infrastructure wireless mesh IP radio network was the backbone for uninterrupted communications between the cameras and radio nodes for the mobile command center and video display. A wired solution was deemed impractical due to the vast distance between cameras over the planned shuttle route. The cameras could be viewed as multiple split screens on police monitors.

We'll increasingly see these kinds of large-scale temporary surveillance set-ups for major events, as much for ensuring the safety and orderliness of crowds – and for dictating where stewards and medical staff are required – as for physical security concerns.

Redefining expectations

Milestone's vision is 'to drive the convergence of video surveillance and IP-based business systems.' This is not only an open acknowledgement of the new direction that video surveillance is taking; it is an assumption of initiative and a rallying call to lead the physical security industry toward video enabling and optimized business processes.

Taking the opportunity to step back and look strategically at the market has enabled us to spot these trends and make informed decisions about the way we can assist our partners to seize the new opportunities they present. It's win-win-win in the sense that end customers are able to use video to help streamline their operations and gather new and useful data, and our partners can generate new business in areas they may not have previously considered. All of these 'wins' are achieved with Milestone at the core of the solutions. It is the fundamental business tool proving the value of video management beyond its use for the defensive and the preventative.

There's another important factor at play here, and that's the public perception of video surveillance. While studies show that most people accept the use of video security to prevent and investigate crime and terrorism, there is also concern that used wrongly, there could be intrusive, 'Big Brother'-type invasions of individual privacy. I think that in general these fears are unwarranted, as physical security systems are in place to detect specific crimes or illegal behaviors, and most countries have privacy legislation to guard against unethical use of video footage. As an industry, we should embrace this sort of legislation, and sign up to codes of conduct and regulation whenever possible, as it helps ensure the public that recorded images will be used legally and non-invasively.

But by encouraging the adoption of video enabling solutions, we're able to show that video surveillance can be positive and useful – helping people and businesses in a very real way. We're showing that video can be more; it can be a positive force in society.

And surely, that is better than dangling from a tall building by your ankles, desperately thinking of what to say to get yourself out of such a dangerous predicament.

7

Creating Demand

One of the challenges of introducing a disruptive technology or concept to an established market is in working out how to create demand for the new product. Advertising and marketing play an important role, certainly – we benefited greatly from the articles and case studies we were able to obtain coverage for in our industry media – but they have their limitations.

That's particularly the case when a new technology comes along – in our case, IP-based surveillance systems – and is perceived as being a threat to the established, analog-centric industry. Getting the convergence message across can be difficult when the dominant manufacturers, distributors, integrators, and media have yet to embrace the possibilities of the new technology.

As I mentioned earlier, it's understandable, in some ways. The physical security industry is inherently conservative, and manufacturers who have invested heavily in the production of non-IP equipment were very reluctant to promote a technology they did not have a stake in. There was skepticism from some influential quarters of the established industry as to whether IP video could produce high enough quality images for customers.

What we were finding in the USA, and also seeing in Europe, was that despite the appeal of our software, and the steadily increasing number of project victories and case studies that were appearing. When we spoke to distributors, they wanted to see increased demand from integrators, before they threw their full weight behind us.

There was interest in the other direction, too, from IT industry professionals who saw IP video security as a new weapon in their network arsenal. We decided to examine the partners who were proving to be the most successful at selling and installing our software and IP physical security systems.

What we found, was that the IT people who were successful were the ones who had acquired knowledge from the physical security industry and understood what physical security meant. It's not just a case of attaching a camera to a wall or ceiling – there are a massive number of variables to be taken into account, such as the way changing light will affect image quality, and making sure cameras are in the optimum location to capture the required images – pictures of peoples' faces, for instance, rather than the back of their heads, are what is vital for evidential purposes.

On the other side, the established physical security companies that were successful with IP were the ones that had acquired additional IT knowledge. They knew everything about physical security regulations, the placement of cameras, integration with analog systems such as access control and building management – then they bought an IT company, or employed someone with IT knowledge, or educated their own people in IT. This IT knowledge meant that they were able to sell their services – and our IP software – to the end customer.

The sales became more complex when IP video surveillance emerged, because for the first time, physical security companies were dealing with both a customer's physical security department and its IT department. In the analog security world, an organization would have a person or a department responsible for surveillance, access control, and perhaps a few other elements of building management. But they operated mostly in a silo, with minimal interaction with other departments. They weren't integrated with the IT department in any meaningful way.

They could, however, make multi-million dollar physical security system buying decisions.

With the advent of IP, the companies who drove the uptake of these new kinds of systems were those that broke the silos within the organizations. They created cross-functional departments and communications, so there were a number of people who could talk to physical security systems integrators and their suppliers. This, in turn, meant that system integrators needed to be fluent in the language of IT, access control, building management, and surveillance.

We discovered that the channel partners who succeeded were the ones who had converged their analog and IT skill sets most effectively. They were not only technically capable, but were equipped with sufficient knowledge to sell these new systems.

A necessary education

We realized that the best, most effective way to create demand in the market – and to simultaneously ensure that end customers received the best possible surveillance systems – was to help educate our partners. We needed to educate the IT people coming into physical security, and the security people who were new to dealing with IT issues.

> By building on our partners' skill sets, and providing them with additional knowledge, we would be able to help stimulate the demand for our product that the distributors were looking for.

They'd have the ability to make the most of the software's capabilities, and recognize its advantages when specifying a system for customers. Those customers would be confident in the performance of their system, thanks to the fully trained integrators installing it. So initially, we started to organize a few training sessions around the U.S. with established partners.

But the response was disappointing. The free training that we were offering was received well by our partners, but few bothered to turn up to the sessions. This cost time and money, and no one was benefitting. Instead, we took a new approach. Inspired in part by Chris Anderson's book Free: The Future of a Radical Price, and the business model Anderson describes (called a Multi-Party Value Exchange System), we came up with a concept, which was new to the physical security industry. We would charge for our training, and in return for attending and passing the certification test, participants would receive some Milestone software.

This proved to be a smart move. The value in receiving the software, and the quality of the training itself, was more than enough to encourage attendance at the one-day events and to make participants work to pass our certification test. Soon, the partners were not only covering their own costs, but also starting to make money for us. Integrators who attended were able to sell the software they received, and make further income through the sale of additional camera licenses, alongside all of the equipment which is able to be integrated with the Milestone software.

The concept was in place and starting to gain traction. But we were still a relatively small-scale operation, so holding these training courses was a big investment of time on our behalf – particularly with such a small team in place.

We approached a company called Security Consultants International – later to become Connex – and entered into a relationship where they would become our training partner.

A new approach

We had recently introduced our Milestone Certification program. This meant that training was compulsory for anyone who wanted to sell our high-end products – which in turn provided end customers with the confidence that their system was being supplied and installed by fully qualified, Milestone-approved professionals.

We created a business model that would allow us to scale out the training program. This was key for us to enable training and certification to flourish as a central part of our ecosystem strategy.

> We were able to offer training classes almost anywhere in the world within ten business days.

All participants took a final test to receive their certification, after which we'd send them the software licenses they had earned by passing the training. The integrators were then able to sell that to an end user, who in turn would need to buy additional camera licenses, cameras, servers and other technology, adding value for the integrator and their distributor. Milestone would end up with additional revenue through the further camera licenses, and pick up more sales as they saw the value of our product and understood all of its features and expandability.

The effect was multiple buy-ins, from the end user to the integrator, and distributor, and on through to Milestone. And this multiplier effect – with Milestone as the magnetic center of this universe – meant that our vendor partners would also benefit from our training efforts, with their products being used as the system's components. Since these courses were able to be organized so quickly, the multiplier effect in the market was felt more rapidly.

Transferring knowledge and skills built loyalty among our partners. Everyone involved in the chain could see that there was value attached to it. It wasn't a cynical exercise. Some consultants and specifiers – the people responsible for determining the attributes a physical security system needs to have, working on behalf of an end customer – even began to state outright that systems could only be installed by those with Milestone certification.

In introducing our certification model, we'd been inspired by IT companies like Cisco and Microsoft. Now the effects were starting to reflect that Milestone certification was perceived as a valuable qualification that could help secure work.

Third party benefits

One of the areas where we've been successful at Milestone is in implementing change. We'll identify an area where we believe that change could be useful, and test it on a smaller scale before bringing the evidence of its success back to the management team. This approach allows us to see how we can implement change across the organization. This was the case with training and certification, where we decided to run the program in the U.S. at first. When it proved to be a major success, I decided to transfer that success to Europe, where we had been running training classes in a different format, using more expensive tutors in a less efficient model.

The new model was predictable, cost-effective, and ensured a high level of customer satisfaction.

This was practical implementation rather than just wishful thinking. And because it was practical, we were able to replicate what we'd done in the U.S. and Europe, in the rest of the world.

Requiring training, as well as certification, was a unique approach in the physical security industry. We also required that customers keep their certification up to date through re-training every two years. By changing the ideas that drove the traditional physical security industry we were able to change the industry itself.

Tender documents soon started to specify Milestone certification as a requirement to submit a bid. Because Milestone was the only source for certification, this strengthened Milestone's bargaining position within the industry and our developing ecosystem significantly.

From this position of strength, we were able to increase our market share and direct the future of the ecosystem.

Knowledge expansion

Our investment in training and certification has proved to be massively successful. Our training course now runs over three days, so we have a full 24 hours in total to really get to know a partner. It's an excellent investment of their time and ours. It's the basis for developing a long-term business relationship. Over the years, we've trained more than 10,000 people. We have strengthened 10,000 individual relationships with Milestone – while at the same time improving the value, in terms of quality installations and service, that it brings to our customers and channel partners.

Our current courses cater to several different demographics. These include the system integrators, both on the technical side and the sales side; end users looking for a deeper understanding of the product and their system; distributors who want to know more about the software; manufacturer partners, so they can understand our features more fully; and all of our own internal Milestone staff, who must take the training. There are three technical tiers, a sales track, and an internal Milestone staff track. We're also in the beginning phases of a self- paced, online-based training.

A key to the success of our training was in recognizing the emergent knowledge gap in the physical security industry. New technology, while offering significant benefits, brought with it a degree of complexity that occurred over a very short period of time. Being trained and certified was a real differentiator for integrators and installers. And if anything, that gap has become wider in recent years, as systems become more complicated at a rate faster than the bulk of the industry can keep up with.

> In the physical security industry today, with the shift from analog to digital, if you don't get training you will get left behind.

And as video enabling becomes a reality, a commensurate expansion in knowledge and skills will also be required. Our training is becoming deeper and wider in its coverage. It's estimated that up to 85 percent of physical security systems are deployed in an ineffective way – a remarkable number, and evidence of the stark knowledge gap. That will have to change. In addition to new challenges created by the need to integrate with non-security systems and functions, there are still many people who require training in the basics of IP-based physical security systems and Milestone's capabilities.

Training and certification will remain central to our business for the foreseeable future.

Beyond training

One of the benefits of developing a close relationship with our partners through training and certification, as well as in our Milestone Integration Platform Symposium (MIPS) and Milestone Partner Open Platform (MPOP) events, is that we are able to talk regularly with them about the features and developments they would like to see in the next generations of our products.

We have Partner Advisory summits, which involve even more direct dialogue with partners to glean feedback for our product management teams. We ask the market how they want new features prioritized.

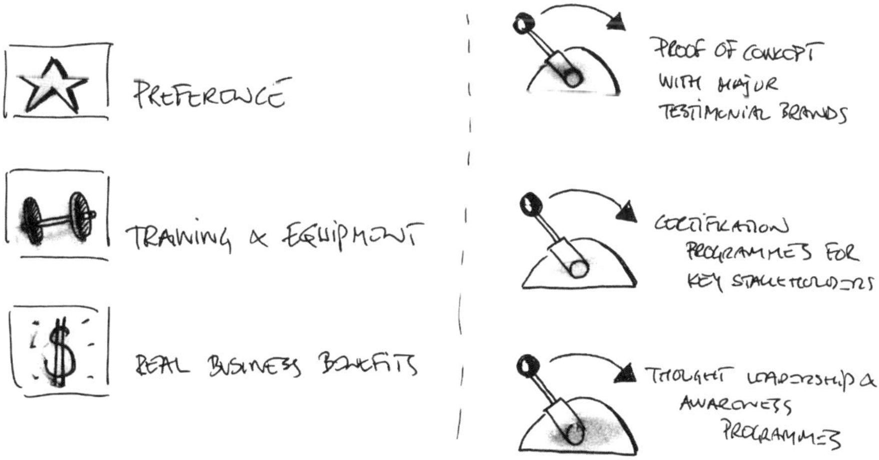

As a new and market-disruptive technology, you'll always have questions from customers on what the product's capabilities are and what we plan to do next. It's an ongoing process – an evolution.

When we sign major deals on significant projects, we use them to drive product evolution as well. New features that have been developed specifically for a really huge implementation can often be the driver for the next generation of software, from enterprise level and across the whole portfolio.

Once again, it is a case of being open to dialogue and discussion – allowing our partners to help us see opportunities along the way. As a leadership team, we have to make the big decisions about the direction we are headed and the changes we need to make. Listening to our partners can help influence and develop our predictions on the direction the market is going, and the changes we can implement to make their jobs easier.

A healthy ecosystem needs an environment in which all the elements can flourish, and that's what we aim to facilitate. The best way to ensure that can happen, however, is by developing and encouraging a culture of excellence within your own organization. And that's an area that I have put significant time and energy into at Milestone.

8

Future-Proofing the Business

This chapter is called 'Future-proofing the business' because, as we know, a strong product or idea with some initial success, can quickly come tumbling down if the company isn't built on solid foundations, with inspiring leadership that can unite a workforce around a common vision.

At Milestone, I think we have been able to harness the strengths of the visionary, U.S.-style technology company model – with innovative product ideas and a focused, inspiring leadership team – and ally them to the strengths of the Scandinavian leadership model, which emphasizes the empowerment of and trust in our employees to be creative and unite around the core values of the company.

'Corporate values' are often seen as meaningless platitudes, or worse, as oxymoronic – saying some nice things in a brochure for public consumption and being perceived as acting in a completely contrary fashion behind closed doors. But when we defined our values, we were looking not at the way outside investors or others would see our company, but at the way we wanted to go about achieving our goals – as an organization, and as individuals.

> That's how we settled on ROIFI: Reliability, Openness, Innovation, Flexibility and Independence.

Reliability applies to our products and our team members, to our reputation as proven and professional, providing solid support to each other, our partners, and end customers.

Being open, as we've seen, is at the very heart of Milestone thinking. Communication is not just a function of our software – it's at the core of what we are about. Communication with our partners in the Milestone ecosystem has been, and will continue to be, the key to our success. We mirror this within the company, through a dedicated internal communications department working to ensure our global team members are kept up to date and feel part of the close-knit Milestone culture.

Innovation we see as essential in our approach to work and in our software solutions. This is motivated by a pioneer spirit, passion, enthusiasm, and ambition. It is inspired by continually increasing knowledge of partners, customers, and new technology, and by sharing our knowledge through training and education.

Flexibility is being able to grow and expand with new people, new markets, and new solutions. It means giving partners and customers the ability to choose levels of product offerings, to scale installations for future needs, and to integrate with other systems. It's closely linked to openness and agility – ensuring that the processes we put in place work to our advantage, rather than slowing decision- making through extra levels of bureaucracy.

Lastly, independence is vital to the way we think – offering freedom of choice to customers and partners in terms of the hardware and devices we support. And for Milestone employees, it means freedom in their working environment and the ability to speak out and take initiative.

These aren't just wishy-washy words to us: they're the cornerstone of our business philosophy, informing our actions and interactions on a day-to-day basis, as well as in our strategic planning for the future.

Timing is everything

One of those strategic decisions about the future of Milestone was taken in 2008. Towards the end of 2007, and into the following year, we had been meeting as a leadership team and a board of directors with an eye on what was happening in the international financial sector. We could see that there was a crisis on the way, and that the boom years for the global money markets were coming to an end.

We were discussing whether we should do something to protect the company in the face of an impending global economic downturn. Remember that the only funding Milestone had ever received was the initial $25,000. We'd always been profitable, and we'd always been growing. That's no small thing, but we'd managed to execute it. We didn't need additional cash, but if we found the right way to do it, it could effectively future-proof us, providing an extra degree of assuredness, and making us an unsinkable ship.

We agreed then, that if the right conditions could be met, we would consider taking some outside funding. 'The right conditions' are very important here – as you know, I have my doubts about venture capital, so any deal we made would need to ensure that we wouldn't run the risk of future issues, such as those I mentioned back in Chapter 2.

Enter Index Ventures

Index Ventures is, I'd say, the top private equity company in Europe, particularly for technology firms. They have funded Skype and MySQL among many others in the high tech and life science industries. Their headquarters are located in Geneva, Switzerland. If you want to have outside investment in your company, Index Ventures is the one private equity firm that you want on board.

> I'd met one of their co-founders, Giuseppe Zocco, five or six years earlier. So I got in touch with him and explained our situation. I put it pretty clearly: I said we were after a silver bullet, an offer we couldn't refuse.

What I meant by that, really, was that any investment should take the form of common stock – share class A, to use my earlier example, where the new investor is on the same priority level as the existing shareholders. It means you avoid any of the complications that issuing preferred stock can cause.

I explained this to Giuseppe, and he said "interestingly enough we've just opened a new Growth Fund on the 1st of January, 2008." This fund didn't require preferred stock. It was a 'growth stage investment,' as opposed to the 'early stage investment' I referred to previously as the entrepreneur's conundrum. A growth fund, for a more established company, allows the investor to be more 'friendly' because their risk is lower. It's about finding the right investor to match the needs of the company. We believed that was Index Ventures, and Giuseppe liked our rationale. The deal was on.

One of the reasons that Giuseppe is so respected, and why I rate him so highly, is that he has real business acumen, and he's able to work quickly. We started talking in March, and by May we had the term sheet, which outlines the conditions of the agreement for investment.

The deal was closed on July 2, 2008. On September 15, Lehman Brothers went bankrupt.

Our timing, it turned out, was perfect. We'd raised enough money that it made sense for us as a one-time deal; we didn't have any intention to seek further funds. In fact, we never spent the cash that we raised. It was a safeguard.

The deal also meant that Giuseppe Zocco took a seat on our board of directors, and he proved to be great to work with. He's able to share the benefits of his knowledge and experience in the info-tech business world with us, and his expertise complemented the rest of our board extremely well.

So if you can find the right investor – who is investing for the right reasons – it's not just the money they bring with them that can be of value. It's their professional insights. And once they've staked money on your success, it's in their interest to help you become as healthy and profitable a business as you can be.

Was there an element of luck to our timing? Of course. But you make your own luck, to a large extent, and good leadership is about being aware of what's happening in the wider world, being open to opportunities, and being prepared to act decisively when those opportunities arise.

This opportunity fits all of our criteria – common stock, future- proofing the business, providing additional expertise and experience to our board – without diluting the Milestone vision or values.

And securing the investment wasn't just about shoring up our own defenses. By this time, our network of partners – the Milestone ecosystem – was extensive. We were able to provide all of our stakeholders with reassurance in a time of global economic turmoil. Much of business is about confidence, and our partners were able to act with the confidence that our future was in good shape financially, so they could feel emboldened as well.

This investment also benefitted from my 'connector' status. Knowing the right person to talk to at the right time was crucial to making the investment happen. It was emblematic of the connectedness that runs through the very heart of Milestone – being open to opportunities and to the expertise of those who can benefit all involved in the ecosystem. I still have my reservations about venture capital. But sometimes the conditions are right, and if you're flexible in your approach and your mindset, you'll recognize that and act on it.

A culture of leaders

Milestone has always thrived on openness, and that extends to the culture we have developed within the company itself. It's reflected by the fact that we have two employee-elected representatives on our board of directors, who have a very strong and real voice as to the direction the company is headed.

We also strongly encourage employees to take ownership and responsibility. One of the aims for Milestone is to be a continually improving performance organization. And one of the ways we are doing this is by positively advocating a culture of leadership within the business.

We have always believed that a focus on professional development and education is fundamental to our Scandinavian management culture.

To sustain our culture of widespread self-determination and autonomy requires that employees are highly educated, so that we can rely on them to make the right decision by themselves.

Again, this isn't just a platitude. Just as we live our ROIFI values, we believe that a dynamic organization can only benefit from encouraging leaders to emerge from within. To make this concept a reality, we have established the Milestone Leadership Academy (MLA).

The idea initially came to me on a flight to the U.S., where I was to attend an industry event and a Milestone board meeting. During the meeting we discussed the concept, saw that it had merit, and conceived the MLA. We then worked with a consultant to build and execute the training and the tools that would comprise the Milestone Leadership Academy.

The program is for all of Milestone's leaders – whether they have one person reporting to them or 50 – which aims to improve the overall leadership quality in the company. The idea of 'leadership quality' could be very nebulous. How do you measure that? My answer is simple. I can rate everyone in the company based on the leadership compass we created.

This leadership compass is at the core of the MLA concept. We focused the course around our compass, making what could be fluffy concepts, truly measurable.

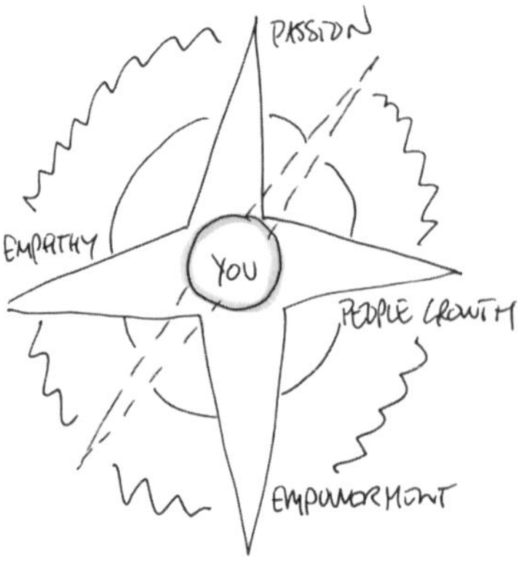

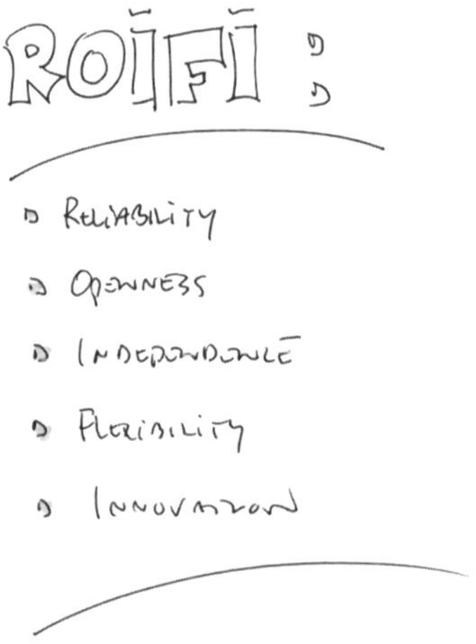

At the center of the compass is the manager. They are asked to live our ROIFI values, to be agile, decisive, to take calculated risks, lead by example – and to think like a Købmand. Around this, on the four points of the compass, are the leadership behaviors that we believe define Milestone leadership. They are:

Passion – the will to win

- Show enthusiasm
- Create involvement
- Be a motivator and encourage leadership
- Be an inspirer and front-runner

Empathy – ethics and work-life balance

- Show genuine interest
- Respect others
- Be present
- Be visible

Empowerment – mutual trust

- Trust people to make the right decisions
- Delegate work and responsibility
- Share information willingly
- Encourage teamwork
- Recognize and reward performance
- Challenge the status quo

People growth – unlock full employee potential

- Promote employee development
- Set ambitious targets and secure commitment
- Learn from mistakes
- Provide constructive feedback
- Enable mobility and exciting career paths

Managers are asked to self-assess on all of these points, and to be assessed by their peers – rating themselves and their colleagues.

Practicality is key – everyone is encouraged to think of concrete examples of real-life situations where they have been able to show passion, or empathy, or any of the key compass points. They do this not just with their peers, but also with others in the company who they may not work directly with on a day-to-day basis. Salespeople team up with R&D people, and managers from our international offices work alongside their Copenhagen counterparts.

We like to employ strong, independent, creative people, and we do a lot of stringent testing as well as interviewing to ensure the best candidates end up working for Milestone. But when you have a vibrant, intelligent workforce – and you encourage them to take responsibility for their decisions – a leadership program such as MLA can help to ensure that these strong-minded people are working in the same direction, achieving our goals in a manner which reflects our values, and is beneficial for them and the people who report to them. It's about speaking with a common voice, and creating a coherent and consistent narrative for the business. It's a structure to ensure that our strong individuals are working towards our common goals.

The program is constantly being developed and improved, making it as practical as possible for our workforce. It's designed to be tangible, which is why we also fly all of our managers from around the world to Denmark to take part in the course.

It has proven to be hugely successful. Not many companies, particularly in times of economic crisis, have invested the amount of money and effort that we have in leadership development programs.

> If people really wanted to, they could copy our products. But it's very difficult to copy the culture of an organization, where the values are really strong.

It takes a long time to build up that culture and values, but once it's there, it's very hard for competitors to emulate. We believe, that in 17 years of business, our culture has proven to be rewarding and effective.

As professor Peter Drucker puts it: culture eats strategy for breakfast, I couldn't agree more … and for lunch and dinner.

Our Chief Financial Officer Lars Larsen, whose previous two roles were with Carlsberg and Microsoft, told me that our leadership program was one of the main attractions to him in joining Milestone in 2010. In contrast to his other, more high-profile employers, the Milestone program focuses on the personal development of the individual, enhancing their 'worth' and effective 'market value' – it's not an off-the-shelf, generic management skills program.

Lars' appointment has proven to be a major boom for Milestone. A strong CEO/CFO relationship is vital to the fortunes of a growing business such as ours, and in Lars I have a trusted ally and member of our Executive Management Team. Lars came through our newly introduced stringent hiring process, including psychological assessments and IQ tests, and passed with flying colors. He brings a real spark to the company, willing to ask tough questions and challenge our assumptions. So his support for the MLA, and our company culture, is valuable – and tells me we're heading in the right direction.

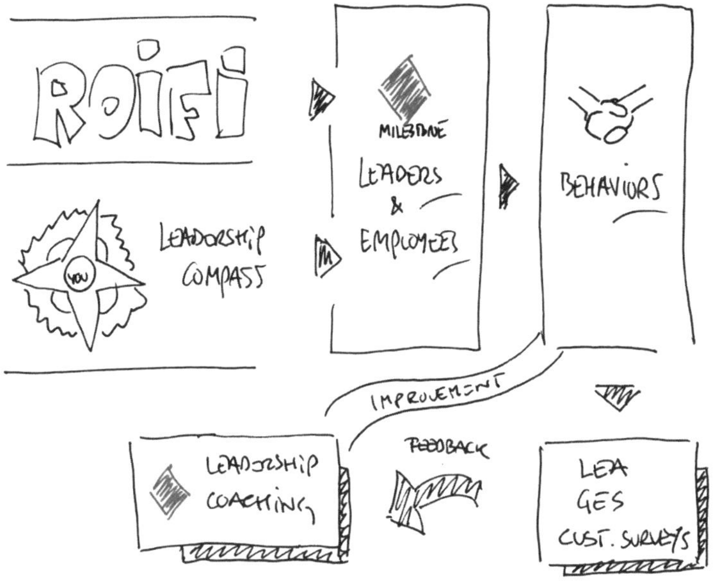

By encouraging a strong, united culture, and a vibrant, dynamic team of leaders, we're able to empower the team with a competitive edge and increased personal market value. They could take this elsewhere if they chose to – and we always say that if you don't enjoy working with us, you're probably better off somewhere else – but the vast majority chooses to stay, and thrive, within the Milestone culture.

In our most recent Global Employee Survey, we asked all Milestone staff to rate their manager based on their leadership behavior, included on the Leadership Compass. I'm proud to say that the result was a very respectable – and objectively measured– 78 out of 100. My goal is to keep driving this figure higher as we expand the MLA and continue our culture of excellence.

Prime Ministers and pillows

One of the greatest attributes a leader can have is to be open to listening to advice from those who have been through similar experiences, and then to use that advice to inform the decisions they make in future. There's a reason for the cliché 'there's no substitute for experience:' it has been proven true on countless occasions throughout the years.

During the process of establishing our Milestone Leadership Academy, I started to ask myself: whom can I think of that had to make a lot of tough decisions in difficult situations? Because surely that person would have something of value to share about the way he or she handled those processes – something that I could learn from and perhaps introduce to my own management techniques, and to the Leadership Academy.

The person that came to mind was Poul Schlüter. He was Prime Minister of Denmark from 1982 to 1993 – the second longest-serving Danish Prime Minister of all time, after Thorvald Stauning. Schlüter came to power at a turbulent time in Danish politics, following the forced resignation of Anker Jørgensen, and he had to stitch together a four-party coalition government. If anything is a recipe for difficult decision-making, it's having to please four different political parties – while being the first-ever member of the Conservative People's Party to be PM, in a country where 20th century politics had been dominated by center-left, liberal and socialist parties.

Poul Schlüter was definitely the man I wanted to talk to. In order to get in touch with him I turned to LinkedIn. If it's used well, the professional network site for business people can be an incredibly powerful tool. You can see the extent of my connections on the diagram below. I have no hesitation in using LinkedIn to organize introductions to people I'd otherwise have little chance of meeting.

Some elements of business are about 'who you know' – but not in the negative way that phrase is often used. It's just a matter of having the confidence to ask people that you do know to introduce you to their contacts; things can snowball from there, and soon your contact list is in the hundreds, or the thousands.

So through my network I got in touch with someone who knew the former Prime Minister, and he provided me with an introduction. Poul Schlüter was very happy to meet with me, and gratefully accepted my gift of cigars and port. We sat and chatted for a couple of hours. He was about 82 at the time, a very smart guy, and he had obviously loved his time as Prime Minister.

I asked him: "what are the key lessons that I, as a manager, can take away from your experience handling such a complex situation, coming to agreements with three other parties, as well as the members of your own? How did you go about it?"

To cut a long story short, he said there were two main tactics he employed. One was to use humor. This helped to defuse potentially tough, stressful situations.

> Poul Schlüter knew he had to negotiate with the same people the next week, and in the months and years to come, and humor was a way of avoiding unnecessary aggression, and of engendering loyalty.

> It's more difficult to be vehemently opposed to someone you find genuinely amusing.

This, I find, is particularly the case in technology companies, where trying to rule by domination, being a brutal business dictator, just isn't effective. The tech industry is a creative business, full of creative people, and being able to show that you have a sense of humor about yourself can encourage as much respect as laying down the law. As with most things, there's a balance to be struck.

The other tactic that Schlüter said he employed was this: he always gave the people he met something to take back to their supporters, to say 'this is the win that I got out of the meeting.' Even when it seemed as if the discussion had produced nothing of value for his coalition partner, Schlüter would go out of his way to ensure there was some small concession made.

It meant that all involved in the process felt there was progress being made, in what was a very difficult situation. No one ever lost entirely, and everyone could go back to their party and their support-base with their head held high, and in a reasonable frame of mind to continue civilized discussion on emerging issues.

It's a technique that can be valuable to all managers, and indeed to anyone who conducts meetings on a regular basis – even if the stakes aren't quite as high as governing a country. It's about respecting everyone who is involved in the decision-making process, and the knowledge that you will have to continue working with them in future.

Meeting with Poul Schlüter proved really valuable. It was a brilliant discussion, and he is an intelligent and friendly guy. It also showed the worth of stepping outside the usual business mindset, and reaching out to someone with the experience to provide thoughtful and innovative ideas.

It also chimed with some of my own thinking about the way you can run meetings productively. I've had a longstanding interest in meeting dynamics – too often meetings can drift aimlessly, sapping the energy and attention of attendees. That means you're not getting the most out of the meeting. You are wasting time.

So at Milestone, I have introduced a few innovations to try to improve meeting dynamics. Perhaps the one that has garnered the most attention is my yelling pillow.

This is a pretty straightforward concept. In a meeting which is likely to be difficult or tense, I equip the room with a small pillow. When people feel frustrated or angry, I explain, they should feel free to release that tension by yelling loudly into the pillow.

This is effective for a few reasons:

- Firstly, by simply acknowledging the fact that the meeting is likely to cause disagreement, you are already helping to diffuse that tension. And you're doing so in a lighthearted manner that suggests, implicitly, that although this might be an important meeting in business terms, it's not life or death stuff. It provides some perspective.

- Secondly, of course, it does actually allow people to release pent-up frustration in a direct manner, rather than let it come out in unmediated outbursts which don't serve any useful purpose in furthering a discussion.

- And thirdly, the moment anyone even gestures that they are going to pick up the yelling pillow is reason for amusement – it can break the tension and make a point humorously, without getting anyone's hackles up, and without even needing to scream into an item of soft material.

The yelling pillow went down extremely well at Milestone, and even caught the imagination of Børsen TV, Denmark's financial WebTV channel, who asked me to come into their studios and demonstrate the yelling pillow technique.

In addition to the yelling pillows, I like to keep people on their toes in meetings, so I'll often have an alarm that goes off every hour. When it goes off I get everyone to rate the meeting's quality, or other specific parameter on a scale of 1 to 10. Then I'll ask how we can improve our rating.

Sometimes I'll get attendees to rate the person to their right on energy and participation. I've been known to encourage people to do 20 push-ups – and I'll do them right beside them. It's all about maintaining the meeting's energy, particularly larger meetings, keeping minds agile and ready to react to something unusual or unexpected. It encourages decisiveness, and the ability to act on those decisions. And it's fun!

Changing for success

The Scandinavian management style usually calls for a very flat organizational management structure – 'tearing down the pyramids,' cutting out unnecessary bureaucracy, and trusting employees with greater responsibility. This was the way Milestone was established, and it has worked successfully for us.

But as we have grown as a company, and as our ecosystem has expanded, demands have changed. And if you're determined to be a leader in your field, as we've seen earlier, you need to observe what's happening in your market – and around it – and think strategically about future demands and trends.

This is what we did in 2012. We'd noticed some interesting developments in the growth levels of different areas of the video surveillance market, and of our products that catered to those areas.

The way we previously segmented the market was based on longstanding research. The traditional way to look at the market is through camera count, in a pyramid model, with a wide market for smaller camera count installations, a mid-level segment, and a smaller, high-end segment at the top. The high-end market is generally considered to be systems in excess of 100 cameras. Mid-level is from 17 to 99 cameras, and low-end is 16 cameras and below.

That's also the way Milestone's product ranges have been targeted, with XProtect® Corporate at the high end, XProtect® Essential at the low end, and XProtect® Professional sitting in the middle. We had seen significant growth in 2012 for our Corporate Product, far outstripping the actual growth rate of the high-end portion of the market.

That doesn't mean that the other half of the market isn't of interest. We still have good growth there, just not at the amazing speed of the top end.

We started to think that it would be useful to look at the market from a different perspective. We began to think in terms of a two-axis model, with complexity on one axis and number of sites on the other. Complexity is about the number of cameras used, but also about the requirements of the surveillance system in terms of integrating with other systems such as access control, and building management functions.

The proliferation of IP-based surveillance systems has also seen an increase in the number of customers with multiple sites – such as franchises of a retailer or different locations of a mining or distribution company – being monitored and operated from a central control room.

So there are two spectrums to consider, and any one project can be plotted along both of those axes. If you draw a diagonal line between those two axes, in the top right area you have the segment we designated 'high complexity,' and on the bottom left, 'high volume.'

We further divided that into nine squares, like a Sudoku puzzle. At the top left you have low complexity, multi-site installations; at the top right would be high complexity, multi-site installations. And we tried to work out the dollar value of each of those segments. We analyzed them, and we found that there is a sustainable market above the line – high complexity – and below the line – high volume.

As a result of this analysis, we took the strategic decision to reorganize the company. We saw the way the market was headed, and we wanted to be able to focus on both areas at the same time. To do so, we moved from a flat organization model to what we describe as a 'matrix organization,' which involves two business units: Corporate Products (covering the high complexity segment) and Professional Products (covering the high volume segment). They both work with our research and development (R&D) and our Sales & Marketing departments. We brought in fresh ideas by appointing new vice presidents from outside the company to head up the two new business units.

It's a hard decision to make, to say: 'We've got a successful company, but we can see that in future, in order to improve on our success, we have to operate differently.' You need to be open enough to listen to what customers and the market say, and to react. You need to be open to being agile, not like a huge supertanker in the middle of the ocean that takes an age to change direction.

You need to be flexible enough in your structures to change course. It's about being prepared for whatever challenges the future may hold. Today, I think one of the things that sets Milestone apart from our competitors is the way we look at the market. Using this in-depth knowledge is part of what makes Milestone a stronger competitor.

That's why we also introduced a third new business unit: Incubation & Ventures, with offices in Silicon Valley and at our Copenhagen HQ. It was a move designed to truly future-proof the business, ensuring we have a channel for new products and ideas to develop, and to make sure that we are able to compete with – and beat – any new entrants to the market.

This is a major move for us. We are doing it to create future business opportunities for our partners. Our ambition is to find game-changing technologies with the potential to accelerate our ecosystem's growth across software, hardware, and cloud services.

We are investing in compelling ideas that will create new value for our partners and their customers. We are investing in the future of our ecosystem.

> We don't see our competitors taking the initiative like this, although we think many would like to. We think this sets us apart in our industry.

Future-proofing is important for any business – catering to your current customer base and partners while being a step or two ahead of the market behind the scenes – but it's absolutely vital in the technology industry, where the next cutting-edge breakthrough could be just around the corner.

9

There's Always the Moon

The establishment of our new Incubation and Ventures business unit is already reaping dividends, both in terms of new products released, and the effect it has had on the company as a whole. This is important, because while you want to encourage growth in the company, the focus on selling your existing range of products inevitably takes up most of your time and attention. Developing new products and new ways of selling into the channel is difficult if you haven't done the business development and made it ready for the sales team first. You need to find a way to get these new ideas into the 'machine.'

That was the thinking behind establishing the Incubation and Ventures unit. It was conceived as a dedicated, independent business unit, able to experiment without the limitations that are necessary for the main business to run smoothly.

The first product to come out of the new team was Milestone Arcus™. This is an embedded video management system which runs on Linux®, Mac OSX®, and Windows operating systems, on network storage (Network Video Recorders (NVRs)) and devices such as cameras themselves.

Milestone Arcus™ was designed with two approaches in mind. In one respect, it is for low-complexity, low-cost physical security installations, which suit our Professional Products division. It is for hardware manufacturers to embed in their products, to be sold by their channel as a ready-to-run, out-of-the-box solution. Products embedded with Milestone Arcus™ will be co-branded with Milestone Systems, offering the additional strength of our brand reputation to our ecosystem partners' products.

This is a new departure for us. Our core product line, the Milestone XProtect® VMS offerings, run on Windows and are sold by our network of channel partners. Milestone Arcus™ features new development code at its core, as well as running on the Linux and Mac OSX platforms. This aspect of Milestone Arcus™ is aimed at the lower complexity end of the market – the smaller businesses that may have yet to make the move from analog to IP surveillance systems. Milestone Arcus™ is intended to make that move fast, and simple.

It also has the potential to go beyond the physical security market into consumer use, through smart TVs, gaming platforms, and almost anything that runs a Central Processing Unit (CPU).

The other important aspect of Milestone Arcus™ is the way it enables advanced integrators to move beyond traditional, centralized conceptions of physical security systems, and toward 'distributed' solutions.

This is a radical departure from current, server-centric systems. In this new type of solution, there is no central point. The VMS exists as a distributed solution across devices, including cameras. Users can log on to any of the cameras (or other devices) and have access to the entire VMS. The processing power sits on these 'edge' devices.

With Milestone Arcus™, a distributed solution like this becomes easy to use because it looks like a traditional system. This is really the technical breakthrough for physical security installers and end users: you can connect the distributed cameras together and manage them as if they were a traditional system that physical security users know well.

Many physical security installers will use Milestone Arcus™ as a way to extend their business to IP without the need to learn network technology in depth.

For the more advanced integrators, who see the opportunity that distributed solutions offer, the combination of the Milestone Arcus™ ease of use and the computing power and storage of advanced cameras means that they can start implementing a distributed solution now. They do not have to wait for hardware to catch up to the type of scenario that Milestone Arcus™ is enabling.
Even today, about 50 percent of the physical security equipment sold is

estimated to be analog, so there is considerable potential business that will be moving to IP networked solutions during the coming years. That could be worth US $6 billion, not including service and maintenance. It's lucrative, not just for us, but for all of our ecosystem partners as well.

Milestone Arcus™ is an exciting new development for us. It's also an example of our openness, and our belief in the strength of partnership and connectedness. We believe that by being upfront about our embedded status in our partners' products – rather than treating it as a white-labeled, OEM arrangement – we can add value through our market-leading position and 15 years of industry experience.

And the impact of the new business unit is obvious. In the short space of time the initiative has been running, it's clear that everyone in our company is excited – by the freedom that the team has to operate, and by the potential for what they might produce. Having both the Silicon Valley and Copenhagen Incubation and Ventures bases is great; the U.S. office gives us access to the latest breakthroughs and the sharpest minds in the technology business, and our Copenhagen Incubation team contribute to that excitement permeating the whole company. People can stop by and see what's happening, or what might be happening in our future. It's tangible and inspiring.

The initiative is the right one at the right time, and a positive move for Milestone as a whole. It's also a move that ensures our agility and commitment to openness is used in the service of new and exciting future opportunities.

The End (is not the end)

This is where I'd originally planned to end this book. It would have marked 15 years of Milestone as a company, and ten years for me in my role as CEO. We'd just embarked on a new stage of the company's evolution, reappraised and reorganized the way we approached the market. Our new Incubation and Ventures initiative was a pleasing echo of John and Henrik's early days, lending the story a nice sense of circularity and renewal.

It wasn't going to finish that abruptly, of course. I wrote about the future of the industry. I wrote: The shape of future technologies can reflect the changes occurring in consumer technology. That's important, and it's a thought that I'll return to.

I also wrote about more imminent security industry developments, such as Video Surveillance as a Service, more commonly referred to as VSaaS. VSaaS is a relatively simple concept: instead of customers paying for servers and associated hardware and storing them on-site in their own facility, they pay a subscription fee – usually on a per- camera basis – for video and its management software and other functions like analytics to be hosted in 'the cloud' potentially by an external provider. When we refer to 'the cloud,' we're talking about the Internet. But what we're really talking about are the servers of the hosting company, or VSaaS vendor, which are accessible via the internet.

In theory, all of the functionality of an on-site IP video system should be available through a VSaaS solution. The critical return on investment comes from saving on the costs of server and associated hardware outlay, as well the overheads for floor space, maintenance, software update patches, virus protection, etc.

And we know there is interest in cloud-based services – a huge proportion of smartphone users are already taking advantage of the cloud to store photos and data, whether they are aware of it or not (as the theft of some salacious, ostensibly private images of Hollywood stars has proven).

But video – and particularly full frame rate video - essential for more complex analytics functions – requires significantly more bandwidth than still images or data. Importantly, this bandwidth needs to provide a high-speed connection for both uploading and downloading. Currently, if you've got a good broadband connection, chances are the download speed is excellent, but the upload speed doesn't compare.

To combat these restrictions, a company could invest in a high-speed fiber optic broadband connection – but this tends to incur large annual rental costs, which amount to more than that of buying and maintaining its own servers.

At present, then, VSaaS is only really suitable for small camera count projects, for home use or very small office requirements. But for a reasonable commercial property, it's just not appropriate yet.

Once the broadband service providers are able to provide reliable, high-speed, two-way connections at the right price point, we predict that there will start to be more significant uptake for VSaaS. That looks likely to happen at some point over the next few years, so it's something we'll be keeping a very close eye on.

As well as VSaaS, I wrote about the lessons that I'd learned over the past ten years at Milestone, about the importance of passion, of independence, of thinking big. Of connectedness and partnership. Of leadership. I wrote about Milestone's three distinct phases. From 1998 to 2003, we were in our entrepreneur phase. Then from 2004 to 2008, we concentrated on growing the business – expanding our scope, establishing our position in the U.S. market, and creating demand via education and training. From 2009 on, our focus has been on leadership. We are now helping to guide the industry into the video enabling era, broadening the very idea of what video surveillance can be and do, and the usage of video as a whole.

But now it's been a year since that original ending was written. In that time the Incubation and Ventures unit has introduced a new range of products, the Milestone Husky™ series. These are Milestone's first steps outside of the software-only world. While Milestone Arcus was designed to be installed on any suitable device, Milestone Husky is a range of hardware network video recorders running preconfigured Milestone video management software that is customizable.

They were conceived in response to a desire from our Professional business unit market segment – those with lower camera numbers, such as small retailers and offices – for a simple, analog-like piece of equipment, where ease of use and installation is paramount. The three Husky models – the M10, M30 and M50 – automatically detect cameras from our extensive integration list onto the network, and automatically install them onto the system.

They're a user-friendly, plug'n'play solution, and as I write this, we are just about to introduce new Hybrid models, which allow a mix of IP and analog cameras. And all of the Husky models look great. They're beautifully designed, in the best Scandinavian tradition.

In addition to Milestone Husky, we've also launched Milestone Interconnect. This is an add-on for our flagship XProtect Corporate VMS software that enables all the other Milestone software products, Milestone Husky NVRs, and Arcus embedded appliances to be, as the name suggests, interconnected, accessed and managed centrally, as well as operating as independent local systems.

Milestone Interconnect is designed for flexibility – because over time, small surveillance installations may expand over multiple sites, requiring more advanced features, centralized monitoring and management. Milestone Interconnect prepares these installations for future growth and enables users to grow their systems to cover multiple locations.

Some other important changes have happened in the past year as well. As I've noted elsewhere that as a leader it's important to be flexible and able to adapt to change, to lead the process and to inspire confidence in your team – and to trust in them as well. As it turned out, all of those attributes proved crucial in the busiest nine month period of my career.

> In my original ending, I asked: what does the future have in store? Where will we be aiming next? Well, there's always the moon, I wrote. And there was.
>
> We decided to take Milestone public.

10

The Next Level

This is how it happened.

May 2013

It began with an approach from a company which was interested in buying Milestone. This in itself isn't unusual. It occurs reasonably regularly, and because of that we worked with a bank, Jefferies, which handled inbound requests.

Often the way it happens is that someone will knock on your door, saying that they'd like to buy your company. Their expectation is that you'll be up for sale very cheaply. They ask what your price expectations are, and you reply with a ridiculously high number, and they come back with a ridiculously low number, and if there's no real reason to meet in the middle, you say your goodbyes.

In this case, the company interested in buying Milestone – which we codenamed 'Moonraker', because, well, why not? – seemed genuine in their intent. But for their own internal reasons they decided not to proceed. So that was that.

Except it wasn't. It made us, the Milestone management team, start thinking about the question of acquisition versus going public via an IPO – an Initial Public Offering – the only process you can control yourself (providing the market is receptive). In both cases you're looking at the evolution of your small company, taking the next step in terms of available capital, scale and visibility. As well as a financial gain for the company founders, of course, who have dedicated so many years of their lives to the business, and the other shareholders. In Milestone's case that included many of our employees as well as the management team.

There are arguments to be made for both an acquisition and an IPO. We initially leaned towards being acquired in the long-term simply because it's easier. We'd heard stories about the IPO process, how difficult it is, and the sheer magnitude of the obligations required of you once your company goes public. To actually get to an IPO, there's the compliance costs, paying lawyers and bankers and PR people, the sheer time and work involved in ensuring that your reporting and processes are up to scratch, all while running your company as normal.

Then once you are listed on the stock exchange, you're scrutinized right down to quarter-by-quarter earnings, which can dramatically reduce your flexibility. That's a big change to make when you're coming from a business founded on and proud of its entrepreneurial spirit. It means that some companies can act pretty oddly in order to fulfill promises to investors or to meet stated targets.

So the management team initially felt that we'd prefer to be acquired simply because it's easier. In that case, then, why would you take your company public? What are the advantages?

From our point of view there were a few key benefits. One is that we'd receive increased visibility and credibility. This is important, as it would mean we'd gain access to new customers who might have doubts about working with a privately held company. As a public company, they'd be able to look at our numbers, and our plans for the future. We'd also be able to attract high quality staff with the prestige of working for a publicly traded company.

Money. That comes into it too, of course. Many companies who go public are looking for capital to invest in future growth. But if you raise a lot of money and you're not sure what you're going to do with it, that can be a problem in itself. If you spend it on marketing and staff and the like, costs begin to increase dramatically. And as a public company you're very much required to be profitable, quarter by quarter – that's what your shareholders demand of you.

There have been some high-profile technology companies in the US where this isn't the case. Some of these companies have had an ongoing deficit and still seen their share price increase. But that's rare, particularly outside of the US context, and particularly for more niche businesses.

So we had to be clear about the money we were hoping to raise through an IPO, and what that money would be used for.

And I'll be honest: regarding primary/secondary planning, the board was conflicted about what we should do. Our chairman, Jesper Balser, wanted to progress slowly, to take our time and assess every factor involved in what would be a huge decision for Milestone, the biggest we'd ever had to make. On the other side of the table was Giuseppe Zocco, our board member from Index Ventures, with his vast experience in helping entrepreneurs and small businesses take the next step in their evolution. He felt that the time was absolutely right for Milestone to go public, and advocated for the value of swift and decisive action.

> One thing was clear. We were going to need some outside advice to help us decide either way.

The foundations

Before I get too deep into the adrenaline and tumult of the IPO process, I want to first look at some of the decisions we made which allowed Milestone to be in this position at all.

Way back in 2003, in fact, when I first took up my role with the company, I said to the other members of the board that I'd like us to be in a position to go public by 2008. It was the classic five year plan. But we hit a bump in the road: the worldwide financial crisis happened, and the markets effectively shut down.

So at that point there wasn't really any thought of the IPO option, instead we hooked up with Index Ventures, which turned out to be a great plan. We got cash (that we did not need) but first and foremost we got access to Giuseppe Zocco. And while the investment they provided in the business offered us a means of strengthening the balance sheet and future-proofing the company, the real, tangible benefit was the presence of Index's Giuseppe Zocco on the Milestone board. He had worked with numerous other tech start-ups and helped them evolve their businesses according to their needs, and his knowledge and experience would prove invaluable to us.

It took us another six years to get to the potential IPO point again.

In the meantime, we'd taken a number of steps that would prove crucial in establishing our readiness to go public. The re-segmentation of Milestone's organization, described earlier, was an important part of that. It not only meant we were at a reasonably advanced stage in our assessment of the market and our place within it, it also meant that our reporting and processes had been improved and, for want of a better word, professionalized.

Another important development was John and Henrik's initial decision to step away from the CEO and CFO roles – to concentrate on their areas of strength, and work with people that are specialists in their fields. That's why they got me on board as CEO, and that's why we brought in Lars Larsen as CFO. Larsen, as he's known to pretty much everyone within and around Milestone, became enormously important to us during this process, which will be evident as we go on.

Christina Bruun Geertsen is a partner at law firm Kromann Reumart and has worked with Milestone for a number of years. She was closely involved with our IPO preparations, as she has been with a variety of other businesses, and agreed that getting your business structure right is vital for companies who might be thinking about going public at some point in their future.

"When you have a company like Milestone, founded by two entrepreneurs, it's often a struggle to be adequately prepared," she said. "And it's a boring thing, but having your documentation ready actually means a lot. Apart from making your processes efficient, it also provides credibility for the team you're assembling to help you go public, and for potential investors."

Christina advises that entrepreneurial businesses should start thinking about making sure their processes and documentation are in place as early as possible.

"Small companies mature and add employees, and often they don't get around to setting up the necessary systems. There are many good reasons why you don't focus on that when you're a young start-up, but at some point you really need to put some resources into it – because every start-up has ambitions of going public or being acquired, and your business will need to be documented."

For us at Milestone, it was when Index invested in the company that we were forced to document our processes to a higher standard. And Christina confirms that having founders who were prepared to step away from the CEO and CFO roles was critical.

"That is one of the things that goes wrong in many businesses, that the original founders keep controlling the company and don't realize that what they're good at involves, usually, new ideas – and they should leave the rest of the stuff to someone who's much better at it," she says. "And that's not something you can do when you're really small – you don't have the funds, so you have to do it yourself. But as soon as you get a bit bigger, it can help you a lot especially when it comes to the scalability and predictability of your company.

> "Attracting the right investors is important, too, but that's not something that you can necessarily plan. So whether it's investors or a CFO or CEO, someone who can bring in capabilities that you do not already have yourself is very important."

This idea of working with specialists, allowing them to come on board and work with you to do what they do best, allowing you to focus on what you do best, not only makes sense in terms of the best use of available resources; it also echoes and reaffirms Milestone's central philosophy. Selecting quality partners and enabling them to focus on their specialties is our business model, that's business magnetism. It makes sense that our business structures and decisions should reflect that.

Another way of thinking about this preparation, early on, is as the way that a teenager might go about getting ready to date. You know you don't really have a chance with girls; you're young, you're gawky, you've got acne, your voice is breaking. And when you do get a chance to talk to a real girl, you're awkward, and you have no idea what to say. But you make sure you wash regularly, you start to shave, you practice your smooth talking and your smooth dancing in the mirror. Because you know that someday, you'll be the right age, and there'll be a girl – or a whole room full of girls – whom you are desperate to impress, and the last thing you need is to have them write you off immediately because you stink, or you have nothing to say to them, and no confidence in your dance moves.

Preparation is everything.

Summer 2013

Over the summer of 2013 we assessed our options. With the board not entirely sure whether we wanted to go public, the decision was made to bring in some experts who could advise us on our best course of action. We put out a request for proposal, and spoke to three different organizations. In the end we settled on the Rothschild Group.

Rothschild is a hugely respected and long established finance business. We engaged them out of London. Giuseppe had experience working with them on a number of projects over the years.

Giuseppe says: "Getting Rothschild involved helped by providing an independent third-party opinion, which could guide the company through the process. At Index we don't always do that but in this case it made sense, particularly as there were differing views from the board as to when or if the IPO process should go ahead."

We codenamed the IPO 'Project Odin'. In Nordic mythology, Odin is the god of gods and ruler of Valhalla.

Rothschild helped us to assess what the opportunity was, taking a high-level approach and allowing us to come to the conclusion that yes, this was something we wanted to pursue. We didn't have to commit to it fully, but market conditions were beginning to look favorable and Milestone's business was progressing as planned. If we wanted to be in with a chance of making it work, we had to put our team together.

Autumn 2013

Rothschild rolled out a process that we needed to follow in order to be prepared for an IPO. There are a number of components you need when you're preparing to go public: bankers, lawyers, and a public relations agency, as well as the team members from within your own business.

In October 2013 the Board agreed to prepare for an IPO, and the process began in earnest. This involved producing Request For Proposals (RFPs) for the required lawyers and bankers – the potential IPO process team members – and the end result of that is a lot of presentations which you need to assess.

To deal with that process we formed a sub-group of the board called the M&A & IPO Committee. This committee effectively acts as advisers to the board, making recommendations and pitching to the board about those we thought we should work with.

In our case, putting the IPO team together was an even more cumbersome process than it might have been for others, as we had decided that we wanted to have a share offering in the USA – called a 144A offering – in addition to the offering in whichever market's exchange we decided to list on (more details on this later). We needed our own lawyers, the underwriters – the bankers – needed their lawyers, and with the American offering, we also needed American lawyers to ensure we complied with the rules there. It all added up to a lot of conference calls and a lot of paperwork.

Around this time the issue of secrecy first raised its devious head. At this point only the Milestone board and our four-person executive management team and my technical assistant, Mark Wilson, knew about the IPO plans. Rothschild had advised us – urged us, really – to keep it amongst this core group. "Don't tell anybody," they said.

Even at this early stage this secrecy was beginning to create issues. Because of the preparation we were doing, we needed to go to our managers for information on the way their departments were run, really quite detailed information which we wouldn't normally need to ask for. They knew something was going on.

Rothschild were insistent, but I felt that keeping this secret wasn't my style. It wasn't Milestone's style. It was antithetical to the Scandinavian management style of inclusiveness that we had built the company upon. The advisers at Rothschild said that informing the wider leadership team would create fear, uncertainty and doubt, and causing more problems down the line.

But I felt that there would be even more uncertainty if we didn't tell them. In other companies, in other corporate cultures, it's often the case that even as a manager you find out about important decisions once they've already been finalized. If that's part of your company's culture, you run the risk of whispers circulating around the business for months. And that uncertainty is more of a disincentive than being trusted with important information. Milestone's managers knew something was up. By telling them what that was, we were able to eliminate that speculation and worry.

So on November 6, 2013, I gathered the Extended Leadership Team, a group of 12 people running the company, together. I wanted to make sure everyone was focused on the discussion, so – like an irritable schoolteacher – I went around and physically collected everybody's phones and laptops. These days it's the only way to guarantee undivided attention!

The news that we were thinking of going public was well received. The ELT were as excited about it as we were – nervous, certainly, but excited. To be a part of a business taking that next step up was galvanizing, I think. The thrill was infectious, and they were very much on board with us. Letting them in on the secret proved to be a very good move, because they would go out of their way to help us obtain any information we needed as the process went on.

It also meant we needed to start our list of 'insiders' – the official list of those informed enough of our intentions to be restricted in various ways, not the least of which is buying and selling stocks – insider trading.

> The last thing we needed was a Martha Stewart situation on our hands.

November 28, 2013

We held a board meeting at the Turning Torso building in Malmö, Sweden, across the Öresund strait from Copenhagen. It's the tallest skyscraper in Sweden, and an architectural marvel; it's called Turning Torso because it looks like a twisted body, contorting to look behind itself. It's impressive, but also disorienting. Which is somewhat appropriate, as the next meetings we were about to have were disorienting in their own way.

We were at Turning Torso to meet with our banker candidates, who would work with us on the IPO preparation process. They were JP Morgan and Carnegie Investment Bank, who were both eventually selected. That was a crucial decision, but the meeting itself was nothing compared to our board meeting a couple of days later. We were in Sweden again, meeting with our chairman Jesper Balser, approving budgets for 2014. It also happened to be the day of the worst storm to hit Denmark for a decade.

As the meeting went on, we could see that the weather was getting worse – darker and windier by the minute. The problem for us was that if the wind got too bad, they'd close the bridge between Sweden and Denmark. So the key decisions on budgets were made, we cut the meeting short, and took off immediately. In spite of that a few people didn't get to the bridge in time. It closed, and they were forced to take the ferry across the strait. It's a short journey, but in this weather it was long enough for a number of passengers to suffer from seasickness.

We all made it safely home in the end, but we were hoping that the storm wasn't some sort of omen about the months to come!

December 23, 2013

Rothschild had been working with us on a 'management presentation' which was for the Joint Book Runner team, or JBR. The JBR team were the bankers working with us on the IPO, responsible for selling our share offering to investors. This presentation would help them to build our 'equity story'.

Rothschild had taken the information we'd given them and put it together in this document, which they wanted to review with us. Unfortunately, they wanted to review it on the day before Christmas Eve. Also unfortunately, I was away skiing with my family, and out of phone range. So I had to leave it to Larsen and my technical assistant Mark Wilson to take the conference call with Rothschild to go through the presentation.

Rothschild are accustomed to the IPO process, and used to 150% focus once the process is underway. But Milestone is a relatively small company, and most everyone was on vacation. I was skiing with my family, out of phone range, so Larsen and Mark had to take the call – lasting four hours, going through every page of the equity story document – while they were both away with their families. It's another example of the value of surrounding yourself with high quality people who you can trust to take care of business on your behalf.

It highlighted one of the challenges we would face at the dawn of the New Year: continuing the day-to-day operation of Milestone while devoting a huge amount of focus to the process of taking the company public. This Christmas break was the calm before the storm. 2014 would be intense.

January 7, 2014

We headed over to London for the JBR team 'beauty parade'. This is kind of what it sounds like, except there are no swimsuits, thankfully. The bankers and lawyers who had responded to our RFPs were brought in to meet us. It's an important process because you're going to be working with these people over the next six or eight months, so even if you know they're qualified to do the job, you want to know that you'll be able to get along with them while you do so. And you want to know that they're eager to do it, too.

> It's like dating – you want to meet someone who is as interested in you as you are in them. It's not always the case.

One of the banks that we talked to had a very odd view of the whole thing. In our initial meeting they sent a very junior team. This row of bankers sat lined up opposite us, with a phone in the middle of the boardroom table. Their CEO was on loudspeaker, and his team didn't say anything. If we asked them a question, they would defer to this disembodied voice on the phone.

They didn't seem particularly interested in Milestone as an IPO, which was surprising, as we thought it would be good for them. But the way they answered our questions was so non-committal, it was funny. It emerged later that they were annoyed by the involvement of Rothschild – they felt a bit threatened over their turf. In the end, though, we selected our team, and six days later, the Milestone board said we were good to go.

January 30, 2014

From here on in, everything got really busy. Crazily busy. The first step was to continue the build-up of the management presentation, as we were due to show that to the JBR team at the end of January. They would use this as the starting point for what is called the 'equity story'.

The equity story tells investors what Milestone is about, and answers the question: Why should I invest in this company?

It's the foundation for everything else you do during the IPO process. It's not just a run-of-the-mill presentation. It drills down to specific details, to the real DNA floating in the backbone of your company. Who are you? Where do you want to go? How do you want to do it?

So we'd been working on the management presentation for a month, with the idea being that we would show this to the JBR team and they'd use it to start building the equity story. The management presentation is our version of the Milestone story, and we'd invited the JBR team to our head office to see the company.

At this point the process was still secret. In Milestone, only our extended leadership team knew about it. And now we had about 40 people descending on our offices, in a bus from Copenhagen airport. For a meeting that officially wasn't happening.

Larsen sent an email to Milestone staff saying that he'd been receiving a lot of press enquiries, so rather than do individual interviews, we'd invited media representatives to our offices to update them on the company story. We also asked the JBR guys not to show up in suits and ties – nobody at Milestone comes to work dressed that formally, so anyone who walks around our hallways dressed in a suit really stands out. So the Danish JBR team members came dressed ultra-casually, while the Brits couldn't help themselves and came in suits, but with their jackets off, and their ties in their pockets just in case...

On top of all of this, I had to tell people to refrain from leaving the meeting room and making calls in the hallways – which, of course, they ignored. They were on their phones really loudly saying, "Hi, I'm at Milestone Systems and I'm advising on their IPO. I just have a few questions..." I learned a couple of things that day. One is that you can try to control or manage people's behavior, but it's just not possible. The other is that bankers talk a lot about the importance of secrecy, of confidentiality, but they don't seem to practice it themselves very often. This would become even more obvious as the process went on.

The actual management presentation was a full day of talking the JBR team through the company, our products and plans. We managed to excite the team, to get them fully on board with us. This is crucial, because you want to attract the best people from the banks to work with your company. Often they'll send the senior people to win your business, but the junior guys are the ones who are sent to execute it. So for us to motivate them with a professional presentation was vital. And it worked, we got the best people!

They responded with their plan for how to approach the next seven months, with a planned early September date for the stock market listing. There were ten work streams that had to be tackled: company preparation and governance, due diligence, financial disclosure, prospectus and listing process, legal and other documentation, business plan, valuation and capital structure, marketing and marketing materials, offer process and execution, retail offer, and communications and PR. We were going to be busy.

February 2014

Less than a week after our management presentation, I flew into Orlando to speak at our MIPS partner conference – a major annual event for Milestone. The evening before my keynote address at the event, Sky News in the UK ran a story with this headline:

> 'Big Brother' CCTV Firm Joins City IPO Frenzy
> The 'Big Brother' CCTV Firm was Milestone, of course.
> Our plans had leaked.

The report, by Sky News' City Editor Mark Kleinman, wasn't a complete surprise, as Sky had been in touch a little earlier to ask us for a comment, which we sent them. But then nothing happened, and we weren't sure if they were going to publish at all. And then suddenly we were on the front page of their business section.

The story claimed we were going to list on the London Stock Exchange, which was something we had discussed but had not made a decision on yet. We're not sure where the leak came from, exactly, but it was someone who had been fairly close to the process.

The immediate effect was that I needed to say something at MIPS the next day. Not only were many of our partners there, a large number of security industry press were in attendance as well, and one of the more prominent websites had run with the Sky News story. I needed to nip the speculation in the bud as it risked overwhelming the message of the conference, which was the work we were doing with our partners.

We put together a statement, approved by our banking team.
This is what I said onstage:
"You have most likely seen today's home page of the website that is one of the prominent industry watchers in our business. As you can see they are asking a question about us – is Milestone going to IPO?

"Milestone is a successful company with a 17-year solid track record in our business. Our primary focus is the continued development of our business but we are also lucky enough to be at a stage in our growth where IPO is one of the options available to us. But it's just one option and no decision has been made.

"There is nothing more to say at this point but you'll be the first to hear when and if we have something more to announce. For the next two days my concern is about our partners. What I do want to tell you is that my intention is to continue to grow Milestone's business and build on the successes we have seen to date. We are focused on:
"Strengthening our products, you saw several new and innovative products from us last year.

"Expanding our business ecosystem. This is our 9th annual global partner conference on Milestone technology.

"Keeping Milestone as a global leader in our business.

"I care about the fact that you have taken time out of your schedules to travel to Florida so that you can be here with me at MIPS. And I want to make sure that both myself and my team do our best to give you the maximum value from your time here.

"So, here's the deal. I do not want to add to the speculation, I will close this topic of discussion now. After this slide you will not hear me talk about it again for the rest of MIPS. And this goes for my team, our partners and the press that are here with us."

It worked. But it was another example of the way that our day-to-day operation of our business could be potentially undermined by the focus on our IPO. As we saw it, it was a good reason to keep quiet about it, even if that secrecy was at odds with our usual policy of openness.
It also led us to recruit a specialist IPO public relations company to handle this kind of situation in future.

March 2014

Around this time the Milestone board was in heated discussions over where we should list. For starters, should it be Denmark as part of NASDAQ –OMX, or elsewhere?

After considering the US and deciding against it, we eventually settled on a choice between the Copenhagen, London and Oslo stock exchanges. Oslo's a bit of an unusual one, but Norway's a wealthy country, based on its oil reserves, and there seemed to be an interest there in relatively smaller IPOs, of whatever nature: salmon, tech, medicine, or flowers – they don't seem to care.

So we had a long, long back-and-forth discussion about the right venue. Looking back, I'd say we wasted a lot of time on this decision. In the end we settled on Denmark, for a number of reasons. One was that we'd prefer to be the bigger fish in the smaller pond than the reverse. We didn't think we'd gain any additional valuation by listing outside of Denmark, and there'd also be higher compliance standards and more requests for information. And the Copenhagen Stock Exchange is part of the NASDAQ group, so we would still be able to sell our stock within that structure. So there wouldn't really be any limitations placed upon us.

The downside is that Denmark's a small market, and we needed to be sure there'd be enough interest in us. Which is where pilot fishing comes in.

Pilot fishing is also known as 'early-looks', and it's essentially asking a smaller group of potential investors if they would be interested in our offering and getting an idea of the sort of price they would be prepared to pay for our shares.

On March 19 and 20 we held early-look presentations in Denmark and London. They went really well – the market reception was positive and reinforced our decision to go with the Copenhagen stock exchange. But what really sticks with me is the London event, which was held at the offices of some of the potential investors we were visiting. Now, bear in mind that these events are still meant to be secret, and that our IPO hasn't been announced officially. And what do I see when I walk into the reception of this busy building? A huge screen, and on it is written: "Welcome to Milestone Systems for pilot-fishing!"

They may as well have put an advertisement in the paper saying that this IPO is happening. It's astonishing, really, how little confidentiality is valued. The first thing I did after laughing was take out my phone and snap a picture of it, because it was so absurd, yet entertaining.

April 2014

At the start of April an article about Milestone's IPO appeared in Berlingske, Denmark's venerable national newspaper. Once again they approached us with some information, which they really shouldn't have had, but we thought that the time was right to acknowledge that Milestone going public was on the horizon. I didn't say much, but indicated that the listing would be on the Copenhagen stock exchange.

The story appeared on April 3rd. That was also the day that we started drafting the prospectus – a vitally important part of the process. The prospectus is a legal obligation and it has to contain all the salient facts an investor would need to make an informed decision about whether or not to buy shares in your company. Our prospectus was due to be filed with the relevant authorities on Friday, July 11. We planned for five drafts of the document to be revised over the next three months.

Then we got a call from Rothschild. They'd been approached by a company which was interested in talking to us about an acquisition, after hearing rumors in the market that we were looking to go public. That company was Canon.

As I mentioned earlier, it's not unusual for us to be approached by a potential acquirer.

> We had no idea how serious Canon was in this approach.

They had a relatively small presence in the security industry with a fairly small range of cameras, which is a tiny part of their total business as the world's biggest imaging manufacturer. But every approach is worth taking seriously, so we put a small, three-person team together to look at this Canon deal, and arranged to meet with them. We codenamed the Canon approach 'Colorado'. So alongside the day-to-day operations of Milestone and the IPO process, we now had a third track running. Things were getting hectic.

A few days later we had our Annual General Meeting (AGM), and delivered our best-ever annual report. That's expected of you, when you're looking to go public; otherwise your valuation is affected.

The day of the AGM, April 8, was also my birthday. So in addition to the good numbers I got a cake and a rendition of Happy Birthday. It was a welcome bit of light relief during a pretty stressful period.

The IPO dilemma

It's worth taking a moment here to discuss what I call 'the IPO dilemma'. This is centered on the way that primary and secondary shares are divided up. When a company goes public, there's a split between primary shares – new shares created for the listing – and secondary shares, which are those shares already held by existing stockholders and are being resold from these private stockholders to the public. The introduction of these new shares dilutes the existing shares.

At the same time, if you're not looking to raise huge amounts of money via the IPO, you have an issue with 'free float'. That is, if there aren't many publicly tradable shares available, your share price can be volatile, as a large trade could have a big impact on your share value. So getting the balance right for available primary and secondary shares is important. Bankers need a certain amount of free float – available shares – to have liquidity in the stock, and they tend to ask for that to be somewhere around a third of the company. Half of that might come from existing shareholders, and half from new shares.

Added to this is the share valuation. This is done by the banks, and it almost inevitably starts high – as they want to win your business – and slowly gets lower, as they are underwriting the IPO and want to limit their risk.

So working out how to distribute between primary and secondary shares becomes difficult. If the valuation is low, then the primary offering will also be low – so existing shareholders will want to sell less than their 15 percent of the third that has been agreed upon. So they may want to sell 5 percent, which means you need to raise 25 percent via secondary shares. Suddenly the amount of money you are looking to raise – as opposed to that going to the existing shareholders – is a lot more than you suggested in your equity story. You originally said that you didn't need to raise a huge amount of money from the IPO – but now you are. What will all of this money be used for? What are your plans? The market says: 'We need to have confidence that you know what you're doing or what we won't invest in you in the first place!'

What can you do? You can either change your equity story, which is bad, because you've just explained this to potential investors at your early-look meetings – so you probably don't want to do that. Or you can put more primary shares up for sale, so the secondary shares are reduced, and the money you're raising looks more realistic. But with a lower valuation, of course the existing shareholders aren't happy, as they're selling at a lower price than they think their shares are worth.

It's a Catch-22 situation, and over the course of this process it caused some very painful conversations. The only way to avoid it is if the bankers are totally realistic from the outset with their valuation – which is unlikely as they want to paint themselves in the best possible light and of course win your business – or the market just happens to be going through the roof during that whole period from when you decide to go public until you actually list. Then it's not so tough. But you'd have to be very lucky for that.

It's a real dilemma, one that I hadn't considered before we got into the process, and looking ahead I can see how it could completely derail an IPO.

April 22, 2014

The IPO PR agency arranged for me to do an interview with Børsen, Denmark's financial newspaper. It seemed to go fine, although they also insisted I pose for some photos which involved me staring at surveillance cameras, bowing as a camera was held above my head, manhandling surveillance cameras – basically anything they could think of that involved me and a camera. They were more odd than arty, and the more bizarre posing proposals I declined.

Three days later the story came out. The translated headline read:

"Founders of IT surveillance firm expect big payday from IPO"
And this was precisely the message we didn't want going out. We didn't want the focus of all of our work to be reduced to this narrow focus on money for the founders and shareholders. We wanted to tell a Danish technology success story.

The Scandinavian mindset, too, was a factor. We knew that Danish readers wouldn't be thinking, "what a success story for a Danish company", they'd be thinking, "the original owners have made a lot of money." It's perhaps different in the US or elsewhere in the world. But here it's similar to what the Australians call 'Tall Poppy Syndrome' – cutting down the flower that stands highest in its field. There's an element of positivity there, in that it suggests supporting the underdog, but it's mainly negative: resenting someone for their success.

So it didn't help our relationship with our PR firm. They got in touch when the story came out, saying what a great article it was. Which was completely at odds with what our communications objectives were.

In this case the damage wasn't too bad. It was contained. But it also served as a warning as to what we could expect as a publicly traded company. Once we were listed, our visibility would be raised dramatically, and we'd constantly be under scrutiny by journalists. To be totally honest, it wasn't something I was looking forward to.

The effect was to make the Canon approach look more appealing in contrast.

May 2014

Rokus van Iperen is President and Chief Executive Officer of Canon Europe, Middle East & Africa. I had spoken with Rokus on the phone, and we'd earlier organized to meet in London on May 7 to discuss Canon's interest in Milestone.

But when the Børsen article came out, it contained a quote from me saying that I wasn't interested in selling Milestone to a big, boring conglomerate. When Canon's Danish advisers picked up on that, Rokus was on the phone to me immediately.

"What's going on? Don't you want to be acquired?" he asked.

I said: "I actually mean what I said there. I do think that being bought by a big conglomerate and being swallowed up would be really bad, and it would be boring. It needs to be a different arrangement."

Rokus agreed with me. He said that was not the intention, and that if Canon acquired Milestone, it would be under the condition that Milestone is able to operate as a stand-alone company within the Canon Group. It would be what is known as a 'Chinese Wall' situation.

A Chinese Wall is a term that derives, presumably, from Beijing's Forbidden City (although Wikipedia claims it's the Great Wall of China) – where the surrounding and much larger city is not privy to the workings and the goings-on of the Forbidden City itself. So in our case, it would mean that Milestone would be able to operate as a stand-alone business within Canon, were the acquisition to take place. It's also used in financial circles to refer to a barrier to prevent conflicts of interest. In this sense, there was also a Chinese Wall between our IPO team and the small group working on the Canon deal. The IPO team had no knowledge that we were speaking to a possible acquirer; we wanted them fully focused on the task at hand, and there was no guarantee that the Canon approach would go further than other potential acquirers in the past.

Bearing this in mind, we met with Rokus and Darren Rayner, Canon Europe's Chief of Corporate Development EMEA. I started by asking, in all seriousness, if we're acquired by Canon, would we still be able to work closely with our partners that were Canon competitors? They're very important to our business. Rokus said that there would be no problem – that the Chinese Wall arrangement would mean we would operate as a stand-alone business, and that we would be able to continue our relationships with our partners – also the ones that are Canon's competitors – without interference. I was impressed by the conceptually elegant solution to a difficult problem.

We entered into a month-long exclusivity period where they would have access to a virtual data room – a cloud-based repository of all of our relevant company documents where specific permissions can be granted to different users – so that they could do their due diligence investigations. The exclusivity arrangement meant that we weren't able to speak to other potential acquirers who approached us once news of the IPO was public, but they would be able to come back to us with their offers once this period was up on June 7.

Later in the month, I flew to the US for our early-look presentations in San Francisco, which seemed to be really well received, then I headed to the Napa Valley in California for the Index Summit, where our investor Index Ventures gathered together a large portion of the CEOs in their portfolio of about 150 companies to network and learn.

Speakers included LinkedIn CEO Jeff Weiner and Twitter CEO Dick Costolo. Asked what keeps him awake at night, Costolo said: "I sleep like a baby. I wake up every second hour crying." Unsurprisingly, even though this was a joke, being the head of one of the most visible tech companies in the world is pretty stressful, and another reminder of the pros and cons of going IPO.

Also onstage were three of the Index companies that had recently gone public, of which two had Danish origins. One was Just Eat, which started up in Denmark then went global, listing in London. The other was customer service software company Zendesk, which also started in Denmark and moved to San Francisco. So two of the three onstage had Scandinavian heritage, and we were looking at an imminent IPO ourselves. Giuseppe, our Index board member, was there as well, and winking to each other discretely, we commented on the way that the Scandinavian welfare model economy was still producing these successful tech companies. It looked like The Economist was right: the Vikings are coming.

May 28, 2014

Here we need to talk briefly about the valuation of our offering – that is, the initial share price that we would offer to the market the first time we were listed. What tends to happen is that the banks you work with look at your company, at all the documentation you've provided, and do a combination of peer group analysis and metrics, like price performance, cash flow and sales. They come back with their valuation, which tends to be pleasingly high.

Then, as the process goes on, this valuation starts getting lower. It makes sense to them, as they're underwriting the IPO and they have to deal with the risk. But they also need to provide reasons to underpin their lower valuation, and in this case they pointed to a North American competitor of ours (whose share price at the time was spiraling downwards), and their CFO had resigned. So they said that they were being forced to lower their valuation as a result of this market activity.

At the same time, the primary/secondary discussion that I mentioned earlier was really heating up, and obviously not helped by this new, lower valuation.

So we fed back our disappointment to the banks. We said that if this was the way it was going to be, they may as well forget it. Why should we go public at all? Some fairly direct language was used.

This was compounded by the level of information they wanted us to provide for the prospectus, and as a consequence, for our future reporting. As underwriters, they want to protect themselves by providing as much in-depth information to prospective investors as they can, to avoid miscommunication or being sued down the line. On the other hand, we'd rather keep our reporting at a higher level than to drill down, to give ourselves flexibility and the chance to react to situations with the same entrepreneurial spirit, which has always guided us.

We decided early on that we would report revenue at the level of our four regions – Americas, EMEA, APAC, and other - which includes certification and miscellaneous items. That would be the extent of our reporting segmentation.

But the bankers wanted us to claim that we had a recurring revenue element that was significant – that if we landed a high-end customer there was a direct correlation between that and expanding revenue from them over a five-year period, buying further licenses and the like. Which isn't necessarily untrue, but there was little way to finally prove it. They also wanted to say that there was a predictable revenue source in our software upgrade path and maintenance and support agreements. We didn't want to discuss either of these in the prospectus, because they simply aren't that predictable, and we didn't want to get tied down to making these revenue numbers each quarter if they aren't, in reality, that regular.

And this is where Lars Larsen, our CFO, really took charge, and stood his ground. The bankers were incredibly persistent, determined that they were going to get him to provide this information about 'recurring revenue', and he just refused, time after time. He'd worked previously for publicly traded companies, including Carlsberg and Microsoft, and knew that allowing this level of detailed scrutiny over details which we weren't comfortable with would only lead to difficulties further down the line. So he stood up to them, wave after wave of insistent bankers. I was really impressed, thanks Larsen.

The bankers' response was to say again that if we couldn't provide this information, then we couldn't argue for a higher valuation. We pointed to US tech companies, which were actually losing money, but still had high valuations.

This was all building towards June 19, which was the scheduled date for what's called the 'analysts' presentation'. The banks have their own sector analysts, separate from their finance teams. They work independently, and build their own models based on the presentation the JBR team provides. The bankers' rationale was that without the recurring revenue information, the analysts' models would be less predictable and would result in a lower valuation recommendation.

The Milestone team said we understood, but it would put us in an impossible position for the future.

> We refused. I'm proud of the way we stood together on this. A weaker management team would have caved in.

The Canon approach was beginning to look more appealing by the moment. In fact, it was a bit like a teenager who is courting a girl. She's interested, but then he spots another young lady. She's prettier, he thinks. And she's got a lot more money.

May 29

Both processes were now hitting maximum velocity. Canon's people had been doing their due diligence, going through our documents, and each Friday we asked them to come back to us and re-confirm their offer. Each Friday, they did.

At this point we didn't know which way we would go: acquisition, or IPO. Acquisition was what we were beginning to favor, thanks to Canon's assurances of being managed as a stand-alone entity, but there was always a chance something could derail the whole thing at very short notice. So we needed to continue with the IPO, preparing the analysts' presentation and meeting all the relevant deadlines.

It was like being a secret agent for a little while. I'd be in a JBR team meeting, and excuse myself to take a phone call, which in reality was an excuse for me to head into another meeting, or a conference call, about the Canon deal, or Colorado to call it by the codename we used for it.

So in this spirit of confidentiality, we held secret meetings with Canon at Milestone HQ on a public holiday. This was done under the assumption that the acquisition would take place, and to look at post-acquisition planning – what we needed to do in terms of communication and that sort of thing.

After that was the final drafting session for the analysts' presentation. The way this came together was interesting. What happens is that you begin the prospectus and the analysts' presentation in parallel, and they're put together separately, but feed into each other. They're constantly being updated so both match up, and the equity story is consistent. The analysts' presentation is essentially a visualization of the prospectus, over 100 pages long. This was a round-the-clock, four-month process.

Once you've presented that information to the analysts, they come back with feedback that is incorporated into the prospectus. The analysts take the information we've provided them, build their own models, then go and speak to their clients, the investors, and educate them about the opportunity.

Earlier in the month we created a separate presentation to show the team from Canon, which included more than 40 people, both Canon staff and advisers. On the IPO track, there were up to about 70 people involved. The sheer numbers meant that working out what you'd spoken about, to whom, and when, was incredibly complex and at times confusing.

May 31, 2014

Canon's exclusivity arrangement with us expired on June 6. If that date came and went, we would have been able to go out into the market and quietly invite competing bids, with the idea that a bidding war might ensue. If Canon wanted to make certain that they would be able to complete the acquisition, that first Friday in June was when it would have to happen.

They'd been coming back each Friday confirming their offer, until the last Friday in May. At that point they said they'd discovered some details which meant that they wanted to change the composition of the deal. Their new proposal wasn't what we were hoping for, so I took it to the M&A committee, and I suggested we abort the deal. They agreed.

On the Saturday, I sent Rokus an email saying that based on Canon's feedback, there's no deal. The agreement had changed, and it no longer worked for us. We were going to pursue the IPO option.

He called me, saying that he thought they could find terms that would work. He would fly into Copenhagen on Monday.

John and I met with Rokus, and we sent him back with no deal. But by the Tuesday morning enough compromises had been made, in terms of cash component and the other elements of the deal, that we felt they had adequately complied with our requests. The deal was back on.

It's important to state here that it was Rokus' decisiveness that made this deal possible. Without his determination to make it happen – to fly in personally to talk to us, to show his true desire to make the acquisition work for both parties – things could have been very different.

But there were still a few days to go. Things can change very quickly. We had to continue with the IPO track, just in case.

June 6

The negotiations with Canon were set to be completed on Friday, June 6, then the deal would be signed on the Monday. Then a problem emerged. Due diligence is a detailed, legal process through which the acquiring company investigates the business prior to signing a contract. The process had gone very well for both Canon and Milestone, then – wouldn't you know it – there was a problem. The due diligence team had seen the problem earlier and at the time they felt it would be solved by the time we got to signing. Suddenly it came back to haunt us.

We'd spent a long day doing some fairly intense negotiating with the Canon team, and by 8pm or 9pm, everyone agreed that we were done with the commercial discussions. Someone on the Canon team said, "oh, and this is just a detail, right?"

"WHAT!?!" I seem to recall was my response. "No, it's everything!"

For reasons of confidentiality, I will not go into details, other than to say that it felt like we had hit a brick wall.

I want to stress to any young entrepreneurs reading this: you need to be over-zealous in scrutinizing every small detail as early in the negotiation for your business as possible. It will save you an enormous headache, and possibly quite a lot of money.

The Canon team quite rightly pointed out that the issue had a significant bearing on things, as they wanted to be clear on exactly what it was that they were buying. It looked, at the last moment, like the deal would have to go through further due diligence, which would take time, and would push us right up against the official dates for filing our prospectus with the relevant authorities to still have the IPO option – or the deal might be off altogether. It was a nightmare situation.

Back at Canon HQ, they hadn't heard any of this, and obviously thought everything was still going fine – so much so that we had received a text message from Mr. Mitarai, Canon's chairman and CEO, and one of the most powerful men in the world, according to Forbes magazine. The message, which came through at the point when we were at our most fraught, said: "Congratulations! I'm looking forward to working with you!"

At that moment, it was hard to laugh at the irony. Late that night, I said: we have to find a different way to work around the issue.

I decided that we needed to do an accelerated round of due diligence ourselves, and we spent the weekend in discussion with advisers pouring over the details of the issue. It was exhausting. But eventually we got there. The consequences would only be a couple of days delay in the signing.

By Tuesday, June 10, it was finalized, and we informed the Milestone HR team. They were the first to know outside the 10 of us working on the Canon deal. Two days later, on June 12, 2014, the deal was signed at our board meeting.

Milestone Systems had been acquired by Canon Europe.

11

To infinity and Beyond: Enabling Visionaries

June 12, 2014

The Canon deal was signed at Turning Torso, the strange building twisting to peer back at Milestone's past, or forward towards its future. I knew which way I was looking.

We called a meeting with our extended leadership team at 5:30pm and explained that Milestone had been purchased by Canon. It came as quite a surprise.

June 13, 2014

We aborted the IPO process. This was a finely orchestrated process, with emails and other communications scheduled and sent at very specific times.

I texted Martin Gren at Axis, saying I needed to meet him at 8am. He responded immediately, and we met up so that I could give him the news. We have always had a very close and fruitful relationship with Axis, so it was important that Martin be amongst the first to know. He was also surprised, but balanced in his response – it turns out Axis and Canon have had close ties for many years, back in the days of their print server business.

Milestone spoke to other important partners that morning, and Canon had to talk to their banks in Japan.

At 10:15am, we called our bankers.

At 10:45am, we sent out an all-hands announcement to Milestone staff for a meeting at 11am.

At 10:50am, we sent messages to our lawyers and the rest of the JBR team.

At 11am, we sent out a press release announcing the acquisition.

> At 11:01am, I made the announcement to our staff in Copenhagen and via webinar to our global offices. This was repeated in the evening for those in different time zones.

At 11:30am, we spoke to key media and secured interviews.

After that we sent guidelines to everyone in the company on how to answer questions about the acquisition. Then, on the spur of the moment, we decided to give everyone a bottle of champagne to celebrate, which involved quickly finding and buying a few hundred bottles of Taittinger. It was very well received!

June 17, 2014

A few days later, we headed over to London for the IFSEC International security exhibition. There we held a reception for press, analysts and partners at the Canon booth, and Canon management presented us with a commemorative plate. After the show finished we were back in Copenhagen for the annual Milestone summer party, where we were joined by Rokus for what we called a 'fireside chat' with our staff. This involved me interviewing him onstage, using questions we'd solicited from our employees. Rokus did well, and came across as an excellent statesman as he is.

Then we went dragon boat racing. It was a great party, and exactly what we needed at that point, after a long intense first half of 2014, easily the busiest and most intense nine months of my career, yet this time I didn't fall off my chair! On the IPO track alone there were probably several hundred meetings; when we were doing the early-look investor events, we'd have eight or 10 meetings in a day. Now, after it's all done, I can find myself thinking that I've had a quiet day when I've only been involved in three meetings! One thing I learned is that it's almost impossible to have a meeting with investment bankers without 20 people in the room.

Another thing I learned about the investment banking community: they have a kind of self-propelling, high-octane, ultra-hyped atmosphere surrounding themselves at all times. Everybody panics about everything, and everybody calls one another to tell them about it. They love it. It's an industry based on confidence and adrenaline and very interesting and exciting.

Some of the Rothschild team was aware of the Canon deal, of course, since they had facilitated the approach yet had no sell-side mandate. But both Carnegie and JP Morgan were not aware, until we let them know on Friday June 13, no superstition. Their reactions were interesting: they accepted it of course, assumed we had a very good offer, and congratulated us. We were expecting a different response, something like "You can't mean this! We've put in so much effort here!" It would have been an understandable response, but this is what they do for a living and they are highly professional. Furthermore, it was a pleasure working with them during the process.

A quick note here, too, on the odd way that the bankers are paid, as I was a little surprised by it. They receive a fee, as you'd expect, but then there's also what they call a 'discretionary payment' – which can be up to 100% of the fee. And it's up to you as the client as to how much of that you'll pay them. Hence 'discretionary'. It's like tipping at a restaurant or in a taxi, except, of course, that it can be somewhat more expensive than that.

It's odd, but in some ways it's worthwhile. On the rare occasions when we felt that they were not engaged to the level that we expected during the process, it was useful. We were able to say that there were certain things we expected them to be doing in order to earn the discretionary fee. Suddenly, they were very amenable.

July 7, 2014

After just a weekend of vacation, which was sorely needed by this stage, we gathered again on the 7th of July when the deal with Canon was officially closed. It was a particularly warm July in Denmark, so we celebrated by providing ice cream for everyone in our Copenhagen HQ.

There were a number of meetings with Canon to finalize the roll-out to Milestone and Canon regional teams, before a proper summer break, one I hadn't planned on being able to take when the IPO still looked likely. A few weeks off, and finally a chance to relax with my family and our new puppy. I went to the coast, sailing and kayaking, recharging my batteries. There was nothing hanging over me at all. I felt more refreshed and rejuvenated than I had for many years.

And at the end of July, it was time to head to Japan, a country that in many respects I am very fond of.

Meeting Mr. Mitarai

Canon is a huge company, the biggest imaging business in the world, with over 200,000 employees. It was founded back in 1937. As well as their famous consumer products – cameras, camcorders, printers, scanners, lenses and binoculars – Canon has a massive presence in the business solutions sector, with printers, copiers and scanners of all types, as well as medical, optical and broadcast products. Their security business is a drop in the ocean in comparison.

I was in Japan to meet with chairman and CEO Fujio Mitarai – known to all as Mr. Mitarai – and Canon CFO Toshizo Tanaka.

I got to spend five or six hours with Mr. Mitarai, much longer than I expected. Obviously acquiring us meant they were interested in Milestone, but I didn't know how much he was involved in – relatively – small-scale acquisitions in niche industries like security. It turns out he's very interested in all areas of Canon's business.

Mr. Mitarai is 79 years old and going strong. He's the Honorary President of the Tokyo 2020 Olympics, and he's full of insight, vision and energy. He lives and breathes Canon. And he was very supportive of our independent status under the Canon umbrella. He has the utmost respect for Rokus, and Rokus is the one who had introduced the

'Chinese Wall' concept to the acquisition process. It's his signature, and has been proven to work already with Onyx, which they acquired with its specialization in commercial printing software and solutions.

In fact, I'd say it's crucial that we are a stand-alone business. The open platform approach is the cornerstone of Milestone's success, and the fact that Canon understands that augurs well for the future. Canon hasn't just bought Milestone the business, they have bought Milestone's philosophy and approach to business. They want to support it because they see that it works.

Independence is one of our core values so when we say stand- alone, we mean stand-alone. If Canon Japan wants Milestone software, they can choose to do so: by being a distributor, or coming to an OEM or other commercial arrangement. They can't demand that we deliver something to them for free.

They don't have access to certain areas of our facilities. They don't have access to our servers. They will have one seat on the board of directors, but if critical or confidential information is discussed at board meetings, we can send the Canon representative out of the room. For example, if we're discussing cooperation with one or more of their competitors. This also applies to any subsidiary of Canon.

So we have a handful of basic rules. They don't want to micro-manage us. Mr. Mitarai and Rokus have both told us that what they want to preserve is our freshness and entrepreneurial spirit. They don't want to run roughshod over that. We're looked upon as a young, exciting opportunity for Canon.

And because Canon's presence in the security market isn't huge at the moment, there's potential to grow. They don't have a rigid system in place for the way they operate in security, so they can be flexible, and we can offer them advice based on our experience in the field.

Visual services: the next revolution

Since we were acquired, people have been asking "Why Canon?" In some ways the question's understandable, because of Canon's relatively small presence in security. But in other ways the question's a little narrow-sighted. For us, it's all about the bigger picture. It's a panorama that includes security, of course, but it goes well beyond that. Canon is a company that has a 200-year plan. Literally. That's big-picture thinking.

We've been musing for a while at Milestone about the future of video. That's probably no big surprise – managing video has, after all, been our business for the last 17 years. But we've been thinking about the way that video has the potential to knit together some of the key technological trends that we can see dominating over the next decades.

These trends are the cloud, big data, social media, and mobility. We're already seeing cloud services begin to proliferate. It's in its infancy, but there are a huge number of opportunities for the ways that will be used.

Big data takes advantage of the petabytes of information stored globally – a zettabyte is equivalent to one billion terabytes – to make analyses previously thought to be impossible. It definitely has a darker side, in terms of the information stored about individuals, but there is amazing potential as well, not least in areas such as medicine, where health trends can be spotted on a scale we could never have dreamed of just a few years ago.

Social media includes networks like Twitter, Facebook, YouTube – and whatever new phenomenon is just around the corner.

And mobility is the way we access all of this now – on smartphones and tablets, wherever we are, at any time.

> We believe that video can be the thing that binds all of these disparate technology trends together, and we call the way those elements are brought together 'visual services'.

Because here's the thing: according to YouTube, over six billion hours of videos are watched each month, and 100 hours of video are uploaded to the site every minute. And that's just on YouTube, never mind on Facebook, Vine, Instagram, Vimeo or other video vehicles.

To make any sense of that, other than searching for a specific video via keywords (which need to be entered by the uploader) requires analytics. Deep integration of video and analytics will be key in the world of visual services.

The thinking behind visual services conceptualizes video as a sensor. Video as an enabler. It won't just be used as something to look at – although that will be important, of course – it will take visual information and use that to help perform other tasks.

Think of it this way: the mobility of cameras and devices embedded with cameras will soon allow video to be continuously streamed and recorded via cloud services. There is no way that there are enough hours in the lifetime of every person on Earth that all of those images can be physically viewed by a living, breathing person. But as the quality of those images improves, so too does the information that can be retrieved from them. And there are endless creative ways in which that information can be used.

A simple example would be to take tiny cameras and attach them to – or have them sewn into – the shirt of every football player in the World Cup, or the English Premier League. Or in any other sport, in much the same way as Formula 1 cars have a number of cameras attached to them now, constantly streaming video to broadcasters. Then viewers could choose to subscribe to the view from their favorite player. This isn't far away from happening – it's just a matter of the size of the battery or power unit being small enough to be unobtrusive. After all, the camera in your phone is tiny. For sports, particularly, there's likely to be major advances in solar microcells to power cameras and other equipment.

That's using video in a pretty familiar way. That's how it will begin.

To give you an idea of the way that video can rapidly evolve, you need look no further than casinos. Casinos are driven purely by money. They make their profits on the advantage they have via probability and statistics: in other words, through data. They are driven by data, and their use of that data is what allows the house to always win. It's also what allows it not to lose.

Security, of course, is an overriding concern at gaming houses. High-definition surveillance video was first used widely in casinos. 360-degree overhead cameras came from casinos. Facial recognition software was pioneered by casinos, allowing them to automatically detect people registered as barred from their premises. If you want to see the future of surveillance video, look to the casinos.

These developments always happen first where money is paramount. There have even been trials of IBM's Smart Surveillance Software (SSS) architecture, which aims to do what they call 'expression analysis'. This is automated analytics software which is designed to detect facial expressions of gamblers to see if they're happy, or bored, or upset. Imagine sitting at a gaming table, thinking that you're about to leave, when suddenly a cocktail waitress appears with another of your favorite drinks, and you have a sip, and you think, you know what? I might stick around for another hour.

What has happened is that the software, which is monitoring all of the video being recorded at the casino, has detected from your expression that you were happy when you last had a drink of a certain cocktail delivered by a certain waitress or waiter, who is wearing a tiny micro-camera in their uniform. Sometime later, another camera has detected that you are bored, or perhaps unhappy. Automatically it sends an alert to the bar directing the same staff member to bring you the same drink, and at the same time it pumps a little extra oxygen from the vents above your table, and amazingly, with your fresh drink and your cute waitress and a bit of pure oxygen in your bloodstream, you're happy again and keen to continue trying your luck. All of this has happened automatically, with no human intervention, just video and POS data compiled and analyzed by applications plugged into video management software.

> Video and analytics can be used in more altruistic ways too, of course.

An elderly Alzheimer's sufferer may be prone to repeated, cyclical activities through memory impairment. Getting up to go to the fridge, not realizing why they are there, and repeating the action time and again. Video analytics that can automatically alert a caregiver that this sort of cyclical activity is taking place means that help can be made available efficiently and effectively.

Visual services aren't restricted to traditional video, either. There have been great leaps made in the development of thermal cameras in recent years, so that what were prohibitively expensive heat mapping devices are now affordable and network-ready. High-end car manufacturers are already using them to alert drivers to the presence of roadside animals that would not have been detectable using conventional cameras. In Sweden, there's a good chance that this can save you from an incident with a moose, which would be unfortunate for both parties.

Visual services sits neatly within the Milestone open platform philosophy. We want to be the hub that helps experts, visionaries in their own respective fields, develop revolutionary new applications for video in the age of the Internet of Things – where devices connect and interoperate to fulfill functions without the need for human involvement. We want to be the magnet that draws all these elements together, business magnetism. And we believe that we can do so.

Both Rokus and Mr. Mitarai agree with our thinking behind the visual services concept, and are keen to help us develop it further. With Canon's support and expertise in imaging combined with our video management knowledge, we will be able to lead the video and technology industries into the new phase of visual services.

It's not something we could have done on our own. This is not just about the narrow confines of the security industry, it's much wider, and will have an impact on everyone's day-to-day life.

The opportunity is enormous. We want to be the ones to take it.

CCTV 2.0

The combination of Canon's backing with the open platform makes Milestone the strongest VMS player in the industry.

However, looking at the market we see that bundled solutions look as if they are making a comeback. I call this CCTV 2.0. These are end-to-end solutions where the customer is locked in to using products from a single manufacturer, both for today and for the future. A one size fits all approach if you like. This is a return to Proprietary Jail, a term that Milestone coined to describe the consequences that these one size fits all, bundled solutions hide from customers. And just like real jail, once you are in Proprietary Jail, it can be difficult, and very expensive to get out.

The advantage of the open platform approach is that customers keep their options open. If it turns out that their initial manufacturer no longer supports their future plans, they can change manufacturers. This is a huge benefit for customers in both the high-volume and high complexity market segments. Today, customers have to plan their installations over longer and longer periods and they are feeling the pressure to get it right. After all, who can really predict the future, a perfect solution today, may not meet requirements in two to three years. This is especially true for high-volume customers, they may not be able to afford the consequences of making a wrong decision. Open platform solutions give security customers a cost- effective way to adapt as their requirements change.

Milestone has always felt that this is an intelligent way to work with our customers. We respect the fact that customers understand their own situation better that we do, they are smart people, and that one size does not fit all. In my experience with real situations, the only thing you can predict is that requirements will change shortly after you have finalized your design. Customers need the flexibility to change their minds if, or most likely when they need to.

Customers are not stupid

This need for flexibility is something that CCTV 2.0 does not take into account. On the contrary, with its one size fits all solutions it is much more egotistical. CCTV 2.0 seems to be saying to customers, your business is not that special, and we know what you will need for the future. Just leave it to us, we'll force fit your requirements into our one size fits all methodology.

Customers are not stupid. They will see this for the arrogant approach that it is. It may look like CCTV 2.0 with its one size fits all method is coming back, but let me tell you, in the long term CCTV 2.0 is dead. Look at the IT industry, they invented the open platform, can you imagine IT managers going back to the proprietary solutions of the 1990s? No way.

> Customers are smart people, they will not go back to Proprietary Jail. They have already seen the benefits that Milestone and the open platform brings them.

Where next?

This year marks Milestone's 17th anniversary, and my 13th with the company. It's the dawn of a new era. We are leaders in our field, and with Canon, we believe we have the team and the leadership which can take video management, and visual services, into a new and exciting future – without sacrificing our core strengths: innovative Scandinavian management style, visionary employees, faith in our ecosystem partners, education, and a culture of entrepreneurship, creativity and reliability.

So, where next? As my old pal Buzz Lightyear from the Pixar movie Toy Story says: to infinity and beyond!

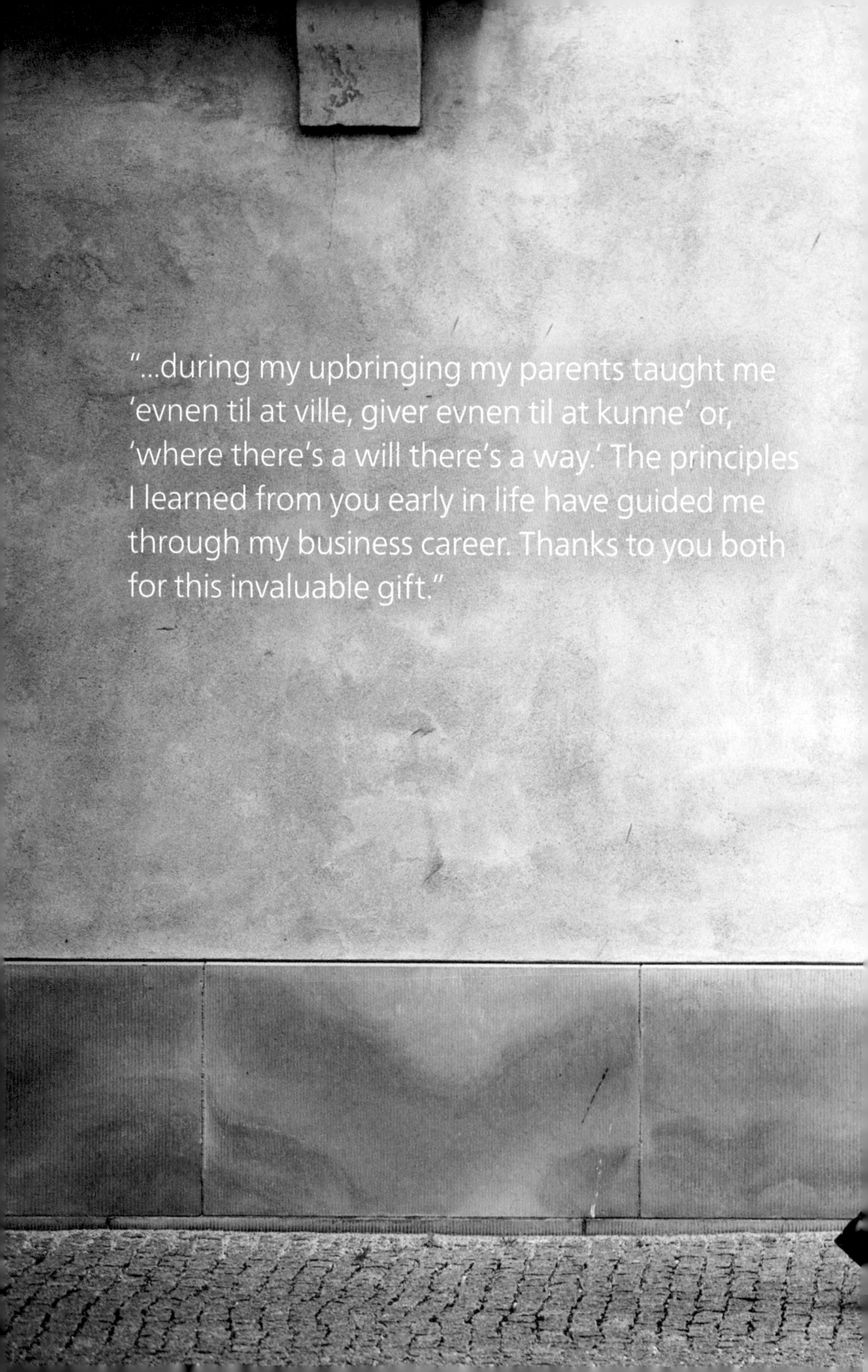

"...during my upbringing my parents taught me 'evnen til at ville, giver evnen til at kunne' or, 'where there's a will there's a way.' The principles I learned from you early in life have guided me through my business career. Thanks to you both for this invaluable gift."

TEAM APPROACH

This book would not exist without the efforts of Milestone's brilliant, creative, and dedicated employees. I feel lucky to work with them every day. Milestone's people, around the world, are the driving force behind our success, and I'm grateful for their passion, their enthusiasm, and their sense of fun. They make Milestone a fantastic place to work.

Thank you all:

Adrian Adolfsson, Ahmad Saleh Al-Haider, Aleksandar Denkov, Alex Knapik, Alex Yoon Seong Je, Alexandar Maliuk, Alexander Nikolaev Dinkov, Alexey Zatvornitskyi, Ameen Yehia Abdallah, Amer Mattar, Amine Sadi, Amit Sarkar, Anders Bent Christensen, Anders Johansson, Anders Marker, Andreas Pettersson, Andrew Moren, Andrew Start, Anee Jayaraj Schmidt-Olsen, Anette Bisgaard, Angelo Salvatore, Anirban Das, Anja Erntgaard, Annette Christiansen, Ann-Katrin Kofoed Andersen, Antony Joseph, Armando Giovanni Ferraz, Artur Gadomski, Artur Gevorkovic Magaljan, Ashley Kirk, Asparuh Trudolyubov Petkov, Assen Kirilov Stoyanov, Ava Parissay, Barbara Erickson, Bence Makkos, Benjamin Østlund, Bent Kenneth Ejlif Jensen, Bertha Fischer, Betina Trolle Thomsen, Bill West, Birgitte Halse Lilmose, Bjørn Juul-Pedersen, Bjørn Skou Eilertsen, Blagovest Petkov Peshev, Bo Ellegård Andersen, Bo Jepsen, Boian Georgiev Kolev, Boris Ivanov Georgiev, Boris Krassimirov Mitev, Borislav Trayanov Traykov, Borislav Vandov Dinkov, Boyan Angelov Boyanov, Brad Cary, Brent Holtorf, Brian Reimer-Nielsen, Brian Salling, Brian Troelsen, Carl Emil Thinggaard, Carlos García San Miguel, Carsten Bøgelund, Celine Menou, Chad Palmquist, Christen Carle, Christian Bergholdt Kvorning, Christian Keinicke Jensen, Christian Martelli, Christian Morana, Christian Ringler, Christina Hampson, Christina Hetkamp, Christopher Benefiel, Christopher Larson, Christopher LeGrice Whitting, Claudia Lillebjerg Simonsen, Claus Rønning, Courtney Dillon Pedersen, Craig Le Cesne, Cristian Sánchez Rodríguez, Cristina-Elena Saitan, Cuauhtemoc Romero Nava, Damyan Atanasov Zhuklev, Dan Kottal Pedersen, Daniel Cisneros, Daniel Freppert, Daniel Johnson, Daniel Talbot, Danielle Joynson, Danielle Quinones, Dario Liu, Darrick Felise, David Carranza, David Dollas, David King, David Kocmick, David Schaub, Denis Gordienko, Dennis Schou Jørgensen, Derek Young, Desislava Blagoeva Jensen, Doncho Angelov Angelov, Douglas Wittner, Edgardo J. Lopez, Edward Cutts, Elin Starup, Elisabeth Wallberg, Elson Lim (Lim Leng Kang), Eric Moe, Erik Friis Mondorf, Euripedes Lopes Magalhaes, Evan Stuckless, Evgeni Stefanov Nunev, Filip Petrov Slanchev, Filip Rusak, France Laliberte, Frances Simon, Frederikke Løkke Pedersen, Fredrik Wallberg, Galin Georgiev Grudov, Gary St. Arnauld, Gary Thomas,

Gavin Archery, Gbedolo Gbeyetin, Geoffrey Gilchrist, Georgi Yasenov Tonchev, Gergana Boykova Ivanova, Giam Vien, Gitte Ines Steenstrup, Greg Willmarth, Gunilla Wildey, Gyulyay Alev Baadi, Handan Anar, Hannah Holz, Hannah von Ascheraden, Hans Jørgen Skovgaard, Hans Olsen, Hans Roed Mark, Heinfried Maschmeyer, Henrik Brix Kronborg, Henrik Friborg Jacobsen, Henrik Høj Pedersen, Henrik Jakobsen, Henrik Kenneth Nielsen, Henrik Lüneborg, Henrik Sydbo Hansen, Hrisimir Dakov, Hristo Vladimirov Yontchev, Ibrahim Mohammad, Ida Graulund, Inger Holm Vinther, Inger Marie Brink, Ish Ishkhanian, Ivan Piergallini, Ivan Tenev Tenev, Ivo Krasimirov Krastev, Jack Lim, Jacob Krog, Jacob Palmqvist, Jaime Durbàn Diez de la Cortina, Jakob Sloth, James Asmussen, James Bryon Glenn, Jan Gray, Jan Lindeberg, Jana Sherer, Jane Moesche, Janne Jakobsen, Jared Tarter, Jasleen Kaur Rehal, Jasmine de Guzman, Jason Fugate, Jathin Jacob Abraham, Jawaid Chotani, Jay Shah, Jaye Deveraux, Jeanette Schrøder, Jeanette Vedding Lysemose, Jean-Francois (JF) Montpetit, Jens Berthelsen, Jens Klarskov Jensen, Jens Ole Steen Svendsen, Jeppe Jensen, Jeremy Scott, Jesper Aaes-Jørgensen, Jesper Benfeldt Ehlers, Jesper Højbjerg Jakobsen, Jesper Johansen, Jesper Køppen, Jesse Huber, Jessy Mak Yin Vei, Jianxin Liu, Jimmi Bendtson, Jimmy Ege Pedersen, Joakim Lagerholm, Job Rabinowitz, Joe Beede, John Blem, John Borman, John Hertel Rasmussen, John Madsen, John Welch, Jomy Abraham, Jonas Lund, Jonathan Sandquist, Jorge Alberto Guzman Michua, Jørgen Christensen, Josh Hendricks, Juan, Carlos George, Julie Nylander, Jurate Beniulyte, Justin Butterworth, Justin Hawes, Kalin Ivanov Stoychev, Kalina Ivanova Milcheva, Karim Abdelkader Zeroual, Karl Erik Traberg, Kasper Lyngh Dalby, Kasper Reiter Kirk, Katherine Anne Shallcross, Kennedy Jones, Kenneth Hune Petersen, Keven Marier, Kevin Tart, Khuram Shazad Bhatti, Kitty van der Sluis, Klaus Klausen, Klavs Pontoppidan, Kliment Villy Todorov, Krasimira Kalinova Nenova, Kristian Kristoffersen, Kuldip Kaur, Lars Andersen Yde, Lars Bjørn-Petersen, Lars Hammer, Lars Larsen, Lars Nordenlund Friis, Lars Wilson, Lawrence Sydney de Guzman, Lena Lundsgaard Christensen, Leonie Bourgeois, Lina Maria Alfaro Arrieta, Linda Chan, Linda Volfing, Line Byssing, Lisbeth Cornelius Jensen, Liselotte Christensen, Lo Yew Seng, Louise Marie Østerby, Lukasz Skomial, Mads Holmsgaard Eriksen,

Mads Landgren, Manjana Shrestha, Manuel Nylén, Marco Schwitz, Maria Laue Christensen, Maria Sarmiento, Mark Eggett, Mark Pauley, Mark Swanson, Mark Wilson, Mark Wollen, Marta Malgorzata Magiera, Martin Aleksandrov Kenov, Martin Dam, Martin Kostadinov Minkov, Martin Mihaylov Mihaylov, Martin Qvist Romme, Martina Dobreva, Martina Valerieva Parvanova, Max Goldberg Ottosen, Max Simonsen, Maxim Valerievich Zapryanov, Megan McHugh, Michael Baburin, Michael Brogaard Munkemose, Michael Brown, Michael Ching, Michael Flanagan, Michael Hegelund, Michael Holm, Michael J Bjerggaard, Michael Leslie Metcalfe, Michael Terp-Müller, Michael Wahlstrøm, Michalina Duda, Mikael Roger Jensen, Mike Sherwood, Mike Tarras, Mike Taylor, Mike Tice, Mogens Nielsen, Monika Zaicevaite, Morten Bach Sommer, Morten Boysen, Morten Engel Kristiansen, Morten Kjær Jensen, Morten Koimaru Skaarup, Morten Lundberg, Morten Rosenkrands, Mugees Ahmed, Muhammad Haider, Myrna Baker, Nalika Lekamge, Naomi Little, Nathan Gruss, Neli Georgieva Georgieva, Neli Valentinova Stoyanova, Nencho Hrissimirov Neikov, Nevena Dimitrova Milanova, Nevena Vasileva Stancheva, Nicolás Emilio Diaz Ferreyra, Nicole Goodman, Niels Sander Christensen, Nikola Yordanov Sivkov, Nikolai Holm Borup, Nikolai Mitev, Nikolaj Mortimer Salvén, Odette J. Malkoun, Ole Lennert, Olga Kryva, Ove Lilja, Paolo Blem, Pascal Pia, Patrick Cooke, Paul Jaroszewski, Paul Messenger, Per Kristensen, Petar Todorov, Petar Veselinov Vutov, Peter Biltsted, Peter Bo Jacobsen, Peter Currie, Peter Forchhammer, Peter Grubauer, Peter Højfeldt Flittner, Peter Irgang Jørgensen, Peter Jacob Rosengren Sørensen, Peter Kristian Storgaard, Peter Lintzeris, Peter Möller, Peter Posselt Vergmann, Petko Anatoliev Petrov, Petko Iliev Pedev, Petya Lozanova Lozanova, Petya Stoilova Mintcheva, Philippe Colas, Philippe Rostock, Piotr Milczarek, Plamen Gospodinov, Plamen Parvanov, Poul Vendel, Preben Holm Nielsen, Rachelle Basaraba, Radoslav Popov, Rafik Lamri, Randi Byrnes, Rasmus Jensen, Raul Amador, Raul Delgado, Ray Tienter Santos, Raziel Bareket, Rebecca Ching, Reem Raid Rady, Reeve Xu Chao, Reijo Harkonen, Reinier Tuinzing, René Meschke, René Rasmussen, Reni Kirilova Tchifilionova, Robert Fitzsimmons, Robert Nunez, Ronald Yu, Rune Allan Petersen, Rune Holstvig, Ryan Chamberlain, Sandesh Kaup,

Scott Paul, Sean Christopher McDonnell, Sean Ellison, Shane Loy, Shaun Ford, Shiva Sohrabi-Nejad, Simone Cosmano, Sophia Anna Charlotte Bunemann, Søren Eschricht Jensen, Søren Løfvall Jensen, Søren Stilling, Stan Ewy, Steen Strandskov Andersen, Steffen Striib Sveegaard, Steffin Burton, Stephan Redon, Steven E. Floyd Jr., Steven Moore, Stoyan Todorov Todorov, Stoyko Neykov Neykov, Sunil Gowda, Sunny Kong, Suzette Oskam, Svetlana Krasenova Ulyanova, Syed Budden Mansoor, Tamara Abdallah-Choueiri, Tanja Myhrvold, Tas Maniatis, Thomas Haase, Thomas Larsen, Thomas Lausten, Thomas Mangaard Christiansen, Thomas Mortensen, Thor Irgens, Tim Bækstrøm Laursen, Tim Palmquist, Tima Pilgaard, Tina Bergmann, Todor Valentinov Petkov, Tom O'Connell, Torben Gjaldbæk, Torben Striboldt, Torsten Thießenhusen, Tracy Little, Trine Voss, Troels Kristian Kruckow, Troels Larsen, Tsvetan Vasilev Filev, Tsvetomira Petkova Georgieva, Ture Reinholdt Nielsen, Tzveta Kanazirska, Van Anh Tran-Schwartzmann, Veselin Yordanov Petev, Vesselin Kostadinov Nikolov, Vibeke Uhrenholdt Olsen, Victoria Jayka, Villads Nygaard, Vladimira Georgieva Girginova, Vsevolod Viatcheslavov Starchov, Walter Coady, III, Wendy Magnuson, Will Ramsay, Yana Boyanova Valchanova, Yasen Hristov Angelov, Yasen Zdravkov Peychev, Yesenia Andrade, Yuliya Gorbundova, Zdravko Georgiev Bankov.

Lars Thinggaard, June 2015

"If people really wanted to, they could copy our products. But it's very difficult to copy the culture of an organization, where the values are really strong."

WHY MAGNETISM?

In physics, magnetism has changed our fundamental understanding of the universe. Because magnetism is for our economy and growing the human-scale challenges [illegible]

Stranger in the Shadows

Stranger in the Shadows

Angela Gordon

Thorndike Press • Chivers Press
Thorndike, Maine USA Bath, England

This Large Print edition is published by Thorndike Press, USA and by Chivers Press, England.

Published in 1998 in the U.S. by arrangement with Golden West Literary Agency and Robert Hale Ltd.

Published in 1998 in the U.K. by arrangement with Robert Hale Ltd.

U.S. Hardcover 0-7862-1343-4 (Candlelight Series Edition)
U.K. Hardcover 0-7540-3226-4 (Chivers Large Print)
U.K. Softcover 0-7540-3227-2 (Camden Large Print)

The text of this Large Print edition is unabridged.
Other aspects of the book may vary from the original edition.

Set in 16 pt. Plantin.

Printed in the United States on permanent paper.

British Library Cataloguing in Publication Data available

Library of Congress Cataloging in Publication Data

Gordon, Angela, 1916–
Stranger in the shadows / by Angela Gordon.
p. cm.
ISBN 0-7862-1343-4 (lg. print : hc : alk. paper)
1. Large type books. I. Title.
PS3566.A34S77 1998
813′.54—dc21 97-49448

Stranger in the Shadows

Chapter One

The second time Lynne saw him he was standing in the failing light staring out at the wayward sea. The first time had been at the spice-scented store of Morgan and Tallant. That time he had noticed her, but this time he didn't; she moved up the walk towards the porch, and turned, up there, to study him.

He was a lean man with rusty-auburn hair, thick and curly and too long in back. He was as young as any man who had clearly been burnt teak-tan by wind and sun and salt-sea spray, ever was. She remembered her grandfather, who had never looked different to her from the time she was six until her seventeenth birthday, when he had died at seventy-seven. And her father, too; men who raced for the Orient trade and manned the Yankee clippers, never seemed to have the time to age. She guessed him to be thirty. She was nineteen so he was an 'older man'.

He was good-looking; she had noticed that at Morgan and Tallant's, but not in the ordinary way. And he was not handsome because there lay a depth of obvious strength in his eyes, and in his expression, that marred any chance of masculine beauty, but his features were good, neither too thin nor too coarse, nor too pinched or too flaccid.

She had to wonder about him. In a place like Smithsport people were entitled to be curious. It was not a large place and most of the people were descendants of seamen who had settled there two centuries and more ago. Of course strangers arrived; almost every ship that sank anchor in the Sound, brought strangers, crewmen picked up along the way, but with the running of the tide they were gone again. No one stayed in Smithsport who did not belong there; there was commerce but very little industry, and it was almost entirely owned and operated by local people. Unless a man lived by the tides and seasons, or unless he was the third or fourth generation to operate one of the trading companies or the local stores, Smithsport was practically closed to him.

The ships that lay by this time of year for re-fitting and overhauling had long since seen the last of their crews. A few clippers still sailed the sullen wintery seas but as a rule when winter was settling in upon the coasts of New England, the companies used the time when risks were greatest making the vessels ready for the keenly competitive springtime runs.

She could of course ask who he was, but not in a place like Smithsport where the attention that was turned seaward during most of the year, was turned inward this time of year.

She watched him standing alone upon the edging of the granite seawall with the leaden sea out front and the torn and tattered grey sky curving above until it met the sea far out. There was a chilling wind, part of this season, but it seemed to scurry past without troubling him, almost as though it neglected to touch a soul that had trouble enough.

The beating sea struck hard at the stone wall, and fell back to try again. Ever since she could remember at this time of the year, there had been that relentless contest. In summertime the sea often ran blandly to the wall, a greeny depth of unpredictable capriciousness, but always gentler then. Even the massive wall, worn smooth over the generations, seemed less formidable, more willing for people to walk its ten-feet wide topmost parapet.

Where he now stood, Lynne Harding had stood a hundred times, first as a child clutching someone's hand, then as a boyish-built lithe girl, and later on as she stood now upon the broad sweep of verandah, tall and slim and rounded in a muscular way with short taffy hair and dark eyes and brows, with her late mother's heavy mouth and strong jaw, and her father's quietness and his dark-eyed resolution. Her great-grandfather had been Portuguese; there were tales in the family of him. An Azorean by birth, a seaman from age twelve, very fair except for black hair and eyes, a large man remembered chiefly for fearlessness, and a great love for the family he had sired by his Yankee wife.

There were portraits of him, of her grandfather, and of her three uncles, all dead now, in the study her father had had panelled from the teak of the *Celeste Gloria* which had been the family ship until it went down with her uncles off the Sandwich Isles more than half a century before. The panelling had been salvaged after the *Celeste Gloria*'s last refitting.

Her mother had once said she had somehow resurrected the passion and the temperament of her Azorean ancestor. At the time, Lynne had been too young to understand and too disinterested to ask what that meant. But in more recent years she had looked from the old portrait in the study to the mirror in the hallway, seeking a similarity. She had found none, unless perhaps it was in the eyes or possibly in the broad forehead. She did not have the hawkish nose nor the slightly predatory look of Great-Grandfather Harding — originally Huertado — but what her mother had probably meant, in that moment of exasperation when she made the comparison, was that Lynne had the kind of temper that could charm people, or chill them to their bones, which was the competence Great-Grandfather had acquired in his long life in an untamed and savage environment.

She was tall for a girl, but not actually noticeably tall among New Englanders whose women were hereditarily tall, and usually angular and lean as well. Her face had strong and pleasant contours, the dark brows were heavy and arched, the eyes direct and stone-steady, the nose finely flaring, as her mother's nose had been. She tanned more readily than some of her friends. Some of those 'friends' smiled knowingly about this; there was that 'taint' back a few generations. There were a few other families in Smithsport, in fact the length of New England's Atlantic sealine, with the same taint, and some covered it up by claiming respectable French descent, but that fooled no one; the French were closer, no farther away than Quebec to the north, but the French had never been the seamen the Portuguese were. Names likes Soares had over the genera- tions become Sears, Reyes had become King, Huertado had become Harding.

She had high colour now, from the chill wind. Her skin coloured like ivory, changing with each season. Now, it was dusky pink and ivory white. Later, when summer arrived, it turned the gold of dawnlight.

Richard Tallant had once compared her summer tan to the golden locket she wore. In fact, Richard had once told her that even in the islands, he had never seen a girl who filled his mind and memory so.

Fred Morgan, second officer on his father's ship the *Yankee Pride* had wanted to marry her when she'd barely turned seventeen, and although early marriages were anything but unusual, her father had dug in his heels. He had said that once a woman was married her whole world shrank down to walls and ceilings and lines of drying diapers, and it remained that way the rest of her life, so there was no hurry.

She had almost died that night, soaking the pillow with salt tears. And three months later just as she was beginning to recover,

Fred Morgan married a leggy pale girl from down at Martha's Vineyard, and had smiled benignly at Lynne the next time she saw him, passing her by on the walkway out front of the chandler's shop on King George Street.

That shock had been as bad, worse actually, in a different way, than the loss of her great first love. It had left its own lesion, too, not the same as the earlier one, but just as vivid and permanent. She had learned a bitter and wrenching lesson about men from that. Her father had never said he was pleased, but she could tell that he had been satisfied; he had once told her that the most important lessons were learned *after* schooling ended.

But the man on the seawall, the stranger in the dusk, was not so much a man as he was a curiosity. Why was he in Smithsport, especially this time of year, what had been his business at the Morgan and Tallant store, why did he stand out there now in the turning shadows looking out towards the tilted sea?

She turned, eventually, and went indoors. The house was warm, almost too warm in fact, and it smelled of the tangy pipe-smoke that seemed to be as much a part of her father as his smile and his very faint limp.

She went to the stone kitchen to start supper. The house had an upstairs which hadn't been used since Lynne had been very small, when her grandfather had kept a room on the sea-side, up there. She and her father lived downstairs; two people did not need any more room than that.

The house was old and weathered, but as solid as the seawall. It had survived as many storms too; they had both been built in the same decade well over a century earlier. Everyone who had lived in the Harding house had left an imprint. Lynne had said often that it was like living in a museum, at times. At least the house had no haunt; some of the Smithsport residences had them, and down at Martha's Vineyard there had been several notorious ones of long standing.

She smiled at the stove. Right now, upstairs in her grandfather's old room, which had not been touched since his passing, the wind made windows rattle and if a person's imagination were strong enough it would probably be possible to hear other sounds, *inside* the room.

Wooden houses 'worked' as her father called it; they were never totally motionless. In summertime they shrank, in wintertime they expanded, when the wind blew they groaned and when the sea beat with its hundred-ton fist against the seawall, there were reverberations inland for a long distance that sent faint shudders up through the walls.

Haunts, Fred Morgan had told her, were more of the old heritage from England. He had told her that one night when they had seen fox-fire inland near the Marion Swamp and she had been almost breathless with fear, or something very much like fear, and had clung to his arm.

That was the night he had kissed her.

Out front someone stamped across the porch and entered and afterwards closed the door. She had known that hard-down footfall ever since she could remember. Her father was a solid, thick man about six feet tall who had been on every sea and who had done very well in the trading business which he now owned and operated. As a youth aboard one of the Morgan clippers he had broken a foot under the fluke of a great anchor. Everyone knew the story; he had refused to say a word, had finished out the entire four-months cruise in agony as the bones mended imperfectly, rather than report sick and see old Captain Morgan's sneer. Since that day to this, her father had walked with a slight limp, and she knew the foot bothered him now and then when the seasons changed, but she had never heard him complain, only swear now and then.

She raised a wrist to push back a taffy curl and with biscuit dough to her wrists went to the dining-room doorway to greet him with a smile — and there he stood waiting for her appearance, with that silent stranger from the shadows standing beside him.

So *that* was why the stranger had been standing out there; he had been waiting for her father.

Chapter Two

Lynne's father had been named for the Apostle-builder of Tarsus, Paul, and later in life after he knew who he had been named for, had once told his daughter that if Lynne's devout grandmother had thought about it, she probably would have given him the great apostle's Jewish name of Saul.

He was a friendly man, grey at the temples, who had not been to sea now for something like twenty-five years. He owned a trading company and a chandlers works on King George Street in the heart of town, and although the chandling business was not now as good as it had been in his youth, at least the trading company still prospered. Would, in fact, like all the other New England trading companies with alliances among the clipper captains and owners, continue to prosper.

He introduced Lynne to Thomas Dorset with a twinkle in his eyes; he knew how indignant she would be later, when they were alone, because he had not let her know they would have a visitor that evening, and he was correct. The first excuse that came to mind she used as her reason for fleeing back to the kitchen where she stood at the window with her anger; she had flour on both hands, her hair hadn't been combed, and there *he'd* stood gravely by way of the rear corridor and got looking down into her face, at the flour smudge on one cheek!

Later, when supper was ready, she went to her room presentable, then she had summoned them to eat and as her father had stepped past and their eyes had met, she glared. He smiled.

Tom Dorset was not a New Englander, she learned at dinner. He had been born in Jamaica and had gone to sea in his 'teens, first in French ships, and then in American vessels. He had been First Officer on the *Bengal Lancer*, sailing under the American Registry but owned by Liverpool investors, when it had broken apart on the coral reefs in the Sandwich Islands two years past, with a loss of life and cargo that had impaired the investment syndicate to such an extent that it had not as yet recovered.

Since that time Tom Dorset had not been to sea. He did not explain why; of course it was a blemish on an officer's record that he had lost a ship, but as her father said the next day, most officers who sailed the Orient route for any length of time had seen their share of disasters. If there was no personal blame assessed by a seamen's tribunal Tom Dorset could get another berth — if that was his wish, but her father turned silent about that, the way men did when they had groundless but private adverse feelings about something.

She was over her pique by morning; hardly mentioned bringing Tom Dorset home for supper unexpectedly, and he had smiled away the last of her annoyance, as he had always been able to do. She loved him very much.

'But he stood out on the seawall for more than an hour last night, in the cold wind,' she told him. 'All he had to do was walk over; I'd have let him sit in the parlour to wait.'

Her father said, 'Well now, I can't answer for Tom Dorset, but that seawall has seen a lot of lonely people in its time, and I doubt that the wind bothered him.'

'Lonely . . . ?'

'The *Bengal Lancer* broke up, and the following year his wife died of malaria in New Orleans. I'd say a man like that standing on a seawall alone, wouldn't feel the wind.'

It had never occurred to Lynne that Tom Dorset would be a married man. But of course he would; strong men were *always* married. Anyway, he was too old not to have been married.

'Why is he in Smithsport?' she asked, and saw her father's gaze turn gently curious, gently pensive. She added a sentence: 'It's simply that he's a stranger.'

Paul Harding answered dryly, 'It's the wrong season for strangers, of course. Well; he didn't come right out and tell me this; my impression is that it's taken him this long to crawl out of his shell. He's looking for work on shore. He had an offer from Cibula Hermanos in Patagonia, but he doesn't want to go down there. He's been travelling up the coast. It's a long way from New Orleans, isn't it?'

She caught the implication; it was indeed a long way from Louisiana to New England, and if a capable First Officer had been enquiring about positions all that distance — why hadn't someone hired him? She said, 'If he doesn't want to go back to sea . . . ?'

Her father gently shook his head. 'It'd have to be something else. There are dozens of trading companies, Lynne, who could use an experienced man.'

'He has no experience in warehouses and counting rooms, then.'

Her father smiled. 'Try again. He'd be capable of overseeing loadings; cargomasters ashore are as valuable as First Officers at sea. Or he could handle the ladings and the warehousings.'

'What, then?' she asked, frowning slightly. 'Something personal?'

'Probably. I can use him. I need a loading-master and a warehouseman.' Her father put aside his cold pipe. 'I don't know. I've handled men all my life; when I've run into one like this, I take them next door to the tavern. Dorset didn't want a drink. He's not a drunkard then, is he? I showed him the chandler's shop, the store out front and the warehouse behind. He wasn't bluffing, he knew as much as I did.'

Lynne sat back suddenly. 'Then there isn't anything. You just think there *might* be. Hire him.'

Her father's gaze drifted round the warm, snug parlour, rested momentarily upon the fine oil portrait of his late wife above the great oaken mantel, then dropped back to her again. 'There *is* something. I told you, I've handled a lot of men. I can't afford risks with people who have the run of the building. The safe in my office belonged to your great-grandfather; it only looks as strong as the Rock of Gibraltar.'

She was aghast. 'A thief! No! I don't believe it.'

Paul Harding's calm dark eyes lingered an extra moment on his daughter, then slid to the sidewall window where wind-driven droplets of rain-spray struck. 'If you're that good a reader of character, then *you* tell *me.*'

She answered quickly. 'I just did tell you.'

He shook his head again. 'It's not imagination. Sure, it's something I can't explain away, but it's there and I've had the same feeling with other men. It was right those other times. I don't want to take the chance, Lynne. I don't need him that badly. Maybe I don't need him at all, except that the damned stone floor is beginning to make me — want to stay off my feet when I can.'

A gust of wind made the house shudder, then it fled inland. She did not heed it; a sad thought had come gently to her. Her father was not an old man; not in the sense people usually meant when they used that word. New Englanders withered and got bent and gnarled, but they did not really age the way other people who lived in less bleak environments aged.

It wasn't his age, it was the abuse his body had sustained, that seemed to be coming now to exact its toll. Not just the maimed foot, but the broken ribs and arms, the old scars and strains, the lifelong stresses that had driven him ashore before she had been born; they had allowed him twenty years or so, then they had started coming back.

She was sure of none of this. It was something she *felt.* People could hardly live in the same house as she and her father had, for so long, and be as close as they had been, and not develop a kind of precognition about each other. It was more than rapport, more than understanding, it went deeper than that. It was a kind of mystical thing, like an invisible umbilical. She knew his moods as well as he knew hers; she could guess the *reasons* for his moods.

She said, 'Please hire him.' Her tone was different, which he probably noticed. She did not use the arguments women used elsewhere; she did not say he'd earned time off to travel or perhaps go fishing. Those were ridiculous suggestions to make to a man who had seen all the world and who had lived for years on end on cod and flounder and salt mackerel.

He reached for a fresh pipe from the rack beside his chair. 'I wrote some letters yesterday.' He stoked the pipe and tamped it. 'If he's still around in a week or so when the replies come back, maybe I'll take him on.' He lit up, puffed a moment, then winked at her. 'Nothing like a little brandy on a stormy night.'

She arose and went out to the pantry to measure him two fingers from the knobbed old brandy bottle. She could not stand the stuff; it not only seared like acid, it had a peach-like flavour that seemed to have been added as camouflage. She returned and handed him the glass without a word, then returned to the kitchen to do the dishes.

What lingered in her mind was Tom Dorset's smile and his calmness. She kept trying to fit that to what her father had shocked her with: She no more knew how to classify a thief than she knew how to classify a philanderer, but she made up her mind that whatever Tom Dorset's problem was, it had nothing to do with any kind of inherent dishonesty.

She pitied him, and while she worked she began to consider him the way she would have considered an uncle. She didn't have one; the only living relative she had was her father. Oh, there were some distant cousins in Maine, connected on her mother's side some way that she did not now remember. They were, she remembered her mother saying one time, woodsmen. All the time she'd been growing up; she'd half associated woodsmen with trappers or hunters, people like that. Now, she knew better. Woodsmen worked with trees and made the timber that came on rafts and wagons to Smithsport to be loaded as cargo, either on consignment or bought on the docks by shippers and traders.

But she'd only met those distant cousins once, as a small child. Otherwise, her nearer kin were in the stony cemetery with her mother. But even if there'd been more family, Lynne was not the kind of person to become very engrossed. Without knowing it she had matured as one of those people who could not share loyalties nor loves, which was why it had been so hard when her father had refused her permission when she'd wanted so desperately to marry Fred. It was also the reason the shock had been so deep and lasting when Fred had married another girl three months later; she had been perfectly willing to wait a year or two. Even five or ten years. But that was her temperament, even if it hadn't been his temperament.

It was the same temperament that made her worry about her father now. She saw Tom Dorset as an opportunity more than as a man. When she pondered over the little mystery of the man, she was curious, not interested.

What she wanted was relief for her father,

and in that context, when she finished in the kitchen and returned to the warm parlour, hair freshly brushed back, no longer wearing the apron, ready to resume their discussion, and found him sound asleep with the newspaper in his lap and his bad foot propped upon an ottoman, she leaned and kissed him then went to stir the fire, willing to hold in abeyance whatever else needed to be said on the score of Tom Dorset, until he awakened. She did not allow things to go unfinished. She had never been a procrastinator. Neither had either of her parents, so at least she came by that honestly.

But when her father finally opened his eyes, looked around, saw her reading a book, saw the fire dying down to coals, he yawned and growled and got to his feet with a rueful grin. 'Good night,' he grumbled, and limped out of the room, and she did not have the heart to detain him.

At breakfast the following morning he told her he would probably be late for supper because he had to go down to Gosnold, a town fifteen miles south, and even if he could transact all his business without delay, the coach ride usually took half a day going and coming, and this time of year he did not trust the little coastwise shallops most people used, which were quicker — and also a lot less trustworthy.

The subject of Tom Dorset did not come up again.

She did not press the issue anyway. It was important, but not *that* important. A day, a week, perhaps even a month, never seemed to make a great amount of difference in things of this nature. There was no real reason why she should think otherwise. Her life had been the same for almost twenty years; her father went down to the warehouse each morning and returned each evening. She minded the house, made the meal, and had her personal outside interests. Sometimes she served as a teacher's aide at the grammar school. Other times she helped with the church bazaars. It was no exciting life but it had been a satisfactory one. She had only once looked to a different kind of life, and that had ended so disastrously she had become a little withdrawn — although *she* did not know it.

Chapter Three

The storm passed inland. They always did, this time of year. In full winter they hovered over the town, over the entire New England coastland in fact, making the days dismal and the nights excessively long, but in early spring they struck, then broke up to re-form elsewhere, always inland. This one did that, and with its passing the sun came with a pleasant thin warmth.

Lynne went out back and found that the scented violets were spreading fresh, dark green against the stone foundation of the house. They were always first in springtime, and whether being protected in the lee of the house had something to do with it, or not, they always had the first flowers.

It was a good sign. She was pleased and turned to look eastward and to the north where Marion Mountain was a constant lodestar in the deep north-east; shipmasters had been using it as a bearing-point for centuries. Its dark firred slopes were stiff-topped with great trees. Early spring always lingered, breathing winter's breath and gusting winter's winds. True spring was likewise unpredictable, but at least it had more sunshine and less wind.

Most people disliked wind. No genuine seacoast New Englander could afford that luxury for the wind filled topgallants and mainsa'ls and scudded the rolling sea beneath the tight low sterns of the clipper ships on their way out and back. Lynne had never known much else but wind and sea-spray. She'd read of places like the Sandwiches, and had heard the stories of the Polynesias and the other sultry outward-bound groups. The nearest she had ever come to real heat was during the brief, midsummers when it was muggy and still and breathless, if one went far inland, and she had never liked that heat nor that kind of turgid humidity.

She stood near the violets looking at Marion Mountain, though, and was perfectly willing for summer to arrive; it had been a long winter, as were all New England winters.

She heard nothing, was conscious of nothing, until her attention faltered. Then something vague and disturbing intruded and she turned. Fred Morgan was standing by the side of the house. Her heart had a spasm of pain, and it passed.

Fred was blue eyed and had curly black hair. What had always intrigued her was the occasional grey hair among the black ones, even though he was still in his twenties.

She had loved him with all of her heart and soul, and as he smiled now, looking calmly over at her, she felt the twist of the knife all over again, but now it wasn't just the haunting wonder of something she'd felt, it was also the agony of what he had done only a couple of months after swearing he would love her until the day he died.

The Morgan family was one of the wealthiest clans in Smithsport. Fred's ailing father, 'Jay' (for Jeremiah) Morgan, ran the trading company, as well as the two ships, the *Hound* and the *Hare.* Fred was First Officer on the *Hare*, his cousin was Captain, but he had confided in Lynne the previous autumn that soon *he* would be Master and his cousin would take over aboard the *Hound.*

She smiled and wanted to run into the house, but he was closer to the door than she was. 'I didn't hear that you were back,' she said. 'The last I knew you'd taken lumber to New Bedford.'

He corrected her. 'New London.' His eyes roamed over her. 'You're the same, Lynne.'

She bit her lips against a sharp retort. Why should she be different, it hadn't been that long ago. With female malice she said, 'How is your wife?'

He strolled towards her. 'Fine. She's visiting her parents down the coast a ways. How's your father?'

She knew the blood was flooding upwards to her throat and cheeks and could not stop it. 'He's fine . . . He's thinking about taking on a new man.'

He stopped ten inches away and never once allowed his gaze to drift from her face. 'Yeah, I know. Dorset. He tried us first. We can't use outsiders. Didn't want Dorset anyway.'

The way he said the name that last time caught at a corner of her consciousness, but she was looking at Fred, and Dorset was something floating adrift almost beyond heeding.

He raised his arms slowly and touched her waist. The fingers slowly closed into talons and dug into her flesh. 'I've missed you, Lynne,' he said, and seemed to be teetering forward and backward a little, as though undecided.

She forced herself into a backward step free of his touch but the feeling remained. A ruffle of wind brought a sweet breath of springtime chill. She pulled it deep into her lungs, held it, then slowly let it go.

She did not believe what his eyes were signalling. She did not believe what his hands had told her or what her own hungers were responding to from him. She stood as silent as stone and although nothing had really happened she felt as though it had, and she was dirty because of it.

If *she* had been his wife and the other woman had been the one he'd gone casually to see like this. . . .

He said, 'You look like you aren't feeling any too well.' He still had the same look. In another moment he'd step closer again.

She said something, hardly conscious of it until the words sounded, then it was so inane she wanted to turn away. 'What is it you want, Fred?'

'You,' he said quietly, and took that onward step she'd anticipated.

She raised a hand and pushed, hard. It stopped him. 'No you don't,' she exclaimed, in a tone of cold anger. 'How long did you wait? Three months!' She hurled it at him. 'You were going to love me to your dying day!'

He did not show any anger or indignation, not even any shame. He kept right on smiling down into her eyes. 'I can still do that. I'm willing, Lynne.'

She said, 'You make me sick,' and rushed

past him to the house, ran all the way to the fireplace in the front parlour and stood rigidly there, staring at the tall-masted schooner her grandfather had spent an entire winter whittling out, years before she'd been born. It had been a full wind astern and the sails were straining at their grommets, but there was not a soul at the rigging nor on the decks, which was something she had marvelled at as a child although her parents had seen nothing unusual about it. Not on a scale-model clipper.

She heard him whistle as he walked back down the slight hill at the edge of town. It was a keening sound that acted like a release for her emotions. She went to the side window and watched him, head high, curly hair tawny in the spring sunshine, hands thrust deeply into the pockets of his shipboard trousers, and this time her heart did not cry its yearning for his quick return, this time it beat with a heavy drumroll, as steady and dull as a requiem.

My God but she *would* have. She felt as though she *had.* The thought, evidently, was as bad as the act. She had wanted to for that second or two before she'd stopped away from him.

So the love wasn't dead after all.

It took a little while to watch him go down

into the cobbled streets where dray wagons and powerful horses stood as clear in each detail as Dresden art work. Then he became another figure among other moving figures down there, so she went to wash her face and after that, to lift a window in her bedroom and catch another deep-down breath of that thin, sweet springtime air.

What a terrible thing for a man to do to a woman. Not to *her,* to that other woman, the one Lynne had only seen a time or two from a distance. His wife.

She closed the window, sat on the bed, and felt the turmoil slowly drain out until she was as limp as a lily pad. She knew, not from what the older people had said when she's inadvertently come upon them over the years, but from the heavy silences and their expression, from their *thoughts* which they hadn't been as capable of shutting off when a child entered the room, how some of the men behaved on long voyages. Not her father, not old Mister Morgan, not even Richard Tallant before he'd left the sea and gone into the store. But some of the others. Fred Morgan, for example. Married less than a year, and wanting her as though nothing had intervened. If she had married him, and afterwards a few years, had found out . . .

She arose and went listlessly to the kitchen. Her father would be along soon, in another hour and a half, probably. No he wouldn't; he'd gone down to Gosnold. He wouldn't be along until late. But she started supper anyway to have something to keep her mind busy.

New England women were good cooks. Not fancy nor elegant cooks, just good cooks. They knew more ways to prepare fish than anyone in the known world. They could make turnips and parsnips taste like something far less mundane than they were, and if they had the time, as Lynne had that evening, they could prepare a meal no man who spent his days in the chill and watery brilliance of New England coastal days could possibly turn his back on.

Their men had been bringing back recipes from places most Americans had never heard of for a hundred years. Lynn Harding could make Spanish dishes, Taurog meal and Luzon curry. She could make rice dishes from the Orient that tasted like roast chicken. She could baste with amber wine and sauté in burgundy, but what she was preparing when the light fist rolled across the front door was grilled halibut with garlic sauce and mushrooms, something her father strongly favoured.

At the first knock her heart had stopped stone still. It wasn't possible, though, that he would come back. She wiped her hands, touched her hair, pulled off the apron and went resolutely out to the entry way. But when she reached for the heavy brass knob it took a little effort. She couldn't look at him again.

It was Thomas Dorset. He nodded in his grave way and held his hat in one hand looking down at her. His eyes kindled slowly with friendship. 'No flour-biscuits tonight' he said, and she turned loose all over with a sense of relief.

She stepped aside. 'Muffins tonight, Mister Dorset. My father isn't home yet. He had to go down to Gosnold today.'

He did not seem large until a person standing close enough to sense his breadth and height. But he still was no taller than her father. Nor was he quite as heavy, but his solidness was arranged differently, as it would be in a man almost half as young as her father.

Dorset fished inside his jacket and drew out a bent envelope. 'Would you give him this, please?'

She reached. 'Of course. If you'd like, you can wait for him in the parlour.'

He did not even hesitate before answering.

'No. I'd better get back.'

'Have you had dinner, Mister Dorset?' she asked with a boldness that even surprised her.

He considered his answer. She saw the shadows come and go before he replied. 'No, but I only came up to give him the letter.' He looked at it in her hand. 'It's a recommendation from a man I worked for a few years back. I should have given it to him yesterday.'

She was curious again. 'But you forgot?'

His blue eyes rested again upon her face. 'Not exactly. I — well — when a man looks for work, he does as much sizing-up as the employer does. I wasn't sure, yesterday.'

'You're sure today then?'

'Yes. It's a good town.'

'Are you looking for a job, Mister Dorset, or a town?'

He smiled a little indulgently. 'One goes with the other, I think.'

That was correct, but she'd never thought of it like that. 'You're right, of course,' she murmured, and was piqued by the strong lines of his face, by the purpose in the way his lips lay closed in a locked-down way.

He said, 'Well . . . I'm sorry if I interrupted anything,' and reached for the knob and stepped out into the failing light of late day.

He smiled back at her. 'I'm obliged.'

She watched him go down off the porch and swing towards town beyond the white-painted gate, then she closed the door and went back to the kitchen. When she put the envelope beside her father's place at the kitchen table, she tried to guess something about the man who had handed it to her.

She could quite often do that with people, but not this time. There was more in his expression than any one emotion could stamp there. In the end, she thought he was altogether different from Fred Morgan — or was he? Was *any* man?

Chapter Four

Her father arrived late and he was not only tired, his limp was more noticeable. She deduced from that, that he had done a lot of walking during the course of whatever business had taken him down to Gosnold. She had only just re-filled the lamp upon his reading table in the parlour, had lighted it and polished the painted globe a moment ahead of his heavy tread across the porch.

She waited in the archway leading into the parlour and when he let himself in, she smiled as he turned to drape his hat from the rack beside the door and to shed his heavy shipmaster's coat with the anchors etched upon each button. He smiled back. 'I've had enough coach-riding for a year,' he said, 'and I couldn't find Flannagan, the lad in town who has the buggy he hires out, or I wouldn't have walked home.'

She knew it was his foot but she kept silent. They never talked about it. Only once, and that had been before her mother had died when he had confided in her that it always seemed to bother him more if he thought about it. She took him out to the kitchen, got a glass of his favourite peach brandy, sat him at the table and completely forgot Tom Dorset's visit until he frowned downward and said, 'What's this?'

The envelope. She explained, so he withdrew the letter and read it first to himself, then aloud to Lynne. It was a very good recommendation. She had never for a moment thought it would be otherwise; a man wouldn't leave a derogatory letter with a prospective employer.

It was so glowing that she said, 'How can you resist?' and laughed as she went to the stove. Then she remembered the way Fred had used the name Dorset, and turned back. 'Fred Morgan came by this morning, Father. He told me that Mister Dorset had also applied for work with them at the store.'

Dorset seemed to suddenly become secondary as Paul Harding's dark eyes considered his lithe daughter. 'What did he want?' he said in a flinty tone.

She suddenly knew *exactly why* her father had absolutely refused to allow her to marry Fred Morgan. It was a shock. *Her father knew Fred Morgan!* 'Well . . . to ask how you were. To tell me about Tom Dorset seeking work at their company.'

Her father sat with one thick hand holding

his brandy glass, regarding her thoughtfully. Finally he said, 'How long has he been married now, Lynne?'

She knew to the week, but all she said was, 'About a year.'

Her father nodded. 'I'll tell you something about Fred Morgan. The new wears off awfully fast with him. He's been like that ever since he was a small child. His folks made him like that, but that's their burden. Now, he's old enough to see himself — well — let's not discuss that.'

She was right about her father's feelings. 'I think we should discuss it,' she said. 'Is that why you were so difficult last year?'

He made a death's-head grin. 'Difficult? Sweetheart, I'd have rather seen you marry an inland farmer than Fred Morgan.'

'But why didn't you tell me?'

'How? Sweetheart, you cried yourself to sleep over that lad more than once. I heard you through the wall. How would it have sounded, then, if I'd told you? You'd have despised me for it, and you wouldn't have believed one word I'd have said.'

'I would now,' she said quietly.

Her father took a swallow of brandy. 'That wasn't all he came by for today, then, was it?'

She had a bitter taste in her mouth. 'Let's

get back to Mister Dorset. Fred said something, I don't remember the exact words, something about they wouldn't have wanted Tom Dorset *anyway*, even if they had needed someone. I felt that Fred knew something about Mister Dorset.'

Paul Harding and Jay Morgan were lifelong acquaintances, almost friends; they were too different in philosophy to have ever been very close, but they had never fought nor argued. Paul said, 'I'll go talk to Jay in the morning. And I'll probably hire Mister Dorset.' He glanced at the letter lying under his hand. 'If Fred comes around here again when I'm not home, let me know.' He picked up the letter, carefully folded it and tucked it back into the envelope. Then he finished his brandy and did not look at his daughter again until her back was turned and she was busy at the stove. He ran a glance up and down and tiredly shook his head. He would not tell her what he knew about Fred Morgan and had known since before Fred had started seeing her, nor would he ever mention lying awake in an anguish of despair when she would go buggy-riding with him in the evenings, nor how he had felt as he had watched her falling in love with Fred Morgan.

The town knew Fred. Not all the crewmen

of the *Hare* were outsiders, but even if the junior officers hadn't been local men, a man whose reputation grew with each sailing out and back would have got the kind of notoriety crewmen and others enjoyed telling and re-telling. Probably Lynne and Jay Morgan were the only ones who *didn't* know. That might have been ironic or just plain interesting, but not to Paul Harding.

The brandy worked its surfeiting benevolence. By the time she served dinner her father was loose and garrulous. He had, he told her, done about half again as much business down at Gosnold as he'd expected to do, which was pleasant, but it had been colder down there, for some reason, than it was at home, and moreover a new company in Gosnold, owned by someone named Livermore, had just lost a ship in a spring squall somewhere near Cuba, and because all hands were local men, there was gloom in every office and warehouse.

He ate like a starved man and afterwards settled thickly in his chair over coffee and smiled across the table. 'They have a woman in the counting rooms down at Gosnold. She's the widow of a cargomaster who served the O'Hara company for twenty-eight years. I thought about that on the ride back.'

She stared. 'Me?'

Her father laughed. 'They do it now in the cities. A traveller told me last summer about a company in Boston that has three women in its office, and I read in the newspaper about the Great Eastern Trading Company in New York employing them. I do a lot of business with Great Eastern.'

She thought of the Morgans, of Richard Tallant, of the shipmasters and buyers, of the community, and imagined their shocked expressions. She smiled at her father. 'Even if I knew the work, Smithsport would go to church the very next Sunday and pray for my soul.'

'Be nice to have Smithsport pray for *something*,' said her father, and struggled up out of the chair, eased his weight down gingerly and paused a moment like a ship in a troubled sea, then set his course for the doorway leading to the dining-room, and beyond, across the wide entry-way to the parlour. He wasn't drunk but he was not entirely sober either. Lynne watched his erect, rolling progress and decided that giving him that extra dram of peach brandy was responsible. He was a three-finger man, evidently.

She worked for an hour in the kitchen, then went down the back hall to her bedroom, turned up the lamp, noticed the wick smoking a little, told herself tomorrow would be a good day to go round the house trimming *all* lamp wicks, then brushed her hair, scrubbed her face, and went out to the parlour fully expecting to find her father fast asleep.

He wasn't. He hadn't touched the newspaper either, which was how he usually spent his evenings after dinner. He was sitting comfortably, one foot propped upon an ottoman, gazing into the fire and smoking his pipe. As she entered he brought his attention back from wherever it had been, and said, 'I think we can make a special corner in the office — the outer office — and set up a place for you there. I'll see about it tomorrow.'

She hadn't been sure he had been serious, in the kitchen, but evidently he was. She went to the sofa and looked at him with a little sensation of regret; he should have had a son. 'I don't know anything about the company,' she told him. 'The warehouse awed me as a little girl, and I still feel that way when I go there. It smells wonderful, but it's such a big, gloomy old place, with all the bales and barrels and crates. . . .'

Her father brushed that aside. 'I felt the same way, years back. You'll manage well enough.' He removed the pipe and looked at her. 'You know, your mother used to do a lot of the bookwork.' His eyes twinkled. 'I lived in terror for fear Morgan or Tallant or some of the others would find out. The companies have always been for men; even boys in their teens weren't allowed in our warehouses. But I'll tell you what I think: Jay Morgan's wife used to be around his office a lot; I think she was watching over things too, but no one ever dared breathe a word about any such a thing.'

Lynne smiled but without feeling much like it. She felt like someone balancing upon an abyss. Worse; if she failed — and she had a very real feeling that she would — it would be a disappointment to her father, and while he would never acknowledge such a thing, *she* would know, and that would be the worst thing she could imagine. She did not want to fail him, ever.

The solution, then, was not to fail. She sat stiffly upon the sofa telling herself that no matter what was required of her, she would do it; she would learn whatever had to be learned.

She was soberly disturbed and afraid, so she twisted to watch the dancing flames at the hearth, not willing to trust her face to conceal from her father's shrewd, kindly eyes, what might show there.

He heaved a great sigh. 'I hope Tom Dorset works out.' That was all he said for a while. When he spoke again it was about something altogether different. 'I've contracted the cargo of Jeptha Coggins from Martha's Vineyard. It's mahogany and coffee from Bolivia. There was word down at Gosnold today that Coggins should be sailing on in within a fortnight. A shipmaster down there saw him in Turtle Bay two weeks back and he was running on schedule. You know, the call for coffee is growing greater each year. I would have been glad to split the cargo with someone at Gosnold, but no one wanted the mahogany very badly. But it'll move well.' He smiled at the fireplace. 'Mahogany stores well and keeps well. It's only that a company doesn't want its money tied up too long in warehoused goods. Well; I could burn it and still make out well just on the coffee. You'll see how those things work.' He got out of the chair, limped to the hearth to knock dottle from his pipe, and afterwards he straightened up and gazed a moment at the sailing ship atop the mantel. '*Celeste Gloria.* It was her loss that drove the Hardings to the land.' He turned about. 'It was our greatest disaster — then — but now I think it was the making of us. We've done better at trading than we ever did at sailing.'

After that he left her in the parlour and

went off to his room. She sat looking up at the ship atop the mantel, too, for a long while, thinking back to the twists and turns of fortune that had dictated the course of the lives in her family. She was the last Harding. The heritage would probably, someday, mingle with other blood just as hardy, but the name would end with her.

Her father probably thought about that once in a while. She pitied him and thought again that she should have been a boy, a man.

The fire burned down, the moon soared across its high curving, yonder in the silvery night a great sea rolled, and the old house 'worked' as the heat went out and the night chill settled in.

Fred Morgan came insidiously into her mind so she arose also to retire. If her father had told her. . . . But he was perfectly right; she not only wouldn't have believed him, she would have been crushed to think her father would make such accusations simply to try and destroy her love for Fred.

Being a human being was not an easy thing; being a woman was hardest of all. She went off to her room, turned down the lamp, blew it out, opened her back-wall window and got ready for bed. Her mother had instilled in her a habit of undressing in the dark and of quickly donning her nightgown; it was sinful for a woman to view her naked body.

She didn't even think of that; she simply went through the routine as she had been taught to from earliest childhood, and afterwards got under the goose-down quilts and lay back upon the flannel sheet. Fred had been replaced by the new challenge; what worried her far more than being the first woman to work in the company counting room, was not being able to succeed at it. That would be even worse. She could close her eyes and visualize old Jay Morgan grinning maliciously at her father and saying he had known all along women didn't have a head for weights and figures and ladings.

She would do it if it killed her!

Chapter Five

She worked like a demon the following day cleaning house, not just because it was time for the spring cleaning but also because whenever she was troubled, like the tormented holy men of old she had discovered that the next best thing to yielding to anxiety, was physical exhaustion. But her worry was different; she felt no temptation of the flesh, she was anxious about her father's proposal.

What made it more than ever frightening was the fact that her father often mentioned business, but always only in a very general way. He might mention buying a cargo, or selling particular warehoused items, but he had never spoken in detail, which meant that she was so ignorant, actually, that she did not even know what, exactly, he dealt in, or who his customers were. He would occasionally mention a company by name, or a shipmaster, or perhaps an investment syndicate, but they had always meant so little to her, actually, that she only remembered a few of them, the ones he had mentioned more than once.

When he arrived home that evening he was cheerful. He had brought in one of the warehousemen and between them they had begun to re-order the outer office to make a place for her. He had confided in his ancient clerk, Cuthbert Emory, that he was going to bring Lynne into the business. His eyes twinkled in reflection. 'He sat there looking like I'd just announced a blight had struck the country.'

She knew old Bert Emory well. Not only had he been her father's book-keeper and company clerk for thirty-one years, he had also been her father's shadow, mentor, and crutch. He was older than her father, a wispy, slightly bent man with thick eye-glasses, snow-white hair, and an elfin look, but he had also sailed with her grandfather in his youth. He was as much a part of Harding Company as the gloomy old office or the big warehouse. His reaction was important.

She said, 'He didn't like it, the idea I mean?'

Her father laughed. 'Probably not, but he didn't say anything. He just sat peering out at me from behind his glasses. He was shocked, I suppose. People never change very readily. Especially old people. Well; I also gave him another bother. I hired Tom Dorset this afternoon.'

She was interested. 'What did Jay Morgan say?'

Her father went towards the kitchen and his pre-supper sip as he replied. 'Gossip. Seamen are worse than old women, but then it's a long time between landings, sometimes, and they have to talk about something.' He got the knobbed decanter and poured in two fingers, went to the kitchen table and sat down. 'It always smells good in here,' he said, and did not meet her eyes.

She got his signal. He was not going to discuss whatever it was Morgan had told him about Tom Dorset. While she mulled that over, with all its dark implications, she started supper.

When a man refused to discuss another man with a woman, there would be a reason that meant the man felt either chagrined or embarrassed at this prospect. Her father had told her of legal disputes, even brawls in the tavern, but he never mentioned men and other women, not in the context that she suddenly suspected would be the case this time.

Of course Tom Dorset would have known women. He was one of those ruggedly interesting men who seemed to attract them. Lynne was neither old enough nor experienced enough to understand all that this could mean, but she *suspected* most of what it *could* mean. New Englanders who lived beside the sea knew a lot more than people thought; men did not sail the high seas without bringing back customs acquired in many places. On the surface, New Englanders were just as granite-like and unbending as their rock-girt coasts; as hard and puritannical as other people said they were, but that was only on the surface.

Her curiosity made her say, 'Whatever it was Mister Morgan told you must not have been very convincing.'

For a moment her father studied the contents of his glass, then he downed the brandy and put the glass aside as he got to his feet to go wash and prepare for dinner. 'Convincing or not, sweetheart, it's outside the ken of the company, and what I'm hiring is a man who knows the business.' He started for the door. 'A man's personal life he leaves outside when he walks through the company's doors.'

She continued working after her father had departed. She was a little surprised, but not terribly so. Her father used a particular tone of voice when he had made a decision that he would not alter nor defend. He had used it just now as he'd passed from the room. He had hired Tom Dorset and that was that.

Lynne was content to accept this; in some indefinable way she was pleased. If Tom Dorset was as knowledgeable as her father felt, he could probably help her at the office. She had no illusions; she was going to need all the help she could get. Bert Emory would be helpful, but she remembered something from years back about Bert Emory; he was an irascible man, quick-tempered and short of patience. He had always been kindly towards her, but that had been as a child or as a young girl, and this time when she appeared it would be as a clerk in the same office, and that would be something altogether different.

When her father returned and she put his meal upon the table he was cheerful again. He seemed to envision something that held promise, perhaps a lessening of the burden of business. At least she connected his hiring of Tom Dorset with his pleasant mood. When she came to sit opposite him, he said, 'It will be Monday morning.' He did not say she would start working Monday morning, or that they would leave the house together Monday morning, but that was what he meant. This was Wednesday, so she had four more days to agonize with herself. But she didn't do that, she started her education then and there by firing questions at him. By the end of the meal he was gazing quizzically at her, considering her as though he had made a discovery and couldn't make up his mind whether he liked it or not. Finally, he said, 'You think like your mother thought. It's about the way men think, except that your mother used to reach out and include more facts. I've always traded on the basis that futures were most important in relation to what's available. Like the Coggins' cargo; I need the coffee but not the mahogany. It was your mother that got me into the habit of taking those other things, if I could get them almost for the price of ballast, then warehouse them and wait for a decent market.' He smiled across the table. 'You think like that too.'

It was probably a compliment, but when men discussed female methods that was not always the case, she knew. Men could be contemptuous and indulgent at the same time.

Her father changed the subject, after one final casual statement. 'You'll make out all right, Lynne. Don't fret.' Then he said, 'Fred is shipping out Friday for Jamaica to take aboard a cargo of molasses and rum for New York. He'll be gone a month or thereabouts.' As he said this her father was busy with his dinner, but she knew what he was trying to convey. Not that it mattered whether Fred came or went, or even whether he remained ashore. He had become something objectionable to her, and almost effortlessly. She hadn't thought much about him within the past twenty-four hours, less along towards the end of that period than at the beginning of it, and in some mysterious way her mind had made an independent judgement. Fred Morgan, whom she had loved to the point of distraction so short a while ago, had now become an epitome of something that made her feel unclean just thinking about it.

She brushed that aside, and she did it in the only way a man would have really believed it. She did not mention Fred, only his cargo. 'Is New York the best market for molasses and rum? Don't the Morgans usually sell rum through the warehouse, or through Morgan and Tallant?'

Her father tasted his coffee. 'Richard finished buying out all the Morgan interests in the store over a year ago, Lynne. It's still called Morgan and Tallant, but it's Tallant now. As for the rum, yes, Morgan would have a good market, but he may already have enough at his warehouse. Sometimes a company makes more money by selling a cargo on board than in warehousing it, and later on marketing it case by case.' Her father finished his coffee. 'Tom put it right: Why handle a cargo more than once if you can profit as much by offloading it on someone else's dock?'

There was a basic sameness in this aphorism and in what her father had been saying, and there wasn't anything very complicated about it. Consider all aspects of selling, then progress along the course that would make the most money. Simple, she told herself, and derived a good bit of encouragement from this.

But of course there would be a lot more to learn, and although it would all boil down to this one law of business, it would still be detailed, complicated, and difficult. She did not, right then, even think about the uniqueness of a woman in one of the company offices.

It had been a delightful day, warm, almost hot in the afternoon. The drab elms — originally brought from China — showed lively new growth, the crocuses and tulips were burgeoning, and out across the cobbled wide roadway beyond the massive sea wall, the sea had been flirting with the warming land, turning blue and silver and soft emerald in all its most alluring variations. The sun had departed reluctantly, a little later than usual. The wind had not come at all, probably because spring was building its own invisible bulwark against the atmospheric pressure fronts, and even after dinner when Lynne and her father went out front to the verandah, as they both often did in mid-summer, it was pleasant enough for an hour or two, for them to sit there in comfort.

Down the slight hill Smithsport showed quaint and solid in the gloaming. Many New England seacoast towns were built of stone. It was the one commodity close at hand which was easily available, but there was also another reason why most of the coastal towns had been made of it; unless a wooden house was strongly constructed and cared for, it did not usually last more than a couple of generations in New England's hard climate.

Originally, Smithsport's wide avenues had been dirt, and before they were cobbled people put up with it, but afterwards the cobbling of the streets had marked an innovative era; they had even brought water into an underground pipeline for some of the residences, and the more prosperous had painted their stores and homes.

But from the slight elevation of the hill where Lynne and her father sat, gazing back down towards the town, nothing looked very different. In her father's lifetime there had been changes; most of the critical innovations had occurred then. But in Lynne's lifetime nothing seemed to have changed at all, except that the Morgans had erected a new stone jetty and the Episcopal church, which had caught fire one Christmas Eve eight or nine years back, had been rebuilt.

She had always felt something like affection for Smithsport, and it was not altogether because she had never known another town, nor did her affection spring from heritage. It was a pretty village, bigger than Gosnold and frequently as bustling as any port town for a hundred miles in either direction, up, or down, the coastland, but still a village. People knew each other. They also seemed to know one another's business with uncanny accuracy.

As she sat looking down there she said, 'I can't imagine Smithsport ever looking any different,' and her parent, who was lighting his pipe, squinted through the evening and studied the rooftops and chimney pots, the worn-flat cobble of King George Street, and puffed up an adequate head of smoke before commenting.

'When I was a lad there'd be as many as fifteen clippers tied along the docks or at anchor offshore. Now we have five or six.' He kept puffing and gazing over on the east side of town where the companies had their stores in front and their great warehouses down the backwall towards the docks. 'There's been change, I can tell you that.'

She looked at him in surprise. He had sounded solemn, almost as though he were lamenting something; she'd never known him to do this before. He caught her expression even in that poor light, and spoke as he smoked.

'When I was a lad Yankee clipper ships dominated all the Orient trade. There was no faster vessel afloat. We could make it out to the Philippines and back with a cargo before the Europeans could make half the crossing. But New Orleans was closer, and now it's San Francisco, which is three thousand miles closer. There's no way to build a ship that can overcome that kind of a handicap — unless we could make it fly.'

She looked back down along the eastern seawall. There were three great sets of masts down there, the *Hare* drawn close broadside to Morgan Company's new dock, the other pair at anchor in the roadstead, the natural harbour out front of Smithsport. She had an uneasy feeling, and yet *she* had noticed no decline. Everything looked to her as it had always looked.

Chapter Six

Monday came, and Monday went, and although she was certain old Mister Emory had spared her a good bit of the detail and trouble, she felt elated as she and her father began the walk homeward in a dazzling glow of sunshine.

Twice she'd spoken to Tom Dorset. The first time he'd come to ask Mister Emory about some receipts, and the second time Mister Emory had stopped into the outer office to see *her.* That time Mister Emory had stepped into her father's office for mid-afternoon tea, a long-standing custom, and although she had been invited, she knew perfectly well Mister Emory had not wanted her to intrude upon this daily tradition, so she had declined and had sat at her bench examining some ladings.

Tom turned out to be a source of a surprisingly vast and varied amount of information, not only about ship's schedules, but about more pertinent things, such as markets and warehousings, and something she had never heard of before — trading between companies. He told her, for example, that Great Eastern down in New York City, had a form-letter out for two hundred barrels of brined fish, and were offering in exchange an equivalent in market value of raw silk in bolts.

She related all this to her father on the walk uphill and he limped along at her side, thick and quiet and thoughtful, but with his stern lips slightly lifted at the corners, as though he were complimenting himself inwardly about something; maybe about her, maybe about Tom Dorset. Possibly even about them both.

'Originally that's how it worked,' he explained. 'The companies traded and bartered rather than sold, but that was in my grandfather's day. Now, we trade when we get something as a landslide ballast — like Coggins' mahogany — if we think we've held it long enough and there's still no market. But that's a sideline; our business is to sell.' He looked up as though to estimate how much farther they had to go. 'Bert told me this afternoon that you reminded him of your mother.'

She thought, again, it was probably meant as a compliment, but men did not always mean their candid remarks about women in that way, so she said nothing.

At home, she learned something else about being an employee; she was also still a housekeeper. Her father hoisted his foot to the ottoman, stoked his pipe and read the paper, but she had to go change, then make dinner, and although she had been sitting most of the day, she still felt a little in need of rest, but less so, apparently, than her father, but he was much older.

The evening passed as had the day, pleasantly and without stress. They had dinner, then sat a while in the parlour, and later, when she went to bed, she smiled in the darkness; it hadn't been like stepping into an alligator pit after all.

The next day was about the same, too; she could cope with the things Mister Emory and her father brought over for her attention. The only really noticeable discordant note came on Thursday; she overheard two of the warehousemen discussing her. Not personally, but that would have been easier to hear. They were agreeing that her father was getting old, and that the business would very shortly now need new direction. They deplored her arrival and thought it was something her father had felt compelled to do out of desperation.

They said nothing at all about Tom Dorset, and later in the afternoon when she thought about that, it seemed probable that the warehousemen had accepted him without reservations. From there, she speculated, once again, on what it was in his past that had made the Morgans leary of Tom.

She did not see Tom every day. By the end of her second week, when the Coggins' cargo arrived, she knew why. The only way a company throve was through ceaseless activity, and at Tom Dorset's level that meant constant attention to the inventory. The warehouse was large, almost cavernous in fact, otherwise it would never have been able to accommodate three and four cargoes at a time. Tom not only had to plan so that the offloadings could be housed, but he had to do it in such a way that every corner of the warehouse was utilized, and the centre of it was available for offloadings, sortings, and stacking. He had four shoremen working for him, but with the arrival of the Coggins' cargo all five of them had to work like Trojans.

It was all done by hand, except of course for the horse-operated winched cargo nets at dockside.

Captain Coggins was a Gosnold man, but he had kin in Smithsport, and one of them told Lynne's father that Fred Morgan had put in at one of the key isles around Bermuda to refit after encountering a storm on his Jamaica run. Even in late spring and summertime the southward run from New England to the Caribbean was hazardous. Some ship's officers held that late springtime was the worst time, although most believed wintertime seas were more treacherous.

Gradually, Lynne's life changed. She was glad to reach home at the end of each day, but her mind remained down at the George Street place of business, and at the end of the third week her father laughed at her, one evening on the verandah, and said she was beginning to sound like a lifelong company employee.

She liked it. The original fear had never turned into anything more substantial than apprehension. She and old Mister Emory got along; he was courteous, short, and patient — for him — with her problems. No doubt about it, though, if she had not been a Harding regardless of anything else, it would have been different. She told her father Mister Emory reminded her of a wizened goshawk and he smiled, saying something that intrigued her.

'People have to belong to something, Sweetheart. Maybe it's something the rest of us don't think much of, or maybe it's something we understand, but they have to belong to something. And the older they get, the more the world passes them by, the more they cling to it. Bert will die with the company, and that is only right.'

Her father never talked of death, and he rarely ever philosophized; at least up until she had gone to work in the office, she had never heard him do it. But then she had noticed another subtle change in their relationship as well; he called her 'sweetheart' as he always had since her earliest recollection, but more and more now, he used her first name. At the office that was the only way he addressed her, and now at home, at dinner, he did the same thing.

She suspected that he was, perhaps unconsciously, beginning to think of her as a *person* more than as a daughter; as another adult.

They only kept the business open half a day on Saturday, but just before her father and old Bert Emory went down to the tavern to sit over a glass of sherry and discuss the week's transactions, as had been their habit for more than a quarter of a century, her father told her Tom would be along with some correspondence on the Coggins' coffee, and as soon as that had been handled, she should go along home.

Tom came, and in the soft sunlight, they sat at ease and talked for over an hour, without once mentioning the coffee. It was quiet inside as well as outside. The gloomy old office with its worn oiled planking floor, was mellow. There was a faint little breeze at the front window, which was open, and except for an occasional shod hoof striking down over the cobbles downstairs, where dray wagons were pulling out with their loads, heading, perhaps, for the steam-car terminus down at Gosnold where goods were shipped — or were railroaded — throughout the country, Smithsport was already beginning to drowse.

Tom was hatless. He did not wear his sea-jacket any more, now that the weather was warmer, and in his grey turtle-neck jersey his torso showed bulges of muscle. When he pulled over old Mister Emory's stool and perched upon it, she thought he looked about as out of place as a man could look. He belonged on the wheelhouse deck of a sailing vessel. She took a chance and said something like that. He studied her face and shrugged. 'How many of us are where we *ought* to be?'

She caught the implication immediately. He thought she should be at home. 'My prospects are limited, but yours aren't.'

'Sure of that, are you?' he asked softly.

She knew the ice was getting very thin

beneath her feet. 'No. Well; about the coffee. . . .' She became brisk and squared round at her counting table.

He sat hunched like a thick stork atop Mister Emory's stool and made no move to hand over the papers in his hand. 'Do you know the country hereabouts?' he asked.

Of course she knew it. She'd grown up here; as a child and a young girl she'd been into the mountains, and westerly out across the rural countryside. 'I couldn't help but know it,' she replied, and turned to look. At once she knew his thoughts, but it was too late, he had led her into his trap as casually as though she were a child.

'I haven't seen much of it this past month. I was thinking about renting a rig tomorrow and going for a drive towards the hills.'

She smiled. 'Do they have mountains in Jamaica?'

'No. They have hills.'

'In New England we have mountains.'

His smile came slowly. 'Excuse me. Mountains. Anyway, I was thinking of a two-seater.'

He kept looking at her. She started to redden so she reached, took the papers from his hand and turned back to the table. She felt his eyes while she studied the ladings, which had to be matched to the orders atop her desk. They would tally, of course; her job was to arrange for the allocations, make out the proper shipping orders, and balance the inventory sheets for what remained of the coffee.

He got off the stool and stood there. She could sense the finality of that movement. He had decided not to press his oblique invitation. She felt sorry for him without knowing exactly why, unless it was because he was strange to the area. She turned and said, 'If you keep to the roads you'll see a lot of lovely country.'

He nodded thoughtfully, then a small impish grin came up. 'I might get lost.'

It was a relief to be able to laugh. 'You could get one of the lads around town to show you round, I'm sure.'

He grinned. 'That's not what I had in mind.'

Their sparring was no longer awkward; humour had made it pleasant. 'What do you imagine might be a suitable alternative?' she asked, which was as much encouragement as any man should need.

He leaned down on her desk. 'I wondered — if your father wouldn't object, maybe you could go with me.'

She didn't even think of her father. 'I go

to church until mid-morning, Mister Dorset.'

He tugged gently at an ear lobe. 'I could drive up after that, perhaps.'

'Ten o'clock?'

'You pray a lot,' he murmured, then said, 'Ten o'clock. And just in case — I don't think there'd be any hamlets — so I could fetch along a picnic hamper.'

She had yielded, and because she was a Harding, having committed herself she did not procrastinate. 'No. I'll pack the hamper.'

He smiled. He had one of the gentlest smiles she had ever seen. 'I think your father is at the tavern.' When he paused she knew what else he would say, so she spoke first.

'My father won't object. I'm almost twenty, Mister Dorset.' She blushed because that had sounded almost ridiculous.

But he did not show any indulgence. All he said was: 'Ten o'clock,' and walked out of the office. The building was so quiet she heard his light lope down the stairs.

She looked at the papers he had left and could only think of that silly thing she'd said. He was probably thirty. At least he was close to it, give or take a year. What would a man of that age, having been married and having been to sea, being, in fact an experienced person, think of a girl who had thrown the fact in his face that she was *almost* twenty?

Later, on the way home, she was still thinking of that when she raised her head and saw the wide sail coming head-down toward the Smithsport roadstead. Her step faltered when she recognized the pennant. Fred Morgan was back.

Someone had said he would be delayed in the Caribbean; but that was the *Hare.* She had known both the Morgan ships all her life, and without being aware of it, she had picked up a considerable store of ship-lore.

Her mouth flattened. Perhaps Fred's delay hadn't been the result of leaks or torn canvas. Perhaps Fred Morgan had put in at one of the islands near Bermuda for personal reasons. She walked briskly the balance of the way home and entered the house without another look beyond the sea wall.

Chapter Seven

She told her father that evening at dinner, and immediately sensed the change in him even before he said, 'People who work together have to guard against familiarity. Otherwise it leads to unnecessary and sometimes even unpleasant relationships. My practice over the years has been never to mix my social and business affairs. Not even with Bert. It promotes respect on both sides, and harmony at the store.'

If he had come flat out and said what he knew, or at least what Jay Morgan had told him about Tom Dorset, she could have handled that, but what he *had* said was not only true, about familiarity leading to contempt, it was also something she could put forth no valid argument against.

But she had to defend herself some way, so she said, 'I need the outing,' and her father said no more on the subject. Later, when she finished in the kitchen and went to the parlour he was smoking and reading. He watched her cross to the sofa and pick up her book, then removed the pipe to speak.

'You could show him the old miller's wheel up near Chickopee Falls. I'm sure that would be interesting to someone who probably hasn't seen many things like that.'

She smiled, and relented towards him. He was making amends for the lecture at supper. 'That's a fine idea. . . .' She opened the book then let it lie in her lap. 'What is it that Jay Morgan told you about Tom Dorset?' At his sudden clearing of the throat and rattling of the newspaper she said, 'If I'm old enough to run your house and work in the office, then I'm old enough to be treated as a grown woman.'

Her father sucked on his pipe a moment longer, eyes roaming over the newspaper's opened page. 'He killed a man,' he exclaimed, and looked over the paper at her again.

She was shocked, but not outraged, and what shocked her was that when she thought of Tom Dorset, now, she thought of his gentle smile. Then her father added another short sentence, and that *did* stun her.

'. . . Over a woman.'

When she recovered she went over to Tom's defence. 'You said it was gossip.'

Her father gravely inclined his head. 'Yes, that's exactly what I said. But I finally got an answer to those letters I wrote a few weeks ago. . . . It is true, Lynne. Tom killed a man in a fight over a woman named Jeanette Stuart. In the South they do those things.'

'In the South?'

'Louisiana. It happened the year following his wife's passing. There's a lot down there we wouldn't tolerate in Massachusetts, but they're a different kind of people. You know that from reading about the War between the States. They — well — they have a lot of French influence, down there. Their, ah, morals, are different from ours.'

'What are the details?' she asked, feeling a little towards Tom Dorset as she had felt that morning out back towards Fred Morgan — terribly disillusioned.

Her father did not know the details. 'I didn't get any more than I've told you. Well; there's one thing more: The man was prominent in a place called Bayou Biscayne. Came from a wealthy family of planters and shipowners. His name was John Loudon.'

For a while a depth of silence settled, then Lynne closed her book and set it aside. She wanted to offer another defence, but she was too honest to make the attempt. 'We don't know Tom's side of it, do we?' she murmured, and when her father said, 'No, we don't,' she was neither satisfied with her question, nor with her father's answer. Perhaps, if he'd lectured her again, but this time on the evils of killing, she could have rallied a little, but he simply sat there.

She excused herself and went to her room to prepare for bed, and took with her a feeling of emptiness. As she blew down the lamp mantle and plunged her bedroom into darkness, moonlight came through the rear-wall window and half replaced the lamplight.

She undressed and got ready for bed, then she stood a while at the window gazing out over the garden where every bush and shrub and tree was now in full bloom.

The moon was full, the night was pleasant, the hush was endless and deep. Smithsport retired early and arose the same way; even this time of year when all human activity was approaching a peak, the town and its environs were never noisy after supper.

She turned, eventually, and went to bed, and because she knew so little, her imagination conjured up a dozen different ways that Tom Dorset had killed that man in Louisiana, and every one of them was ugly. Maybe if there hadn't been that other name — Jeanette Stuart — she could at least have imagined a clean death for John Loudon, but the woman made it sordid, made it evil and unclean. She could even imagine Tom drunk and dishevelled and shooting down a rival named Loudon.

It did not make her sleep easy, when it finally arrived, and when she awakened she lay a moment wondering which excuse to use in avoiding the drive to the mill wheel with Tom Dorset.

Her father rarely arose early on Sunday. When her mother had been alive he'd had to, but now, without her to goad him into correct church attendance, and with his daughter grown and not as outwardly religious as his wife had been, he lay abed sometimes until eight or nine o'clock on Sundays.

Lynne, though, had been cursed with her mother's vigour and self-discipline. She not only arose the same hour on Sunday as on any other day of the week, but she also bustled round making breakfast, setting the parlour to rights, doing a little dusting, and by the time her father finally appeared, she had his breakfast ready and was on her way to church without him.

She seldom asked him to accompany her because she realized he did this, when he went at all, as a duty, and her opinion of worship, unlike her mother's opinion, was in no way related to saving his, or anyone else's, soul. She was concerned primarily with her *own* soul; she was not, as her mother had been, a zealous proselyte.

She arrived at the church attired in a dove-grey dress that fit loosely at shoulder and breast, and which fell to her ankles, and a shade lower. She wore white gloves, and a little hat to match both gloves and dress, and perhaps because of the other thing on her mind she failed to sense the distance of the men who gravely nodded to her on the way in, and the mixed reception she got from their wives and daughters. Some of the women smiled very frank encouragement and admiration, as though she were some kind of local suffragette, some kind of local hero of a woman's liberation movement. The other women seemed to either resent her, or to feel sorry for her.

But there was no difference in the masculine faces. Every expression showed distaste, and some showed frank hostility.

She only understood this gradually, as the services progressed and she caught people gazing at her from time to time. When it finally dawned upon her what was happening, in a sudden brief moment of dazzling clarity she saw the future: People would of course eventually hear the gossip about Tom Dorset — he had killed a man; they might even eventually learn that he had killed a man *over a woman*. And Lynne Harding, who had gone buggy-riding with him, was the same girl who was trying to break down the barriers in the world of shipmasters and businessmen by working in her father's offices. She could imagine their words: 'Well, if you ask me a girl who'd want to work around *men* at one of the company stores, has to be a shameless wanton.' Or: 'It's a good thing her poor mother didn't live to see *this:* Her daughter flaunting herself with a known dissolute woman-chasing killer!'

Usually, she stayed throughout church and put in a little time in the Sunday school department with the small children. Not today. She left by a side-door as soon as she decently could and walked briskly back up through town without encountering a soul, all the way back up the slight hill and when she crossed the verandah, she hoped her father would not be in the parlour, otherwise as she went past on the way to her room she'd have to stop and say something, which she did not wish to do right at the moment.

But her father was out back with a hoe, stirring the gravelly soil around her mother's lilac bushes. He was working with his sleeves rolled to the elbows, without his coat or jacket, and without his hat too. The sun was warmer where it bounced back from the rear of the house. She saw him through her bedroom window and he was slightly flushed in the face and perspiring. It was good for him to get that exercise; at the office the most exercise he ever got was to hike down to the warehouse once or twice a day, and climbing stairs was unpleasant for him, and therefore really did not count as exercise. Nor did he hike up and down the stairs any oftener than he absolutely had to.

She stepped out of the dove-gray dress, almost unconsciously selected a white blouse that fit snug at bust and shoulder, and a dark tan skirt, suitable attire for buggy-riding in the countryside on a warm summer day.

She hadn't really made up her mind to go; in fact she was still considering excuses, but since she had to wear *something,* and this attire was equally suitable for Sunday loafing, she put it on, buttoned up, after bathing and powdering, then sat for a while at the dressing-table re-arranging her taffy hair, which was turning more gold again, as it did each summer.

She unconsciously listened for the sound of horseshoes over the cobbles out front, half hoping they would not arrive, and when she was finished making herself presentable, she went to the kitchen to make something cool for her father, and took the glass out to him. He looked at her, seemed not aware that she had changed clothes, accepted the glass and drank deeply, drained it in fact and passed it back, then he said, 'You know, these blasted lilac bushes used to make your mother's and my bedroom smell like the inside of a sachet, and I hated it. My idea of sweet air was just honest, salt-breeze. But now I don't think I could go right off to sleep in summertime without the lilacs out here.' He laughed. 'If people keep doing something long enough, even though they don't like doing it, eventually they'll like it, then they'll want to do it, and finally they won't be able to make out very well unless they are doing it.'

She smiled at him. 'Is that what you've been thinking, hoeing the flowerbed?'

He looked at her for a moment without answering. 'Partly. Mostly, I suppose. You're a grown woman now. If I keep worrying about you, it'll get to be that kind of a habit. That wouldn't be healthy for either of us, would it? Well; are you going buggy-riding with him?'

She started to say that she wasn't, when out front they both heard the horseshoes rattling with loud echoes up the silent, morning-drowsy roadway. A man was whistling out there.

Her father resolved the problem with one look, and one sentence. 'Happiness is a day like this, and nothing to do but shape it into a pleasant memory.'

She stood a moment or two listening to Tom's approach and gazing at her father. 'I don't know how it can be done,' she murmured.

'Maybe it won't be done,' he replied to her. 'Maybe you'll look back on it as a bad experience. But at least it *will* be an experience, won't it? And that's what folks your age need more than anything else. Go along now.' He lifted the hoe, turned his back, bent and went back to the lilac-bed work.

She wanted to kiss him, but instead she said, 'I'll be back about sundown, I suppose.' Then she went hastily back to the kitchen, rinsed the glass, put it aside and when Tom knocked she was poised in the doorway between kitchen and dining-room.

Perhaps her father was right. She had never really tried to define what youth was, except health, and perhaps that it was also a difficult time of transition for girls, but she had never thought of it as the period for having experiences. Still, what else could it be?

She went to the entry-hall, swung back the door, and saw his strongly handsome face with its kindly smile.

It was very easy to be critical of someone

when they were not present, but when they were standing in front of you showing pleasure, showing admiration and anticipation, it was not easy at all.

She smiled, stood aside for him to enter, and left him waiting while she went for a shawl and a wide-brimmed hat. Sometimes she freckled in summertime. That hat would be protection against that. Anyway, the buggy tied out at the iron post beyond the front-garden fence had a top on it.

She looked one last time at herself in the mirror, said, 'You're going to have an experience,' then marched resolutely back to the entry-hall.

Chapter Eight

She had entirely forgotten about the picnic hamper!

She did not remember this until, as he was handing her up after first untying the horse, he looked back towards the house as though half expecting someone to bring something out.

She raised a hand to her lips with a tiny gasp. He looked up, understood, and laughed. 'Folks eat too much anyway,' he said, and came round to his side of the rig.

'I'll only be a minute,' she exclaimed, but he reached and detained her by the arm. Then he flipped the lines and swung the buggy completely around heading back down the hill as he said, 'I'm not hungry and you probably aren't either. Let's worry about it when we are. Maybe we won't even get hungry.'

She was enormously chagrined with herself, but as they levelled off at the flat part of King George Street, which had been named during provincial times and for some abstruse reason had never been given another name, she heard the solid echoes go bouncing back and forth along the storefronts as they went north through town.

There were a few people, but very few, out walking. Some appeared to be those who had remained at church until the last peal of the churchbell, others were simply young girls and their equally young escorts. Some looked up, some even grinned and waved, but there were several other couples, with children trailing them like minnows in a creek, who became engrossed with things they saw in store windows and managed to be quite oblivious to the shod-horse sound as the buggy rolled past.

Tom noticed, but until they were nearing the upper end of Smithsport he said nothing.

The buggy smelled of leather-soap and the rump of the sleek bay horse between the shafts rose and fell with a steady, tireless cadence. It was a beautiful day in the countryside, and a person never had to progress beyond the end of the cobbled roadway more than a half mile, in any direction from Smithsport, to be in the countryside. There was the enormous cresting bluish sea on their right, the slightly rolling, rocky land on their left, and dead ahead were mountain slopes that looked close enough to reach in an hour or two, but which kept retreating the farther they drove.

Tom said, 'It's a healthy country.'

Because she had expected almost any comment but that one, she looked over at him. He saw her expression and grinned. 'Well; of course it's beautiful too. It has a kind of briskness you only find in places where the winters are severe. What I meant was you don't ever feel as listless as you do down south, where the air's hot and muggy most of the year.'

She knew better, but she asked the question anyway. 'Did you spend most of your time in the south?'

He sat hunched a little, a line in each hand, looking around as they drove. His answer was given while he was looking away from her, to the left. 'Enough of it.' He offered no elaboration.

She was tempted to press the topic, but didn't. 'Do you see that farm in the swale on your left; the one with the faded old red-stained barn? My great-grandfather lived there for a long time, before he moved to town. He didn't sell the farm even then. My father was born there, then his father built the house in Smithsport.'

Tom was interested. 'I thought your great-grandfather was a seaman?'

'He was. But according to my father, where he came from the people were only allowed to work the land providing they gave half of every harvest to a lord, and when they had a bad crop, the lord took it all and they either starved or went to sea. He went to sea; but he never lost his love of the land . . . I suppose you could say he was a frustrated farmer who did best at something he only did because he knew how to do it. Sailing and trading. He established Harding Company. And, oh yes; in case you hadn't been informed by the local gossips, his name was Huertado, not Harding. He was Portuguese.'

Tom turned with an exaggerated expression of horror. 'And all the time I thought you were descended from the glorious knights of St George.'

He was teasing her. She said. 'Partly. The other part were descended from the serfs of — well — whoever is the patron saint of the Azores, of old time Portugal.' She smiled. 'And they weren't knights, as far as I know, they were peasant farmers.'

A little farther along they came to the watercourse. It was called a creek, but it was easily twenty feet across and she knew, having gone swimming in it, having in fact, learned to swim in it, that it was just about that deep as well. 'Chickopee Creek,' she told him. 'That old stone bridge ahead to the left is Chickopee Bridge. If you cross it and bear right on the other side, we'll eventually get to a bluff and a waterfall.'

He said, 'Called Chickopee Falls, naturally.'

She laughed. 'Naturally. But before that I want to show you where they had a water-wheel long ago. Everyone took their grain up there to be ground to flour. At one time there was a settlement at the mill, but nothing's left now but a few old stone houses and the mill-building. The wheel was of wood, so it disappeared long ago. My father said it rotted away, but I think some of the townspeople who needing planking for a cow barn or a house, helped it rot.'

They clattered over the bridge, swung right, and Tom looped the lines and allowed the bay horse to meander at his own gait, which was an ambling walk. Tom blew out a huge breath and sank back. 'It's the way I thought it would be; green and stony and old, and kind of sleepy; kind of — what's the word? Permanent?'

'Tranquil,' she said, knowing his mood because she'd had the same sensation many times.

'No matter what happens, wars, bad times,

ships lost at sea, it's still here and always unchanged.' He looked out towards the fir-greened slopes. 'By the way, I can't quite put my finger on it, but within the past week I've sensed a kind of change around Smithsport. When we drove up through town an hour ago, it was stronger than ever. Don't they like outsiders?'

She answered easily because he had inadvertently provided her with enough of a half-truth to make her reply palatable. 'No, they don't. We have friends who've been here twenty years, and they're still referred to as "those other people". Those "outsiders". Those people from New York, or Boston, or wherever they're from.' She kept looking out between the horse's ears as she spoke.

Tom saw the mill through the trees and other growth and raised his arm. 'It's like a calendar painting, the big old stone building and the little stone houses here and there.' He leaned to pick up the lines. 'Can we drive in there?'

She showed him how to pick their way until they eventually reached what had once been a well-travelled roadway, and that, in turn, became the central avenue of the hamlet.

Birds scolded from rooftops of grey slate, from the roofless second-storey of the ancient mill, and also from the treetops. There were earth-creatures too, but they had long since scuttled for shelter at the sound of the buggy's approach, so, except for the birds, the little abandoned village was hushed and drowsy, in a fretwork of sunshine and soft shade.

They left the horse standing out front of what had once been a forge, anchored to the ground by a teatherweight, and she took him along a narrow path to the stone decking where the huge old water-wheel had once turned. Here, when they spoke, echoes came like lonely ghosts from the doorless windows of the stone-walled building nearby. All the windows were without glass and most were also without sashes, evidence that the process of dissolution had had some helping hands — human ones.

The stones were worn smooth from shoe-leather where the giant grinding wheels had once turned, inside, and high above was the cloudless sky.

She saw him standing, hands on hips, feet wide-planted as though he were upon a pitching deck, looking at the rusty old saw-toothed gears. She came closer to see what interested him and he said, 'Imagine the labour and the sweat that went into casting gears that size. They did everything by hand in those days.' He looked down at her. 'Men didn't perspire in those days, Lynne, they *sweated.* Only after they were gone did men perspire.' His eyes were shadowed with thoughtful irony as he said this. 'What happens to a country when it can no longer sweat, and can only perspire?'

It was not a nice topic so she didn't answer, but moved slightly to one side where the mighty stone grinders were still in place, and pointed to a slot where the grain went in above, and where it came out below into a rotting wooden trough, as meal or flour. He came over and leaned to look. His head was close enough for her to catch the spice-scent from him; it was a familiar fragrance to her. Every man who worked in the company warehouses had that tangy scent. I got into their clothes and did not come out; fortunately, it was pleasant.

They went back to the empty, crooked little street. Nothing remained of the houses but the walls and partitions and roofs. Everything else had been hauled away by people from round the countryside in need of something with which to build the later homes. But from the centre of the light-shadowed roadway, the cottages looked exactly as they had looked a hundred years earlier. Stone walls and slate roofs were not only guarantees against New England's rainy springs and autumns, they were also guarantees against the dry-rot that ate up wooden residences.

When he strolled up towards the nearby north-westerly end of the roadway, she paced along at his side thinking that, somewhere back on the road, she had lost her bad premonition about him — if that was what it had been. Anyway, she liked this; enjoyed being in the ghostly, poignantly lonely place in his company.

He stopped and said, 'They weren't all millers.' There was a painted name over a small stone shop, and the single word 'Gunsmith'. That word brought it all back to her in a flash. She could have closed her eyes and seen him pulling the trigger, could have seen the other man falling dead.

He turned to say something, and was smiling. He stopped the words and lost the smile as he studied her expression. 'Are you all right? Lynne, are you feeling ill?'

She shook her head. When something caused inexplicable uneasiness people said someone had just walked across their grave. She said it now, forcing a wan smile, then she took his sleeve and tugged him along as she walked ahead.

When they found a cottage with a bakers' oven built of stone into one wall, which still had the iron grating in place, they peeked through a glassless window and discussed the oven's capacity, then he took her by the shoulders and turned her to face him.

'If you aren't feeling well we'll go back.'

She smiled and gently eased from under his hands. 'I'm feeling fine.'

'But back there outside the gunsmith's shop . . . ?'

'I said I'm feeling fine, Tom.' She tugged him along again, then they came to the forest and underbrush at the end of the hamlet, and had to turn back. She stood gazing back down along the crooked little street. 'If someone walked out of a house now in buckle shoes and a plum-coloured brocade waistcoat, wearing a three-cornered hat, would you be surprised?'

He said, 'I'd faint.'

They started back. He felt for her hand and closed his fingers around it. She did not resist; it didn't mean anything. And it was pleasant, walking through the shades and shadows, among the hushed buildings still redolent of simple work and simple pleasures, and practical, honest people. He squeezed and she squeezed back. Then he let go and they covered the last couple of hundred feet in an easy and companionable silence.

The horse was drowsing. They hunted for a trough to water him at before starting back, or going elsewhere, and found one that still had water running into it, and over and all around it, from a tiny uphill spring. The horse drank, they returned to the doorway, climbed into the buggy and went at a slow walk down through the hamlet towards the trail that would lead back to the main thoroughfare.

She regretted leaving. So did he, but she wouldn't have said anything about this. He was different; he was a man with more basic and open opinions.

'You can't even hear the ocean from here. Through the trees you can't even see it. People in those days must have lived much closer than we do now.'

'Simpler,' she agreed. 'Without the complications, I imagine. They didn't live for gain, but simply to spin their cloth and raise their animals, and have their harvests.'

He looked at her with a twinkle. 'Write me a poem, some day.'

She blushed, but his smile was easy to respond to, so she smiled back at him. 'Would you like to see Chickopee Falls?'

He would. ‘Turn right when we get back to the road, then. It’s about two miles up-country.’

He turned, and they passed deeper through a sylvan world of bright and dark green.

Chapter Nine

The name, or word, Chickopee, had something to do with the old-time Indians who had at one time owned Massachusetts, had at one time owned all of New England, and although Lynne was certain she must have heard an interpretation of the name at least a dozen times since childhood, when Tom asked what it meant, her mind was blank on that topic.

'I don't remember. It had something to do with the Indians, probably the Wabenakis.' She looked slightly apologetic. 'I'm sorry.'

The reason he asked was because, when they first saw the water-fall through a cleft in the trees, where the road meandered slightly inland to get farther from the creek, it seemed to just suddenly appear out of the sky, a great, white-frothed cascade of snow-white water; he guessed that the name probably had some reverential significance. 'At least,' he said, gazing up there at the falls, 'that's the way I'd have named it.'

She studied his lifted profile. From things

he had said, she did not think of him as a man with much reverence in him. And from what else she knew about him . . . She put that out of her mind with a sudden fierce thrust of will.

They had to leave the buggy at the roadside and walk about a half mile back towards the creek to get at the great pool at the base of the falls, and here again, they were surrounded by a lush and flourishing, spring-awakened forest of trees and flowering undergrowth.

The falls were two hundred feet tall. She knew that. They were active year around and were fed by some great mountain peaks hundreds of miles inland and northward. She had to raise her voice to explain all this to him because where the falls struck down into the roiled pool, the noise was one long, continual drumroll of throaty sound.

A mist kept all the verdant growth on both sides of the pool adequately watered. There were tough-stalked slender plants up there with leaves twice as large as a man's hand.

They stood back at the extreme end of the pool. He suddenly pointed. 'Fish, by golly!'

She had to smile at his sudden tenseness. He did not have to tell her he liked going fishing. 'My father used to come up here fishing. I suppose most of the men from town probably learned to fish here.'

That only indirectly interested him. He turned and looked back down the creek where the steamy water rushed in a tumultuous gush southward. 'How do the fish get up here?'

She had no idea. It suddenly struck her that, actually, she was not a good guide at all. She said something about this. He looked down into her tilted face with the sunshine on it, and said, 'I didn't want a guide, I wanted a friend.' Then he leaned over the bank seeking more fish, and she watched him, thinking that he was half-boy, half-man, and that when he said something, it came from this half-and-half composite, and was essentially frank in meaning as well as the way it sounded. He was the kind of man who did not pay compliments because he thought someone wanted them; if he said he wanted a friend, that was exactly what he wanted.

She stepped closer and also leaned down. If there were fish in the cold depths of the gray-green water she did not see them, but evidently he did because he pointed out moving objects to her.

Then they picked their way round the pool to the far side. There was a small path, evidently used rather often because although it was still early summer, other people had already been tramping through here.

She showed him a stand of old trees that grew in a perfect square. Her father had showed it to her, and his father had showed it to him. The Indians used to string vines between those trees, planted especially for their purpose, and every time they speared a fish, they cleaned it and hung it on the vine-work to slowly cure under the summer sun.

There was one other thing worth seeing. She took him right up on to the falls, stepped across two slippery flat boulders and leaned against the wet rock. She could not be heard over the noise, so she beckoned him closer and when his head was beside hers, she pointed. There was a perfect, narrow stone walkway beneath the falls. Except that the footing would be extremely hazardous, a person could, if they dared, pass from one side of the pool to the other side by walking behind the waterfall.

Then she went back where the spray couldn't reach them and told him the legend of the Indian princess who had escaped her husband's relentless pursuers by using that secret passageway as she fled to her lover. At his rueful expression she laughed.

'I didn't believe it either, but the ledge is there, so naturally someone had to think up a myth for it, didn't they?'

He agreed, and paused to wipe spray from his face. He leaned and also wiped her face, then they headed back around the pool at the lower end, and started down the forest path towards the roadway and their buggy again.

When they reached the thoroughfare he paused to look up one more time at the awesome spectacle of all that water roaring over the abrupt dark lips of stone and falling out of sight beyond the trees. 'Beautiful,' he said. 'The people in the hamlet downstream would have come up here on warm days.' He offered her his hand as she got into the buggy. Then he went to the head of the horse, freed it, and as he looked back he said, 'Do you know how to swim?'

She did, but there was an inhibition, too. 'I suppose so,' she replied, with no enthusiasm at all.

He strolled back, climbed up beside her, flicked the lines and as the horse headed back down the lane he said, 'Well; maybe someday . . .' and let the subject die.

She liked him. She didn't want him to feel — whatever it was he would feel, regret, sadness, resentment, whatever a man would feel when he suggested something and a woman was cool about it — so she said, 'I can swim, but that water at the pool is awfully cold.'

He hauled back a little on the seat to face her. 'Do you know a better place?'

She did. There was a local swimming hole inland about five miles from town, to the west, and there was a more secluded one about parallel with the waterfall, several miles from where they now were. She told him of them, then, because she was afraid he'd mention the local spot, which was usually full of people on Sundays during the summer, she said she preferred the secluded one. He agreed at once.

She wondered, on the leisurely ride back to town, why she was allowing herself to get so involved with him. The answer came unbidden: Because she liked him. He was nice, easy to know, pleasant to be with. What other reasons would she need?

She knew exactly what other reasons there were.

When they passed the path leading to the mill he said, 'If it wasn't so far from Smithsport, what a wonderful place to buy and live in.'

'You're not the only person to think that,' she exclaimed. 'I remember a couple that tried it, when I was in high school. One winter, and they sailed with the first ship bound back to New York.'

He sat back and allowed the horse to find the way; the horse knew where home was from just about any direction and this one was simplest of all. The liveryman had told Tom when he set out, that in the event he got confused in the countryside, to simply turn the horse around and give him his head.

Tom related this bit of advice to Lynne. Her response was quick and light. 'Then you weren't ever in much danger of being lost, were you?'

She was referring to what he'd told her the day before at the office. He knew it and laughed softly. 'I hadn't met the horse yesterday.' He turned a little. 'It wouldn't have been at all the same. It will never be the same again, either.'

She saw a flash of brilliant orange in the trees ahead. 'What kind of a bird is that?'

He did not look away from her. 'I don't know.'

She dropped her gaze. 'By now you'll be hungry.'

'I didn't expect to be, and I'm not.'

His eyes were gentle and, when she did not look away as she'd been doing up until now, she could see something else deep in their depths; a kind of soft-sad haunted look.

She spoke evenly and quietly from some inner need to do so. 'Tom; when you applied to the Morgans and they didn't hire you — what did they say?'

'The Morgans? Jay Morgan? Oh, nothing much. They didn't need a supercargo, something to that effect.' He did not take his eyes off her. 'I think now it was because I was an outsider.'

'It was more than that, Tom. I think among seamen it's a little like it is among the gossipy old women around Smithsport. My father said something to that effect anyway, and I think he was probably right.'

He looked at the horse, then looked back. 'What else was it?'

'Trouble in Louisiana,' she murmured, no longer mindful of the trees or the sunshine, or the fern-growth and the summertime fragrance on both sides of them as the horse ambled along. 'A place called Bayou Biscayne.'

He settled slightly at the shoulders and lifted a hand to drift it without feeling through his hair. Then the surprise passed and he said, 'How did that ever get up here? How did it ever get up here, so that they'd know about it when I walked through the doors?'

'I just told you what my father said, Tom.

Seamen are clanny, I suppose; they don't know anyone but other seamen.'

'It didn't happen at sea, Lynne.'

'I know. But they knew who you were. One of them; another ship's officer.'

He dropped the hand to his lap where it lay like a dead bird. 'What else?'

'That's all.'

'I mean — what else have you heard about me?'

'You were in a shipwreck . . . and your wife died.'

He sounded fretful when next he spoke. 'Hell; that's all there is to know.'

She doubted that. The name Jeanette Stuart dominated her thoughts. But she was a woman, which meant that she could be prudent.

He suddenly made a hard little snort of a laugh. 'That's why Morgan turned me down.' He blinked suddenly. 'Your father knows?'

'Yes.'

'Did he know when he hired me?'

'Yes, he knew.'

They stared at one another. Tom looked away, brushed a bug off his arm and reached for the lines. Just when she was sure he was not going to speak again, he did speak.

'Are you curious, Lynne?'

She had to first, define her own feelings. Of course she was curious; she was a woman. But actually it was more than that or she would never have brought up the subject. As for giving him an answer, she couldn't; not without letting him know she was more than curious, and she was certainly not going to admit only to curiosity. He looked over when she did not answer, saw her expression and after a long moment, offered his gentle smile.

'The shipmaster was howling drunk. He drowned with most of the crew. At the Board of Enquiry I simply said he'd made a miscalculation. What was the purpose of saying anything else? He was gone and so was everything else . . . My wife — died of cholera in a town on the Gulf of Mexico. She was — the same age that you are — or that you shortly will be: Twenty.' He looked ahead and watched the curved old stone bridge drawing nigh. Until they were turning to cross it he did not mention that other thing.

Then he said, 'The man I killed was named John Loudon. It wasn't murder. Is that what they say in Smithsport?'

As far as she knew, now, Smithsport did not even know Loudon's name, only that Tom Dorset had killed *a* man. 'I haven't heard what they're saying,' she told him.

They clattered up over the bridge and went

down the far side heading back for the main roadway. He gave her a crooked, humourless, grin. 'In a place like Massachusetts it would be damned near impossible for me to make it sound right. New England is as different from Louisiana as heaven is from hell.

'I killed him in a duel. In the South it's called a meeting of gentlemen, and the place you meet is called the field of honour. It's something left over from two hundred years ago in Europe, but in Louisiana they're very serious about their honour. He fired first. I didn't want to kill him; I hardly even knew the damned idiot. He nicked my thigh — and I killed him.'

Chapter Ten

In New England self-defence meant that someone probably killed an Indian or two, years ago, defending his home. Or it meant the shooting of desperadoes who either attacked a man, broke into his residence, or molested his womenfolk. But as far as Lynne Harding knew, duelling had never been popular, and if it had occurred at all, within several hundred miles of Smithsport, it must have occurred a long time ago because she had never heard any stories of duels.

That evening while she was getting dinner, and while her father was in his room cleaning up after a day spent gardening, she had an idea that if her father knew the details of the killing, he probably wouldn't object to it very strongly. He wouldn't approve of it, exactly, but the matter of how it had happened, with both men armed and facing one another, would probably amount to a degree of mitigation to him.

As for herself, she believed it was justified, but she did not delude herself. The reason she believed that, was because Tom Dorset was a friend, and people with even the smallest smidgin of loyalty in them, sought reasons for excusing their friends' actions.

Eventually, when her father came in looking tanned and fresh and fit, to enquire how her excursion had gone, she told him how Tom Dorset had killed John Loudon. He took a cup of tea to the table, sat squarely down over there and asked how Tom had happened to tell her. She then had to admit that she had asked him. Her father looked his strong disapproval; in fact he seemed more immediately concerned with what he said was 'rudeness' than with the killing. But after mildly scolding her, he turned back to the duel with a slightly scornful expression.

'I was down there, not very long after the war, and as I've told you, they are completely different from us. I heard about their duels. Never saw one but I heard about them. Seems the men pride themselves on duelling.' Her father sipped his tea. 'I'll tell you something, Lynne: If I'd never left New England, I'm sure I'd be about like some of the hidebound farmers who live inland, but once a man's seen strange people and strange places, and heard about customs as different from ours as night is from day, he doesn't have to *approve* of them, but at least he understands how they got started.' He finished the tea. 'Killing a man with a gun because you disagree with him always seemed damned foolish to me. If you knocked him down, then you got personal satisfaction, and you didn't make any widows or orphans.' He pushed the cup forward on the tabletop. 'Duelling is ridiculous,' he concluded.

'But it wasn't murder,' she said, and her father raised his eyes.

'I never for a moment thought Tom Dorset had murdered anyone. I wouldn't have hired him if I'd thought that.' His eyes narrowed a little. 'Is that what you thought?'

'I — don't know. Probably.'

'Then will you tell me why you went buggy-riding with him today?'

She felt helpless. His masculine logic had not just stripped her motive bare, it had made her appear foolishly reckless. 'I suppose I was — curious.'

Her father grunted. 'Curiosity kills a lot of cats.' He changed the subject. 'Where did you go?'

'To the mill and the falls. It was beautiful up there.'

'It is, this time of year,' he conceded, and said no more until she'd put his plate before him and had re-filled his tea cup. 'He's a likeable man, isn't he?'

She looked around suspecting a trap, but

her father was concentrating on his meal and did not meet her gaze. 'Yes, he's good company. He's also a lonely man.'

Still without raising his eyes her father said, 'Well; don't make the common mistake of feeling sorry for him.'

She brought her plate to the table and sat opposite him. As she ate her mind went back to the sunshine and shadow, to his smile and his interest, not just in her but in the things they had seen together. Feel sorry for Tom Dorset? He wasn't the kind of man women felt sorry for. Nor had he given her much reason, really, to feel sorry for him. Except perhaps that she could sense his quiet loneliness. But he certainly hadn't *said* much to inspire that kind of feeling in her.

Still, she was honest with herself, and she *did* feel sorry for him. But she was too wise to say it at the supper table.

Her father told her of his day. He had, he thought, perhaps over-done it a little. He'd had to sit down and rest a couple of times. Manual labour was hard for him, because of his foot, but he was one of those physically strong men who revelled in it once in a while.

After dinner he took her out back and showed her which trees he'd pruned, which flowerbeds he'd harrowed with hoe and spade, and where he'd tied up the new shoots of her mother's lilacs and other climbers.

It was mellow that evening. Her father assured her that the bad weather was now past by saying that he'd been plagued by bees, which was a sure sign only warm weather lay ahead.

Eventually, as day ended, his mind seemed to gradually get back into harness, perhaps in preparation for the next day. He asked her about the inventory of that warehoused coffee, and whether any responses had come in concerning his letters about the mahogany. They spent the balance of the evening discussing mundane things, and although she was tempted to tell him what she thought the gossips were saying, not only about her but also about Tom Dorset, she did not do it. This didn't really bother her very much; perhaps it would never amount to anything, and there was no real reason to burden her father with it.

Later, after she had retired, she went back in her mind over the long day, and one thing in particular stood out: Tom Dorset's expression of exasperation when he'd learned that the people around Smithsport already knew he had killed that man down south. In retrospect, she thought he had seemed frustrated, as though perhaps he might have expected no one to know, in a place as distant as New England.

Then she slept like a log.

In the morning when she was getting breakfast, her father came to the kitchen with a smile for her, and said he felt as good as new. From this, she inferred that perhaps he *had* over-done it yesterday, digging around out back. But their talk was of business and by the time they left the house to walk down the hill she had forgotten all about her father's over-exertion. So had he. He told her that despite the fact that he'd been doing this self-same thing for a lot more years than he cared to think about, he still enjoyed it, still looked forward to getting back to his desk. He said that she would learn to be that way, too, in time.

She already felt that way; she was anxious to get back to the office too, but not for the same reason, but wild horses couldn't have pulled that declaration out of her.

The day was beautiful. It started out that way very early. It seemed to possess a magic ability to touch everyone with its pleasantness, too. Old Mister Emory gave Lynne an old-fashioned slight bow and a smile as she put aside her hat and gloves and went to her desk. Briefly, she wondered what someone like Mister Emory did on their Sundays.

At ten o'clock Jay Morgan came up to see

her father. He was a grizzled, grey man, with eyes like chips of blue ice. His bearing was almost regal, marked only by a slight stoop. Lynne saw him shoot her a stare as he came through the opened door, then he turned his back and told Bert Emory to announce him to her father. It did not have to be a deliberate slight, but she had no illusions about that. Nor did she believe Jay Morgan's erect and proper coldness was due entirely to the fact that she was working at a man's job; it was also because she hadn't married his son. She remembered what Fred had told her about that. His father had gloated a little; if the Morgan and Harding companies were combined, they would not only have ships as well as warehouses, but they would also be able to pool their techniques and their sales lists, and dominate the export-import trade around Smithsport. They would in fact become one of the larger and more prominent trading establishments on the New England coast.

Bert Emory scuttled back to unctuously say Mister Harding was waiting, and Morgan pivoted without a glance in Lynne's direction, strode purposefully past her desk and disappeared beyond the frosted glass door of her father's office. She saw Mister Emory looking at her, and smiled.

‘It was a bit chilly in here for a moment,’ she said, and old Emory laughed.

‘You must not expect old dogs to learn new tricks,’ he replied. ‘He won’t be the only one.’

She went back to work, set her back firmly to the closed door, and balanced the warehouse notations against the inventory to arrive at the correct amount of coffee still remaining to be sold. Later, she found a tentative query about the mahogany from a company in Ohio among the letters Mister Emory had sorted and distributed. She reacted to it with sharp interest, then smiled at herself; she was already beginning to develop predatory instincts.

Tom did not appear. From time to time she caught herself listening when masculine footfalls sounded downstairs in the warehouse, near enough to the stair-well for the sound to come up.

She had no curiosity at all about Jay Morgan’s visit. He was such a thorough trader that he could only be visiting her father because he had something to sell, or because her father had something Morgan wished to buy. She had almost forgotten he was in there with her father, when he emerged, stood a moment behind her, then walked briskly to Mister Emory’s desk, leaned down and whispered something. She was not aware of this unusual procedure until Bert Emory shot up out of his chair, then the noise attracted her attention. Mister Emory went scuttling to the stairs and bounded down them.

She looked after him, puzzled and intrigued. Old men *never* moved like that. Morgan stood a moment at Emory's desk, then he kept his back to Lynne and went to the front-wall window, clasped both hands behind his back and stood gazing dolorously downward where the usual clumsy dray wagons with their enormous harness horses were moving, and where a scattering of dark-clad seamen mingled with bonneted women whose skirts nearly dragged the ground, and bearded and moustached men, mostly storekeepers or employees of the companies and warehouses along King George Street, moved about, either idly or briskly.

Lynne finally said, 'Is something wrong, Mister Morgan?' and he turned, very slowly, still with both hands behind him, to gaze solemnly over at her. He did not speak for a moment, then he said, 'It's your father, Lynne. He's very ill.'

She was stunned. Morgan's deep voice and his slowly-uttered words were like sounds of doom. She arose and turned towards the half-open door. Morgan said, 'Just wait. I sent Mister Emory for Doctor Clavenger. There's nothing anyone can do until he gets here.'

Lynne suddenly felt the shock pass. She rushed to her father's office. He was lying out full length upon the quilted black horse-hair sofa that stood against the far wall, and the tangy, familiar scent of his pipe smoke filled the room, although he hadn't been smoking when he'd gone over to lie down, or had been helped to the sofa by Jay Morgan.

He did not open his eyes to her touch and his breathing was guttery and shallow. He did not look pale, but then he probably wouldn't have anyway, with his freshly-acquired sunburn, but when she knelt at his side and took hold of a hand, he moved his lips slightly and his eyelids flickered.

She felt the rough-gentle hands lifting her away by the shoulders. It was Jay Morgan, and the doctor was already stepping past. Old Mister Emory was hovering in the doorway; he was paler than Paul Harding and seemed near collapse himself.

Morgan steered Lynne back to her table and eased her down. He let a hand lie a moment, heavily, upon her shoulder, then he turned back without a word and went into the private office and closed the door in Mister Emory's face. Her father never would have done that to anyone, but then Jay Morgan was not Paul Harding.

Mister Emory went to his counting table and hunched over there on his stool. When Lynne turned to him, she was too numb with shock to notice that the old man had his head in both hands.

'What is it?' she murmured. 'Mister Emory . . . ?'

He did not hear her, or, if he heard her, he did not heed her.

Chapter Eleven

Albert Clavenger had not been practising long, and although he was outwardly confident, inwardly he was not very pleased at being called to look at Paul Harding.

Clavenger was a native Vermonter, which made him a little more acceptable to Massachusettsmen than if he'd come from the south or the west, but he was not a native of Smithsport. What made him acceptable was that he happened to possess the only degree in medicine in the entire coastal and inland community. But still, he was younger than people liked their physicians to be. He was about thirty-five and looked less than thirty. Particularly, the womenfolk shrank from his visits.

He and Tom Dorset lived in the same rooming house on the east side of King George Street, near the upper end of town. In fact, Doctor Clavenger and Tom Dorset were friends. They shared an occasional drink at the tavern and sometimes, on warm evenings, sat out front on the porch playing chess, a game New Englanders by and large did not care much for, preferring checkers.

Lynne knew Bert Clavenger too, but only passingly, and when he came to the door of her father's office looking for her, she responded without waiting to be summoned. Clavenger did not take her inside. In fact he eased the door closed at his back and stood barring it as he said, 'We can't move him for a while, but I think you might go home and prepare for his arrival. And Miss Harding . . . I'm afraid he won't be back here for a very long while, if ever.'

That 'if ever' had very frightening overtones. She said, 'What is it, Doctor?'

He replied succinctly. 'Heart. How old a man is he?'

She wasn't exactly certain. 'Fifty, I think; maybe a year or two more. That's not old, Doctor.'

He agreed. 'Not old at all, and heart seizures don't always have much to do with a man's age. It's his general condition. Your father is a sedentary man. He doesn't get much physical exercise.'

'Yesterday,' she said, 'he worked all day in the garden doing physical work.'

Clavenger nodded. 'I believe you. That's the point, Miss Harding; sedentary men his age who feel fit usually over-do it. And this is what happens.'

'Is he — will he recover?'

Clavenger was careful when he answered. 'Let's wait a few days before talking about that. Right now, I'd say he has a reasonably fair chance. It wasn't a massive seizure, nor anything like that, but there is no such thing as a commendable heart attack, and there will be permanent damage to the muscle. Otherwise, if the medicines I've administered work on him, I'd say he has a good chance of recovery — but — he can't work again for a long time, and very probably he'll never be able to work again. Now then, if you'll go home and —'

'Can't I see him?'

'He's sleeping, Miss Harding. You'll see him tomorrow.'

She did not want to be separated from her father by the distance which separated the office from their home. She stood looking at Albert Clavenger, and he continued to stand blocking the doorway. Finally, she turned and went heavily past the desk towards the stair-well. As she was descending she heard men's voices behind her in the office. Jay Morgan was one of those speakers, she recognized his low-pitched tones. The other one was probably Doctor Clavenger.

She did not see anyone as she turned towards the street door and had the knob in her cold fingers. He had to call three times, and to finally walk over and touch her arm before she twisted and glanced up. It was Tom Dorset wearing a worried, puzzled expression.

She told him what had happened upstairs. He was astonished, then he recovered and held the door for her, guided her listless feet to a nearby buggy, handed her up in and without a word turned the rig and snapped the lines so that the big sorrel horse went clattering towards the hill at a quick trot.

He said nothing and neither did she. Something kept pulsing in her mind: Her father, as long as she could remember, had always been there, had always looked the same, had been so reliably indestructible. She had thought very little about immortality, but if anyone had ever asked her what it meant, in personal, physical terms, she would have thought of him. It had never crossed her mind that a man as solid and strong as he was, could in one moment be stretched helpless — and perhaps helpless for whatever remained to him of his life.

Tom helped her out of the rig and up to the verandah, and there, finally, the dam burst. She leaned a little, his arms came up around her, she buried her face against his chest and the storm raged.

Two women drove past, looked, then looked harder and were borne away by their buggy wheels. Neither Tom nor Lynne were aware of them at all.

He got her inside to the parlour, loosened her tight little jacket, loosened the high-necked collar of her blouse, then went to the pantry and rummaged until he found the knobby decanter and poured some peach brandy into a glass and took it back. She didn't want it. She didn't want anything except to be left alone. He insisted, and eventually she sipped the brandy. It had no taste at all. It still burned in her mouth and throat, but not as it usually did.

After a couple of moments she looked up at him. He handed over a folded, clean white handkerchief which she took and used to dry her eyes. Then she said, 'You've been kind, Tom.'

He shrugged that off. 'What did the doctor say?'

'That it was a heart seizure. That my father would probably never be able to work again. That he overexerted himself. Tom; that was my fault.'

Dorset looked surprised. 'Your fault . . . ?'

'He worried about me yesterday, when I went out to the falls with you. He went out back and worked it off by digging round in the garden.'

Tom Dorset sat in silence for a while, then he arose and said, 'Are they going to fetch him along home?'

'Yes.'

'Then I'd better find you a woman to help, hadn't I?'

She looked up. 'You don't have to do that.'

'You'll need one for a few days, Lynne, and right now you don't look to me like you're capable of doing much. Just relax. Go wash your face in cold water, then go lie down. I'll find a woman and send her along. Then I'd better stay close to the office for a day or two. And whatever else you do, don't blame yourself.' He leaned and kissed her flushed cheek, then left.

She sat a long while on the sofa in the parlour, but eventually his advice predominated. She went to bathe her face. The brandy helped although she was not aware of this right then. But she did not lie down, she went to her father's room to change the bedding, to open the windows so he could smell the lilac-scented breeze from the garden, and she got sufficiently involved with work round the house to eventually become reconciled to what had happened. It had been a terrible blow; the worst in her life, since the death of her mother years ago.

He had kissed her!

That sudden blinding recollection stopped her in midstride, feather-duster poised to sweep across the night-table at her father's bedside.

The astonishment passed; it had been a sympathetic gesture, a brotherly token, the kind of a kiss an uncle or a cousin might give someone in a time like this. The duster descended, made its flourish, and moved on.

She was no longer aware of the dazzling day nor of the fragrances, and when Mrs O'Hara arrived, a thick, bosomy older woman with the bluest of eyes and hair like plaited flax, Lynne welcomed her because she knew Tom had sent her.

Mrs O'Hara was, most recently, a widow, but she had been married four times and it was a source of dry amusement around Smithsport that, devout Catholic that Mary O'Hara was known to be, not all her husbands had died. Some had fled to sea and had never come back.

Mrs O'Hara knew, of course; by this time everyone in town knew about Paul Harding's collapse. Mrs O'Hara also knew something else.

It had never once occurred to Lynne to wonder about Tom having that buggy out front, the one in which he had brought her home. Mrs O'Hara told about that with spiteful relish as she shed her shawl and stood in the entryway looking about as though taking the measure of an adversary. 'We'll have the house ship-shape in no time,' she assured Lynne. 'And if Mister Morgan, the auld skinflint, comes round, he'll get what Mister Dorset jist give him out front of your father's place.' Mrs O'Hara turned her very blue eyes to Lynne with an expression of enormous pleasure. 'An' what did the auld devil expect, you in your trouble and all, except that a body'd take the first rig he seen? Any man worth his salt'd have done the same, I tell you.'

Lynne faltered. 'Mister Morgan and . . . ?'

Mary O'Hara nodded vigorously. 'Put him flat down, he did, in the roadway, when auld Morgan said he'd ought to be locked up for stealin' his buggy an' horse the way he done. Didn't scarcely allow the lad a chance to explain, the auld scoundrel. And I've got cause to know about them Morgans. Overbearin' lot they are. My late husband, may the good Lard mind his poor soul — wicked though it was — sailed aboard the *Hare* and told me later niver did he know such a taskmaster as the young Mister Morgan.

Wouldn't take him on again, neither, and my poor Mike was a willing man to work. Thim Morgans saw to't poor Mike niver sailed out o' Smithsport again, too.'

Lynne tried to steer the conversation back where it had been before 'poor Mike' diverted it. 'Did they argue, then?'

Mary O'Hara snorted. 'Argued? Naw; only Mister Morgan argued. He'd been standin' outside there, gettin' madder by the minute, when young Mister Dorset come up and started to apologize about commandeerin' the buggy. Auld Morgan lit inter him hammer and tongs, said something about a no-good 'un with a turrible reputation, and a thief inter the bargain. He was beside himself, he was. Mister Dorset tied up the horse, and walked over, caught auld Morgan by the coat, and boosted him off his feet and flung him out inter the roadway. Miz' Grady, who was right there and saw the whole thing, said it did the cockles o' her heart a world o' good.'

Lynne thought past what Jay Morgan had said, to what she, herself, had told Tom the day before; the reason the Morgans hadn't hired Tom. She knew that had been in Tom's mind when he'd attacked Mister Morgan. She had a feeling of having ~~ten~~ been partly responsible for someone else's trouble

— again. First, her father, and now Tom.

Mrs O'Hara sidled to the arched parlour entrance and peered in, roamed her experienced glance around, then said, 'Place looks as neat as a pin to me, Miss Harding. You'll be needin' me more as a nurse than as a scrubwoman, then?'

Lynne nodded. 'Yes. To look after my father. They'll be along with him shortly now.'

Mrs O'Hara gave her plaited flaxen hair a pat at the entry-hall mirror and said, 'And where'll his room be, then?'

Lynne showed her, and Mrs O'Hara brushed a finger across the top of the night-table, crossed to peer out the window, then turned round and expertly assessed the bed. 'It couldn't be any better,' she announced. 'Maybe if we went to the kitchen. . . .'

Lynne took her on down the rear hallway and Mrs O'Hara beamed. She was evidently a woman who believed that a woman's place, as well as her next best appeal to the flesh, lay in her culinary abilities. She stood in the centre of the room looking about and back again. 'Now this,' she told Lynne, 'is the kind of a place where a woman wins about half her battles. *Half,* I said, Miss Harding. But you're unmarried so you'd not know about the other. Well; I'll set to makin' some good beef broth, and when they come along with 'im, niver you fear. I've nursed 'em, and scolded 'em, and done most everything else to 'em. If your father's able to hold his head up just a wee bit, Mary O'Hara'll do the rest.'

Lynne went to the entry-hall on her way to the parlour, but the sound of men outside stopped her cold. She went up and threw open the door. They were bringing her father from the buggy out front. Tom, Doctor Clavenger, and two men from the company warehouse. Her father still had his ruddy colour, but his lips were loose and bluish, and his eyes were slack-closed as they carried him up the stairs to the verandah. Her heart almost stopped at the sight of that strong man inertly helpless in the arms of his bearers.

Tom said, 'Which is his room?'

She led the way, moving automatically, and afterwards she remembered nothing of any of this even though she stood in the doorway and watched them put her father down upon the bed as gently as though they were handling a newborn child.

Chapter Twelve

Tragedy was never something people had to *learn* to live with, Lynne discovered after the third day; it was something that they could not *avoid* living with. But on the third day it became bearable because that was the day her father smiled at her after his mid-morning nap.

Mary O'Hara had done perhaps as much for Paul Harding with her care and spicy broth and good-humoured remonstrances, her mother-hen attitude, as Doctor Clavenger had done with his medicines.

Her father was sleeping again, in late afternoon, when Lynne saw Tom Dorset striding up the hill and went out front to meet him. From the foot of the verandah stairs he looked up enquiringly, and she smiled. 'He's much better, Tom. We visited a little this morning.'

Mary O'Hara came round the far side of the house, saw them, and ducked back from sight, all in an instant. Neither one of them saw her as Tom came up onto the verandah.

He said, 'That's the best news I've had all day.'

She immediately sensed something. Neither she nor her father had been in town since Paul Harding's collapse. She said, 'Is there something wrong at the store?'

He looked a little ruefully at her. 'That's what scares me about you, Lynne. I'll never get accustomed to having a woman rummaging round inside my head. No, nothing that won't take care of itself. Damned old Bert Emory's going round like a pallbearer, sniffling and blubbering. I'd like to kick his . . .' He checked himself up short. 'It's been a busy day,' he said, by way of apology.

She held the door but he stood back until she had entered, then followed her to the cool and peaceful parlour. She asked if he'd like some coffee or tea. He declined, and went to stand gazing down towards the town from a window. Without looking back he said, 'I'm very glad your father's better. Clavenger and I had dinner together last night, at the tavern.' Tom turned and gazed over where she was sitting. 'He said it was nonsense for you to feel guilty. The way he explained it was that these things are not actually as sudden as people think; they are coming on for a long time, years he told me, and if his seizure hadn't come on Monday, it probably would have come on Friday, or some other day, but it would have come shortly. He also said your father has to lose about thirty pounds, and he will have to *drive* up and down the hill, if he gets back onto his feet.' He stood over there, sunlight at his back, smiling down at her. 'How is Mrs O'Hara?'

She smiled back at him. 'She's a jewel, Tom. I don't think anyone could be as perfect for the job. They argue, and she always wins, and I think my father likes having a woman nearer his own age around the house.'

'Why shouldn't he?' Tom demanded boldly. 'Your father's neither a hermit nor an old man. I hope Mrs O'Hara flirts with him.'

She said, 'Tom!'

He laughed and crossed to her chair, leaned down and kissed her cheek exactly as he'd done that other time, only now it wasn't a compassionate kiss. Still; she didn't blush, and in some indefinable way she didn't feel satisfied at all, she felt cheated. This time, it had been a brotherly kiss. When she looked up, he was crossing to the sofa. From over there he said, 'Well; of course you've heard that I borrowed Mister Morgan's buggy that day, and afterwards he was nasty about it.'

'And you struck him, Tom.'

He looked surprised. 'Struck him? No; he's older than your father. I just picked him up and threw him out into the road beside his buggy.'

'I heard the names he called you. Tom; if you hadn't known what he had learned before you applied to him for a job, if he'd just been an angry man, you wouldn't have assaulted him.'

'Wrong,' he exclaimed. 'The names he called me still would have earned what he got. I didn't think about that other thing at all.' Tom paused, then said, more pensively, 'But if there hadn't been people standing around who heard every word of it, I probably could have just walked away . . . It's awkward, Lynne, but that's how it is among men. You may not *want* to have to defend your honour very hard, but if there are witnesses, you just about have to.'

She thought she knew what he was talking about. It didn't have as much to do with Jay Morgan as it had to do with John Loudon down in Louisiana. She accepted his argument in any case; in fact, she had come to accept just about all his judgements.

Then he went on about the Morgans, but in a different manner. 'I made a bad enemy, no doubt of that. I found it out today, and so did old Mister Emory.'

'How, Tom? What happened today?'

'That company in Maine that wanted the mahogany . . . You remember their letter, don't you?'

'Yes.'

'They sent a man down to look at the wood. I showed it to him. He knew mahogany; he said it was as fine a shipment as he'd seen in years and asked the price, so I took him upstairs for Bert to talk to. While I was standing there, the man from Maine agreed to the price and said he'd go and see about arranging for the drayage . . . He came back later in the afternoon and said he'd changed his mind. He'd found another warehoused cargo; the mahogany was not of the same quality, but he could not afford to buy both lots, and the inferior lot had been offered to him at less than one-third of what Bert had quoted.' Tom leaned back. 'It was Morgan's mahogany he bought.'

'One-third the price?' she said, troubled because she knew the market price as well as the cost, and her father's lot had been marked down to the minimum selling price because they had already profited from the coffee which had been included in that same cargo, and her father wanted to move the mahogany out and not have his capital tied up in it indefinitely.

Tom confirmed that. 'One-third. Old Emory told me after the buyer had gone, that the only way the Morgans could do that, would be to sell at a loss and make it up on something else.' Tom sighed. 'He also told me he thought the Morgans wouldn't have done that unless they had a very good reason, because they were successful, profit-minded, businessmen. In other words — according to old Bert — Jay Morgan took his loss to force Harding Company to lose a sale — and I'm responsible.'

Finally, she understood his resentment towards Bert Emory. She could also excuse her father's old retainer. Whatever happened to her father also happened to Mister Emory; he was an old man. Another company would not hire him. He was frightened, and with good reason. She said, 'Tom; I'll come down tomorrow. Mister Emory's old and what happened to my father will have upset him badly.'

Dorset did not deny this, but he did not see it as the salient issue. 'It's not Emory, Lynne, it's me. Morgan had no use for me before, but now he's got a lot less. And on the hike up here this afternoon something else crossed my mind. Morgan isn't a man who feels sorry very long — if he feels sorry at all. With your father flat on his back, Morgan wouldn't be in character if he didn't recognize an opportunity. You and Mister Emory and I are now the people who will have to keep the company healthy. Me, I'm not even altogether familiar with the cargoes yet. Mister Emory is a very old man — he could keel over tomorrow. You . . .'

'I'm a woman,' she murmured. 'Mister Morgan made that very clear without saying a word about it, the day he found my father slumped at his desk. Afterwards . . . I think you're right, Tom. Afterwards, he did not offer a single word of sympathy. I think you're probably right.'

Mary O'Hara came to say Lynne's father had awakened and was asking for her. Evidently the older woman saw the quick shadow of apprehension come and go because she added a reassuring remark. 'Naw, it's nothing bad, Miss Harding. It's just that the man wants to see his daughter.'

Mary O'Hara beamed over at Tom Dorset, as Lynne arose and went as far as the doorway before looking back. 'Would you like to see him?' she asked, and Tom also rose.

Paul Harding's recovery was slow, physically, but mentally he was as alert as ever.

He had not yet come to accept his new role as an invalid, and there was an excellent chance that he would never learn to accept that; he had been a strong, active man all his life; the only thing that had tried to restrict him was his crooked foot, but he had been fighting that for so long it hardly counted any longer.

What seemed most unique to him, now, some days after that band of hot steel had squeezed his chest with a spiral of pain, was that he felt about as he had always felt. His heart did not palpitate, his mind was perfectly clear, his body felt the same, and yet he had to tell himself that he was *not* the same, and would never again be the same.

This was the hardest thing to accommodate, and when Lynne entered the room softly, with big Tom Dorset behind her, he smiled at her, and nodded affably at Tom. To Dorset he said, 'I'm ashamed of having dumped the warehouse workload on you like this, Tom.' To his daughter he said, 'I didn't know you had a caller or I wouldn't have sent for you. I don't want anything; I just thought you might play me a game of checkers.'

She was relieved, the way she felt every time she answered his summons and found it to entail nothing more momentous than this. With a flash of inspiration she moved to the chifferobe-top to get the checkerboard and said, 'Tom will play you. I've got to help Mary for a little while.' She did not look at Tom as she set up the board on her father's lap, made certain he was adequately supported in back with pillows, then handed him the small black box that held the checkers. She looked up only when she was at the door.

Tom had a cheerful expression on his face, but when he met her eyes she wanted to laugh. He looked hang-dog. She left them. The last sound was her father directing Tom to pull up a chair.

Mary O'Hara was shredding carrots and cabbage and potatoes into a copper pot on the stove to make a stew. She had already boiled the meat and the kitchen smelled as wonderful as Lynne had remembered it smelling when her mother had been alive. Lynne seldom made stews because, to her knowledge, her father was not overly-fond of them. But she kept this to herself. Moreover, she was sure she had never made a stew that smelled like this one. Mary O'Hara was a fine example of a real New England cook, although there was good reason to believe she had not laid eyes upon the coasts of America until she was well grown.

When Lynne went to set the table Mary O'Hara watched briefly. Normally, only she and Lynne ate dinner. Now, there suddenly appeared three settings. But Mary O'Hara was the soul of discretion. She went back to her work and hummed to herself. It was indeed a pity that a girl with the looks of Lynne Harding hadn't already had three or four children. Mary had never had any, but that was not her fault. As for Lynne, they'd be fine youngsters, with a good, tall size and heft to them, and with those handsome, flashing dark eyes and that taffy hair.

They might o' course look a bit like their father. Mary O'Hara had no difficulty rationalizing about that either.

And he was a foine-looking specimen of a man, too.

Lynne had to speak twice to capture Mary O'Hara's attention. 'I'll ask Mister Dorset to stay for dinner, Mary. There'll be plenty, won't there?'

Mary O'Hara's intensely blue eyes widened. 'There's always plenty for another mouth, Miss Harding. The surest way to their hearts is through their stomachs. It's an old saying. I think 'twas Saint Patrick as said it.'

Lynne nodded. 'I'm sure it was,' she said,

and went out of the room blushing. There were some things about Mary O'Hara — well, *one* thing at least — that Lynne would just as soon had been left out of her make-up. Lynne was *not* trying to captivate anyone through their stomach, or any other way.

Her father had beaten Tom two out of three games and was pleasantly cheerful and a little tired when Lynne entered the room. She laughed at Tom's face, leaned to feel her father's cheek, then said she thought he'd had enough for now, and took away the checkerboard. Her father was willing, but before she herded Tom from the room her father, usually anything but a demonstrative man, made a gesture that surprised her; he offered Tom his hand, and as they shook, her father looked steadily into the younger man's eyes, and Tom looked down, and smiled his easy, gentle smile.

Lynne, watching this, had a sudden inkling that this was how strong men really communicated their trust and faith, and liking, to one another. She was right, that was exactly how they did it.

Chapter Thirteen

Her intention had been to go down to the office early, but she did not even leave the house until shortly before ten o'clock.

After dinner the previous evening she and Tom had sat upon the verandah. Nothing startling nor tumultuous had happened. They had discussed the company, and when she had said it was her intention to operate it as her father would have done, he had stared into the treetops out front for a long while without commenting. That was the only moment of discord. He hadn't said a word but sometimes silences were louder than words.

Otherwise, they had talked of many things, and she had been impressed with his wide knowledge of subjects. Perhaps she shouldn't have been; after all, at one time he had been a far-ranging seaman. But she did not think of him in that context. Probably because she had never known him when he'd been a ship's officer. Somehow, she thought of Tom Dorset as a man of nature and also a man of business. If the two did not necessarily go together, that was not her fault. His image in her mind had been formed at the falls, at the abandoned old mill, and also at the office upstairs above the company warehouse. From these things her mind had pieced together her impression.

Of course there was another side of him. He had killed a man. But she had reached an accommodation with that, based upon his explanation.

There was one element that had jagged corners, and of which she knew nothing because he had never volunteered anything, and she had shrank from asking: Jeanette Stuart.

Each time the name cropped up, she scolded herself. Tom had been married; he had know other women too, no doubt of that. He was a ruggedly handsome man, strong and active and — virile. What he had done before coming to Smithsport was not really any of her concern anyway. . . . Except that it *was*, because she would want to know about someone named Jeanette Stuart; she *had* to know, before she could ever make any kind of a commitment to Tom.

At the office she found Mister Emory hunched at his desk, and someone — no doubt Mister Emory — had put a black ribbon across the frosted panel of the door to her father's office.

That angered her. She went over and yanked the ribbon down, then she turned, but Mister Emory was buried in work and did not raise his eyes.

She put aside her hat, loosened the buttons of her smartly tailored smoke-blue grenadier-type jacket, and went to her desk. At once Mister Emory came padding over with a sheaf of papers, letters, invoices, ladings, all the accumulation of work both she and her father had previously taken care of. He put the pile in front of her.

'These are the things I don't have the authority to take action about,' he said, pale eyes swimming in liquid. 'How is your father?'

'Very much better,' she answered, without looking at him. 'In fact he beat Tom at checkers last night, and ate a good dinner.' Now, finally, she raised her face.

Emory smiled weakly, almost as though he didn't believe her. 'I'm glad,' he muttered, and as they looked at one another Lynne saw something she had never seen before: Old Bert Emory was not as fierce as she had always thought. In fact he was the opposite. He was actually a fearful, timid man, and could *appear* fierce only when he knew someone with strength was behind him to give support and direction.

She suddenly felt very sorry for this wizened old man. Her father surely had known, and yet he had never said anything to her about his relationship with Cuthbert Emory.

She smiled. 'Nothing will change, Mister Emory, except that for as long as my father can't make the decisions, I'll make them.'

He ducked his head. 'Yes.' He seemed to derive strength from her positivism. He became brisk again and slightly scowling, which was how she had always known him to be. 'Well, Miss Harding, we've had a couple of reverses. First, we lost a mahagony sale.'

'Tom told me. What else?'

'This morning, early, the man from Rampart and Friday — that's the company that does most of our drayage — came in to say he was scheduled for the next four months and could not haul for us.'

Lynne knew the drayage company only indirectly. She had seen their great wagons, with the name in elegant script done in red paint upon the sides, going and coming from her father's warehouse, since childhood. Rampart and Friday, in fact, were the major draymen in Smithsport. What business they did not handle in the hauling line, a few little independent haulers handled, but the independents did not have the means for moving very much cargo, or very heavy cargo.

She said, 'To whom are they scheduled, Mister Emory?'

He pulled a death's-head grin. 'Morgan Company, ma'am.'

She wasn't surprised because she'd anticipated his answer. Tom, it seemed, had been only partly correct; the Morgans were not only squaring off against him, they were also squaring off against her; against Harding Company. She said, 'Thank you,' and turned back to the sheaf of papers. Bert Emory padded back to his desk and became busy.

She felt both fearful and apprehensive, and the longer she sat there the more those two feelings blended. Jay Morgan was a wealthy and powerful man. He was the last person in Smithsport to have for an enemy. If he had decided to punish Tom Dorset for assaulting him by striking at the company, there was the obvious solution, but evidently it went deeper than that, evidently Jay Morgan meant to cripple the company regardless of Tom Dorset, and he may have arrived at this decision separately — unless, of course, he was doing it because of her; because he wanted to destroy a company run by a woman. It wasn't entirely rational, she was certain, but she was equally certain that a vindictive, fierce man like Jay Morgan was quite capable of irrationality.

She finally left the desk and went down to the warehouse. Tom was standing at an upright desk near the huge doors working with a pencil. He heard her coming and turned slowly. Then he smiled and half her anxieties vanished. But the other half were too real, so they remained.

She asked if he knew about Rampart and Friday. He knew. 'Yes, but I think it's ironed out.'

'How?'

He was patently reluctant to explain, but he did it anyway. 'Jonas Friday, Doc Clavenger and I have a Saturday night card session. It's been going on sometime now. I went up and talked to Jonas this morning right after his father or old man Rampart sent their chief clerk round to give Mister Emory the bad news. Jonas said he would send wagons and teams any time we needed them.'

Lynne was relieved, but not entirely so. 'By any chance, would this have been brought about by Jay Morgan?'

He put down his pencil and leaned upon the table when he answered. 'Of course. I told you, he hates the sight and thought of me.'

'Did you tell Jonas Friday that?'

'Yeah, I told him.' His eyes brightened with a hard look of masculine amusement. 'But I can't repeat what Jonas said, beyond the fact that he said he'd send us wagons whenever we wanted them.'

'Jay Morgan will be furious with him, Tom.'

Dorset kept the same, hard, amused look. 'We discussed that. Lynne, did you know that the Morgans are pretty heartily disliked around this town?'

She could believe it, but she hadn't known it. How could she have known it, she'd never been involved on King George Street before. 'No, but regardless of that,' she replied, 'they have wealth and power, Tom.'

'Maybe it'll take more than that,' he exclaimed, and called to a passing workman to start moving the rice cargo forward for loading. Then he looked down at her again. 'Made a sale this morning before you got down here.' He picked some papers off his table and scanned them briefly before handing them over. 'Haven't had time yet to run upstairs and give these to Mister Emory.'

Clipped to the invoice and the order was a substantial cheque. It was half payment in advance. The balance would be remitted, according to the signed agreement, upon delivery of the rice down at Gosnold. It was actually a large transaction. When she looked up Tom had stopped out front to stand in half-sunshine, half-shadow, looking down the roadway. As she watched he turned back and strolled almost up to her, then signalled for two more of the warehousemen to help with the rice sacks. Then he said casually, 'Three Rampart and Friday wagons coming.'

She leaned upon his high desk. She never could have done this by herself. She sought for some kind of appreciative expression, but he simply paused, winked, then went on back where the warehousemen were concentrating upon those mounded rice sacks.

She went back upstairs, dropped the papers atop Mister Emory's desk, and did not wait to see his eyebrows spring up like a pair of caterpillars. She returned to her desk, sat a moment doing nothing and thinking nothing, then she went to work upon the correspondence and did not leave her desk, even for the usual mid-afternoon tea, until after five o'clock.

Mister Emory got his hat and coat promptly at five, put them on while studying Lynne's back, then, from the head of the stair-well he said, 'Good night,' and went skipping downward liked a gnarled gnome.

Tom came, which was what she had been

waiting to have happen, but during the long interval she had become current with all the filing and all the correspondence, so when he stamped up the stairs with the drayman's receipt for the rice, that was the only un-filed paper atop her desk.

He dropped down over at Mister Emory's desk looking tired but contented. 'Quite a day,' he said, looking at her in a way that made her conscious of the unbuttoned little jacket. 'A little while ago, right after Emory went scuttling for home, a buyer came in looking for coffee. I probably should have sent him up here.' He fished in a pocket and flipped a crumpled paper down upon Emory's desk. 'I took his order, and his advance, for all of that Coggins coffee we have left. It's to be hauled north first thing in the morning. I went down to see Jonas. He'll have a wagon up here at six in the morning.' Tom heaved up off the stool with a grunt, took the papers over to her desk, and leaned to place them in front of her.

'I was thinking: If I could hire a buggy Sunday . . . That place you mentioned where we could swim . . . ?'

She felt the furious blush coming in time, and dropped her head towards the desktop so she could pretend to be studying the papers there. 'Ten o'clock?'

He smiled and reached to gently lift her chin with a curled finger. 'Ten o'clock . . . Lynne; don't listen to old Emory. Don't listen to anyone — not even your own fears. The Morgans aren't going to cause any more trouble than we'll allow them to cause. You and me.' He removed his hand, pulled back to stand straight, and very gradually her heart resumed its normal cadence; for a troubled moment, when he'd had her face tilted, had his face so close, she had been sure what he was going to do.

But he hadn't done it.

'I'll walk you up the hill, if you like,' he said. 'It'll be dusk before long.'

She said, 'No thank you. I'll be leaving in the next few minutes. . . . Good night, Tom. I'm grateful. Believe that, please.'

He winked that half roguish, half-challenging wink of his. 'There is nothing really to be grateful about, Lynne. I'm supercargo of the warehouse. I'm only doing what I'm paid to do — and what loyalty dictates. Tell your father I think I've figured out those moves of his at the checkerboard, and if I may, I'd like to come up again some evening and try him again.'

She watched him cross to the stairway and disappear down it, then she rose slowly, buttoned her jacket, got her hat, and went over to the front window as she put the hat on, to watch him go striding up the quaint old roadway, northward.

Finally, because she was the last one out, she looked up at the streetside, and started homeward. It was a mellow, soft summer evening, not yet twilight but close to it. She could see the Harding house simply by lifting her eyes where the cobbles rose slightly to go up the gentle slope.

Her father would be pleased, and probably relieved as well, that they had got rid of the last of that rice, not to mention the balance of the Coggins coffee. Of course they still had the Coggins mahogany, but she lifted her chin a little as she strode past the huge, cavernous Morgan warehouse, with Richard Tallant's store out front, and told herself that they would also sell the mahogany.

Then she smiled at herself. She was actually doing the same thing old Mister Emory did; she was relying for *her* strength on the greater strength of someone else: Tom Dorset.

Instead of feeling inwardly guilty about this, or perhaps humiliated, she liked the idea. The more she walked, the more she thought, the better she liked the idea.

Chapter Fourteen

Fortune *could* smile. Lynne sold the mahogany on Thursday to an order-buyer from Bangor, Maine, who had heard of it from that previous buyer who had ended up purchasing the Morgan mahogany. Lynne's buyer did not go down to the Morgan warehouse, not that it would have made any difference because the Morgans had no more mahogany.

It was a fairly large shipment, but that was not what occasioned the cortège of Rampart and Friday wagons; mahogany also happened to be one of the heaviest of woods, and where most lumber seemed to lighten the older, and drier, it got, mahogany, like locust-wood, seemed to get heavier.

Lynne stood with Mister Emory at the upstairs window watching those four wagons pulling out of the warehouse over the cobblestones. The little old man was enormously pleased. For the first time, he acted as though he might really accept her, and to Lynne, that was almost as important as seeing those wagons depart.

Richard Tallant dropped round shortly before noon to visit. Actually, he had in mind a trade. Because he was closely associated with the Morgan Company, had in fact once been financially allied with it through his late father, what his proposition amounted to was an inter-company transaction. He had, he told Lynne, bought heavily in commodities that weren't, actually, disposable in great amounts, through his store. He did not operate a company, only the store, but what he had bought from the Morgans he could not expect to sell back to them, therefore, he wondered if she would consider a trade.

She was wary. Across the room old Emory was sitting hunched upon his stool, little beady eyes watching her. She could not afford to fail, especially with Mister Emory waiting like that, to see whether she would fail. It wasn't the trade that troubled her; it was her ability to meet a man — in this case Richard Tallant — on an equal footing, and not be bested.

'What are your commodities?' she asked, and Tallant unctuously spread his hands as he said, 'Bolt goods. Silk, brocades, Irish linen. I won't sell three bolts a year of anything except the linen, but as it happens I have seventeen cases of Irish linen.' He smiled winsomely. 'I probably wouldn't live long enough to sell that much, and meanwhile I've got my capital tied up in it.'

She had a sale for the brocade, providing there was enough of it, and perhaps a sale for the silk. This was how her father traded. He had once told her it was like buying a live horse and getting a dead horse thrown in to seal the bargain.

'What did you see downstairs that you liked?' she asked.

Tallant, sensing a trade, leaned forward upon her desk. 'Tom Dorset showed me some Jamaica rum, the end run of a small lot, and some English pewter picked up in Bermuda.'

It required no great skill to understand what Richard Tallant had in mind, because clearly, his bolt goods and Irish linen were worth more than her odd-lots of rum and pewter. She forestalled his request that she pay the difference in cash by saying, 'I doubt that we'll get together on those lots, Dick. Is there anything else?'

She could almost hear old Emory's silent laughter.

Tallant gazed at her, drummed softly upon the tabletop, and finally said, 'Even trade, Lynne. My forty-six lots of the cloth, seventeen each of brocade and silk, plus twelve of the Irish linen, for your pewter and rum.'

She did not have to calculate her costs to know she was going to profit handsomely, so she did what her father had always done, she offered him her hand. He shook, then arose with a smile.

'But you'll have to make the transfer.'

Finally, she saw what he thought he had done. Obviously, he did not know Rampart and Friday were still doing Harding Company's hauling. She met his smile easily. 'I'll have Tom take care of it, Dick.'

His smile faltered. 'When?'

'This afternoon,' she replied, praying hard.

Tallant turned and walked to the stairs. Old Emory vigorously polished his eyeglasses and nearly broke his face smiling. Then he ducked down and resumed his work, without another glance in her direction, and not a word of congratulation, but the triumphant little smile did not leave his face even after Lynne had allowed Richard Tallant enough time to leave, then went hastily downstairs in search of Tom.

She told him what she had promised, slightly breathless at her own daring, and he took it in stride. 'All right. I'll have the transfer made right away. I've got an idle man to send up for the wagon.'

She said, 'On short notice?'

He looked down into her lifted face. 'Jonas will do it. No one likes short notices, Lynne, but I'd say from your expression this is important to you?'

She explained about the trade and he agreed that this time, at least, the short-notice was justified. Then he laughed at her.

'You'll be the next one to have a heart seizure.'

He left her standing there and went in search of the man to send for the wagon. She returned to the upstairs office and found that Mister Emory had already accomplished the papers for her transaction.

The balance of the day passed without event, and when she left that evening, although she hesitated downstairs in the huge warehouse looking around, she did not see Tom, so she went home without thanking him for coming to her rescue, and when she arrived there she found Doctor Clavenger sitting comfortably upon the verandah sipping a lemonade, hospitably provided by Mary O'Hara. He arose as she came up the stairs, and when she took a seat upon the old swing, he sat down again, all without smiling.

'Walking is good for you,' he said. 'I watched you up the slope. You have a good stride, Lynne.' He drained his glass and set it aside. 'You also have a good housekeeper.

I also walked up here, and it's thirsty work from the north end of town.'

She let him get all this said before making her pointed enquiry. 'How is my father?'

Albert Clavenger gravely nodded his head. In another twenty years he would be one of those portly, greying, imperturbable physicians people put great faith in.

'He's coming along very well. But he's not going to lose any weight unless you convey the idea to Mrs O'Hara that he absolutely *must* do that. I know her type; I've been battling them ever since I went into practice. They operate on the old fashioned idea that if it's not a cold you feed it like you'd fatten a calf for butchering. Well; that's not the way any longer, Lynne. We know weight is a directly contributing factor to seizures such as your father had. That's why I waited for you to come home this evening. It's useless for me to talk to your father about losing weight; he said he's weighed the same for the past thirty years, and I don't doubt it for a moment, but this is an altogether different situation. From now on, he *must* trim down. As for Mrs O'Hara. . . .' Clavenger rolled up his eyes. 'I've heard all their arguments. So — it's up to you. You'll have to lay down the law to her. I can't do that. You'll have to. Otherwise, you can expect your father to have a second seizure. He may survive it, but he won't survive the third one.'

Clavenger arose, picked up his little black satchel from the floor beside his chair, and stood looking at her. Finally, then, he smiled. 'Tom Dorset is of the opinion there's nothing you can't do. I hope, for your father's sake, Tom is right.'

He was poised to depart but she did not want him to leave just yet. 'Doctor; about Tom. . . .' She suddenly felt guilty over what she had wanted to do: Pump Clavenger. She stood up. 'Nothing. I — I've changed my mind.'

Clavenger looked out towards the roadway and the yonder seawall. 'Just as well,' he murmured, and hefted the little satchel in his right fist. 'I'll be back in a day or two. Mind you, Lynne, he's *got* to lose weight.'

She stood watching the physician pass beyond the little picket gate and go walking briskly back down towards town, then she took his lemonade glass to the kitchen, removed her hat, put the glass down firmly and said, 'Mrs O'Hara, we're going to have to devise a way to help my father get rid of about thirty pounds.'

Mrs O'Hara looked aghast. 'Thorty pounds, you said?' She raised her hands in horror. 'Ma'am, the poor man's flat on his back. You'll have him t'weak to stand without help. It'll be the death of 'em, starvin' him down like that.'

Lynne was very patient. 'Part of the cause of heart seizures is being over-weight, Mary, and if he can't exercise but lies there eating as though he were still able to exercise, he'll gain more weight, and it will eventually kill him.'

Mrs O'Hara looked very sceptical but before she could argue Lynne spoke again.

'Please help me. He won't like it at all, and I can't be here to watch him. I need you very much.'

Mrs O'Hara's expression underwent a subtle alteration. 'Don't you worry yourself a bit. If he's got to lose the weight, then depend upon Mary O'Hara to see as he does it. Now then, go change and come back, and we'll have a cup of tea together, and plan our strategy. Never let it be said two women wasn't the match o' a man.'

Lynne went to change, and afterwards she visited with her father. It was becoming a kind of small, personal ritual between them. He was pleased to see her, and he looked closely at her as he smiled his welcome, then he asked her about the company. She had not told him about the abortive Rampart and Friday trouble, and he had not heard, at least from her, about Tom Dorset's set-to with Jay Morgan.

She felt guilty about withholding things from him, but she did it for what she knew would be his own good. Their positions were reversed; he no longer shielded her, she was shielding him.

But this particular night she had something special to recount: Her manoeuvring with Richard Tallant. He was delighted. He liked Richard, had known his father very well, but it was only natural that he should be especially pleased that his girl had bested Tallant's son.

She had previously told him about the mahogany deal, and about some of the other transactions. He lay back looking quite satisfied, then, finally, he asked about Tom.

She raised her eyebrows a little. 'He's doing a wonderful job, if that's what you meant.'

Her father's dark gaze drifted to the window, and beyond, out into the twilighted garden yonder. 'He'll be a help to you, of course, Lynne.'

She sensed something and waited for him to say more, but he didn't, he continued to gaze past her, so she seized the initiative.

'He *is* a help to me. Both he and Mister Emory.' She related old Emory's reaction to her small triumph over Richard Tallant, and although her father smiled his appreciation, he looked back out into the garden again.

'We call them "stores" and "companies",' he said, as though musing aloud for his own benefit rather than hers. 'But they are really family enterprises, sweetheart.'

She knew all this, had known it ever since she'd been old enough to be aware.

He rambled on. 'Tallant died and his son got out of Morgan and Tallant, keeping just the store. Jay has young Fred . . . but I don't envy him that . . . and now Harding Company has my daughter.' He swung his eyes to her face. 'Strange isn't it? Three of us; two with sons to take over, one with only a daughter; the sons don't equal the daughter. That will be hard for old Jay to live with.'

Lynne thought to herself that 'old Jay' *wasn't* living with it, very well, but she said nothing.

Her father held out his hand and she took it in both her hands. 'But you can't spend your life down there,' he told her, and it finally dawned on her what he was trying to convey.

She released his hand, got up and said, 'I've got to go help Mary . . . And there's something else: Doctor Clavenger insists that you have to lose weight. Starting tonight, then, you get a light meal.' She leaned and kissed him, then hastened from the room before he could organize his arguments and issue his ultimatums. She stopped midway to the kitchen to ponder.

If her father had been on the verge of saying what she *thought* he was going to say, it was probably one of the most profound reverses he had ever made in his life, because although he *had* hired Tom, he had, she knew because she knew her father, done it only because he'd had no alternative. For him to now suggest something else, a more close alliance between Harding Company and Tom Dorset, was something she could only accept if she also agreed that her father feared for her, without masculine direction to keep her going.

She did not like that idea at all.

Chapter Fifteen

Sunday arrived a day early. Lynne was still, as her father would have said 'hock deep' in work at the office when five o'clock arrived on Saturday. Tom had gone down to Gosnold at her request and would not return until quite late. Old Mister Emory did something he'd never done before, he brewed a cup of tea and brought it to her desk. She didn't especially want tea, but she surmised that this was his gesture, his tribute to her, so she asked him to sit down, and at five o'clock they were drinking tea together when Albert Clavenger climbed the stairs and nearly gave her heart failure, he looked too solemn. But he simply had a note for her from Tom. She read it while Mister Emory scuttled to fetch a third cup of tea, and Doctor Clavenger sat and drank it.

This note said, quite simply: 'Ten o'clock tomorrow morning and this time don't forget the hamper.' She smiled and put the note into a pocket as Mister Emory returned with the tea. Clavenger gazed at her, thanked

Mister Emory, and said, 'I never write notes lovely women smile about when they read them.'

She laughed. 'You probably don't write notes, only prescriptions.'

Clavenger agreed with that. 'True.' He switched his attention to Cuthbert Emory. 'Tell me,' he said, peering over, 'when was the last time you had a complete physical examination, Mister Emory?'

The old man's pale little eyes showed a sudden flood of consternation. 'Don't I look all right, Doctor?'

Clavenger sipped his tea before replying. 'It's rude to counter a question with a question, and I should think you'd know that, Mister Emory. I asked — when was the last time you had a physical examination?'

'Well,' muttered Emory, shooting Lynne a look of appeal. 'It was a time back, come to think about it.'

'When — a time back, Mister Emory?'

'When they come for me to join the Union army.'

Clavenger looked across his tea cup. 'The Union army? Man, that was —'

'I know when it was,' snapped the old man. 'I never been sick a day in my life, except for the hives a time or two, and a bad tooth Mister Heffler the wheelwright pulled for me eight or nine years ago.'

Doctor Clavenger arose to finish his tea and place the cup atop Lynne's desk. As he did this he winked at her, then he stepped across and lightly laid a hand upon old Emory's shoulder as he said, 'May the Good Lord continue to watch over you, Mister Emory, but if the day should come when you need a more temporal kind of reassurance, stop in at my rooms.'

Lynne called her thanks as Doctor Clavenger went clumping down the stairs. Mister Emory said nothing until he heard the door close downstairs, then he sniffed. 'All they think about is ways to get into a man's purse. You'll be flabbergasted when you get his bill for your father. There ought to be a law against 'em, I say.'

Lynne drained her cup and arose to take it away, but old Emory was quicker. He took all three cups away, and called back that he would see her Monday morning, and also went down the stairs.

She sat alone and quite at peace for a time, then arose and went to the frosted door of her father's office. She had not entered that room since she'd seen him in there on the horsehair sofa. The moment the door glided inward and she saw everything as it had always been since as far back as she could remember, even the tangy scent of his pipe smoke, she had a bad feeling, almost as though he had died that day.

She closed the door, got her hat, and left the building. The sun was still up, which made it seem a little odd. Usually, the sun was either going down or quite gone. Summer had arrived, evidently, and within another month or two, darkness would not come until almost ten o'clock at night.

She saw Richard Tallant across the way speaking to another younger man. He waved, she waved back. A man she had known since childhood, Barney Oldham, who did smithing and wheelwrighting and, occasionally, on order, buggy and wagon building, removed his hat and gave her an encouraging grin as they passed.

'Good health to you, and tell your father you'll have them all eating out of your hand before it's done with,' he said, and kept on walking in the direction of the tavern, which did a land-office business on Saturday evenings and Saturday nights.

Lynne paused and looked around, but Barney Oldham was picking up momentum as he got closer to the tavern. She resumed her way wondering what, exactly, had prompted him to say that.

It intrigued her mid-way up the hill, then

she put it out of her mind and wondered how she was going to make going swimming with Tom Dorset in the morning sound to her parent as though it were something everyone did after church.

In the end, she did not tell him she was going *swimming*, she only mentioned that Tom would be by with a rig in the morning, and breezed on out to the kitchen to help Mary O'Hara.

Later, when she returned with her father's tray, she asked how he felt, and almost betrayed herself by mentioning that Doctor Clavenger had come by the office this late afternoon.

Her father looked eagerly at his meal, then yielded up a groan and sank back against his pillows. 'How much weight did that confounded sadist say I had to lose? Mary said something like thirty pounds, but of course that is preposterous.'

Lynne smiled sweetly. 'Thirty pounds is absolutely correct, love.'

She set the tray down and waited briefly for him to adjust his logs under the blankets to balance it, then she went for a little chair and sat at his bedside to tell him everything that had transpired on King George Street today. He only half listened; most of his attention was directed towards the meagre portions of food on his plate.

She was half-way through mentioning an offer the company had had from a New York shipmaster who was on his way up the coast with a cargo of thread and leather and canvas, when without any warning he said, 'Two Sundays in a row with Tom? People will begin to talk.' He did not sound very upset. In fact, she did not believe he was the least bit upset, because he continued to study the meal, then he went to work on it with knife and fork.

To test him she said, 'If you'd prefer I'll stay home. There's plenty to do round here.'

'The time to avoid something,' he told her, truthfully, 'is when you see it coming, not after it has arrived. If you agreed to go, it wouldn't be honest to give some kind of excuse now, would it?'

She smiled as she said, 'No, it wouldn't,' and arose to return to the kitchen. She had to begin thinking about what she would put into the picnic hamper in the morning. Her father nodded absently and she departed.

Mary O'Hara, who had began to adopt an aunt-like attitude towards Lynne, knew of her forthcoming outing, perhaps from Lynne's father, and had suggestions to offer for the picnic, but not once did Mary O'Hara make a personal observation nor ask a personal question.

On the other hand Mary was a veritable fountainhead of local gossip, and while they were together in the kitchen she told Lynne of a fierce upheaval among the Morgans. It appeared that Fred's wife had somehow learned that her husband had been seeing a girl down in Gosnold. She had threatened him, and all this got back to Jay Morgan, who had become embroiled because he knew that if anything of this nature became public knowledge, it would damage the Morgan reputation and image.

Mary did not know what the final results were. She had heard it all from a woman by the name of Halloran who did part-time housework for the younger Morgans, and when Mary O'Hara's friend had returned the following week, although there had been a noticeable coolness, evidently the issue had been resolved because nothing more was said in her presence.

Lynne was neither very interested nor very sympathetic. She did not know Fred's wife, but she knew Fred and she knew his father. Her private view, one she did not share with Mary O'Hara, was that eventually there would be other scenes like the one Mary O'Hara's friend had witnessed. She put the entire matter out of her mind, and later, when she returned for her father's dishes, she was beginning to feel tired. It had been a long day.

A unique aftermath of her father's collapse and subsequent illness was that he had somehow or other lost his love of pipes. He was doing something, when Lynne entered the room, she could not recall ever seeing him do before; he was sitting propped up reading his newspaper without a pipe in his mouth.

As she gathered the plates he pointed to the column on the last page which recorded the arrival and departure of ships. The *Hound* was due on schedule from Barbados with a cargo for Morgan Company, and the *Hare* was scheduled to sail for Spain, Gibraltar and France within a fortnight. The article did not say what the *Hound* was bringing back, which interested her father. Not that he could benefit from the cargo, but as he said, if Harding Company knew what Morgan Company was warehousing, duplication could be avoided. Sometimes the newspaper column offered this information, but not always; it was gratuitous information and not all companies were willing to part with it.

Lynne was not as interested as her father was. 'Sugar,' she said, hazarding a guess. 'Rum possibly,' and picked up her father's tray as she watched his keen interest when he studied the column. Her father would never cease being involved, whether he ever again left his bed or not, and in a way this was a good thing. She kissed him tenderly and left the room.

He continued to study the column, which was actually only three or four paragraphs long, although at one time, during his youth, it had not only been much longer, it had also appeared on the front page. Finally, when he had gleaned as much information as he possibly could, he carefully folded the newspaper, put it aside, sat a moment listening to the quiet house, then threw back the covers, twisted until he was sitting upon the edge of the bed, and after a moment of that, he got to his feet, long nightshirt hanging loosely to his ankles, and crossed slowly to the rear window where he peered out at the treetops, at the pale stars and the ghostly moon, then he turned back and made a sort of ritual circuit of the big room.

He had been doing this for several days, testing his heart for reaction. The first day there had been a slightly ominous palpitation, but from the second day on his body had seemed to adjust to the slight additional exertion, and now, this particular night, there was no increase at all, that he could feel with his palm, so he increased the length of his stride and also the duration of his barefoot pacing.

He felt better, after he had done this, not only physically but mentally. He realized that taking one's own pulse was not a very accurate way to measure a heartbeat, but he was also of the opinion that his mental attitude was something he, and not Doctor Clavenger, could best assess, and at least in that area, he was quite satisfied. Each evening after he paced the room, there was a sense of cautious jubilation which gripped him.

He knew next to nothing about heart attacks, but he had never felt quite as ill as Doctor Clavenger appeared to think he should feel, and, working from this basis, he had just about convinced himself that he had not suffered the permanent damage Clavenger said was the customary result of heart seizures.

But most of all, Paul Harding had resolved that whatever his actual condition was, he was *not* going to accept Clavenger's gloomy prediction; if he was indeed dangerously ill, then he was not going to give in to that and spend the rest of his life — whatever of it was left — lying in a damned bed reading newspapers and being waited on like a small child.

Clavenger had told him that the next seizure might very well be fatal; that people seldom survived more than three attacks. Well; rather than lie there and wait, Paul Harding had made up his mind that he would continue to *live* right up until that second or third one came, and that was the underlying reason why he was secretly testing himself, was quietly and privately fighting to come back again.

Death was inevitable in any case, for the ill or the robust, but yielding to gloom and composing one's self to await its arrival was alien to his spirit, and this particular night, when he finally ceased exercising and got back into bed, it seemed farther away than it had seemed since his collapse at the office. He was almost convinced that Doctor Clavenger had been overly pessimistic.

Chapter Sixteen

Sunday morning was not quite as clear as the previous few days had been. It dawned sultry with a high, veiled mist before the sun. On her way to church Lynne became aware of the mugginess, and afterwards, on her walk home again, too.

It was cool at church, and it was also cool inside the house after church. Actually, probably because the Harding residence had the upstairs area, all dead-air space, to mitigate it, downstairs it was never too warm.

As she lugged the hamper to the porch then went back to change clothes, to put her swimming suit on beneath her outer attire, she thought of the hot drive up to the pond. Even in a topbuggy it would be uncomfortable, and once they got into the woods northwest of town, the shade wouldn't mitigate the high humidity.

But swimming would be pleasant, more so than on just a hot day, because a person could usually find relief from pure heat, especially if there were a forest nearby, but sticky, hazy heat was something else.

She went to look in on her father. He was busy with a pen and some notepaper figuring available Harding capital for re-investment, while at the same time studying several week-old out-of-town newspapers for clues as to what commodities would be most in demand across the land. It was an old game of his; Lynne had seen him do this before, many times, and it looked about as much like black-magic divination to her now, as it had then. She went and sat upon the edge of the bed amid the clutter and reached to comb back his thick mane with the bent fingers of one hand.

'What does the Oracle of Delphi tell you this morning?' she asked.

He was not offended. 'Guns,' he said, looking up at her. 'Guns to trade out, and staples to bring in.' He looked very serious. 'The trouble with this country is that it's got mills and factories and foundries all the way out to California, by now. When I was a lad the companies grew rich supplying forged and machine-shop commodities from overseas; the farther west people went, the farther they were from manufactories. They would buy almost anything. But now it's got to the point where they can make all those things themselves.' He leaned back, still gazing intently at her. 'Maybe the time's come to think more about the *export* end. For example, without looking at the trading and commodity pages of the newspapers, but looking at the front, feature, pages, we might find a key to something.' He reached and slapped a paper. 'The Spaniards are having the devil's own time of it in Cuba, for example. Those confounded people are rebelling by fits and starts. Lynne, within a few years they're going to have an insurrection down there.'

She looked at her father, slightly puzzled. 'Are you saying Harding Company should buy guns here, in the United States, and sell them to the natives of Cuba?'

He was completely unabashed. 'Why not? Didn't the French and Spanish do that for us when we were organizing against the British a hundred years ago.'

She did not have an answer, but by instinct she recoiled from the idea. She recoiled even more when her father spoke again, very frankly.

'I don't think the French and Spanish were all that concerned with our freedom, back in those days. They weren't great champions of democracy — how could they have been, they were both monarchies? — I believe they were motivated by cash sales. Well; so is Harding Company. People may say we're doing our Christian duty and all that, Lynne, but we will be more honest, won't we? If we can sell guns to the Cubans, it will be for profit. We're never going to be hypocrites.'

Mary O'Hara appeared at the door with a silent nod for Lynne, then silently withdrew. Lynne did not want to leave her father, right at this instant; she was troubled about what he'd said, but because she'd never thought about selling guns to the Cubans, or to anyone else for that matter, her thoughts were only instinctively opposed, so she could not have put up much of a protest. Not on rational grounds anyway, and she knew men well enough to realize that no other kind of protest would mean anything.

She got off the bed, smiled, and left the room. Her father reached for the nearest newspaper almost before her last footfall had died.

Tom was in the entry-hall. He had already taken the hamper to the buggy out front. He looked more tanned and fit than usual. His collar was open to expose a powerful neck and a muscular throat. He smiled down at her, scattering her other thoughts. 'As usual,' he said, offering his first compliment of the day, 'you look cool and handsome.'

He held the door, closed it after himself,

and took her arm as they went down the stairs and out to the rig. It was, as she had known it would be, quietly and oppressively hot even in the shade. Neither of them commented about this until they were heading back down the hill, then he said it would be a wonderful day to swim. He also said the glass was in trouble, a seafaring man's reference to the changing mood of a barometer.

Beyond town they had several miles to traverse before reaching any appreciable amount of shade. The horse's sides darkened with foam, collecting where the traces touched and where the collar-pad and breaching rubbed. Lynne removed her hat and estimated the distance they had yet to cover.

Tom did not seem affected by the heat. When she said something about this, he answered easily. 'If you'd been raised where I grew up, you wouldn't suffer as much from it. And later, I shipped out of the southern ports from Washington south around the bight of Louisiana to the Gulf of Mexico. It's all hot country; most of it is even hot in wintertime. And heat at sea is worse than heat on land. The water reflects it back at you.' He drove a quarter mile then said, 'Heat changes people.' He sounded as though he'd been thinking of something in particular, but although she waited, that was all he said.

They reached the woodlands, and although the high humidity remained, exactly as she had known it would, the direct rays of sunlight were blunted, so that helped a little.

She showed him which roads to take, and along the way he pointed something out to her which she otherwise would not have noticed: There were no other wheeltracks going up through the woodlands; not since the last spring rainfall.

To reach the pond, which was actually a small lake, they had to change course often. Tom said he never would have been able to find the place unguided. Lynne knew that very few strangers ever visited the pond, and because there were other watering places closer to Smithsport, and less difficult of access, their destination was never, even at the peak of summer, visited very much.

More fishermen went up there, she told him, than swimmers.

They finally came over the top of a low, flat hillock, and the pond was below them no more than a hundred yards. He stopped the buggy and looked around, then he drove on down to a shaded, grassy place, took their horse from the shafts, pitched the harness upon the floorboards, haltered the animal and set it to grazing.

While he'd been doing this, she went to feel the water. It was cold, but not terribly so. She went back to report, as he carried their hamper to a cool place in some flowering bushes, and as he faced around she saw the expression of peace upon his face. She was pleased.

He went with her to the water's edge. On all sides shades of green, from pale to very dark, marched down in tangled profusion to the shoreline. The pond was about a half mile across at most places, and its steel-blue burnished surface reflected the clouds and the veiled sun with the fidelity of old glass.

He said, 'Beautiful,' and reached for her hand to cling to. 'I've always had an idea that New England was about like this in the summertime.'

She felt a faint defensive stirring, so she said, 'Wintertime in its own way, is just as wonderful. But you have to like snow.' She freed her fingers. The water was very inviting. 'You go that way,' she said, pointing, 'and I'll go this way.'

He laughed at her with a teasing look, but said nothing. She returned to the area where he'd put the picnic hamper and shed her outer clothes over there. Afterwards, she glanced downward at herself. She was not a heavy girl, but swimming suits even on lithe women, left little to a person's imagination. For a moment she was hesitant, then she overcame that and went down to the water. She did not see him coming, at first, because she was testing the soggy lake bottom, and even when she knew he was getting close she did not look around right away. A man, a *strong* man, could never really conceal his feelings when he looked a certain way at a woman; it was better not to look up and have to face this.

His shadow fell across the water, thick at the shoulders and chest, leaner elsewhere, and this time when he felt for her hand the breath hung up in her throat for a second. She told herself it was because the water was cold as they moved forward into it, but she knew better.

For a second she wished she had not come; wished she'd told any lie at all to avoid coming.

He released her fingers and dropped forward cleaving the water with scarcely a ripple. Where he surfaced, he rolled once, looked back at her, then he completed the roll, sank from sight and all she could see was a powerful tanned body skimming along the placid lake bottom for a few moments before he was lost to sight.

He was an excellent swimmer. Of course he would be, having been raised in a place where people swam all year round.

She went deeper, felt the buoyancy take over, and also swam. As a child she'd loved swimming, loved being in water. As a young girl she'd had fewer opportunities to go swimming, but it was something a person never forgot. She swam out, sank to stroke back towards the shore underwater, and when she re-entered the shallows, and surfaced, he was already there waist deep, waiting and laughing. His hair was plastered almost flat and his face shone. His arms and chest were like polished brass in the muggy light. She trod water until she found the bottom, then stood up and threw back her head to get the drenched hair out of her eyes.

'It's like glass, down there,' he told her. 'You can see the fish. Where I grew up beside the sea, the surf is never that clear.'

She said, 'I'll bet it's warmer though.'

He expostulated with an outflung arm. 'This isn't cold. This is about the same temperature as the Pacific, this time of year.' When she raised up standing clear of the water he noticed, of course, and she had known he *would* notice, but he turned away and went over sideways to plunge down deep again and head out towards the centre of the pond, so that moment of acute self-consciousness for her was actually minimal, and this made it easier for her to suppress the inhibitions that were always there, no more than arms' distance away.

She swam after him, on the surface, and the unused muscles responded as though this were not her first swim in several years.

Because she was lithe and supple and muscular, her passage across the water was swift and graceful. She revelled in her strength, untried for so long. The heat no longer existed; nothing existed, in fact, but her freedom and her sense of physical prowess. She did not see Tom again, but the pond deepened gradually the farther one got from the shoreline; it was murky the farther down it sloped.

Finally, she turned back — and he was upon the shore watching her. She had no idea how he had managed that. He hadn't been able to swim all the way back underwater but she hadn't seen him surface either. She smiled as she started back. He was better than ordinary, by far.

When she felt the mud underfoot and eased down to stand a moment at breast-depth to allow her lungs to recover, he turned and went over towards the flowering bush where the picnic hamper was hidden in cool shade.

His legs were lean and muscular. They were slightly lighter than his torso, as though he might have spent more time under a hot sun naked from the waist up, than from the waist down.

His chest was thick and powerful, as were his shoulders and upper arms. He had a beautiful physique, she thought, then reddened as she turned purposefully to look elsewhere.

They had the entire pond to themselves. Except, of course, for the drowsing horse over under a huge chestnut tree, and some noisy little birds who flitted anxiously in and out of the flourishing undergrowth that stood back a dozen or so yards from the slope of grassy shoreline.

He called, and she came slowly up out of the water to go over where he was trying to decide upon the best place for their picnic. As she walked towards him, he turned and watched, and she lifted her eyes to his face expecting to find that special expression there.

It was. And she did not care.

Chapter Seventeen

She had devilled the ham and had minted the tea. She had also added a few drops of peppermint, which made tea taste cold even when it was not cold.

Where they ate beneath a giant locust tree, at least he said it looked like a locust to him and she could not dispute this because she had no idea what kind of tree it was, the pond's reflection did not reach, and because they were wet, it seemed fifteen degrees cooler to them.

They sat upon the laprobe from the buggy, side by side, facing the pond. She saw a distant flight of ducks and pointed them out to him. In the fall of the year men from town came up here for waterfowl hunting. She asked if he liked to hunt, and saw the momentary shadow pass across his face before he wagged his head and answered.

'I'm not much of a killer, Lynne.' He made light of this. 'Maybe I wasn't born with the correct instincts, or perhaps they just never developed.' He smiled at her. 'When a man has to kill. . . .' He shrugged as though to say that was something different. 'But just to come up here and kill ducks because a man owns a gun and has the time to use it. . . .' He did not finish, instead he reached for the jar and re-filled both their glasses with tea.

She thought of the duel he'd fought, wondering if he'd felt the same way about killing *before* that. He surprised her by saying, 'But I suppose a man who kills because he really believes it's a sport, has more in his favour than two men who stand up about a hundred and fifty feet apart and try to commit murder.'

She thanked him for re-filling her glass, then looked up at him. 'Tom; is that why you allowed him to fire first? Because you didn't want to kill him?'

He didn't balk, as she half expected. 'Not exactly. It's true I didn't want to kill him, but there was another reason. . . .'

She took down a shallow breath, then said, 'Jeannette Stuart?'

His blue gaze came around slowly. 'I thought you said all that was known up here was that I'd killed a man.'

She hadn't anticipated being caught like this; she hadn't even thought ahead when she'd mentioned that name. Jeanette Stuart had been a tantalizing wraith, now, for a long while. She had made her utterance, not as he probably thought, out of curiosity, she had made it out of a strong, involved, interest in him.

'Before my father decided to hire you, he talked to Jay Morgan to find out why Morgan had not hired you. That was when he learned about the killing. My father wanted you, Tom, but he didn't want to embarrass either of you, by asking questions, so he wrote to acquaintances in Louisiana. They wrote back.'

He said, 'I see. Then you knew all along about Jeanette Stuart.'

Lynne set aside the tea glass. 'No. All I know is the name.'

'But your father knows?'

'If he does, he's kept it to himself.' She didn't want to pursue this further. 'I'm sorry.' Her mind darted round for a fresh point to start from. 'You haven't eaten enough.' She reached to put more devilled ham on his plate and he caught her wrist.

'Jeanette Stuart was the mistress of John Loudon,' he said softly but incisively. 'I did not know this. I met her at a Creole ball.' He released her wrist. As she drew back he said, 'The next morning when we were having breakfast on the gallery, a man I never saw before arrived and handed me a note. It was Loudon's challenge. That was the first

I knew Jeanette even knew who Jack Loudon was . . . I knew, because I'd shipped aboard his family's ships in the Orient trade.

'I went out to the Loudon estate to try and explain. John Loudon refused to see me and had me put off the place.

'I went back to try and get Jeanette to go see him. She refused. I looked up the gentleman who'd brought the challenge and he laughed at me; in fact he said I should feel honoured that Loudon had challenged me, instead of sending his coachman to horsewhip me.

'So — I went out there. I've never since been able to explain even to myself how I felt that morning. The last thing I wanted to do was shoot a man. Jeanette had a three-year-old son.'

Lynne said, 'Loudon's child?'

'Yes. I kept thinking of that, too, and when we stepped up to the line, I made up my mind not to shoot back . . . Then he turned, I saw the hatred and contempt on his face, he fired, I felt the pain where the ball gouged my thigh, and I fired back — and he fell dead.'

Those distant ducks were taking wing again, calling back and forth as they lifted off and headed northward. Otherwise, Lynne was conscious only of Tom Dorset's strained expression, and the shade where they sat, which seemed now to be more sad than it was benign.

She said, ‘I’m sorry I mentioned it, Tom, but at least I know now.’

He loosened where he sat, a little at a time. ‘There is one more thing, Lynne: I was blackballed among the companies and the shipmasters. That’s why I finally headed north. That’s why I went to Morgan; he was the only shipowner in Smithsport.’

She had a sinking sensation. ‘That’s what you want — to go back to sea, Tom?’

He leaned back with his shoulder brushing her. ‘I did. I didn’t believe I could amount to anything in any other way. I’ve always been a seaman. But maybe that’s not true; with Harding Company I’ve discovered that the ships are only a part of it.’ He turned, looking long at her, then raised a gentle hand to her shoulders and said, ‘And of course there is you.’

Her heart stopped. Intuition was taking over, intuition and instinct. She could manage the one but the other was overwhelming.

‘That day I came up the hill with the letter for your father . . . Did you feel anything that day, Lynne?’

She had, but she’d refused to admit it. Since then she’d felt things too, and she’d also refused to admit that. When she'd been surest had been those few times when he'd touched her; it had been a combination of anguish and longing, of fear and want, which was exactly how she felt this instant, with his arm around her shoulders.

'Something,' she murmured, and felt his arm tighten. Weakly she said, 'You haven't eaten very much, Tom.' He twisted from the waist. She saw his head and shoulders starkly blocking out a portion of sky and treetops; she stiffened to resist but otherwise did not move back, and when his lips touched her mouth everything swam.

She closed her eyes, raised her arms, and held back as much as possible from responding to him. Warnings came and went, weaker each time. He was gentle but she felt his need, and when he slowly pulled back she dropped her head into the curve of a powerful shoulder and clung to him.

Now, there was no way back. She knew it. She also suspected that he knew it too.

The silence hung on, water lapped the shoreline, birds came and went in the treetops, and when the storm subsided in her she forced herself to think rationally. It wasn't an easy matter, with his shoulder against her cheek and the sturdy sound of his heart pulsing against her.

She thought of something irrelevant and said it aloud. 'My father doesn't know we went swimming. Only that we went driving.'

His answer was wiser. 'Your father knows, sweetheart. If I had a daughter as lovely as you are, and she went driving with a young man — I'd know. Especially if she went driving with him *twice.*'

It was probably true. As close as she and her father were, there had always been things they did not discuss. She sighed and relaxed in his arms. 'You think it was easy, don't you?' she asked, keeping her face pressed tightly against him.

'I think it was inevitable. I'll tell you something about love, Lynne: It's something you *feel* long before you *know.* It's kind of like that 'faith' the preachers talk about. It's something deep down inside a person that doesn't have anything to do with rational thought. You *feel* it, and later on, you rationalize it, and *know it.* Easy? My God, if there's anything in this world that *isn't* easy, it's love.'

He pulled her back and tilted up her face the way he'd done once before, with a curled finger beneath her chin. 'I'll tell you something about Tom Dorset: He is a man who can only love once.'

She saw the darkening shadows in his eyes. ‘Your wife?’

‘My wife,’ he murmured. ‘And for a long time after she died. I can’t love as other men love. That’s what I tried to prove that night with Jeanette Stuart . . . The next morning I knew . . . That was another reason why I left the deep south, went clear away from everything I’d known . . . And now it’s you, and that doesn’t make it any better, really.’

She didn’t understand. ‘Doesn’t it?’

He released her and said, ‘No, because when I leave Smithsport, you’ll be leaving right along me — as a sort of ghost.’

She reached up to push back his tumbled hair. ‘Suppose, when you leave, I would leave with you, *not* as a ghost?’

He looked at her. ‘Would you, Lynne?’

She would. Without thinking, without reconsidering, she would. ‘Yes.’

He let out a rough breath and raised both arms. She went willingly inside them. This time, without a single dread or inhibition, or sense of shamelessness, she drew him down to her, met his lips with her hot-eager mouth and clung with a fire that matched his fire.

She had lived almost twenty years inside a band of proper restraint. The rare few times she had even permitted her imagination to soar, she had kept it tethered so that it never could soar *this* high. For the past five or six years she had been aware of herself as a woman, as a girl who had matured early and had become a woman long before even her father had suspected this was so.

She had wanted this to happen and had almost given up hope that it ever would. She had seen the maiden ladies of Smithsport; shrivelled and parched and made acidy and caustic with their unslaked thirsts. They had frightened her more than the eternal hell-fire and damnation she had heard every Sunday from the Episcopal pulpit, because she had seen herself moving inexorably down this same road towards that other agony.

And now it happened.

She yielded to him softly and willingly, and he met her with his gentle needs. She told him she loved him and although she had always thought that love was not this tumultuous, that it came only gradually in a soft-sweet way, as late springtime turned to summer, now she knew that if this were so with some, it was *not* so with her, nor with him.

He was not a boy, he was a man. His feelings were not clumsy nor half-strangled by fear. His palms did not feel clammy against her flesh, they felt warm and softly wonderful. When she opened her eyes to him, he smiled in a way she could never forget, and leaned to brush her lips with his mouth. *He* was what she had never been able to quite imagine, except in a kind of twilight of formless shape; but now he was real, and he was what she wanted from life, she knew it with that same kind of instinctual perception he had mentioned.

He was love and life, breath and thought and feeling. She held him close with her eyes closed, fully conscious that this was what life was all about.

Chapter Eighteen

Monday morning was not, as the novelists say, wakening to a new world. For Lynne the *world* was the same; what she wakened to was a new *life*, a new Lynne Harding. She had her breakfast, visited briefly with her father, kissed his cheek, told Mary O'Hara she would try to be home early, and left the house on the hill with Smithsport's roofs and chimney pots and faint sea breeze at the base of the hill as they had always been. It was all the same, but *she* was not, and never could be, the same again.

Mister Emory had already hung his coat upon the round peg behind the door and was at his desk when Lynne climbed the stairs. Just before starting up she had paused to cast one scorching look around the vast warehouse. *He* was there, somewhere, but she had not seen him.

Mister Emory said there was a letter from New York City; the master of that ship carrying thread and leather and canvas had been compelled to put about and return to New York for some minor repairs. He would appreciate a prompt response to his earlier enquiry.

Mister Emory waited patiently but Lynne could not make that swift a decision. Of course she *could* have, but she wasn't going to. Intuition told her the thread would be merchantable; it always was, but not in large amounts. The leather, being from the Caribbean area, would not be the equal of imported British leather, and although it would sell for less money, it would not be easy to dispose of. The canvas was in a different category. There was always a firm demand for canvas.

She went downstairs looking for Tom. He was at his counting table near the front doorway. When he turned, she felt her heart miss a beat. He smiled, then looked around and when he saw no one close he said, 'I didn't sleep a wink last night.'

She blushed furiously. 'I'm glad you didn't,' she said. 'Misery likes company. Tom . . . ?'

He didn't take his eyes off her. 'I'm not even thinking straight today,' he murmured.

She looked away. 'Tom . . . ?'

'Every place I look, I see you and everything I touch — I feel you.'

'Tom!'

'Yes?'

'There's a cargo of leather, thread and canvas in New York. We've had a letter of enquiry . . .'

He pulled back slightly to lean upon the desktop. 'The canvas sounds good. Where was the leather cured?'

'In the outer islands.'

He softly shook his head. 'Poor quality, sweetheart.'

It was impossible, looking at him, hearing his voice, sensing his thoughts, and trying to talk business too. 'I know,' she replied, 'and we've never been able to sell thread in large amounts.'

He said, 'You're strikingly beautiful . . . Well; then it's a marginal cargo, isn't it? You can profit on the canvas, tie up capital in the thread and over a period of time make fair interest on the money, and the leather is ballast. . . . Will you tell your father I'm in love with you?'

She struggled, hard. 'The canvas. . . .' She gave it up. 'I wanted to tell *someone,* last night. Anyone at all. Tom; I'm not even thinking right today.'

He reached and furtively touched her, then drew back his hand. 'Yesterday, when you said those things. . . . Do you still feel the same way this morning?'

'Yes. More so. I love you, Tom, I'll do

whatever you want me to do.'

'Marry me?'

'I said I would, didn't I?'

He straightened up off the table. 'Do you want me to tell your father?'

She didn't know; she couldn't think beyond the need to resist whatever it was his magnetism or something like that — while they were in plain view at the warehouse doorway. She said, 'Come by this evening. We'll talk about it.'

He was willing. 'All right.' He kept gazing at her. 'You'd better go back upstairs.'

She obeyed, and when she got back up there she hoped that if Mr Emory noticed her flushed face he would attribute it to the stairs.

He evidently did not notice because as she was sitting down he said, 'I looked through our files, Miss Harding, and we've done very well on canvas. The low-quality leather we've handled in the past, has been sold to a commercial belting company in Pittsburg. I found a letter from a Delaware company dated last summer, asking about thread.' Emory arose and crossed to her desk and put the letter in front of her. 'What did Mister Dorset say?'

She gave a little start and quickly looked up. The old man was smiling. 'I thought you went downstairs to ask what he thought about this cargo.'

She said, 'Yes, I did,' and picked up the year-old letter of enquiry. 'He said — about what you've just mentioned, Mister Emory.' She handed back the letter to be re-filed. 'I'll write the shipmaster for his prices.' She smiled then turned her back and Mister Emory retreated.

Writing the letter did not take long. She signed it as she had been signing all letters lately: 'Lynne Harding for Paul Harding, Harding Company, Smithsport, Massachusetts.'

She began noticing the heat by the time she was finished with the letter and removed her jacket. That hazy overcast was thicker today than it had been yesterday. It was almost tropical in its thick, cloying, hot humidity. She went across to open the roadway window, something that was not done as a rule because the noises from the roadway were distracting.

But that did no good. The heat was the same, inside or outside. As she turned Mister Emory patted his wizened face with a folded handkerchief. 'Saps a body's strength,' he commented and would have said more but someone coming up the stairs with a solid strike of boots made him turn and crane in that direction, glasses slipping down to the end of his nose.

Lynne went to the wall-peg, got her jacket and put it on again. She had reached her desk before the visitor appeared in the doorway. It was Jay Morgan, his face slightly flushed, and with perspiration faintly darkening the edges of his collar, but otherwise looking as formidable as always.

Lynne was surprised. She had not thought he would step inside Harding Company's building again now that they were enemies. Then she became fearful. If he had come, it was not for any good purpose. She said, 'Good morning, Mister Morgan.'

He turned towards Cuthbert Emory and said, 'Good morning.' Then he turned towards Lynne and bleakly inclined his head without uttering a sound.

Mister Emory sat poised like a wizened bird in the presence of a snake. He seemed scarcely to breathe.

Morgan crossed nearer to Lynne's desk and although she was tall, for a woman, she had to look up. She expected to feel fear, but instead she felt mild antagonism and something else which she could not define, but which was not fear. Perhaps it was the stirring of a slow rebellion; something like that.

Morgan said, 'I went up to see your father this morning, but he was sleeping. The housekeeper refused to waken him.'

Lynne remained impassive and waiting. 'His rest is important,' she murmured.

Morgan took no notice. 'The reason I went up there was to make him a business proposal. But I suppose I'll have to make it to you.'

Lynne felt her colour rising and bit her lip. Very few people had ever talked 'down' to her. Those other times she scarcely recalled, but *this* time it was different.

'I had in mind some kind of subsidiary association between Morgan Company and Harding Company.'

She had no idea at all what this meant. She smiled and said, 'Please sit down, Mister Morgan.'

He remained standing, but Lynne sat. 'Morgan Company,' he went on to say, 'could monopolise all the trading in Smithsport. We are the only company that still puts ships to sea, and our volume of trade as well as our capitalisation, make it possible for us to control the trading. For example, Miss Harding, you probably got a letter of enquiry from a New York shipmaster with thread, leather, and canvas aboard.' Morgan paused, studying Lynne's face. Evidently he could read nothing there because he said, 'Well, did you?'

Lynne confirmed that she had indeed received such a letter.

Morgan's stormy look passed, and a flinty one tinged with contempt replaced it. 'And you may have replied favourably. Well; yesterday I sent a man down on the steam cars from Gosnold to give the shipmaster a voucher for his cargo. It will belong to Morgan Company when you see the sails approaching.' Morgan paused, his hawkish old bleak eyes like rapiers. 'Do you see? Morgan Company can dominate the Smithsport trade. Also, Fred is due in any day with a private cargo for us.'

Lynne considered all this boastful talk. She said, 'Now that I'm enormously impressed with the prestige and distinction of Morgan Company, Mister Morgan, perhaps you will explain just what exactly a subsidiary association is.' She looked steadily up into the fierce old man's uncompromising face.

She had stung him. For a moment he looked upon the verge of lashing back at her. It may have been that unyielding look she gave him, or it may have been personal restraint, based perhaps on something as old fashioned as rough gallantry, but in any event he finally said, 'If you knew business, you'd understand,' and with this mild and figurative wrist-slap, he then said, 'My proposal would include using the Harding Company facilities — warehouse and offices, plus sales and trading records, and stocking them with Morgan Company commodities. Morgan Company could then expand, take over all the Smithsport export-import trade, and substantially increase our business.' He paused and Lynne thought he had said it all. Then he spoke again. 'Morgan Company would control both firms while your father, who will be unable to return to work, will be paid a fair sum according to the leasing arrangement.'

Lynne sifted through this last bit and came up with its essence. 'You want to lease the warehouse and office, offer my father a pension providing he agrees not to keep our company alive — and you want to fire me.'

Morgan's gaze flickered for the first time. 'If you wish to put it that way, by all means do so.'

Anger came up very slowly in Lynne. As a general rule she had no difficulty controlling her temper. In her entire lifetime she had not actually erupted with anger more than twice. This was the third time. She arose and leaned on her desk and said, 'You go to hell!'

Jay Morgan had seen her colour rising so he had not been caught entirely unprepared, but he had not expected *this.* It was not done. Probably in Jay Morgan's long lifetime he had not been sworn at by more than half a dozen women, if that many, and they had certainly not belonged to Lynne Harding's category.

Cuthbert Emory winced.

Lynne did not allow Jay Morgan a chance. She said, 'My father wouldn't accept that proposal, and I'm not going to discuss it any further with you.' She stepped clear of the desk and went to the front window for a breath of air. There was none, the day was more leaden than ever, the sky was turning an unpleasant shade of hazy gray, and the heat lay like a solid substance everywhere.

Morgan went to the stairs and down them without another look or word. When his footfalls were no longer audible Bert Emory squeakily cleared his throat, sat a moment waiting for Lynne to turn back, and when she didn't he finally resumed work at his ledgers and files.

It took a while for Lynne's heartbeat to return to normal. Morgan hadn't been able to intimidate Tom, he had failed in his attempt to cripple Harding Company by cutting off the draying, so he had come round with this offer of a pension for her father, and his scorn of her.

She was still angry five minutes later when she turned and said, 'I think I'll go home, Mister Emory. There's nothing that needs doing anyway. I'll be back first thing in the morning.'

Old Emory grinned and bobbed his head. He would have said something encouraging, perhaps something congratulatory, but the look on her face kept him from it. But after she had departed Emory left his stool, went to the window to look out, and he chuckled to himself. She was enough like her father to be his son, instead of his daughter. Her father would have reacted the same way. Old Emory hadn't worked beside Paul Harding all those years without learning that upon rare occasions the Harding temper could surface; it was the kind of fury that rooted a man to the floor.

Emory saw her striding up the roadway. lithe and erect, and although it went strictly against his lifelong grain as a male, as a *superior* male, he did not hold back on his admiration.

Then he scuttled downstairs to find Tom Dorset and tell him what she had said to old Jay Morgan, *verbatim*.

Chapter Nineteen

She should have reported to her father as soon as she arrived home, but instead she went to take a cooling bath, to change into light, summer clothing, and to afterwards sit a long while brushing her hair.

For one thing, she had cheapened herself by swearing. For another, she had ensured for herself a mortal enemy. Finally, she just might have done something that could not be un-done; if Harding Company got involved in a trade-war with Morgan Company, and lost, which was entirely possible, there would be no way, not even if she went begging on her knees, to get Jay Morgan to make his offer again.

Her father knew she was home, and although she would have preferred not having to face him, if she did not go to his room he would know something had happened. He was anything but a simpleton.

But first she went to the kitchen for a cup of peppermint tea, and listened to Mary O'Hara's complaints about the muggy heat, and the way it drained away all her energy.

She also learned that her father was up to something. Mary did not know exactly what it was, but she had taken his luncheon in a bit early, and as was her custom had knocked on the door first, before entering, and he hadn't called out for her to come in until after she heard something that sounded very much as though he were scrambling across the room back into his bed.

Lynne promised to look into this, and went down the back hallway to her father's room and walked in without knocking. He was sitting propped up in his bed looking as normal as though he had never been ill a day in his life. She glanced towards the window, saw his slippers over there, saw his robe where a careless hand had hastily draped it across a chair, and guessed what he had been doing. But she did not mention that. Not right then, at any rate.

She pulled over a chair and smiled as she sat down. 'You're looking much better,' she said.

He agreed. 'I feel much better too. Maybe Albert Clavenger. . . . Well, he *is* a young man, Lynne. Doctors aren't infallible, are they?'

She kept right on smiling, and she did not like having to be blunt with him, but she was. 'They aren't infallible, but neither are you, and Doctor Clavenger knows at least a *little* more than you do, about heart trouble.'

Her father took that without a murmur, then changed the subject. 'Bad weather. What are they saying in town?'

She did not know what he meant. 'Saying about what? The weather?' She hadn't heard anyone say anything about the weather, but then she hadn't been out of the office. She leaned to punch his pillows into shape. 'It's hot and muggy and very unpleasant. But it will pass in a day or two.'

He leaned until she was finished, then settled back. 'Any sails in the roadstead?'

She hadn't noticed any. 'No.' Then she remembered what Jay Morgan had said. 'The *Hare* is due, though.'

Then it struck her.

She should have suspected. She had lived beside the greeny sea all her life; had seen it before. Her only reason for not knowing was because something else had come to completely overwhelm everything else, for her.

She looked steadily at her father. 'A storm?'

It seemed to irritate him a little. 'Well, of course. Go look at the glass in my study. It's been dropping steadily over the past twenty-four hours. The signs are as plain as the nose on your face. And a bad one.'

How did he know that glass had been dropping in his study, unless he had gone in there to look? She had her earlier suspicions confirmed as to what he was up to, but she still said nothing about that.

Her father spoke briskly. 'If there are any ships in the harbour they'd better put to sea. Fred won't arrive.' He stopped a moment, pursed his mouth in thought, then changed that. 'Not if he's got the sense God gave a mouse, he won't sail in. But who can say what Fred Morgan will do?'

She overcame the presentiment; she had been through many storms, not ordinarily so late in the season, but many storms nonetheless. Smithsport had been built, and re-built, to withstand storms. Two and more centuries of learning where the weaknesses were and correcting them, had made the town almost immune.

Storms battering the seawalls until the earth shook under the impact for a mile inland, were never pleasant, but neither had Lynne Harding ever seen any genuine disaster result. Besides, there was something more important on her mind.

'Tom will be by this evening,' she murmured, looking at the untidy stack of newspapers upon his bedside table.

Her father must have detected something in her tone because his brown eyes drifted to her face and remained there through a moment of silence before he said, 'His visit won't have anything to do with the company, will it?'

She kept looking at the untidy stack of newspapers; she wanted to smile. She should have known he would have sensed something more than a friendly house call.

'No, it won't have anything to do with the company,' she replied quietly, and raised her eyes to him. 'He told me about the duel — and about the woman, Jeanette Stuart.'

Her father faintly inclined his head. 'Yesterday, of course.'

She remembered what Tom had said: Her father would know. He had been right. Her father *did* know. She arose and stepped to the window with her back to him. 'The woman was the — lover — of that man he fought the duel with.'

'I see. Fighting like tom cats over a female cat,' exclaimed her father, and she turned to face him.

'No. Tom did not know about the woman.' Lynne swallowed. 'He met Jeanette Stuart at a ball. . . . The next morning John Loudon challenged Tom. He tried to dissuade Loudon. He did all he could — then they duelled. Tom let Loudon fire first. Tom was wounded slightly in the hip. And he killed the man. Then he left and came north — and you hired him.'

Her father sat back relaxed, watching her face. 'Sweetheart, tell me truthfully: What are your feelings?'

She held her lower lip between her teeth for as long as was required to force a calmness, then she answered him. 'Truthfully: I love him.'

Her father sighed, but otherwise showed no particular emotion. 'Jeanette Stuart . . . ?'

'I didn't know him then, and he didn't know me. . . . Do you think he's another Fred Morgan, with women?'

'No,' answered her father, dryly. 'I'm that much of a judge of men. He's not another Fred Morgan. . . . Well; does he love you?'

'He asked me to marry him.'

Paul Harding, who had been feeling progressively better, now felt — not worse — just old. He had suffered torments through her first infatuation, when she'd still had freckles, but this time he knew in his heart, as a woman, not a girl, she was willing, and of course she was very vulnerable.

What could he say? What could any father say? She stood over in front of the window, round and supple and ready; he had taught her all he would ever be able to teach her, and if it hadn't been enough, or if he hadn't taught her the right things, why then it simply was too late now to attempt any amends.

He was not happy with the thought, though, even when he recognized all the signs and knew that no matter what he said or did, she was not going to deviate. It occurred to him, not as any consolation, that every father of a daughter who had ever lived had probably suffered through exactly what he was suffering through. They had survived it, so he would also survive it.

He smiled. 'Bring Tom in when he comes.'

Lynne took this as her dismissal, and in a way she was relieved to be able to escape, but as she went to his bed she leaned on impulse, threw both arms round him, and kissed him hard on the cheek. Then she pulled back and halted at the door to say, 'How did you know the glass was falling in your study?'

He gave her a blank look, then cleared his throat and scowled darkly.

She left the room, went without thinking to the study, stopped in front of the large ship's barometer upon one teak-panelled wall, and saw how correct he had been. The delicate little black arm with its fluted-arrow pointer, was down as far as the 27th degree, while the humidity gauge was steadily sinking behind its rounded glass shield.

An hour later a light wind came, high enough to ripple across the rooftop but otherwise not noticeable. Mary O'Hara was out back at the clothes line gathering dry sheets and pillow cases against her full bosom, and came muttering back to the pantry with her hair slightly askew. When she saw Lynne through the doorway in the kitchen she said, 'And now it'll be coming. Step out and smell the air.'

Lynne filled two cups with tea and offered one to Mary. 'The barometer is down about as low as I've ever seen it.' They took their cups to the kitchen table where Mary patted her hair back into place.

'I've lost two men t' the sea,' she told Lynne, looking grim but resolute. 'I was sixteen the first time, and I near died from the grief of it. Then I emigrated to here with a promise to m'self to go inland so far I couldn't even smell the salt.' She snorted and drank her hot tea. 'And how far did he get?' She pointed towards the front of the house. 'A quarter mile.' She dropped her arm, sat a moment, then became cheerful again, with an effort. 'Did your father tell you I gave him tea instead of coffee for his breakfast, and he didn't like that?'

Lynne arose to go for more tea. 'He didn't mention it, no.'

'But y'see, tea's better for his blood,' explained Mary O'Hara.

Lynne brought the pot over but Mary O'Hara declined a second cup. 'It's the bloody weather,' she exclaimed. 'Takes m' appetite away.'

The wind came again, lower this time, against the front of the house, bringing with it a peculiar scent of metal. Mary O'Hara wrinkled her nose. 'Brimstone.' She arose to go back where she had left the piled sheets and pillow slips in the pantry, and called from out there. 'I'll make certain the windows is all closed upstairs.'

Lynne finished half her second cup of tea, then went to the front of the house to make certain the windows were closed on the ground level. After that, she stepped out front upon the verandah. Until she did that, she did not realize that the wind had strength to it. Inside the massive, sturdy old house, which had been built to withstand the worst nature had to send against it, there was no sensation of a building storm — yet.

Across the distance to the far sea wall trees as big around as the church steeple at the upper end of town, stirred uneasily at their tops, but at their bases they were immovable.

Lynne saw birds scoot up the front of the sky and make a big roll backwards with folded wings, to be borne swiftly inland. None tried to return.

The sea was not turbulent, but it had a peculiar listlessness, a kind of heavy, weighted pitch and heave, but like molten lead, not water. The colour was, as normally was the case, a reflection of the streaked sky. She had seen most of this before, but the rawness was lacking. There were no cresting tons of froth to strike at the topmost slick stones along the sea wall, and the wind, which usually came from the south when a high sea ran, was coming across the roadstead in fitful bursts that had stinging, invisible bits of water in it.

The wind changed, then, and came from the south as was customary. Lynne noticed this and felt a slight, almost an unconscious, relief, because she now had seen it all before, and could make a prediction.

But the sea did not break up. There were no whitecaps. That immense, overwhelming mass of water boiled like mottled oil running parallel to the land with a sound as of a deep-down continuing explosion. Only when one of those fitful bursts of wind came across the water, stippling its surface, did the sea appear to respond with a slight lee-ward list. Then the sea wall caught the full force, the land trembled, and Lynne felt as insignificant, as small and inconsequential as one of those wind-flung birds — except that the birds could ride the high thermals for five or ten miles inland, for as far as the wind ran on, and escape, and Lynne was held to the front of the weathered house by the same force and could not elude it.

The sky did not darken right away, but the sun very gradually dimmed out, and by one o'clock it was like early dusk. It did not change from that hue, not even when Lynne went back indoors to get a cardigan, and by then there was a steady wind-whipped squall of water beating over the house, the town, and the surrounding countryside for a mile or two inland, and that stifling, muggy heat was gone, replaced by a salt-water chill.

Water streaked the windows, wind made the house groan, and as steadily as it was inescapable, the storm came nearer.

Mary O'Hara took Paul Harding's noon tray back to the kitchen with her shawl around both shoulders, and afterwards she called Lynne to a dining-room window, her face as grey as putty, her doubled fist pressed to her mouth. When Lynne came, Mary pointed.

There was a ship riding ahead of the gale, masts bare, sails furled, now high enough for the red-leaded parts of its hull to show, now bow-down ploughing a white-spumed furrow.

The *Hare*! Lynne recognized its figurehead even at that distance. She might have been able to recognize the Morgan pennant too, except that it had been torn away hours ago.

Chapter Twenty

When the capricious wind shifted, slashing with full strength crossways towards the land, the helpless ship did not turn, did not even heel over, it seemed to pause and shudder like an injured thing rousing from a crouch, stunned and in pain. Then, when it finally would have yielded, the fitful bursts died and the howling wind from astern pitched the *Hare* fully onward again.

Rain pelted downward in a wild swirl, sometimes obscuring the sight from the dining-room window, sometimes sweeping the glass as clean as crystal, which was when Lynne could see the ship best. It stood upright, huge and out-sized, like something from a nightmare, alternately straddling the heaving swells, then falling back again.

She was not aware of anything else, until a gust of cold, damp wind came through and she turned to see Tom standing in the dining-room archway. She went over to him and was engulfed in his arms. She said, 'Did you see it? That's the *Hare*, a Morgan ship with Fred. . . .'

'I know,' he said quietly. 'I know. And I've got to get back down the hill.' He kissed her forehead. 'Stay inside, Lynne. Within an hour the wind'll be able to hoist you right off your feet. Batten down and stay inside.' He looked over where Mary O'Hara had not moved, and still had the white-knuckled fist against her mouth. 'Tell your father it's a bad blow but not to worry.' He smiled at her. 'I'll be back later, if I can.'

She clung with both hands. 'Where are you going? You might as well stay with us, Tom.'

He shook her loose gently. His hands were cold. She only just now noticed that his face was wind-reddened, that his seaman's jacket was wet and that his hands holding hers, were chilly and damp to the touch.

'Down the hill,' he said, without offering any more explanation than that. 'That damned fool should have known better than to bring his ship in.' He leaned down and brushed her lips, then dropped her hands. 'Remember what I told you: Secure the house and make certain no one tries to go out.'

She went swiftly beside him as he paced back towards the entry hall. 'What can anyone possibly do, Tom? You're not going to try and put a boat out? You'd be swamped ten feet from the wall.' She grabbed his arm at the doorway. 'Tom . . . ?'

He turned to soothe her. 'No one's foolish enough to try and put out a boat, sweetheart. Maybe there's nothing anyone can do, but I'll go down there and wait with the others. And don't fret.' He opened the door, fought it closed; the gust of squally wind rocked her back, then it died and he was gone.

She did not return to Mary at the dining-room window, she went instead where she had always gone when life had become too much for her. When she opened the door she saw her father buttoning himself into a thick black seaman's coat. He was fully dressed, booted and hatted. She closed the door and barred it with her body. They looked at one another. He said, 'I'm going down to George Street.'

She answered in the same tone of voice. 'No, you're not. Tom just left. He said not to allow anyone out of the house. . . . The *Hare* is coming in.'

Her father's eyes widened. 'The *Hare*? A ship in the roadstead this evening — I told you — I suspected that damned fool wouldn't have the judgement to put off for the open sea. Didn't I? Can you see it from the house?'

'From the dining-room window,' she said, and forgot to keep him in his room.

Mary O'Hara had not moved since before Tom Dorset had arrived, except to lean slightly to one side of the window.

Lynne and her father moved up closer. Lynne heard him catch his breath even though winds were pounding the house from all directions, making it moan and creak in every wall.

The *Hare* was closer now. It looked huge, as though it were riding the top of the sea, not riding well settled into the sea. It was even possible to see men like small dolls clutching the lines as they worked their ways fore and aft. Without sail, without power of any kind, there was absolutely nothing the *Hare* could do but ride before the racing sea. She was as helpless out there as though she were a cockleshell. She rode the waters well, but then that had been in the mind of her builder. She was a Yankee clipper, one of the fastest, most manoeuvrable, most sea-wise ships afloat. She would sink no matter how the seas ran, but her salvation — the salvation of any ship stripped bare before a storm — was to ride upon the foremost surge, to run before the storm, to ride it out upon the thousands of unobstructed sea-miles, and what the *Hare* was doing, riding high and free, was running directly towards a distant bight beyond the Smithsport anchorage, where great, rocky slopes came down from high mountains to form a protective arm for the Smithsport harbour.

There was no way for the *Hare*'s helmsman to sheer her off; all the sea was running at full-charge towards that distant rock-belted shoreline. The *Hare* was trapped. She was indeed running ahead of the storm, but towards the land, not the open sea, and once she passed the point upon which the Harding house sat, she was caught as surely as though she were a small animal hazed into a gauntlet.

Normally, ships passed a mile out from the sea wall, hence did not look so huge. But the *Hare* caught those treacherous side-sweeping gusts now and again, and was born in a listing skid across the top of the greasy sea until she was no more than a quarter mile from the sea wall when she came abreast of the house.

Her hull dwarfed the house and her spars were higher than the Harding chimneys. Lynne could not move. She saw the men clinging to their life-lines, as helpless to divert the inevitable as any men ever were. She could feel their terror and their despair. One of the men upon the after deck would be Fred, but they all looked alike in their shiny foul-weather attire. Lynne could *feel* what was in their souls as the great ship paused in one of those senseless side-gusts of wind and for ten seconds stood squarely out front of the house. They were going to die; there was nothing that could be done to prevent it, but they were going to have to ride another four or five miles past their town, past everything they wanted most, unable to be heard when they screamed out, to be swiftly borne along to the furious breaking up of the ship beneath their feet in a roaring discord where that mighty sea struck the massive stone coast with a force neither a ship nor a human body could withstand.

Her father went for a chair and sank down, watching. Neither he nor Mary O'Hara were capable of hearing or heeding anything but the unalterable tragedy they had to sit rooted and watch play out.

Lynne went resolutely to her room, put on her heavy skirt, buttoned herself into a winter blouse that she hadn't worn in several years and which now fitted tighter than it had before, rummaged for the pea-coat and watch-cap her father had given her, half in jest, when she'd been infatuated with Fred Morgan. He had half-jokingly told her at that time that the wives of shipmasters sometimes went to sea, too.

Then she left the house by the rear doorway, gasped at the tearing force of the wind, then got to the edge of the house and started bucking her way down the hill in the direction of town. She did not have any actual idea, except that something had to be done, and since it couldn't possibly be done at that point, since the *Hare* was already that far along, it would have to be done in town.

Three times the gale swept her off course. Twice, she was able to break her staggering drift by finding a great tree. The third time she was almost to the stone house where Jay Morgan's chief warehouseman lived, and fought with all her remaining strength to get that far, before surrendering to let the wind batter her against the wall and hold her upright when she would have willingly gone down to her knees.

A man's rough arms caught at her, pulled her over to a recessed doorway, but when the man said something, his words were sucked out of his mouth and all she could hear was the howling wind and the thunder of fisted raindrops.

She got free, and when the south wind paused to allow one of those cross-currents to gust inland, it was possible for her to get free of the recessed doorway and make her way across the treacherously slippery cobbles to the entranceway of a warehouse. The cross-current could not break through the town because of that solid wall of stone buildings which backed towards the sea wall and the yonder sea.

There were men just inside the warehouse, but the same wind that could not break through from the east, set up such a scream in the cavernous warehouse those men Lynne saw had to scream to be heard, and none of them was more than five feet from the others.

She recognized Tom, and two of his warehousemen, buttoned to the chin in foul-weather attire. Of the other three men, she knew only one; old Jay Morgan. He was hatless, half drenched, and looked to be in a fury of half-wild dementia. He was still wearing the grey suit and necktie she'd seen him in that same morning. It was not the kind of dress for a savage storm but he seemed as unmindful of this as did the men around him.

She clung to the doorjamb, unable to hear a single word that was being said over the unending roar of the wild sea and the maddened wind, and yet she was no more than twenty yards from them.

Tom turned to the warehousemen and yelled an order. They swung away. Only old Morgan stood unbendingly in place. Lynne could see his forbidding profile, but with all its strength, the colour was ashen and the lips were bloodless.

The warehousemen ran past her as though she hadn't been there, and a moment later Tom also turned and came ahead, head lowered, but as he turned, she reached, and at her touch his head came up. He stopped in his tracks.

'What are you doing here?'

She didn't attempt to answer. He took her by the arm and half helped, half dragged, her along. They did not go far; across the road to the backlot behind the town hall. He left her and went ahead where five men were struggling with an iron cannon. She saw Tom stoop, toss three iron cannonballs from the neat heap at the base of the ugly old weapon down its black maw, then he joined with the others and his added muscle was enough to make the old wheels turn. As the men pushed past, straining hard, Tom jerked his head for her to follow along. She did, and when they reached the road, for the first time Fortune did not turn her back; that fitful cross-current wind was blowing inland. The men were able to get the cannon across the road, up the stone drive into the Morgan warehouse, and then, finally, just as Lynne was closing the distance, the cross-current died and the savage south wind resumed.

But they had made it and so had she.

Inside, Tom yelled at the men to lean to it. They wheeled the cannon the full long length of the warehouse, to the stone platform out back where carters' wagons normally stood, loading or unloading, and there, finally, when Tom ran past leaning against the wind to peer round a jutting warehouse wall towards the surging sea, which lay no more than three hundred feet across the dock, Lynne began to have an inkling. But she could not believe it.

Old Jay Morgan stumbled over beside her, but if he knew who she was, or if he in fact knew anyone was beside him at all, he gave no indication of it. He looked like a man in his last anguish. He seemed to be speaking but there was no sound.

Tom ran back, and this time when he yelled to his men, she heard, 'Caulk it so that it fires low. Amos; break into that keg and shirt-tail the powder. Lend a hand and tip her down so the balls will roll out. Hurry, damn it!'

Lynne and Jay Morgan watched. The *Hare* was sweeping close; that last prolonged cross-current wind had brought her within less than her length from the sea wall and the massive old stone dock. Finally, Lynne could make out the twisted faces of seamen clinging to shrouds and lifelines jury-rigged at all angles to keep them from being swept overboard.

She saw the ship loom huge and terrifyingly close, then above the roar of sea and wind the cannon exploded. In a second Tom was cursing the men to get it re-loaded. She saw the ball smash at the waterline, for'ard, but the *Hare* was still rising out of the water in its headlong plunge.

Tom yelled the second time. 'Fire!'

That time the *Hare* was much closer and the iron shot tore across the front of her bow where the red-leaded hull and the black-painted topside met, shearing away as much timber as would ordinarily go to build a small house.

'Re-load!' Tom yelled. 'Amos! The powder!'

The *Hare* was within a stone's-throw, toweringly high above. Lynne's heart stopped when the great clipper ship listed towards the warehouse as though it would die right there and roll upon its side and crush them all.

Tom screamed out for the last time: *'Fire!'*

Chapter Twenty-one

There would not have been time for another shot even if they had possessed another cannonball.

There was a gaping hole at the waterline below the bowsprit and although the *Hare* was racing ahead, when she arose, frighteningly close and enormous, Lynne's fright was not sufficient to keep her from seeing the majestic clipper ship as a huge, sleek wounded monster. Then the bow dipped.

It was as though something under the water had raised a resisting great palm. Seawater poured in a surging flood through the big hole, tons upon tons of it, and the ship shuddered her full length, brought up so hard her stern lifted out of the water. Thinly, over the howling wind, Lynne heard men screaming as they fought to hang to their lines upon the storm-washed deck.

For the first time the ship was not keeping pace with the racing tide, water hissed on both sides seeking to suck the hull along.

The *Hare* sank back at the stern, settled a little, and as her holds filled and the vast weight of all that water rolled rearward, she settled lower, lifted her broken bow so slowly Lynne could see spilt seawater in corded rivulets, like twisted cables, running back out of the hole. Then the stern wallowed and heeled away from the shore, and very gradually righted again, with the bottom settling below the waterline.

The bow dipped, more water poured in, and although the ship moved silently past, like a dying mastodon, it was no longer answering the surge of the running tide, it was moving sluggishly. Someone at the wheel locked the cabled-rudder landward. The *Hare*, dying as she responded, grated her sleek side against the massive stone bulwark between the Harding warehouse and the Morgan warehouse.

Two men on deck ran ahead and pitched out a line. Tom's impromptu cannoneers dashed to catch hold and make their laps round a huge old iron capstan sunk five feet into the dockside rock. But there was far too much weight, and although the hawser was as large as a strong man's forearm, as the ship settled deeper and crept sluggishly ahead, the rope snapped as though it had been nothing more than cordage.

The *Hare* ground her sleek hull along the sea wall, settling lower and lower. Lynne saw

Tom run in close and gesticulate to the crowd of oilskin-clad seamen upon the deck. He was yelling. So were the warehousemen with him. It was not a long drop from the deck, now that the ship was sinking, but at the other end there was stone and mortar, which was unyielding even from a lower height.

A man vaulted the rail and sailed, oilskins taking wing, down towards the dock. Before he landed other men hurled themselves over the side. Lynne heard a piercing scream that went out along her nerve ends like a knife-blade.

Tom's warehousemen were clustering round, and from out in the roadway other men came running. The *Hare* continued to settle, but she also began a heavy list away from the shore, which began to lift the shoreside deck. The last of her crewmen jumped. One plummeted into the oily sea within a yard of the wall and three men at once rushed to entangle him in ropes and drag him roughly upon the barnacle-encrusted side of the sea wall. He was bleeding at the face, hands and chest as they wrenched him up over the wall's top and dragged him clear.

The *Hare* did not sink. If she had there could have been some worthwhile salvage because a century of silt had made the sea just beyond the wall shallow enough so that her superstructure, and perhaps more of her, would have been above water. She continued her lazy, slow and inexorable tilt, with the current fighting to get her bow swung clear of land. She went out to deeper water like this, her masts within a few yards of the higher sea-swells, incongruously floating two-thirds heeled over, yielding to the urging of the sea but no longer mindful of the wind.

Lynne had never imagined anything like this. She had heard sea tales all her life, but none that could equal what she was now witnessing. The ship's concave side, like the wet-shiny gut of a huge whale, was awash. Her keel showed its red surface. The vessel was not answering the pull of her fates very well, though. She only drifted on her side about a hundred yards, northward and slightly eastward, past the Harding Company warehouse.

Instead of pitching high against a pitch-blende sky and being crushed to death in frothy and mountainous seas the way all the great ships died in the lithographs Lynne had seen, the *Hare* gave up the ghost without any farewell at all; she simply slid her bow into the water and kept right on going down. There wasn't even the poignant, sudden up-ending of her stern. She simply slid into oblivion without fanfare.

Jay Morgan made a little throaty sound which Lynne heard distinctly, then he walked away from her in the direction of the rescued seamen. Lynne, too, went over there. She felt as though she had just attended the funeral of a close friend, and now she was going to comfort the bereaved.

She saw Fred with a bloody rag to his face. He had been the one dragged up the razor-sharp barnacles of the sea wall. A man was guiding him away even as old Jay Morgan came up, then stopped stock-still looking after his son. Lynne saw Tom and went over to him. The townsmen were carrying three of the *Hare*'s survivors up to Doctor Clavenger's place. Three more leaned for support on shoremen, injured in the hips, ankles or feet. It had been a hazardous jump, but at least those were men who *could* feel pain.

Tom saw Lynne and came over. He looked cold and haggard. 'It was a miracle,' she said. 'Tom, you were God's instrument.' She hugged his arm.

He grinned a trifle ruefully and did not respond, right then, because Jay Morgan came over. He ignored Lynne, for which she felt no resentment at all. In all his long lifetime Jay Morgan had only once been anything but a man's man, and the result of that one brief lapse was his son Fred. Otherwise, and especially now in his age, Jay Morgan was a man for a world and an environment of men.

He said, 'You were right, Dorset. I was wrong. I apologize for saying you were insane.' It was an apology but to Lynne it sounded more like a denunciation.

Tom did not smile nor offer his hand when he replied. 'It could have failed, Mister Morgan. There was a bigger chance of that, than there was of success. But anything at all had to be better than just standing there . . . I'm glad it worked out. Lynne said it was a miracle; God's work.'

Morgan looked down into Lynne's face with scorn struggling against gratitude. 'God is a damned good cannoneer,' he said sharply to her, 'if it was His hand aiming the piece. But my officers and men, and I too, can't very well shake His hand.' The old man pushed out a scarred old fist. 'You have a friend for as long as I last, Mister Dorset.'

Tom shook, pulled free and took Lynne back over to the doorway leading into the Harding warehouse. One of those freakish cross-current winds slammed inland from the furious sea and struck the stone wall beyond which Tom and Lynne made their way to the stair-well leading up to the offices. He clung to her all the way up, and when the door would not yield, he set a thick shoulder to it and the lock broke. As he pushed her through then followed he said, 'Mister Emory will cluck like a mother hen.'

Lynne laughed in the sudden hush of the office, where no wind could reach. 'Let him cluck,' she said, looking over where a piece of the broken brass lay dully glinting where watery daylight slanted inward from out front. 'Tonight locks can't matter.'

He loosened his jacket, pulled off his cap and flung it atop her desk, sank down upon a wall-bench and shoved wet and muddy trouser-legs out their full length. For the past few hours there had been no order, no organization, no sensible sequence, that he had not forced, and for something as ridiculous as a door-lock to wish to end all that, was preposterous. It was fitting that he should walk right through that door.

Lynne went to the little stove to make a fire and set some water to boil. This was where Mister Emory had always brewed his tea — and her father's tea, as well, for many, many, years.

He suddenly ran a set of crooked fingers through his thick mane, looked over at her, and laughed aloud. 'He was right, Lynne. That old bastard downstairs was right; it was a crazy idea by an insane man . . . Do you know — I *saw* it happen exactly the way it happened. Absolutely the same way. While I was standing at the base of the hill after leaving you up at the house, I watched the *Hare* double the sound and enter the roadstead. I saw the whole damned thing, even that old cannon. That's impossible, isn't it?'

She could easily have said it was not at all impossible; she could have said something trite and lofty. Instead she smiled at him. 'You are a hero.'

'Luckier than I've ever been before in my life, Lynne. Hero my foot. Crazy lucky. It could never happen like that again. Not a one of those damned fools died. Young Morgan should have, but even he made it.'

'Mister Morgan,' she began, then started over. 'Fred just may wish he'd never gone to sea when Mister Morgan is finished with him.'

Tom closed his mind to that. He did not know Fred Morgan, he only knew Jay Morgan, and in his mind he had already put the old man into a niche where he would remain. They had nothing in common. Jay Morgan had wealth, and of course power, one went with the other, but Tom Dorset's world, which lacked both, did not really consider wealth and power as the requisites; he looked over at her and said, 'The *Hare* wasn't lost by a fool as much as it simply died from having over-lived its usefulness.'

She wasn't on his same wavelength, so she turned enquiringly to face him. He made a little gesture and explained what he had meant.

'It's the steam cars, the railroads, Lynne, that are going to make the difference from now on, not the clipper ships.'

She did not have that kind of vision. 'The ships will have to bring the goods, Tom.'

He smiled at her. 'No. Everything this country needs is right here. Mines, forests, farms, all of it. Our future, yours and mine, lies inland. You'll see it happen; the companies that don't start buying from inland factories and shipping the commodities to the West Coast, to the Great Plains, to the South and the South-west, are going to die out. If old Morgan wants to replace the *Hare*, let him. The day he puts a quarter of a million dollars into a ship, will be the day Harding Company can invest the same amount of money in trade goods manufactured right here among our own factories and foundries, and beat him hands down in the trading business.'

Tom heaved up to his feet and crossed to her at the little stove. She filled two crockery cups with hot tea and handed him one. She wanted to disagree with him out of a sense of loyalty to tradition. Harding Company had always faced the sea, had always made its money by the sea. But the more she thought and pondered and speculated, the more correct he seemed to be.

She finally gave it up. Her reason was basic enough; when a woman loved a man she wanted him to be right. Whether *time* would prove him right or not was another matter, but a woman's love was not rational, it was emotional. Lynne wanted her man to be right because she loved him, and that was enough . . . for her, if not for the rest of the world.

She lifted the cup and looked up at him. If he talked like this to her father he was going to run head-on into opposition. But that was between *them.* What lay between Tom Dorset and Lynne Harding could not be touched by anything external.

He drank the hot tea and winked at her. 'How much did you say at home?' he asked, as though he knew she would have told her father *some* of it, which she had, of course.

'That I love you. That you asked me to marry you.'

He looked down into the cup. 'What did he say?'

She couldn't remember, and she'd only told her father a few hours ago. But between then and now an entire historic episode had intervened. While she sought for an answer he slowly raised his eyes.

'He didn't approve, did he?'

She abruptly recalled her father's final words. 'He said to bring you to see him when you dropped round this evening . . . Tom; he likes you. Do something for me — give him a chance to have his say.'

He agreed. 'I'd do that anyway.' He finished the tea, absently set the cup aside and strode to the front window to study the tattered sky. When he turned he was solemn. 'If you're ready to buck the wind, we can walk up the hill.'

She was ready to buck the wind; where she felt faint was in the area where she felt most vulnerable: When the man she loved as a parent sat down with the man she loved as a mate.

But it would not wait. She put down her cup and started for the stairway.

Chapter Twenty-two

Mary O'Hara saw them coming, leaning into the uphill climb with the wind opposing each step they took. She called Lynne's father to the parlour window. He went over, still holding the slip of paper in his hand a Morgan warehouseman had delivered moments before.

In his calmest voice Paul Harding said, 'Mrs O'Hara, go make some chocolate, please.'

Mary hesitated. *Her* men had taken strong tea laced with rum, in weather like this. 'Chocolate, sir?'

He nodded without taking his eyes off the oncoming couple. 'Chocolate.'

Mary obediently went to the kitchen, and was not there when Tom steered Lynne to the verandah, up its broad steps, and held the door for her to enter first. She was breathing hard, her cheeks were red, and as her father came from the parlour, her eyes sparkled with pride and trust when she turned from the man at her side to face the older man.

Paul Harding saw that look; it stabbed through him with a clean, quick pain, then that passed and he smiled. 'Morgan sent me a note,' he told them, walking into the entry-hall. 'There aren't many details.' Harding showed them the paper in his hand. 'He said he finally understood something an old shipmaster once told him: That the man with a daughter has a better chance of getting the son he'd want than the man has who raises a son.'

Lynne was surprised. 'Mister Morgan wrote you that?'

Her father passed over the note. 'A man who makes *some* kind of effort, Tom, is worth fifty men who know what should be done and who do nothing.' He offered his hand. Tom shook it without smiling.

'It's done, Mister Harding. It shouldn't have succeeded. It was too insane, as Mister Morgan said, to succeed. But it *did* succeed, and that was nothing but pure luck.' He dropped the older man's hand. 'I'd like to forget it. There is something else, though.'

Lynne finished with the note and looked at her father with a plea in her eyes. He saw the look; they were close enough for him to understand it. He did not offer her his fond smile as he had since childhood when she looked at him like this, instead he knew that a whole lot more than a great and majestic clipper ship had passed into oblivion with this savage storm; the other thing that was gone was something he had always cherished: her need for him. She could never again run to him for comfort when something in her world had hurt her. From this time on she would ran to another man. All he could hope and pray for was that this man would never betray her. But whether that happened or not, Paul Harding was now a stranger in the shadows. He could never again intervene in the life of his girl.

He said, looking at Lynne, that Mary was making chocolate in the kitchen. 'You'll want to sit where it's warm, won't you?'

Tom did not move. 'I want to marry Lynne, Mister Harding. That's the other thing, the *important* thing. I need your approval.'

Paul Harding turned slightly towards the younger man. 'You don't need it, Tom. You need *her* approval.'

'No sir. I need *your* approval.' Tom smiled his gentle smile. 'I have her approval. Mister Harding, I've been married before. I can say from experience it takes more than love. You're a man, you'll understand that.'

Paul Harding, did in fact, understand that, but his daughter didn't, she stood looking from Tom to her father. She did not believe there was anything that two people needed but love, but Lynne Harding was not quite twenty years old, and no matter how quick a woman was to learn many things, there was a whole lot more she could not possibly know at twenty, until she had experienced it, had lived it, and this required time.

Her father said, 'You have my approval. Both of you. Now, let's go have that hot chocolate. You two look half-drowned and chilled to the bone.'

Mary O'Hara was waiting and the first sip of chocolate made Lynne's eyes water. Mary stood across between Lynne's father and Tom Dorset, her face as smooth and expressionless as it could be. When Lynne glanced up, Mary slowly dropped one eyelid and raised it. That was the only acknowledgement that passed between the two women that Lynne's hot chocolate had been fortified with a wee dram of brandy.

The old house groaned as the storm raged outside, and as the shadows had lengthened inside, Mary O'Hara had kindled the lamps. Stinging raindrops splattered against streaked glass, the wild world beyond those stout walls spent its fury, but it was a tribute to the canny builders of the old Harding house, that not a single lamp-flame flickered.

Paul Harding savoured his chocolate, thinking in a way that was entirely new to him. He had known success and tragedy, but very little melancholy in his lifetime, and never this kind of melancholy. He was losing a child and gaining a woman with her personal mate. It was the loss of the child that saddened him. Sitting with them now he could recall with a special vividness the skinned knees, the thorn-scratched arms, the widened dark-liquid eyes looking up in complete trust.

His daughter had been the only thing that he'd had to hold to after the death of Lynne's mother; that had been a long time ago, and he had re-lived something of his best years through his daughter.

He remembered his wife, always, but not as clearly with the passage of time, because his daughter had filled much of the emptiness. And now it was again his turn to accept loss, to live at peace with that which he could not change. To become the stranger in the shadows.

He smiled over at her. She smiled back. In this way they paid tribute to what each had been to the other, and in this way, too, each said good-bye to something. Then Paul Harding asked for the details of the death of the *Hare.*

She told him as she remembered how the ship had foundered with a gaping hole in her bow. It was vivid enough in her mind so that each detail could be related almost as though it were all happening again. Her father and Mary O'Hara listened. Tom sat back, watching her, his eyes gentle, his wide mouth softly smiling. When she had answered her father's questions, and had drawn Tom into the conversation too, they exhausted the topic and her father arose.

He was tired. Not in the way Lynne thought, but he was willing to have her believe it was physical tiredness. He told them he had to go rest, and left the kitchen. Mary O'Hara made them drink more hot chocolate, but Mary O'Hara, like the wind, was something they tolerated without inward response.

Lynne could feel the nearness and the strength of the man across the table. She finished her chocolate and took him back to the parlour, shed her coat and shook loose her hair, then went to stand at a window with him, hand in hand, and look out where the prematurely dying day was mingling with an early gloom.

He peered towards the great trees out back and gave his head a little wag. 'It all came out right,' he said, turning slightly towards her, 'but this morning there wasn't a hint. Suppose it had all turned out just the opposite?'

She impulsively squeezed his fingers. 'I wouldn't have cared . . . But when you left the house to go back down the hill I couldn't stay in here. Tom, it didn't matter how the rest of it ended. That's cruel, I know, but that was exactly how I felt. I didn't even know whether you needed me, down there . . . I just had to go to you, even if I was in the way.'

He raised a gentle hand to her face. 'As long as you can feel that way,' he said, and dropped the hand without finishing the sentence.

She took him back to the sofa near the fireplace. He was tired. Men, for all their strength and size and courage, were quicker to spend their energy. Lynne had made this discovery with her father, but with the older man she had attributed it as much to advancing age as to anything else. Now, she learned from Tom Dorset, that age was only a small part of this unique characteristic.

She was beginning her second education. It would not end until she'd borne his sons, had watched them grow, had seen them leave, one by one; it would not end until she died.

He forced himself to stay alert. When she sat down beside him he twisted to touch her, and while the storm raged beyond the windows where the dimly-discernible orange lamps of Smithsport showed in a huddled cluster down the hill, she lay back and pulled him to her until their lips met.

Then even the storm faded.

She had experienced this before, and more, but it was like an addiction. It kindled its own heat and sustained its own tumult; it created its own demands, its own recurring needs, and for Lynne there was nothing else in her world.

He smelled of spice and sea-salt. His arms were heavy and powerful. She felt herself as part of that strength, as something less forceful, but more enduringly a part of it.

He lifted his head and smiled down into her opened eyes. 'My mother told me once that when I was old enough, to find an athletic girl.'

Lynne smiled in silence. This was the first time he had ever mentioned his mother. She actually knew very little about him. She didn't even know if he came from a large, or a small, family, if he had brothers or sisters; she didn't even know the place where he'd been born and reared, except that it had been the island of Jamaica.

'I don't feel very athletic,' she murmured. 'I feel like bread-dough, all weak and soft.'

He grinned. 'All woman, is how you feel to me. You never have to be any different — if you don't want to be.'

'I don't want to be, Tom.' She raised both arms to his shoulders. 'Do you know that you really ought to go home?'

He didn't argue. 'If I always did the things I ought to do, I probably wouldn't have ever made love to you.'

That puzzled her. 'Why not?'

'You're . . . Well; I'm older. I've had a wife. My kind of a man wants more than a girl usually understands.'

She did not look away even though she felt the blush coming. 'Was I — did I disappoint you?'

He brushed her lips as he shook his head. 'You couldn't do that, Lynne . . . You didn't, and you couldn't.'

She pulled his head down against her and held him. The wind sang overhead without being heard in the parlour. She could feel the deep sweep of his breathing, could withstand the weight of his body. She thought that if some perverse Fate came abruptly and told her to select the moment out of all the moments of her life which she would be willing to re-live throughout all Eternity, this would be the moment.

But an hour later her arms ached and her shoulders felt weighted with more of a burden than they could continue to bear, so she eased upwards and sideways as gently as she could.

Tom did not respond. He was dead weight. She managed to work free and to let him down gently. He was sound asleep. She straightened his body upon the sofa, covered him with an afghan her mother had knitted, and arose to go look out the north-wall window. There were fewer lights, now, down in the village, and the sea, which she could not discern, did not send forth the same wild sounds, which meant that the storm was abating.

She could still hear the wind, but although it was still steady, it did not seem to have quite the same force that it had had before.

By morning, Smithsport would be brightened again by summer sunlight, and hereafter only the *Hound* would ride in the Smithsport roadstead. When there were two sleek hulls, there was pride, but when there was only one tall stand of masts, there was loneliness.

She turned and gazed at the sleeping man,

wondering if he had been right in his predictions for the future of New England trade. If he *was* right, then their life would be as tinged with security as any life ever could be, and if he were wrong, it did not matter because she loved him.

She smiled to herself. While he slept and was beyond her reach, or she was beyond *his* reach, it was easier to be objective. But it *still* did not matter; a woman fell in love when her time arrived. Fate might be able to determine whether she would get the kind of mate other people liked and respected, and whose sagacity would bring ease, but of only one thing did there seem to be a predictable certainty: When a woman's time came, she found a lover.

It didn't sound very wonderful, put that way, but Lynne, at twenty, was more of a woman than Tom Dorset suspected. She knew what had happened between them had had to happen because he came to her at the precise time when she was ready in every way to love him. Love was part instinct, part need, part longing, and part something else — wonder and conviction, part dream and part hope.

She went to him, knelt down and kissed him, once, gently, and the second time a little more insistently. He did not awaken at once, but she persevered until he did awaken, and looked out at her through a soft, warm glow, opened his arms and she drew close, while at the same time she raised a hand to firmly twist the lamp-wick until it drowned in its oil. Only the wind and sounds of the old house were left. And the darkness, which swooped in.

She kissed him and whispered, ‘Go home.’

He kissed her back and answered with a question. ‘Should I, Lynne?’

She reached with both arms to hold him. ‘No.’

He didn’t.

We hope you have enjoyed this Large Print book. Other Thorndike Press or Chivers Press Large Print books are available at your library or directly from the publishers.

For more information about current and upcoming titles, please call or write, without obligation, to:

Thorndike Press
P.O. Box 159
Thorndike, Maine 04986 USA
Tel. (800) 257-5157

OR

Chivers Press Limited
Windsor Bridge Road
Bath BA2 3AX
England
Tel. (0225) 335336

All our Large Print titles are designed for easy reading, and all our books are made to last.

Discover Your Health Behaviors:

A Self-Assessment and Behavior Change Manual

Peggy Blake
Health Education Consultant
Raleigh, North Carolina

Robert Frye
Health Education Consultant
Raleigh, North Carolina

Michael Pejsach
Health Enhancement and Promotion Company
Ames, Iowa

This is an abridged version of *Self-Assessment and Behavior Change Manual* by Peggy Blake, Robert Frye, and Michael Pejsach.

Random House
New York

First Edition

9876543

Published in the United States by Random House, Inc., and simultaneously in Canada by Random House of Canada Limited, Toronto.

ISBN: 394-35824-4

Manufactured in the United States of America

Preface

If you flip through the following pages, you will notice that they contain numerous tests. But why would students want to subject themselves to more tests?

These tests are all *ASSESSMENTS* of yourself, designed to help you become more aware of your thoughts, attitudes, and behaviors as they relate to your health and well-being now and in the future. Social, physical, mental, spiritual, and emotional aspects of health are all related to your total life style, and these assessments help you see how.

In addition to the assessments included in this booklet, a computer-scored and -analyzed test, the *Health Risk Appraisal Program,* is available through Random House. Ask your instructor for information on how to obtain this health-assessment tool. It can provide you with pertinent information to add to and combine with what you learn in the chapters of this book.

In addition to the assessment tests, this book contains exercises to help you apply what you have learned to your own life. These *PERSONAL APPLICATIONS* develop further self-awareness and, in some cases, suggest methods of changing health-related behaviors.

The book concludes with an *ACTION PLAN*, which will help you put your self-knowledge to work. Included in the plan is a chart to help you select a personal behavior to change.

Your instructor may require you to select a few of your own behaviors to change throughout the duration of the course and to write a contract outlining your goals and methods. Therefore, you might want to browse through this book early in your health course to see if there are particular areas you wish or need to work on.

Ultimately, all assessments and personal applications should be useful to you. Optimal health is a matter of maintenance as much as remeditation; so, even if you are not at risk now, you might want to know how to stay that way. Also, behavior-change techniques discussed in any given chapter usually apply to other chapters as well.

This booklet is a condensed version of the *Self-Assessment and Behavior Change Manual,* which contains many more assessments and is available through Random House.

(Please note that the assessments, personal applications, and action plans in this book are all *educational* tools. They are not intended to be diagnostic or prescriptive and should not be interpreted as such. The assessments allow you to find out where you stand in regard to general factors that tend to influence most people's health. But you are not "most people"; you are yourself. If you are concerned about the accuracy or meaning of your results on any assessments, please consult your doctor for clarification. Under no circumstances should the information you gain from this book cause you to disregard any advice you have received from a professional health practitioner.)

Contents

Introduction

Most people your age are probably about as healthy right now as they ever will be. But if *you* choose, you have a good chance of enhancing your current health status and maintaining it for years to come.

The major techniques of staying healthy are anything but obscure. In fact, most amount to little more than "common sense." Controlling weight, eating a balanced diet, exercising, resting, managing stress, avoiding unnecessary risks (for example, drugs and fast driving), and many other wellness-promoting activities have been taught to us since we were old enough to learn.

We might not know all of the technical facts about health, but most of us are at least generally aware of which of our behaviors are health-promoting and which are not. So, why don't we practice what we know?

One reason, for a person your age, is that you probably feel and look relatively healthy; therefore, you have no motivation to change your immediate life style in order to enhance your health. Or perhaps you take your health for granted and assume little responsibility yourself: You feel that the cafeteria dietitian is responsible for getting the proper nutrients to you, the town water department is in charge of the safety of your water, the school physical education department organizes your physical activity, the student infirmary is there to make minor repairs on you when necessary, the police have the job of regulating your driving behavior and assuring your general safety, and so forth.

The following points might *not* be apparent to you:

- Your body, because of its youth and resilience, can take abuse now that it cannot handle later, but the health-related habits you form now are likely to stay with you.

- Health problems often result from cumulative abuses; in other words, what may not cause much harm if done only a few times can be dangerous if continued over a period of time.

- You might not be as healthy right now as you think, or you might not be aware of how much better you *could* feel and look; optimal health is not the same as "getting by."

- As you age, your responsibility for all aspects of your life tends to become greater, including your responsibility for your own health and that of others, but you could be unprepared to handle that responsibility if you have had little practice.

- Health problems in modern times have to a great extent become the result of *personally chosen* life styles rather than of "natural" and essentially uncontrollable forces.

In summary, your health, now and later, depends in large part on your willingness to *assume responsibility now* and your motivation to *act now*, even though you might think that you look and feel fine. This chapter will help you to determine where you stand in regard to these important factors of motivation and willingness to assume responsibility.

Self-Actualization Inventory

Overview

A self-actualized person is one who is meeting all of his or her needs. Few of us are at that point. However, awareness of the degree to which we are successful in meeting our needs, and awareness of which needs remain, can help us to plan specific actions through which we can approach true self-actualization. The following assessment will help with this process.

Directions

Circle the number that best characterizes you for each of the descriptions below. Use the following criteria:

1 = Never

2 = Almost never

3 = Sometimes

4 = Almost always

5 = Always

Assessment

How often do you feel that you possess the following characteristics:

1. You have a clear understanding of reality.	1	2	3	4	5
2. You have the ability to handle uncertainty.	1	2	3	4	5
3. You have the ability to respond in a spontaneous fashion.	1	2	3	4	5
4. You are comfortable with your surroundings.	1	2	3	4	5
5. You are creative.	1	2	3	4	5
6. You accept yourself.	1	2	3	4	5
7. You are independent.	1	2	3	4	5
8. You are able to give love to others.	1	2	3	4	5
9. You can deal with problems of others and are not self-centered.	1	2	3	4	5
10. You have a zest for living.	1	2	3	4	5
11. You enjoy others but also enjoy serene, alone, and quiet situations.	1	2	3	4	5
12. You have a purpose in life.	1	2	3	4	5

Scoring Add *all* the circled numbers. Your score is the total.

Total ___________

Interpretation

40–60 = Self-actualization has virtually been reached

30–39 = Self-actualization is being approached

20–29 = Average self-actualization

<20 = Below-average self-actualization

The Self-Actualization Inventory, although not reliable for all mental-health areas, does give you an opportunity to take a look at where you are in terms of Maslow's developmental framework.

Abraham Maslow, through his studies of *healthy* personalities, theorized that individuals grow from needing the basics to needing fulfillment through a variety of experiences, very often outside of *self.* A person who is not approaching self-actualization may not be meeting his or her higher needs and hence may experience such things as psychological stress, illness, anxiety, a lack of motivation, and boredom.

The following figure shows Maslow's Hierarchy of Needs. According to Maslow, people tend to work on fulfilling needs at their own level, and most of us are not interested in or successful at fulfilling needs that are much further up in the hierarchy than where we are.

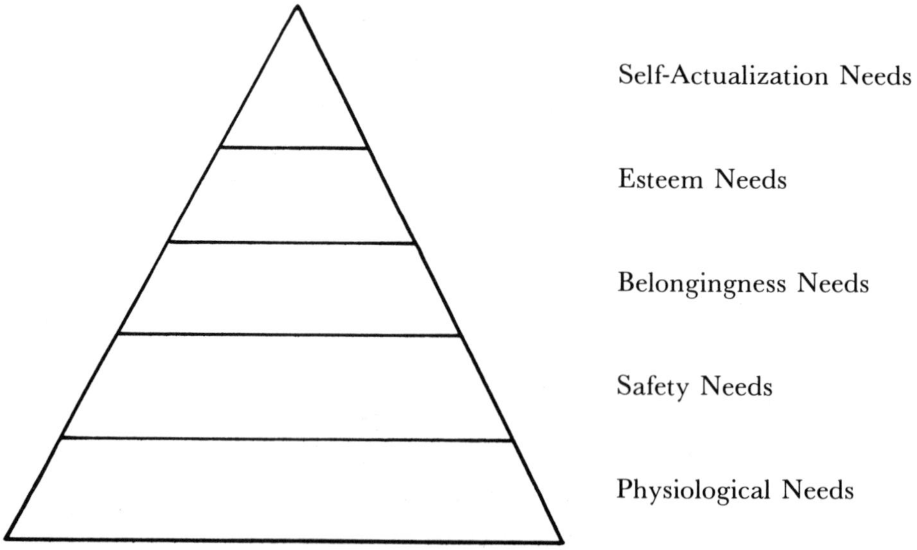

You might notice that health per se is not on the list of needs. This means that few of us strive to be healthy, for its own sake. In fact, we seem willing to risk our own health in order to accomplish fulfillment of the needs that are important to us at our own given level of the hierarchy. An example is the person who partakes of alcohol in order to maintain status in his peer group, even though he may know that alcohol is unhealthy.

If you agree with Maslow that his hierarchy of needs reflects the motivating forces behind most human behavior, and if you agree that health, even if it is not a basic need, is necessary to achieve fulfillment of all needs, then you will agree that *the best course of behavior is to search for healthy ways of meeting our needs.* For example, a person might seek another peer group which does not emphasize alcohol use as a criterion of membership, or might develop assertiveness skills so that membership could be maintained without consuming alcohol.

Personal Application

In the following chart, the needs from Maslow's hierarchy are listed in the first column. Read each need and then determine how you can meet this need in an unhealthy way. Record your answer in column 2. Then determine how you can meet this need in a healthy way. Record your answer in column 3.

NEEDS	UNHEALTHY METHOD OF MEETING NEED	HEALTHY METHOD OF MEETING NEED
Physiological needs		
Sleep	____________	____________
Water	____________	____________
Food	____________	____________
Safety needs		
Security	____________	____________
Safety	____________	____________
Belongingness needs		
Affiliation with others	____________	____________
Acceptance	____________	____________
Belongingness	____________	____________

Esteem needs		
Achievement	______	______
Competence	______	______
Approval	______	______
Recognition	______	______
Self-Actualization needs		
Pursuit of knowledge	______	______
Beauty	______	______
Creativity	______	______

Now answer the following questions.

- Do you tend to satisfy your needs in healthy ways or unhealthy ways? Explain.

- Would you like to change the way you satisfy a need? Explain.

- Why do people often take self-defeating measures to satisfy their needs?

Locus of Control

Overview

Some people seem to feel that their own health is beyond their control. Others are overly confident that they are completely in charge and are surprised when they become ill. These different outlooks reflect different upbringings, different personal experiences, and different levels of health education. This questionnaire will help you to determine the sort of outlook you have and help you decide whether you might want to increase your responsibility in determining your own health.

Directions

For each statement in the following questionnaire, circle the letter that best reflects how well you feel the statement represents your own views. Answer honestly. There are no right or wrong answers.

Assessment

	AGREE	UNSURE	DISAGREE
1. If the government has approved a drug and my doctor prescribes it for me, I don't need to question whether I should take it.	a	b	c
2. I can have an effect on reducing environmental pollutants produced by private businesses and industries.	a	b	c
3. By the time I might suffer from the long-term effects of unsafe health practices, medical researchers probably will have found a cure for them.	a	b	c
4. If none of my friends or roommates regularly exercised, I probably wouldn't either.	a	b	c
5. From my experience, people who never get sick are simply lucky.	a	b	c
6. As long as I have a good health and disability insurance policy, I will have little reason to be concerned about my health.	a	b	c
7. If my physician doesn't tell me to quit smoking, lose weight, or get more exercise, then there is no reason why I should consider doing these things.	a	b	c

	AGREE	UNSURE	DISAGREE
8. Since we all have to die of something sometime, there is no point in trying to control our own health status.	a	b	c
9. I have little say over my nutrition since I can't control what food producers, manufacturers, processors, and preparers do to food.	a	b	c
10. Most people, including myself, are basically healthy or basically unhealthy, and there is little way to change that.	a	b	c
11. Until medical science has advanced further, there is no way I can understand and prevent the causes of ill health.	a	b	c
12. Since the world is full of odd diseases that seem to strike unpredictably, there is no reason why anybody should spend a lot of time and energy trying to stay healthy.	a	b	c
13. When I set health goals for myself, I feel that I can usually achieve them.	a	b	c
14. If a medical authority gave me advice or directives, I would probably challenge him or her or ask questions.	a	b	c
15. If I felt there were something wrong with me but friends and relatives all said I looked and acted fine, I probably would seek a professional opinion anyway.	a	b	c

Scoring

If your answer is the same as the answer in the "Response" column, give yourself one point in each space on the line corresponding to the statement. For example, if your response for number 1 is c, then you would place 1 point in the "General Points" column and 1 point in the "Reliance on Others Points" column.

STATEMENT	RESPONSE	GENERAL POINTS	FATE POINTS	RELIANCE ON OTHERS POINTS	PERSONAL EFFICACY POINTS
1.	c	______		______	
2.	a	______			______
3.	c	______		______	
4.	c	______			______
5.	c	______	______		

STATEMENT	RESPONSE	GENERAL POINTS	FATE POINTS	RELIANCE ON OTHERS POINTS	PERSONAL EFFICACY POINTS
6.	c	______		______	
7.	c	______		______	
8.	c	______	______		
9.	c	______			______
10.	c	______	______		
11.	c	______			______
12.	c	______	______		
13.	a	______			______
14.	a	______		______	
15.	a	______		______	
	TOTALS	______	______	______	______

Interpretation

If you scored 15 or close to it in "General Points," you have a very strong tendency to acknowledge your own capacity and responsibility for determining your own health. If your score is near zero, you probably feel pretty helpless, possibly even apathetic, about the influence you have on your own health.

The statements to which you have responded also can be examined with reference to several areas of control over health status. For example, statements 5, 8, 10, and 12 deal primarily with your attitude toward "fate." Interestingly, if you believe strongly that fate controls your health, it probably will! You would be unlikely to intervene in a process over which you had no control.

Statements 1, 3, 6, 7, 14, and 15 indicate the extent of your "reliance on others" for your well-being. A low score for this set of statements indicates that you don't necessarily leave your health to fate, you leave it to other people! You might, therefore, want to examine the sources of these beliefs and decide for yourself if they are really useful.

The remaining statements concern the degree of your belief in your own "personal efficacy." Thus, a low score on statements 2, 4, 9, 11, and 13 might say that you feel as if you personally have little power to cause change, even if you think that change is possible and desirable. This attitude could be related to your own self-confidence, your opinion of your own will power, your conception of the potential political power of individuals—especially yourself—or even your confidence in your ability to understand new information.

The importance of this assessment lies not so much in your responses to individual questions as in any general trend that may be revealed. For example, if you had practiced every reasonable precaution but still caught a cold that had been "going around," you might as well ascribe it to "fate" as anything else. But if you blame fate for every health problem that exists, you probably are not doing yourself any favor! The more strongly you believe that you are in charge of your health and the more willing you are to take action in your own behalf, the better off you will be.

Personal Application

An internal locus of control is very important in promoting and maintaining your own health. Sometimes it is necessary to rely on others—for example, we rely on others to inspect the kitchens of the restaurants we eat in. But for the most part it is up to each of us to initiate our own behaviors to enhance our well-being. Sometimes we don't realize how many choices we make about our health behaviors.

In order to give yourself an overview of your own role in affecting your health, complete those of the following statements that apply to you. Answer honestly!

- I choose to jog or exercise regularly because ______________________________

  ____ .
- I choose not to jog or exercise regularly because __________________________

  ____ .
- I choose to eat junk food because ____

  ____ .
- I choose not to eat junk food because ____________________________________

  ____ .
- I choose to skip breakfast often because __________________________________

  ____ .
- I choose not to skip breakfast often because ______________________________

  ____ .
- I choose to have regular dental check-ups because _________________________

  ____ .
- I choose not to have regular dental check-ups because _____________________

  ____ .
- I choose to express my emotions and not to bottle them up because _______

  ____ .
- I choose not to express my emotions and to bottle them up because _______

  ____ .

- I choose to take time to relax because______________________________
____.
- I choose not to take time to relax because __________________________
____.
- I choose to smoke cigarettes because ______________________________
____.
- I choose not to smoke cigarettes because __________________________
____.
- I choose to drink alcohol because ________________________________
____.
- I choose not to drink alcohol because______________________________
____.
- I choose to use seat belts in cars because __________________________
____.
- I choose not to use seat belts in cars because ________________________
____.
- I choose to develop a variety of close interpersonal relationships because
____.
- I choose not to develop a variety of close interpersonal relationships because
____.
- I choose to be overweight/underweight because________________________
____.
- I choose not to be overweight/underweight because ____________________
____.
- I choose to get enough sleep at night because________________________
____.
- I choose not to get enough sleep at night because ____________________
____.
- I choose to drive after drinking because_____________________________
____.
- I choose not to drive after drinking because _________________________
____.

- I choose to seek help when I feel depressed because ______________________ ______________________.
- I choose not to seek help when I feel depressed because ______________________ ______________________.
- I choose to worry excessively about things because______________________ ______________________.
- I choose not to worry excessively about things because ______________________ ______________________.
- I choose to prepare (or select) nutritionally balanced meals because. ______ ______________________.
- I choose not to prepare (or select) nutritionally balanced meals because___ ______________________.
- I choose to avoid situations where I might meet and form relationships with persons of the opposite sex because ______________________ ______________________.
- I choose not to avoid situations where I might meet and form relationships with persons of the opposite sex because ______________________ ______________________.

Now consider these questions:

- Do you see any patterns in your responses—for example, lack of will power, ignorance, fear, laziness?
- Are there any behaviors in the list that you feel you absolutely couldn't change if you chose to?
- Do you believe that the person most responsible for your health is you?

The remaining chapters in this book should give you insights into your own behavior, lead you to methods of changing your behavior, and acquaint you with additional information about your health and its value. But the bottom line is: It's up to you!

Assertiveness Scale

Overview

This assessment will give you an idea of your own level of assertiveness. As strange as it may seem at first, most of us are not highly skilled in assertiveness. Many of us, for example, have a difficult time saying "no" in response to another's suggestion, even when "no" is what we would prefer to say. As a result, in our effort to sustain or promote comfort in interpersonal situations, we end up doing things, sometimes risky things, that we wouldn't otherwise do. Another aspect of assertiveness is being able to express our needs and opinions. Many jobs require a high level of assertiveness.

Directions

Using the code given below, indicate how characteristic or descriptive of you each of the following statements is.*

+3 Very characteristic of me, extremely descriptive

+2 Rather characteristic of me, quite descriptive

+1 Somewhat characteristic of me, slightly descriptive

–1 Somewhat uncharacteristic of me, slightly nondescriptive

–2 Rather uncharacteristic of me, quite nondescriptive

–3 Very uncharacteristic of me, extremely nondescriptive

Assessment

______ 1. Most people seem to be more aggressive and assertive than I am.

______ 2. I have hesitated to make or accept dates because of "shyness."

______ 3. When the food served at a restaurant is not done to my satisfaction, I complain about it to the waiter or waitress.

______ 4. I am careful to avoid hurting other people's feelings, even when I feel I have been injured.

______ 5. If a salesperson has gone to considerable trouble to show me merchandise that is not quite suitable, I have a difficult time in saying "No."

______ 6. When I am asked to do something, I insist upon knowing why.

______ 7. There are times when I look for a good, vigorous argument.

______ 8. I strive to get ahead as well as most people in my position.

______ 9. To be honest, people often take advantage of me.

______ 10. I enjoy starting conversations with new acquaintances and strangers.

______ 11. I often don't know what to say to attractive persons of the opposite sex.

______ 12. I will hesitate to make phone calls to business establishments and institutions.

______ 13. I would rather apply for a job or for admission to a college by writing letters than by going through with personal interviews.

______ 14. I find it embarrassing to return merchandise.

______ 15. If a close and respected relative were annoying me, I would smother my feelings rather than express my annoyance.

______ 16. I have avoided asking questions for fear of sounding stupid.

______ 17. During an argument I am sometimes afraid that I will get so upset that I will shake all over.

______ 18. If a famed and respected lecturer makes a statement that I think is incorrect, I will have the audience hear my point of view as well.

______ 19. When I have done something important or worthwhile, I manage to let others know about it.

______ 20. I am open and frank about my feelings.

______ 21. If someone has been spreading false and bad stories about me, I see him or her as soon as possible to "have a talk" about it.

______ 22. I often have a hard time saying "No."

______ 23. I tend to bottle up my emotions rather than make a scene.

______ 24. I complain about poor service in a restaurant and elsewhere.

______ 25. When I am given a compliment, I sometimes just don't know what to say.

______ 26. If a couple near me in a theater or at a lecture were conversing rather loudly, I would ask them to be quiet or take their conversation elsewhere.

______ 27. Anyone attempting to push ahead of me in a line is in for a good battle.

______ 28. I am quick to express an opinion.

______ 29. There are times when I just can't say anything.

Scoring

To score this scale, first change the signs (+ or −) for items 1, 2, 4, 5, 9, 11, 12, 13, 14, 15, 16, 17, 19, 23, 24, 26, and 30. Next, add up all the plus items and all the minus items. Now subtract the minus total from the plus total.

Score ___________

Interpretation The highest possible score is +90; the lowest is −90. The higher the score, the more assertive your behavior is. When this scale was administered to college students, they averaged 0.30. However, more important than someone else's average is your own score. How assertive are you?

**Source:* Spencer A. Rathus, "A 30-Item Schedule for Assessing Assertive Behavior," *Behavior Therapy* 4 (1973).398–406. Reprinted by permission.

Personal Application

Assertiveness is different from both passiveness and aggressiveness. It is not halfway between these; it is different altogether. Passiveness means acquiescing to another's demands regardless of the consequences to yourself. Aggressiveness means attempting to force your desires on another in order to satisfy your own purposes and without consideration of the rights of the other. When you are assertive, you respect the rights of others the same as you expect others to respect yours.

These three types of behaviors are often expressed verbally, as the following examples illustrate.

Situation: You and your roommate are taking the same psychology course. An exam is scheduled for tomorrow. You have been keeping up with your studying during the course; your roommate has not. Even though you feel reasonably prepared, you plan to devote the entire evening to review. Your roommate enters early in the evening and states, "Hey, you've got to help me get ready for this psych test. I'm totally lost. If you could ask me questions for two or three hours tonight, I think I'll get by tomorrow." You respond:

Passive *"Well, uh, I guess I could."*

Aggressive *"You should have thought about studying a long time ago. I'm not wasting my time on you."*

Assertive *"I know that you don't feel prepared for the exam, but I've got to review for it myself and don't have enough time to help you out now. I'm afraid you'll have to find somebody else this time."*

Notice that although the assertive response is tactful, it leaves no room for doubt about the speaker's intentions. It acknowledges the other person's needs and desires and also affirms those of the speaker.

Here is another example of the three different responses.

Situation: While you are walking across campus on a Friday afternoon, a friend stops you and suggests the two of you round up a few other people and go out for beers that evening. You have had a busy week and would like some recreation, but sitting in a smoky tavern drinking beer doesn't sound appealing. You say to your friend:

Passive *"Well, if that's what you want to do—OK."* or *"That sounds great, but I don't have any money. Maybe next time."*

Aggressive *"That would be a dumb way to waste time. Why do so many people think it's fun to get bombed?"*

Assertive *"I'd like to do something together this evening, too, but I'm not really in the mood for drinking. I hear they're keeping the gym open late for anyone who wants to play basketball. Why don't we get some people together for a game?"*

There are four good rules to remember about being assertive:

1. Be tactful.
2. Recognize and acknowledge the other person's needs and desires.
3. Recognize and affirm your own needs and desires.
4. Don't be assertive just to prove you can be. Save your assertiveness for those times and situations in which it is appropriate—for example, when the issue at hand is important to you.

Now answer the following questions.

- Think of a situation that occurred in the last week in which you wish you had been assertive. How could you have responded more assertively?

- Have you ever known an assertive (not aggressive) person? What is your opinion of that person?

- Can you think of any situations that might occur in the near future which would lend themselves to assertiveness on your part? Write some sample assertive responses you might make.

- Have you ever found yourself using drugs, alcohol, or tobacco when you would have preferred not to but were not sufficiently assertive? If so, write some sample assertive responses you could have used.

Depression Assessment

Overview All of us have felt depressed at times; this is normal. But lengthy or severe depression can affect all facets of our lives. This assessment will help you examine the amount of depression in your life.

Directions Read each statement. Decide whether at present you feel this way None or A Little of the Time; Some of the Time; Good Part of the Time; or Most or All of the Time. Check the box that applies to you.

Assessment

	NONE *OR* A LITTLE OF THE TIME	SOME OF THE TIME	GOOD PART OF THE TIME	MOST *OR* ALL OF THE TIME
1. I feel down-hearted, blue, and sad.				
2. Morning is when I feel the best.				
3. I have crying spells or feel like it.				
4. I have trouble sleeping through the night.				
5. I eat as much as I used to.				
6. I enjoy looking at, talking to, and being with attractive women/men.				
7. I notice that I am losing weight.				
8. I have trouble with constipation.				
9. My heart beats faster than usual.				
10. I get tired for no reason.				
11. My mind is as clear as it used to be.				
12. I find it easy to do the things I used to do.				
13. I am restless and can't keep still.				
14. I feel hopeful about the future.				
15. I am more irritable than usual.				
16. I find it easy to make decisions.				
17. I feel that I am useful and needed.				
18. My life is pretty full.				
19. I feel that others would be better off if I were dead.				
20. I still enjoy the things I used to do.				

Scoring In each line of the chart below, circle the number that corresponds to your answer. Then add all of the circled numbers (disregard columns).

	NONE *OR* A LITTLE OF THE TIME	SOME OF THE TIME	GOOD PART OF THE TIME	MOST *OR* ALL OF THE TIME
1. I feel down-hearted, blue, and sad.	1	2	3	4
2. Morning is when I feel the best.	4	3	2	1
3. I have crying spells or feel like it.	1	2	3	4
4. I have trouble sleeping through the night.	1	2	3	4
5. I eat as much as I used to.	4	3	2	1
6. I enjoy looking at, talking to, and being with attractive women/men.	4	3	2	1
7. I notice that I am losing weight.	1	2	3	4
8. I have trouble with constipation.	1	2	3	4
9. My heart beats faster than usual.	1	2	3	4
10. I get tired for no reason.	1	2	3	4
11. My mind is as clear as it used to be.	4	3	2	1
12. I find it easy to do the things I used to.	4	3	2	1
13. I am restless and can't keep still.	1	2	3	4
14. I feel hopeful about the future.	4	3	2	1
15. I am more irritable than usual.	1	2	3	4
16. I find it easy to make decisions.	4	3	2	1
17. I feel that I am useful and needed.	4	3	2	1
18. My life is pretty full.	4	3	2	1
19. I feel that others would be better off if I were dead.	1	2	3	4
20. I still enjoy the things I used to do.	4	3	2	1

Total __________

Interpretation

50 = Within normal ranges
50–59 = Minimal to mild depression
60–69 = Moderate to marked depression
70 = Severe to extreme depression

Personal Application

Depression can be caused or made worse by worrying about things—and often our worries are not even fully logical ones.

In column 1 list three things you worry about. Then for each of these worries determine the worst possible happening. Record this in column 2. Then estimate how likely it is that the worst will occur. Record your estimate on the scale in column 3. Now determine what you can do to prevent the worst from occurring. Record your answer in column 4. This kind of logical thinking can help fight depression.

WORRIES (1)	THE WORST POSSIBLE HAPPENING (2)	LIKELINESS OF THE WORST OCCURRING (3)	HOW I CAN PREVENT THE WORST (4)
		impossible certain 0 5 10	
		impossible certain 0 5 10	
		impossible certain 0 5 10	

Study your responses. What did you learn?

The Glazer-Stress Control Life-Style Questionnaire

Overview

Is stress good or bad? It all depends on the amount of stress and how you handle it. Without stress, we would have little reason to change our lives. We would not grow and develop or reach our optimal level of functioning. However, most of us do not relish an overload of stress. It seems that a moderate amount of stress, successfully dealt with, is an important key to physical and mental well-being.

Stress has been correlated statistically with a number of physical and mental problems, including cancer, heart disease, ulcers, and depression. While it is difficult to prove absolutely that stress can cause these disorders, everyday experience (''butterflies'' in the stomach, blushing, sweaty palms, insomnia, etc.) suggests that stress is indeed related to both physical and mental phenomena.

It appears that the higher the level of stress an individual experiences, the greater the likelihood of illness. Therefore, it is valuable to know what types of life events tend to cause stress and what can be done to control the causes and to alleviate potentially negative consequences. The ability to anticipate or recognize stress combined with specific strategies for coping with it help one avoid self-destructive responses such as drug use, depression, or irrational behavior, and may help prevent physical illness.

The following assessment tests and activities will help you to recognize or anticipate causes of stress in your life, to measure your level of stress, and to design actions you can take to prevent illness.

In the 1970s two cardiologists, Friedman and Rosenman, studied the relationship between excess stress and heart disease. They divided their patients into two groups: Type A and Type B. Type A is characterized as aggressive and competitive. Type B is more relaxed. The cardiologists concluded that Type A behavior is a major contributing factor in the development of heart disease. The purpose of the following test* is to help you determine whether you are more Type A or more Type B.

Directions

Each scale below is composed of a pair of adjectives or phrases separated by a series of dashes. Each pair has been chosen to represent two kinds of contrasting behavior. Each of us belongs somewhere along the line between the two extremes. For each item on the test, place a check mark at the point where you think you belong.

Assessment

	1 2 3 4 5 6 7	
1. Doesn't mind leaving things temporarily unfinished	— — — — — — —	Must get things finished once started

	1 2 3 4 5 6 7	
2. Calm and unhurried about appointments	_ _ _ _ _ _ _	Never late for appointments
3. Not competitive	_ _ _ _ _ _ _	Highly competitive
4. Listens well, lets others finish speaking	_ _ _ _ _ _ _	Anticipates others in conversation (nods, interrupts, finishes sentences for the other)
5. Never in a hurry, even when pressured	_ _ _ _ _ _ _	Always in a hurry
6. Able to wait calmly	_ _ _ _ _ _ _	Uneasy when waiting
7. Easygoing	_ _ _ _ _ _ _	Always going full speed ahead
8. Takes one thing at a time	_ _ _ _ _ _ _	Tries to do more than one thing at a time, thinks about what to do next
9. Slow and deliberate in speech	_ _ _ _ _ _ _	Vigorous and forceful in speech (uses a lot of gestures)
10. Concerned with satisfying himself, not others	_ _ _ _ _ _ _	Wants recognition by others for a job well done
11. Slow doing things	_ _ _ _ _ _ _	Fast doing things (eating, walking, etc.)
12. Easygoing	_ _ _ _ _ _ _	Hard driving
13. Expresses feelings openly	_ _ _ _ _ _ _	Holds feelings in
14. Has a large number of interests	_ _ _ _ _ _ _	Few interests outside work
15. Satisfied with job	_ _ _ _ _ _ _	Ambitious, wants quick advancement on job
16. Never sets own deadlines	_ _ _ _ _ _ _	Often sets own deadlines
17. Feels limited responsibility	_ _ _ _ _ _ _	Always feels responsible
18. Never judges things in terms of numbers	_ _ _ _ _ _ _	Often judges performance in terms of numbers (how many, how much)
19. Casual about work	_ _ _ _ _ _ _	Takes work very seriously (works weekends, brings work home)
20. Not very precise	_ _ _ _ _ _ _	Very precise (careful about detail)

Scoring Assign a value from 1 to 7 for each score. Total them.

Interpretation

110–140 = Type A_1 — If you are in this category, and especially if you are over 40 and smoke, you are likely to have a high risk of developing cardiac illness.

80–109 = Type A_2 — You are in the direction of being cardiac prone, but your risk is not as high as the A_1. You should, nevertheless, pay careful attention to the advice given to all Type As.

60–79 = Type AB — You are a mixture of A and B patterns. This is a healthier pattern than either A_1 or A_2, but you have the potential for slipping into A behavior and you should recognize this.

30–59 = Type B_2 — Your behavior is on the less-cardiac-prone end of the spectrum. You are generally relaxed and cope adequately with stress.

20–29 = Type B_1 — You tend to the extreme of non-cardiac traits. Your behavior expresses few of the reactions associated with cardiac disease.

This test will give you some idea of where you stand in regard to your susceptibility to cardiac illness. The higher you score, the more cardiac-prone you tend to be. Remember, though, even B persons occasionally slip into A behavior, and any of these patterns can change over time.

**Source:* Raymond W. Bootner, "The Glazer-Stress Control Life-Style Questionnaire: A Short Rating Scale as a Potential Measure of Pattern of Behavior," *Journal of Chronic Diseases*, *22* (1969). Reprinted by permission of Pergamon Press, Inc.

Personal Application

Some people believe that identifying oneself or others as Type A or Type B is unrealistic. They believe that a healthy life style incorporates both A and B behaviors as they are appropriate to different situations.

Circle Type A or Type B as the behavior you think would be most appropriate in the following situations:

	TYPE A	TYPE B
1. You are boarding an airplane. You would prefer your pilot to be . . .	A	B
2. You are discussing with your mother the fact that you don't have enough money for next semester's tuition. You would perfer that your mother be . . .	A	B
3. You are waiting in a long line at a bank in order to cash a check. You would prefer that the teller be . . .	A	B

		TYPE A	TYPE B
4.	You go out to a fine restaurant with a date. You would prefer your date to be . . .	A	B
5.	You go to a dentist because you have a painful toothache. You would prefer that your dentist be . . .	A	B

Now review your answers to questions 1 through 5. Did you always circle the same type? Was it always easy to choose a type? Do you agree that behavior should be appropriate to the situation, or do you think consistency of behavior is best at all times?

In the chart below, list three customary behaviors of your own that you think might *not* be appropriate to the situations in which they usually occur. Try to choose behaviors that fit in the A or B categories.

BEHAVIOR	SITUATION
1.	
2.	
3.	

Consider the following questions: How difficult would it be for you to change these behaviors? Is it worth a try?

The Modified Mast

Overview

Do you use drugs? What do you think of when you hear the word "drugs"? You might think of substances such as marijuana, amphetamines, and/or alcohol. But what about cigarettes, caffeine and related chemicals (in chocolate, coffee, some soft drinks, and tea), cold medications, aspirin, vitamins, and birth-control pills? Considering all these substances, how many of your friends and/or relatives use drugs? Are they using them responsibly? Or are the drugs affecting their life styles in a negative fashion, altering their everyday functioning and relationships? Are there any drugs that affect an individual's life in a positive way? What are your personal beliefs and attitudes regarding drugs? What effect do your drug-related behaviors have on your health and well-being?

The purpose of The Modified Mast* is to help you analyze your behaviors related to alcohol and drug use. Here the term "drugs" is used in the narrow sense. It refers to marijuana, opiates or other narcotics, barbiturates and other sedative-hypnotics, amphetamines and other related stimulants, and hallucinogens such as LSD.

Directions

For each of the following questions, circle "yes" or "no."

Assessment

1. Do you feel you are a normal drinker? YES NO ______
2. Do you feel you are a normal drug user? YES NO ______
3. Have you ever awakened in the morning after some drinking the night before and found that you could not remember a part of the evening before? YES NO ______
4. Have you ever awakened the morning after taking some drugs the night before and found that you could not remember a part of the evening before? YES NO ______
5. Do your spouse, friends, or parents ever worry or complain about your drinking? YES NO ______
6. Do your spouse, friends, or parents ever worry or complain about your drug use? YES NO ______
7. Can you stop drinking without a struggle after one or two times? YES NO ______
8. Can you stop taking a drug without a struggle after one or two times? YES NO ______
9. Do you ever feel bad about your drinking? YES NO ______
10. Do you ever feel bad about your drug use? YES NO ______

11. Do friends or relatives think you are a normal drinker? YES NO ______
12. Do friends or relatives think you are a normal drug user? YES NO ______
13. Are you always able to stop drinking when you want to? YES NO ______
14. Are you always able to stop taking drugs when you want to? YES NO ______
15. Have you ever attended a meeting of Alcoholics Anonymous (AA) because of *your own* drinking? YES NO ______
16. Have you ever attended a meeting of Synanon or any other self-help drug group because of *your own* drug use? YES NO ______
17. Have you gotten into fights when drinking? YES NO ______
18. Have you gotten into fights while using drugs? YES NO ______
19. Has drinking ever created problems with you and your spouse? YES NO ______
20. Has taking drugs ever created problems with you and your spouse? YES NO ______
21. Has your spouse, family member, or close friend ever gone to anyone for help about your drinking? YES NO ______
22. Has your spouse, family member, or close friend ever gone to anyone for help about your drug use? YES NO ______
23. Have you ever lost friends or girlfriends/boyfriends because of your drinking? YES NO ______
24. Have you ever lost friends or girlfriends/boyfriends because of your drug use? YES NO ______
25. Have you ever gotten into trouble at work because of drinking? YES NO ______
26. Have you ever gotten into trouble at work because of drug use? YES NO ______
27. Have you ever lost a job because of drinking? YES NO ______
28. Have you ever lost a job because of drug use? YES NO ______
29. Have you ever neglected your obligations, your family, or your work for two or more days in a row because you were drinking? YES NO ______

30. Have you ever neglected your obligations, your family, or your work for two or more days in a row because you were taking drugs? YES NO ______

31. Do you ever drink before noon? YES NO ______

32. Do you ever use drugs before noon? YES NO ______

33. Have you been told you have liver trouble? cirrhosis? YES NO ______

34. Have you been told you have liver trouble? hepatitis? YES NO ______

35. Have you ever had delirium tremens (DTs), severe shaking, heard voices, or seen things that weren't there after heavy drinking? YES NO ______

36. Have you ever had severe shaking, cramps, sweating, excessive nervousness, dizziness, trouble with your vision, nausea, vomiting, loss of sleep, convulsions, itching, diarrhea, chills, goose flesh, loss of energy, severe depression, "flashbacks," heard voices, or seen things that weren't there after heavy drug use? YES NO ______

37. Have you ever gone to anyone for help about your drinking? YES NO ______

38. Have you ever gone to anyone for help about your drug use? YES NO ______

39. Have you ever been in a hospital because of your drinking? YES NO ______

40. Have you ever been in a hospital because of your drug use? YES NO ______

41. Have you ever been a patient in a psychiatric hospital or on a psychiatric ward of a general hospital where drinking was part of the problem? YES NO ______

42. Have you ever been a patient in a psychiatric hospital or on a psychiatric ward of a general hospital where drug use was part of the problem? YES NO ______

43. Have you ever been seen at a psychiatric or mental-health clinic, or gone to a doctor, social worker, or clergyman for help with an emotional problem in which drinking had played a part? YES NO ______

44. Have you ever been seen at a psychiatric or mental-health clinic, or gone to a doctor, social worker, or clergyman for help with an emotional problem in which drug use had played a part? YES NO ______
45. (a) Have you ever been arrested, even for a few hours, because of drunken behavior? YES NO ______
    (b) If yes, how many times? ______
46. (a) Have you ever been arrested, even for a few hours, because of behavior due to drug use? YES NO ______
    (b) If yes, how many times? ______
47. (a) Have you been arrested for drunken driving or driving after drinking? YES NO ______
    (b) If yes, how many times? ______
48. (a) Have you ever been arrested for sale, possession, or use of drugs? YES NO ______
    (b) If yes, how many times? ______

**Source:* M. B. Cannell and A. R. Favazza, "Screening for Drug Abuse Among College Students: Modification of the Michigan Alcoholism Screening Test," *Journal of Drug Education, 8* (1978), 119–123. © 1978 Baywood Publishing Company, Inc. Reprinted by permission of Dr. Cannell, who is in the private practice of psychiatry in San Diego, CA, and Dr. Favazza, who is a Professor of Psychiatry at the University of Missouri—Columbia.

Scoring Using the following chart, list your points beside your responses on the assessment. For question 1, for example, if you answered "no," record 2 points; if you answered "yes," record 0.

	POINTS		POINTS
1. No	2	25. Yes	2
2. No	2	26. Yes	2
3. Yes	2	27. Yes	2
4. Yes	2	28. Yes	2
5. Yes	1	29. Yes	2
6. Yes	1	30. Yes	2
7. No	2	31. Yes	1
8. No	2	32. Yes	1
9. Yes	1	33. Yes	2
10. Yes	1	34. Yes	2
11. No	2	35. Yes	2
12. No	2	36. Yes	2
13. No	2	37. Yes	5
14. No	2	38. Ycs	5
15. Yes	5	39. Yes	5
16. Yes	5	40. Yes	5
17. Yes	1	41. Yes	2
18. Yes	1	42. Yes	2
19. Yes	2	43. Yes	2
20. Yes	2	44. Yes	2
21. Yes	2	45. Yes (2 points for	2
22. Yes	2	46. Yes each arrest)	2
23. Yes	2	47. Yes (2 points for	2
24. Yes	2	48. Yes each arrest)	2

Next, add all of your points for all odd-numbered questions. Do the same for even-numbered questions.

Odd-numbered questions total ____________

Even-numbered questions total ____________

Interpretation A score of greater than 5 for either even-numbered (drugs) or odd-numbered (alcohol) questions indicates the possible existence of a problem. The higher the score, the greater the likelihood.

Personal Application

Below is a list of reasons people use drugs and alcohol. Read each motive, then write several possible alternatives to drug and alcohol use.

MOTIVE FOR DRUG/ALCOHOL USE	POSSIBLE ALTERNATIVES
Example: Need for relaxation	*Playing music; walking; meditation*
To escape boredom	
Peer pressure	
To feel "high"	
Depression	
To feel less inhibited	
Kicks; risks, trying something new	

Now answer the following questions:

- Can you think of additional reasons for using drugs or alcohol? What are they?

- Which reasons might influence you personally? What alternatives, corresponding to these reasons, exist for you?

- If you were trying to convince yourself not to use alcohol or drugs, what arguments would be most persuasive?

- If you were to develop a plan of regular activities for yourself in order to reduce your susceptibility to alcohol and drug use, what would you include? Consider realistically the time, energy, and money that the activities require. Make sure the activities you choose are practical ones for you.

What Is Your Intimacy Quotient?

Overview

Most of us desire close relationships with at least a few other people. Intimate ties, whether they be sexual or not, have the potential to help satisfy many different physiological, social, emotional, and psychological needs. And, of course, need satisfaction is an important aspect of health.

However, close relationships are subject to many challenges. Stress and conflict occur regularly and unavoidably. These sources can include finances, role definitions and expectations, career choices, long-range goals for the relationship, relatives, traditions, and degrees of personal openness to intimacy. Even small, day-to-day irritations and frustrations can be taken out on a partner in a close relationship. Successful close relationships require constant "fine tuning."

This inventory* is designed to measure your capacity for intimacy—how well you have fared in (and what you have learned from) your interpersonal relationships from infancy to the present. At a more general level, it measures your sense of security and self-acceptance, since these qualities are what give one the courage to risk intimacy with another human being and to risk the possibility of rejection.

Directions

Read each question. If your response is "yes" or "mostly yes," place a plus (+) on the line preceding the question. If your response is "no" or "mostly no," place a minus (−) on the line. If you can't decide, place a zero on the line; but try to enter as few zeros as possible. Even if a particular question doesn't apply to you, try to imagine yourself in the situation described and answer accordingly. Don't look for any significance in the number or the frequency of plus or minus answers. Simply be honest when answering the questions.

Assessment

_______ 1. Do you have more than your share of colds?

_______ 2. Do you believe that emotions have very little to do with physical ills?

_______ 3. Do you often have indigestion?

_______ 4. Do you frequently worry about your health?

_______ 5. Would a nutritionist be appalled by your diet?

_______ 6. Do you usually watch sports rather than participate in them?

_______ 7. Do you often feel depressed or in a bad mood?

_______ 8. Are you irritable when things go wrong?

_______ 9. Were you happier in the past than you are right now?

______ 10. Do you believe it possible that a person's character can be read or his future foretold by means of astrology, I Ching, tarot cards, or some other means?

______ 11. Do you worry about the future?

______ 12. Do you try to hold in your anger as long as possible and then sometimes explode in a rage?

______ 13. Do people you care about often make you feel jealous?

______ 14. If your intimate partner were unfaithful one time, would you be unable to forgive and forget?

______ 15. Do you have difficulty making important decisions?

______ 16. Would you abandon a goal rather than take risks to reach it?

______ 17. When you go on a vacation, do you take some work along?

______ 18. Do you usually wear clothes that are dark or neutral in color?

______ 19. Do you usually do what you feel like doing, regardless of social pressures or criticism?

______ 20. Does a beautiful speaking voice turn you on?

______ 21. Do you always take an interest in where you are and what's happening around you?

______ 22. Do you find most odors interesting rather than offensive?

______ 23. Do you enjoy trying new and different foods?

______ 24. Do you like to touch and be touched?

______ 25. Are you easily amused?

______ 26. Do you often do things spontaneously or impulsively?

______ 27. Can you sit still through a long committee meeting or lecture without twiddling your thumbs or wriggling in your chair?

______ 28. Can you usually fall asleep and stay asleep without the use of sleeping pills or tranquilizers?

______ 29. Are you a moderate drinker rather than either a heavy drinker or a teetotaler?

______ 30. Do you smoke not at all or very little?

______ 31. Can you put yourself in another person's place and experience his emotions?

______ 32. Are you seriously concerned about social problems even when they don't affect you personally?

______ 33. Do you think most people can be trusted?

______ 34. Can you talk to a celebrity or a stranger as easily as you talk to your neighbors?

______ 35. Do you get along well with salesclerks, waiters, service-station attendants, and cabdrivers?

______ 36. Can you easily discuss sex in mixed company without feeling uncomfortable?

______ 37. Can you express appreciation for a gift or a favor without feeling uneasy?

______ 38. When you feel affection for someone, can you express it physically as well as verbally?

______ 39. Do you sometimes feel that you have extrasensory perception?

______ 40. Do you like yourself?

______ 41. Do you like others of your own sex?

______ 42. Do you enjoy an evening alone?

______ 43. Do you vary your schedule to avoid doing the same things at the same times each day?

______ 44. Is love more important to you than money or status?

______ 45. Do you place a higher premium on kindness than on truthfulness?

______ 46. Do you think it is possible to be too rational?

______ 47. Have you attended or would like to attend a sensitivity or encounter-group session?

______ 48. Do you discourage friends from dropping in unannounced?

______ 49. Would you feel it a sign of weakness to seek help for a sexual problem?

______ 50. Are you upset when a homosexual seems attracted to you?

______ 51. Do you have difficulty communicating with someone of the opposite sex?

______ 52. Do you believe that men who write poetry are less masculine than men who drive trucks?

______ 53. Do most women prefer men with well-developed muscles to men with well-developed emotions?

______ 54. Are you generally indifferent to the kind of place in which you live?

______ 55. Do you consider it a waste of money to buy flowers for yourself or for others?

______ 56. When you see an art object you like, do you pass it up if the cost would mean cutting back on your food budget?

______ 57. Do you think it pretentious and extravagant to have an elegant dinner when alone or with members of your immediate family?

______ 58. Are you often bored?

______ 59. Do Sundays depress you?

______ 60. Do you frequently feel nervous?

______ 61. Do you dislike the work you do to earn a living?

______ 62. Do you think a carefree hippie lifestyle would have no delights for you?

______ 63. Do you watch TV selectively rather than simply to kill time?

______ 64. Have you read any good books recently?

______ 65. Do you often daydream?

______ 66. Do you like to fondle pets?

______ 67. Do you like many different forms and styles of art?

______ 68. Do you enjoy watching an attractive person of the opposite sex?

______ 69. Can you describe how your date or mate looked the last time you went out together?

______ 70. Do you find it easy to talk to new acquaintances?

______ 71. Do you communicate with others through touch as well as through words?

______ 72. Do you enjoy pleasing members of your family?

______ 73. Do you avoid joining clubs or organizations?

______ 74. Do you worry more about how you present yourself to prospective dates than about how you treat them?

______ 75. Are you afraid that if people knew you too well they wouldn't like you?

______ 76. Do you fall in love at first sight?

______ 77. Do you always fall in love with someone who reminds you of your parent of the opposite sex?

______ 78. Do you think love is all you presently need to be happy?

______ 79. Do you feel a sense of rejection if a person you love tries to preserve his or her independence?

______ 80. Can you accept your loved one's anger and still believe in his or her love?

______ 81. Can you express your innermost thoughts and feelings to the person you love?

______ 82. Do you talk over disagreements with your partner rather than silently worry about them?

______ 83. Can you easily accept the fact that your partner has loved others before you and not worry about how you compare with them?

_______ 84. Can you accept a partner's disinterest in sex without feeling rejected?

_______ 85. Can you accept occasional sessions of unsatisfactory sex without blaming yourself or your partner?

_______ 86. Should unmarried adolescents be denied contraceptives?

_______ 87. Do you believe that even for adults in private, there are some sexual acts that should remain illegal?

_______ 88. Do you think that hippie communes and Israeli kibbutzim have nothing useful to teach the average American?

_______ 89. Should a couple put up with an unhappy marriage for the sake of their children?

_______ 90. Do you think that mate swappers necessarily have unhappy marriages?

_______ 91. Should older men and women be content not to have sex?

_______ 92. Do you believe that pornography contributes to sex crimes?

_______ 93. Is sexual abstinence beneficial to a person's health, strength, wisdom, or character?

_______ 94. Can a truly loving wife or husband sometimes be sexually unreceptive?

_______ 95. Can intercourse during a women's menstrual period be as appealing or as appropriate as at any other time?

_______ 96. Should a woman concentrate on her own sensual pleasure during intercourse rather than pretend enjoyment to increase her partner's pleasure?

_______ 97. Can a man's effort to bring his partner to orgasm reduce his own pleasure?

_______ 98. Should fun and sensual pleasure be the principal goals in sexual relations?

_______ 99. Is pressure to perform well a common cause of sexual incapacity?

_______ 100. Is sexual intercourse for you an uninhibited act rather than a demonstration of your sexual ability?

Scoring

Questions 1– 18, count your minuses _______

Questions 19– 47, count your pluses _______

Questions 48– 62, count your minuses _______

Questions 63– 72, count your pluses _______

Questions 73– 79, count your minuses ______

Questions 80– 85, count your pluses ______

Questions 83– 93, count your minuses ______

Questions 94–100, count your pluses ______

Total ______

Subtract from this total half the number of zero answers to obtain your corrected total.

Corrected total ______

Interpretation

If your corrected total score is under 30, you have a shell like a tortoise and tend to draw your head in at the first sign of psychological danger. Probably life handed you some bad blows when you were too young to fight back, so you've erected strong defenses against the kind of intimacy that could leave you vulnerable to ego injury.

If you scored between 30 and 60, you're about average, which shows you have potential. You've erected some strong defenses, but you've matured enough and have had enough good experiences so that you're willing to take a few chances with other human beings, confident that you'll survive regardless.

Any score over 60 means you possess the self-confidence and sense of security not only to run the risks of intimacy but to enjoy it. This could be a little discomforting to another person who doesn't have your capacity or potential for close interpersonal relationships, but you're definitely ahead in the game and you can make the right person extremely happy just by being yourself. If your score approaches 100, you're either an intimate Superman or you are worried too much about giving right answers, which puts you back in the under-30 category.

If it is convenient, try taking the test with someone you feel intimate with and afterward compare and discuss your answers. It may indicate how compatible you are, socially or sexually. This is one area of interpersonal relationships in which opposites do not necessarily attract. A person of high intimacy capacity can intimidate someone of low capacity who is fearful to respond. But those of similar capacities will tend to make no excessive demands on each other and, for that reason, will find themselves capable of an increasingly intimate and a mutually fulfilling relationship.

**Source:* Assessment, Scoring, and Interpretation excerpted from the book *Go To Health* by Communications Research Machines, Inc. Copyright ©1973 by Communications Research Machines, Inc. Reprinted by permission of Delacorte Press.

Personal Application

Parents, friends, relatives, teachers, and others all play a role in forming the identity and personality of the adult. It is largely through such role models in our life experiences that we develop our attitudes, values, and customs. We develop attitudes about the role for our spouse (or future spouse)—for example, "A woman's place is the home" or "A man should take charge of the family finances." In fact, without realizing it we may have developed a whole list of "shoulds" and "ought tos" for our spouse—for example, "A woman should be submissive," "My spouse ought to attend church," "My spouse should give me a hug when I get home," "My spouse should keep the house clean." We also have developed customs and family traditions—for example, "Thanksgiving dinner finishes with pumpkin pie" or "Presents are to be opened on Christmas Eve." Both partners bring into the marriage—or into any relationship—their own values, attitudes, and customs. Differences in these areas have the potential for discord and, ultimately, for inhibiting intimacy unless they are discussed and resolved. Before you can discuss these areas with your partner you have to be aware of your own values, attitudes, and customs. The following activity will help you gain this awareness.

Pretend you were recently married. You are sitting in the living room with your spouse. Each of you has brought an unopened package. The two packages are filled with the attitudes, values, and customs that you are bringing into the marriage. Included inside are placards saying, for example, "The man wears the pants in the family."

Think about the contents of your package, and then do the following:

- List the values in your package.

- List the attitudes in your package.

- List the customs in your package.

Now review the contents of your package, and answer the following questions:

- Which items would you be willing to discard?

- Which items would you never compromise on? Why?

- Which items would you be able to compromise on?

If you were aware of the contents of your partner's package, how would this reduce stress in your relationship?

Analyze Your Nutrient Intake

Overview

The following assessment will help you analyze your diet to determine if you lack nutrients. It should be noted that there is considerable controversy over how much of the various nutrients we need for optimal well-being. The range of opinions regarding vitamin C exemplifies this controversy. However, a committee appointed by the National Academy of Sciences has developed a Recommended Daily Allowance (RDA) as a nutrient guide for nutritionists. (See Appendix A.) The purpose of the RDA is to indicate acceptable levels of nutrient intake for average people who are healthy to begin with. You should be aware that part or all of the RDA may not apply to you exactly, since you may not be "average." You may need more than the RDA or less than the RDA.

Directions

Record the exact amount of food you eat for a period of three days. Then pick the day that seems most typical of you. For that one day, record the foods and the amounts on the Nutrient Intake Worksheet. Then refer to the chart entitled "Nutritive Values of the Edible Part of Foods" (Appendix B). Record the value of each food in the appropriate columns of the worksheet. Total the amounts.

Assessment

Nutrient Intake Worksheet

FOODS I ATE	AMOUNT	CALORIES	PROTEIN	FAT (mg)	CALCIUM (mg)	PHOSPHORUS (mg)	POTASSIUM (mg)	ZINC (mg)	COPPER (mg)	IRON (mg)	VITAMIN A (IU)	THIAMINE (mg)	NIACIN (mg)	FOLACIN (mg)	VITAMIN B_{12} (mg)	VITAMIN C (mg)
TOTAL																
RDA																
DIFFERENCE (+ or −)																

Scoring Refer to the RDA Chart (Appendix A). On the worksheet, record the RDA for each nutrient. Then find the difference, plus or minus, between your total and the RDA.

Note: Calories are not nutrients. However, a knowledge of the total number of calories you consume may be useful if you wish to diet. Of course, fat is not included in RDA. But your calculation will give you an estimate of your fat intake.

Interpretation Review your results. Which nutrients, according to the RDA, are you lacking?

Personal Application

Refer to the "difference row" of the worksheet, and compile the following two lists.

1. List missing or deficient nutrients.

____

____

____

____

____

____

____

2. List overabundant nutrients.

____

____

____

____

____

____

____

Now review your results. What advice do you have for yourself? Which foods should you add to or subtract from your diet?

Cancer-Risk Checklist

Overview

''Cancer'' is to many people a vague and frightening word. Technically, it is defined as the abnormal, rapid, and uncontrolled reproduction of cells. The cancer may be located in any organ, and it can spread from one site to others. Cancer is second only to heart disease as a leading cause of death in the United States.

There is no unanimous consensus about the causes of cancer. However, most scientists agree that viruses and/or a defective immune system play a role in the development of many cancers. The evidence also suggests that a number of life-style behaviors and/or exposure to risk factors can increase one's chances of getting some form of cancer. As with risk factors for heart disease and stroke, although many risk factors are behavioral problems, it might be years before the disease develops. If intervention takes place and the unhealthy behaviors are changed, then one's chances of developing cancer or dying from cancer may be reduced. Some behavioral factors that may affect the risk of cancer include:

- ***Nutrition***: If your nutrition life style includes eating out often—at fast-food restaurants, for example—you probably have a diet that is high in fat. Low-fiber, high-fat diets have been implicated in two types of cancers: breast cancer and colorectal cancer.
- ***Exposure to carcinogens:*** One of the most significant risk factors is exposure to cancer-producing chemicals and substances, of which several hundred are known. Such substances include asbestos fibers, coal dust, and cloth fibers/dust. Excessive exposure to auto exhaust, sunlight, or x rays may also place one at risk. Generally, the greater the number of years of exposure to a carcinogen, the greater the risk.
- ***Smoking:*** Cigarette smoking is one of the most significant risk factors for a variety of diseases, including cancer of the lungs and the oral cavity. The more you smoke, the greater the risk.
- ***Obesity:*** Obesity relates to fat intake, diet, level of activity, and other behaviors, which, in turn, are related to different types of cancers.

This list is short. Consult your textbook and the daily newspaper for additional factors, but react cautiously to what you learn. Sometimes preliminary results are printed with a zeal that overstates their importance. Test results based on laboratory animals may not always apply to human beings. Unfortunately, some people, feeling bombarded and bewildered by cancer ''scares,'' have adopted the attitude that ''Everything causes cancer, so why worry about it?'' Whatever else may or may not be true about cancer, deciding to ignore it is not a good course! Some cancer-causing factors are very well known, verifiable, and important.

The purpose of this checklist is to increase your awareness of some of the risk factors that have been correlated with cancers that occur at various body sites. While some of these risk factors such as age and heredity are beyond your control, others are behavioral and within your power to change. Regard this list as an educational tool rather than as an absolute indicator of your own personal risk.

Directions Check the items that apply to you for each of the factors listed for each cancer site.

Assessment: Cancer-Risk Checklist

	YES	NO
Breast Cancer		
Risk Factors		
• Age over fifty	______	______
• Family history	______	______
• No children or first birth after age thirty	______	______
• Obesity	______	______
• High dietary fat intake	______	______
• Personal history of endometrial or ovarian cancer	______	______
Cervical Cancer		
Risk Factors		
• Two or more sexual partners in one year	______	______
• More than three pregnancies	______	______
• Began intercourse before age eighteen	______	______
• Bleeding between periods or after intercourse	______	______
• Herpes II infection	______	______
Endometrial Cancer		
Risk Factors		
• Age over sixty	______	______
• Obesity	______	______
• Diabetes	______	______
• Never pregnant	______	______
• Family history	______	______
• Hypertension	______	______

	YES	NO
• Infertility	______	______
• Use of exogenous hormones in high dosages for a long period	______	______
Skin Cancer		
Risk Factors		
• Frequent work or play outdoors	______	______
• Exposure to chemical irritants	______	______
• Exposure to radioactivity	______	______
• Light/fair complexion	______	______
• Skin trauma (especially repeated) resulting in scars	______	______
Colorectal Cancer		
Risk Factors		
• Over age sixty	______	______
• Family history of polyps of the colon	______	______
• Personal history of ulcerative colitis for ten or more years	______	______
• Personal history of bleeding from the rectum (other than hemorrhoids)	______	______
Lung Cancer		
Risk Factors		
• Smoke cigarettes	______	______
• Live in an urban area	______	______
• Work in mines, with asbestos, radioactive material, nickel, chromates, petroleum, arsenic	______	______
• Male	______	______
Prostate Cancer		
Risk Factors		
• Family history	______	______
• Black race	______	______
• High fat diet	______	______
• Alcohol use	______	______

Testicular Cancer

	YES	NO
Risk Factors		______
• Age twenty to forty	______	______
• Family history	______	______
• Personal history of undescended testes	______	______

Interpretation

Examine your checklist with special attention to all items marked "yes." Remember that most risk factors in this checklist are based on correlations, and correlations do not prove causality. For example, there is a relationship (correlation) between gender and lung cancer (males are at higher risk than females), but the primary reasons for this are that, traditionally, a greater percentage of males than females smoked cigarettes and worked in more hazardous occupations. So, the primary causal factors seem to be smoking behavior and occupation, not gender. For many cancer sites, causal factors are less clear, and so correlations are the best useful information available. Therefore, consider these correlations as educational tools with which to analyze your life style, not as definitive indicators of risk.

Please note that although some of the risk factors, such as age or heredity, are beyond your control, others are directly associated with your own chosen behaviors. Even some of the risk factors that you have no choice about are also susceptible to intervention on your part. For example, if you have a family history of a particular type (or site) of cancer, you might reasonably decide to seek regular medical screening for that disease even though your life style does not indicate that you are otherwise at great risk.

As cancer research continues, it is becoming noticeable that general health-related behaviors and cancers of various body sites seem to be related in unexplainable ways. For example, high fat–low fiber diets and alcohol and tobacco use appear to be correlated with cancer at body sites not as obviously connected as smoking and lung cancer. A health-conscious person might form the conclusion that the basic principles of healthful living apply to the prevention of cancer just as they do to many other health problems.

Personal Application

For one twenty-four-hour period or for different segments of a twenty-four-hour day to be studied over a period of several days, describe where you are, what the situation is, and *any* possible cancer risks. If you work at this hard enough, use your imagination, and consult a textbook for a comprehensive list of potential carcinogens, it is unlikely that you will find any time during your day that you are not at risk, even if the risk is extremely slight.

WHERE	SITUATION	CANCER-RISK AGENTS
EXAMPLES:		
Cafeteria	*Eating lunch*	*High animal fat food (pork chop and fried potatoes)*
Second Street	*Walking to class*	*Solar radiation*
History seminar	*Small room*	*Tobacco smoke from other students*

Select the most serious risks you were exposed to. What could you do to lessen your risk—for example, wear a hat while walking to class, ask fellow students not to smoke in class.

Write your list below.

Action Plan

Increasingly, health is becoming a matter of individual responsibility. We tend to cause our own health problems by the life styles we *choose* to adopt, and, since we have more control over our own behaviors than anyone else does, it follows that if we want to be healthy, we must take an *active* role in directing our behaviors toward health.

Behavior-Change Selection

Even though it is not always easy, it is possible to change your personal behaviors. What is truly difficult is to change several behaviors at one time. For this reason, it is advisable to select *one* behavior change to work on.

The following chart will help you make this selection on the basis of which change is most likely to be successful for you. The criteria for success include (1) acknowledgment of degree of risk, (2) personal desire to change, and (3) relative ease of change.

Behavior-Change Selection Chart

Directions: First, review the assessment tests you have completed in this booklet. Select up to five of your behaviors that may cause you to be at risk for illness. Write these in the first column of the chart. Next, in the Health Risk column, rank the behaviors according to your opinion of how serious a risk they pose to your health and well-being. Place the number 1 beside the most serious risk, number 2 beside the second most serious, and so forth. In the Desire to Change column, again rank the behaviors, this time according to how much you *really want* to change them. Again, number 1 is the one you want most to change. In the next column, rank the behaviors according to how easy you think it would be for you to make a change. Number 1 is the easiest to change. (It might be simpler to work backward on this ranking, that is, first find the hardest to change and write the highest number beside it.) In the final column, average your rankings for each behavior.

BEHAVIOR	HEALTH RISK	DESIRE TO CHANGE	EASE OF CHANGE	AVERAGE RANKING

The behavior that has the lowest average ranking is probably the one you should choose to work on changing in order to have a healthier lifestyle. Your next step is to devise a plan of action and write a specific contract with your instructor, friend, spouse, roommate, classmate, parent, or someone else who is important to you. A blank contract form and a sample contract follow.

BEHAVIOR-CHANGE CONTRACT

I,______________________, have decided to commit myself to the following behavioral change:

Behavior change:
More specifically, my goal is:
Date I expect to reach my goal:
Subgoal(s) (include the dates you expect reach of your subgoals):
Action steps and rules to follow that will help me accomplish my goal:
I will get feedback by:

If I reach my subgoals, I will reward myself by:

If I do not reach my subgoals, I will punish myself by:

If I reach my goal by the date specified, I will reward myself by:

If I do not reach my goal by the date specified, I will punish myself by:

Signature ______________________________ **Date** ______________

SAMPLE BEHAVIOR-CHANGE CONTRACT

I,________________________, have decided to commit myself to the following behavioral change:

Behavior change: *To lose weight.*

More specifically, my goal is: *To lose ten pounds.*

Date I expect to reach my goal: *July 10.*

Subgoal(s):

- *I will eat no more than 1,200 calories per day.*
- *I will lose two pounds each week.*

Action steps and rules to follow that will help me accomplish my goal:

- *I will write a three-day menu, which will contain no more than 1,200 calories for each day.*
- *I will stop eating before I feel full. I resign from the clean-plate club.*
- *I will eat carrot sticks and celery sticks for snacks.*
- *I will substitute water for soft drinks.*
- *When I go to someone's house for dinner, I will eat half the portion.*
- *Before going to a party, I will ask my roommate or a friend to remind me not to overindulge.*
- *At the end of each day, I will report my success to my roommate or friend.*

I will get feedback by:

- *Charting the number of calories I eat each day.*
- *Getting on the scale each Monday and charting the results. The chart will be posted on my bulletin board.*
- *Reporting my results to at least two friends.*

If I reach my subgoals, I will reward myself by:

- *Taking a bubble bath for each day that I stick to 1,200 calories.*
- *Buying a record for each week that I lose two pounds.*

If I do not reach my subgoals, I will punish myself by:

- *Confining myself to 1,000 calories for the day after I exceed 1,200 calories.*
- *Depriving myself of a party if I continue to exceed 1,200 calories day after day.*

If I reach my goal by the date specified, I will reward myself by:

- *Buying a new dress.*

If I do not reach my goal by the date specified, I will punish myself by:

- *Not watching TV for two weeks.*

Signature ______________________________ **Date** ______________

Appendix A

Recommended Dietary Allowances (RDA)

Age (years)	Weight (kg)	Weight (lbs)	Height (cm)	Height (in)	Protein (g)	Vitamin A (RE)	Vitamin D (μg)	Vitamin E (mg)	Vitamin C (mg)	Thiamin (mg)	Riboflavin (mg)	Niacin (mg equiv)	Vitamin B_6 (mg)	Folacin (μg)	Vitamin B_{12} (μg)	Calcium (mg)	Phosphorus (mg)	Magnesium (mg)	Iron (mg)	Zinc (mg)	Iodine (μg)
Infants																					
0.0–0.5	6	13	60	24	kg × 2.2	420	10	3	35	0.3	0.4	6	0.3	30	0.5	360	240	50	10	3	40
0.5–1.0	9	20	71	28	kg × 2.0	400	10	4	35	0.5	0.6	8	0.6	45	1.5	540	360	70	15	5	50
Children																					
1–3	13	29	90	35	23	400	10	5	45	0.7	0.8	9	0.9	100	2.0	800	800	150	15	10	70
4–6	20	44	112	44	30	500	10	6	45	0.9	1.0	11	1.3	200	2.5	800	800	200	10	10	90
7–10	28	62	132	52	34	700	10	7	45	1.2	1.4	16	1.6	300	3.0	800	800	250	10	10	120
Males																					
11–14	45	99	157	62	45	1000	10	8	50	1.4	1.6	18	1.8	400	3.0	1200	1200	350	18	15	150
15–18	66	145	176	69	56	1000	10	10	60	1.4	1.7	18	2.0	400	3.0	1200	1200	400	18	15	150
19–22	70	154	177	70	53	1000	7.5	10	60	1.5	1.7	19	2.2	400	3.0	800	800	350	10	15	150
23–50	70	154	178	70	56	1000	5	10	60	1.4	1.6	18	2.2	400	3.0	800	800	350	10	15	150
51 +	70	154	178	70	56	1000	5	10	60	1.2	1.4	16	2.2	400	3.0	800	800	350	10	15	150
Females																					
11–14	46	101	157	82	46	800	10	8	50	1.1	1.3	15	1.8	400	3.0	1200	1200	300	18	15	150
15–18	55	120	163	64	46	800	10	8	60	1.1	1.3	14	2.0	400	3.0	1200	1200	300	18	15	150
19–22	55	120	163	64	44	800	7.5	8	60	1.1	1.3	14	2.0	400	3.0	800	800	300	18	15	150
23–50	55	120	163	64	44	800	5	8	60	1.0	1.2	13	2.0	400	3.0	800	800	300	18	15	150
51 +	55	120	163	64	44	800	5	8	60	1.0	1.2	13	2.0	400	3.0	800	800	300	10	15	105
Pregnant					+ 30	+ 200	+ 5	+ 2	+ 20	+ 0.4	+ 0.3	+ 2	+ 0.6	+ 400	+ 1.0	+ 400	+ 400	+ 150	†	+ 5	+ 25
Lactating					+ 20	+ 400	+ 5	+ 3	+ 40	+ 0.5	+ 0.5	+ 5	+ 0.5	+ 100	+ 1.0	+ 400	+ 400	+ 150	†	+ 10	+ 50

* The allowances are intended to provide for individual variation among most normal, healthy people in the United States under usual environmental stresses. They were designed for the maintenance of good nutrition. Diets should be based on a variety of common foods in order to provide other nutrients for which human requirements have been less well defined.

† Supplemental iron is recommended.

Estimated Safe and Adequate Daily Dietary Intakes of Additional Selected Vitamins and Minerals*

	Age (years)	Vitamins			Trace Elements†						Electrolytes		
		Vitamin K (μg)	Biotin (μg)	Pantothenic Acid (mg)	Copper (mg)	Manganese (mg)	Fluoride (mg)	Chromium (mg)	Selenium (mg)	Molybedenum (mg)	Sodium (mg)	Potassium (mg)	Chloride (mg)
Infants	0–0.5	12	35	2	0.5–0.7	0.5–0.7	0.1–0.5	0.01–0.04	0.01–0.04	0.03–0.06	115–350	350–925	275–700
	0.5–1	10–20	50	3	0.7–1.0	0.7–1.0	0.2–1.0	0.02–0.06	0.02–0.06	0.04–0.08	250–750	425–1,275	400–1,200
Children	1–3	15–30	65	3	1.0–1.5	1.0–1.5	0.5–1.5	0.02–0.08	0.02–0.08	0.05–0.10	325–975	550–1,650	500–1,500
	4–6	20–40	85	3–4	1.5–2.0	1.5–2.0	1.0–2.5	0.03–0.12	0.03–0.12	0.06–0.15	450–1,350	775–2,325	700–2,100
Adolescents	7–10	30–60	120	4–5	2.0–2.5	2.0–3.0	1.5–2.5	0.05–0.20	0.05–0.20	0.10–0.30	600–1,800	1,000–3,000	925–2,775
	11 +	50–100	100–200	4–7	2.0–3.0	2.5–5.0	1.5–2.5	0.05–0.20	0.05–0.20	0.15–0.50	900–2,700	1,525–4,575	1,400–4,200
Adults		70–140	100–200	4–7	2.0–3.0	2.5–5.0	1.5–4.0	0.05–0.20	0.05–0.20	0.15–0.50	1,100–3,300	1,875–5,625	1,700–5,100

* Because there is less information on which to base allowances, these figures are not given in the main table of the RDA and are provided here in the form of ranges of recommended intakes.

† Since the toxic levels for many trace elements may be only several times usual intakes, the upper levels for the trace elements given in this table should not be habitually exceeded.

Appendix B
Nutritive Values of the Edible Part of Foods

Food	Weight g	Approximate Measure	Energy Kcal	Protein g	Fat g	Total Carbo-hydrate g	Minerals: Calcium mg	Phos-phorus mg	Mag-nesium mg	Sodium mg	Potas-sium mg	Zinc mg	Copper mg	Iron mg	Vitamins: Total Vitamin A Activity IU	Thia-min mg	Ribo-flavin mg	Niacin mg	Vitamin B-6 mg	Panto-thenic Acid mg	Folacin (free) mcg	Vitamin B-12 mcg	Vitamin C mg
Almonds, chopped	15	12–15 nuts, 2 tbsp	90	3.0	8.0	3	35	75	40	1	115	0.2	0.1	0.7	0	0.04	0.1	0.5	0.02	0.07	5	0	tr
Apples, raw with skin	150	1 medium 3/lb	80	0.3	0.8	20	10	15	10	1	150	0.08	0.1	0.4	100	0.04	0.03	0.1	0.04	0.2	5	0	6
Apple juice, canned, no sugar added	125	½ c	60	0.1	tr	15	10	10	5	1	125	0.04	0.01	0.6	u	0.01	0.02	0.1	0.04	0.1	1	0	1
Applesauce, sweetened	125	½ c	120	0.3	0.1	30	5	5	5	3	100	0.1	0.01	0.6	50	0.03	0.01	tr	0.04	0.1	1	0	1
Apricots																							
Fresh	100	2–3 medium	50	1.0	0.2	13	15	25	10	1	280	0.04	0.1	0.5	2700	0.03	0.04	0.6	0.07	0.2	u	0	10
Canned, heavy syrup	120	4 halves, 2 tbsp juice	100	0.7	0.1	25	15	20	10	1	235	0.04	0.1	0.4	2000	0.02	0.02	0.5	0.06	0.1	u	0	5
water pack	100	4 halves, 2 tbsp juice	40	0.7	0.1	10	10	15	10	1	245	0.03	0.1	0.3	1800	0.02	0.02	0.4	0.06	0.1	u	0	4
Dried, sulfured, raw	30	4–6 medium halves	80	1.5	0.2	20	20	30	20	1	295	0.04	0.1	1.7	3300	tr	0.05	1.0	0.05	0.2	3	0	4
Apricot nectar, canned	125	½ c	70	0.4	0.1	18	10	15	5	tr	190	u	u	0.3	1200	0.01	0.01	0.3	0.04	0.10	u	0	4
Artichokes, French, boiled	120	1 large (300 g as purchased)	30	3.0	0.2	12	60	85	u	35	360	0.4	0.4	1.3	200	0.08	0.05	0.8	0.30	0.60	u	0	10
Asparagus																							
Fresh, green, cooked	100	½ c cut, 6–7 spears	20	2.0	0.2	4	20	50	15	1	185	0.3	0.1	0.6	900	0.2	0.2	1.5	0.2	0.6	60	0	25
Canned, salt added	100	½ c cut, 6–7 spears	20	2.0	0.4	3	20	50	15	235	165	0.8	0.1	1.9	800	0.06	0.1	0.8	0.06	0.2	25	0	15
Avocados	125	½ fruit, 4-in. long	190	2.0	18.0	7	10	45	55	5	680	0.5	0.5	0.7	350	0.1	0.2	2.0	0.4	1.1	40	0	15
Baby foods																							
Dinners	130	Contents 4½ oz jar																					
beef-noodle			60	3.5	1.5	9	15	35	u	150	205	u	0.1	0.6	790	0.03	0.06	0.6	0.04	0.2	u	0.3	3
beef-vegetable			110	9.5	4.5	8	15	110	u	115	145	u	0.1	1.5	1410	0.09	0.2	2.0	0.10	0.3	4	0.3	3
vegetable-beef-cereal			70	3.5	2.0	10	20	50	u	150	185	u	0.1	1.0	3580	0.04	0.05	1.0	0.05	0.2	u	0.2	1
Fruits and desserts	135	Contents 4¾ oz jar																					
banana-pineapple			110	0.5	0.1	30	30	15	u	10	100	u	0.1	0.3	40	0.01	0.01	0.1	0.06	0.2	1	0.05	3
custard pudding			130	3.0	2.5	25	80	80	u	80	120	u	0.06	0.4	130	0.03	0.2	0.1	0.02	0.3	u	0.2	1
fruit pudding			130	1.5	1.0	30	35	45	u	15	100	u	0.1	0.4	140	0.04	0.07	0.1	0.02	0.2	u	0.08	4
Bacon, broiled, drained	25	2 strips, thick	140	6.5	12.5	1	3	55	5	245	60	1.2	0.1	0.8	0	0.1	0.08	1.0	0.03	0.08	0.1	0.2	0
Bagels	60	4-in. diameter	180	6.5	2.0	30	10	50	u	u	u	0.6	0.2	1.3	30	0.15	0.11	1.3	u	u	u	0	0
Bamboo shoots	100	¾ c	25	2.5	0.3	6	13	60	u	u	630	u	u	0.5	20	0.15	0.07	0.6	u	u	u	0	4
Bananas	120	1 medium	100	1.5	0.2	25	10	30	55	1	440	0.3	0.2	0.8	250	0.06	0.07	0.8	0.6	0.3	25	0	10
Beans																							
Canned, with pork and tomato sauce	130	½ c	160	8.0	3.5	25	70	115	35	590	270	1.0	0.2	2.3	150	0.10	0.04	0.8	0.4	0.1	10	0	3
Canned, with pork and sweet sauce	130	½ c	190	8.0	6.0	25	80	145	35	485	u	1.0	0.3	3.0	u	0.08	0.05	0.7	0.1	0.1	10	0	3
Lima, fresh or frozen, boiled	85	½ c	95	6.5	0.4	17	40	105	65	2	360	0.9	0.4	2.2	250	0.20	0.08	1.0	0.1	0.2	8	0	15
Red, canned	15	½ c	120	7.0	0.5	20	35	140	35	4	335	1.0	0.2	2.3	tr	0.06	0.05	0.8	0.4	0.1	10	0	0
Refried	120	½ c	230	8.5	12.5	25	50	165	35	340	360	1.0	0.2	2.3	tr	0.30	0.07	0.8	0.2	0.2	20	0	0
Snap, green, fresh or frozen, boiled	65	½ c	15	1.0	0.2	3	55	25	15	2	95	0.2	0.08	0.4	350	0.05	0.06	0.3	0.04	0.1	5	0	8
canned	65	½ c	15	1.0	0.2	3	55	25	15	150	60	0.2	0.08	1.0	300	0.02	0.04	0.2	0.03	tr	5	0	2
Soybeans, mature, dry, cooked	90	½ c (1 oz dry wt)	120	10.0	5.0	10	65	160	80	2	490	0.6	0.3	2.5	20	0.20	0.08	0.6	u	u	20	0	0
Bean sprouts. See Sprouts																							
Beef																							
Corned, canned	80	2 slices each, 3 in. × 2 in. × ¼ in.	170	20.0	9.5	0	15	85	20	u	u	2.5	u	3.4	tr	0.02	0.20	3.0	0.08	0.5	2	1.5	0
hash, with potatoes	110	½ c	200	10.0	12.5	12	15	75	20	595	220	1.4	u	2.2	tr	0.01	0.10	2.5	0.08	0.6	u	0.8	0
Dried, creamed	120	½ c	190	10.0	12.5	9	130	170	40	880	190	1.8	u	1.0	450	0.08	0.20	0.8	0.60	0.7	u	u	1
Hamburger, broiled, lean, 21% fat	85	4/lb, raw wt	240	20.0	16.5	0	10	160	20	50	220	3.7	0.07	2.6	30	0.07	0.20	4.5	0.4	0.3	3	1.5	0
very lean, 10% fat	85	4/lb, raw wt	190	23.0	9.5	0	10	195	20	60	260	4.9	0.09	3.0	20	0.08	0.20	5.0	0.4	0.3	3	1.5	0
Roast, chuck, braised	85	3 oz	240	23.0	16.5	0	10	115	20	40	185	3.7	0.07	2.9	30	0.04	0.20	3.5	u	u	3	1.5	0
rib, U.S. choice	85	3 oz	380	17.0	33.5	0	10	160	20	40	190	3.1	0.07	2.2	70	0.05	0.10	3.0	0.3	0.3	3	1.5	0
Steak, broiled																							
round with fat	85	3 oz	220	24.5	13.0	0	10	215	25	60	270	5.0	0.09	3.0	20	0.07	0.20	5.0	0.3	0.4	3	2.2	0
sirloin with fat	85	3 oz	330	20.0	27.0	0	10	160	20	50	220	3.7	0.07	2.5	50	0.05	0.20	4.0	u	u	3	1.5	0

tr — trace amounts
u — unknown thought to be present
0 — Absent or below detection level

Source: Reproduced from C. F. Adams, *Nutritive Value of American Foods in Common Units*, USDA Agriculture Handbook No. 456,1975, updated, as available, from revised USDA Handbook No. 8

Nutritive Values of the Edible Part of Foods

Food	Weight g	Approximate Measure	Energy Kcal	Protein g	Fat g	Total Carbo-hydrate g	Minerals: Calcium mg	Phos-phorus mg	Mag-nesium mg	Sodium mg	Potas-sium mg	Zinc mg	Copper mg	Iron mg	Vitamins: Total Vitamin A Activity IU	Thia-min mg	Ribo-flavin mg	Niacin mg	Vitamin B-6 mg	Panto-thenic Acid mg	Folacin (free) mcg	Vitamin B-12 mcg	Vitamin C mg
Beef stew, with vegetables	245	1 c	220	15.5	10.5	15	30	185	50	90	615	2.4	0.05	2.9	2400	0.15	0.15	4.7	0.3	0.2	7	1.6	15
Beer	360	12-oz bottle	150	1.0	0	14	20	110	35	25	90	0.1	0.2	tr	0	0.01	0.10	2.0	0.2	0.3	25	0	0
Beet greens, boiled	75	½ c	15	1.0	0.2	2	70	20	80	55	240	0.5	0.1	1.4	3700	0.05	0.10	0.2	0.08	0.2	u	0	10
Beets, sliced, canned	85	½ c	30	1.0	0.1	8	15	15	15	200	135	0.3	0.1	0.6	20	0.01	0.03	0.1	0.04	0.1	30	0	2
Beverages. See *Carbonated beverages*, individual entries.																							
Biscuits, from mix, enriched	30	1 of 2-in. diameter	90	2.0	3.0	15	20	65	5	270	30	0.3	0.09	0.6	tr	0.08	0.07	0.6	0.01	0.1	2	0	0
Blackberries, boysenberries, etc., raw	70	½ c	40	0.8	0.6	9	25	15	20	1	120	0.05	0.1	0.6	150	0.02	0.03	0.3	0.04	0.2	2	0	15
Blueberries, raw	70	½ c	45	0.5	0.4	11	10	10	4	1	60	0.05	0.08	0.8	80	0.02	0.04	0.4	0.05	0.1	2	0	10
Bokchay. See *Pakchoy*.																							
Brazil nuts, raw	30	6 large nuts	180	4.0	19.0	3	55	195	65	tr	205	1.4	0.4	1.0	tr	0.30	0.03	0.5	0.05	0.1	tr	0	0
Bread																							
Boston brown, canned	45	1 slice, ½ in. thick	95	2.5	0.6	20	40	70	u	115	130	u	u	0.9	30	0.05	0.3	0.5	u	u	u	0	0
Corn, from mix	55	2½ in. square	180	4.0	6.0	30	135	210	u	265	60	u	u	0.8	150	0.10	0.10	0.8	u	u	u	u	0
Cracked wheat	25	1 slice	65	2.2	0.6	13	20	30	10	130	35	0.3	0.05	0.3	tr	0.03	0.02	0.3	0.02	0.2	3	0	0
French, Vienna, Italian, enriched	25	1 slice	70	2.3	0.8	14	10	20	5	145	20	0.5	0.09	0.6	0	0.07	0.06	0.6	0.02	0.1	3	0	0
Fry bread, Indian, enriched	60	1 piece, medium	200	4.0	7.5	28	80	50	u	305	35	u	u	1.0	0	0.10	0.09	1.3	0.02	0.2	10	0	0
Raisin, not enriched	25	1 slice	65	1.5	0.7	13	20	20	5	90	60	0.3	0.05	0.3	tr	0.01	0.02	0.2	0.01	0.1	3	0	0
Rye, American	25	1 slice	65	2.5	0.3	13	15	40	10	140	35	0.4	0.05	0.4	0	0.05	0.02	0.4	0.02	0.1	2	0	0
White, not enriched	25	1 slice	70	2.2	0.8	13	20	25	5	130	25	0.2	0.05	0.2	tr	0.02	0.02	0.3	0.01	0.1	3	0	0
enriched	25	1 slice	70	2.2	0.8	13	20	25	5	130	25	0.2	0.05	0.6	tr	0.06	0.05	0.6	0.01	0.1	3	0	0
Whole wheat	25	1 slice	65	2.5	0.8	12	25	60	10	130	70	0.4	0.05	0.8	tr	0.06	0.03	0.7	0.04	0.2	9	0	0
Broccoli, fresh or frozen, boiled	85	½ c	20	2.5	0.2	4	70	50	15	8	205	0.2	0.07	0.6	1900	0.07	0.20	0.6	0.1	0.4	20	0	70
Brussels sprouts, fresh or frozen, boiled	85	4 large sprouts	30	3.5	0.3	5	25	60	15	8	230	0.3	0.08	0.9	440	0.07	0.12	0.7	0.4	1.1	15	0	70
Butter, salted	5	1 tsp or pat (90/lb)	35	tr	4.0	tr	1	1	tr	40	1	tr	0	tr	150	tr	tr	tr	0	0	0	tr	0
	15	1 tbsp	100	0.1	11.5	0.1	3	3	tr	120	3	tr	0	tr	450	tr	tr	tr	0	0	0	tr	0
Cabbage, green, headed																							
Raw, shredded	70	1 c	17	0.9	0.1	4	35	20	10	15	165	0.3	0.08	0.3	90	0.04	0.04	0.2	0.1	0.1	20	0	35
Cooked, chopped	70	½ c	15	0.8	0.2	3	30	15	10	10	120	0.3	0.02	0.2	100	0.03	0.03	0.2	0.09	0.1	2	0	25
Cakes																							
Angel food	40	2-in. sector of 10-in. cake	105	2.5	0.1	25	40	50	10	60	25	0.1	0.02	0.1	0	tr	0.04	tr	tr	0.08	1	tr	0
Cheese cake, frozen	85	¹⁄₁₀ of cake	225	6.5	12.5	24	80	80	30	170	90	u	0.04	0.5	200	0.05	0.1	0.3	u	u	u	u	tr
Chocolate, with chocolate icing	90	2-in. sector of 8-in. cake	310	4.0	11.5	55	55	95	20	240	120	1.1	0.3	0.7	150	0.03	0.07	0.3	0.07	0.4	3	0.1	0
Gingerbread	65	2⅜ in. square	170	2.0	4.5	30	55	65	u	190	175	u	u	1.0	tr	0.02	0.06	0.5	u	u	u	u	0
Cupcake, iced	50	1 medium	190	2.0	6.0	30	60	95	u	160	55	u	u	0.4	80	0.02	0.05	0.1	u	u	u	u	0
Pound cake	30	3½ in. × 3 in. × ½ in.	140	1.5	9.0	14	6	25	5	35	20	0.2	0.02	0.2	80	0.01	0.03	0.1	0.01	0.09	2	u	0
Yellow with chocolate icing	70	2-in. sector of 8-in. cake	230	3.0	8.0	40	65	125	15	160	75	0.3	0.07	0.4	100	0.01	0.06	0.1	0.03	0.2	2	u	0
Candy																							
Caramels	30	1 oz	120	1.0	3.0	20	40	35	u	65	55	u	0.01	0.4	tr	0.01	0.05	0.1	tr	0	u	u	0
Chocolate bar																							
plain milk chocolate	30	1 oz	140	2.0	9.0	16	65	65	20	25	110	0.1	0.3	0.3	80	0.02	0.10	0.1	tr	0.03	1	u	0
with almonds	30	1 oz	150	2.5	10.0	14	65	75	u	25	125	0.1	u	0.5	70	0.02	0.10	0.2	tr	u	1	u	0
Fudge with nuts	30	1 oz	120	1.0	5.0	20	20	30	u	50	50	u	u	0.3	tr	0.01	0.03	0.1	u	u	u	tr	0
Hard	30	1 oz	110	0	0.3	30	6	2	u	10	1	u	0.03	0.5	0	0	0	0	0	0	0	0	0
Marshmallow	30	1 oz, 4 large	90	0.6	tr	25	5	2	u	10	2	0.01	0.06	0.5	0	0	tr	tr	u	u	0	0	0
Peanut brittle	30	1 oz	120	1.5	3.0	25	10	25	u	10	45	u	u	0.7	0	0.05	0.01	1.0	u	u	u	0	0
Cantaloupe. See *Melons*.																							
Carbonated beverages, sweet	170	6 oz	65	0	0	17	0	0	0	0	0	0	0	0	0	0	0	0	0	0	0	0	0
Carrots																							
Raw	80	1 carrot, 7½ in. × 1⅛ in.	30	0.8	0.1	7	25	25	15	35	245	0.3	0.07	0.5	7900	0.04	0.04	0.4	0.1	0.2	10	0	6
Boiled	70	½ c diced	20	0.5	0.3	10	25	20	4	25	160	0.2	0.07	0.4	7600	0.04	0.04	0.4	0.02	0.2	2	0	4
Cashews, roasted	30	1 oz	160	5.0	13.0	8	10	105	80	60	130	1.3	0.2	1.1	30	0.1	0.07	0.5	0.1	0.4	2	0	0

Cauliflower																							
Raw	50	½ c whole flower buds	15	1.5	0.1	3	10	30	12	5	150	u	0.1	0.6	60	0.1	0.1	0.7	0.1	0.5	15	0	75
Boiled	60	½ c	15	1.5	0.2	3	15	25	8	10	130	u	0.1	0.4	40	0.06	0.05	0.4	0.1	0.5	2	0	35
Celery																							
Raw	80	2 large stalks	15	0.8	0.1	3	30	20	17	100	270	u	0.09	0.2	200	0.02	0.02	0.2	0.05	0.3	5	0	8
Boiled	75	½ c diced	10	0.6	0.1	2	25	15	u	65	180	u	0.08	0.2	200	0.02	0.02	0.2	0.05	0.3	u	0	4
Cereals, breakfast																							
Ready-to-eat																							
bran flakes, 40% enr.	35	1 c	100	3.5	0.6	30	20	125	u	205	135	1.3	0.4	12.4	0	0.4	0.5	4.0	0.1	0.3	6	0	0
corn flakes, enriched	25	1 c	95	2.0	0.1	20	4	10	4	250	30	0.07	0.03	0.6	0	0.3	0.4	3.0	0.02	0.05	3	0	0
granola	50	½ c	215	5.7	9.6	29	30	170	60	3	180	1.0	0.4	1.6	0	0.16	0.08	1.1	0.06	0.45	20	tr	0
rice, puffed, enriched	15	1 c	60	0.9	0.1	13	3	15	u	tr	15	0.2	0.03	0.3	0	0.07	0.01	0.7	0.01	0.06	1	0	0
wheat flakes, enriched	30	1 c	100	3.0	0.5	25	10	85	30	310	80	0.7	0.3	1.1	0	0.4	0.4	3.5	0.09	0.1	3	0	0
wheat, shredded	50	1 c of spn-sized	180	5.0	1.0	40	20	195	65	2	175	1.4	0.4	1.8	0	0.1	0.06	2.0	0.1	0.4	5	0	0
Cooked, 1 oz dry wt, salt added																							
cornmeal and grits																							
unenriched	120	½ c	60	1.5	0.2	13	1	15	10	130	20	0.1	0.06	0.2	70	0.02	0.01	0.1	0.04	0.2	2	0	0
enriched	120	½ c	60	1.5	0.2	13	1	15	10	130	20	0.1	0.06	0.5	70	0.07	0.05	0.6	0.04	0.2	2	0	0
oatmeal	120	½ c	65	2.5	1.0	12	10	70	30	260	75	0.6	0.04	0.7	0	0.10	0.02	0.1	0.04	0.4	5	0	0
wheat farina																							
light, enriched (e.g., Cream of Wheat)	120	½ c	50	1.5	0.1	10	5	15	4	175	10	0.07	0.04	0.4	0	0.05	0.04	0.5	0.02	0.1	5	0	0
whole-meal (e.g., Ralston)	120	½ c	55	2.0	0.4	12	10	65	35	260	60	0.6	0.3	0.6	0	0.08	0.02	0.8	0.[illegible]	0.2	10	0	0
Chard, Swiss, boiled	70	½ c	15	1.5	0.2	2	55	20	45	60	230	u	u	1.3	3900	0.03	0.08	0.3	u	0.1	u	0	0
Cheese																							
Natural																							
blue, Roquefort	30	1 oz	100	6.0	8.0	0.7	150	110	7	395	75	0.8	0.04	0.1	200	0.01	0.1	0.3	0.05	0.5	0.3	0.3	0
cheddar	30	1 oz	115	7.0	9.5	0.4	205	145	8	175	30	0.9	0.04	0.2	300	0.01	0.1	tr	0.02	0.1	0.3	0.2	0
cottage, creamed	110	½ c	120	14.0	5.0	3.0	70	150	6	455	95	0.4	0.02	0.2	180	0.02	0.2	0.1	0.[illegible]	0.15	15.0	0.7	0
cream	30	2 tbsp	100	2.0	10.0	0.8	25	30	2	85	35	0.2	0.01	0.3	400	tr	0.06	tr	0.01	0.1	0.2	0.1	0
Parmesan	30	1 oz	130	12.0	8.5	1.0	390	230	15	455	30	0.8	0.1	0.3	200	0.01	0.1	0.1	0.03	0.1	0.3	u	0
Swiss	30	1 oz	110	8.0	8.0	1.0	270	170	10	75	30	1.1	0.04	0.1	250	tr	0.1	tr	0.02	0.1	0.3	0.5	0
Pasteurized, processed																							
American	30	1 oz	110	6.0	9.0	0.5	175	210	6	405	45	0.8	0.05	0.1	350	0.01	0.1	tr	0.02	0.1	0.9	0.2	0
cheese spread	30	1 oz	80	4.5	6.0	2	160	200	8	380	70	0.7	u	0.1	200	0.01	0.1	tr	0.03	0.2	u	0.1	0
Cheese fondue	100	⅔ c	260	15.0	18.5	10	320	295	u	540	165	u	0.04	1.2	900	0.06	0.3	0.2	u	u	u	u	0
Cherries																							
Raw, sweet	75	10 cherries	45	0.9	0.2	12	15	15	10	1	130	0.1	0.1	0.3	70	0.03	0.04	0.3	0.02	0.2	4	0	7
Red, canned																							
heavy syrup	130	½ c with syrup	100	1.0	0.2	25	20	15	10	2	160	u	0.06	0.4	80	0.02	0.02	0.2	0.06	0.1	tr	0	4
water pack	120	½ c with juice	50	1.0	0.2	13	20	15	10	2	160	u	0.06	0.4	80	0.04	0.02	0.2	u	u	tr	0	4
Chicken																							
Canned, flesh only	100	½ c	200	22.5	12.0	0	20	255	20	u	140	2	0.2	1.6	250	0.04	0.1	4.5	0.3	0.8	2	0.8	0
Creamed	120	½ c	210	17.5	12.0	7	85	140	u	u	u	u	u	1.1	300	0.04	0.2	4.0	u	u	u	u	tr
Fried																							
breast	95	½ breast	160	25.5	5.0	1	9	220	10	u	u	0.8	0.1	1.3	70	0.04	0.2	11.5	0.6	0.8	2	0.4	0
leg	55	1 medium	90	12.0	4.0	0.4	6	90	10	u	u	1.4	0.1	0.9	50	0.03	0.2	2.5	0.3	0.2	3	0.2	0
thigh	65	1 medium	120	15.0	6.0	1	7	120	10	u	u	1.6	0.1	1.2	100	0.03	0.2	3.5	0.4	0.5	3	0.3	0
Roasted, light meat, without skin	100	3½ oz	170	31.5	3.0	0	12	265	u	65	410	0.9	0.1	1.4	60	0.04	0.1	11.5	0.7	0.8	3	0.4	0
Chickpeas or garbanzos, cooked without salt	125	½ c (30 g, dry wt)	110	6.0	1.0	18	45	106	u	10	240	2.7	u	2.1	15	0.1	0.03	0.6	0.2	0.4	7	0	0
Chili con carne, with beans, canned	255	1 c	340	19.0	15.5	30	80	320	65	1355	595	4.2	0.8	4.3	150	0.08	0.20	3.3	0.3	0.4	10	u	tr
Chili powder, chilis. See peppers.																							
Chili relleno (stuffed pepper)	110	1 pepper	190	10.5	14.0	6	225	195	u	465	270	u	u	1.3	1600	0.08	0.2	0.8	0.1	0.7	15	1.0	55
Chocolate, bitter or baking	30	1 oz	140	3.0	15.0	8	20	110	u	1	235	0.7	0.8	1.9	20	0.01	0.07	0.4	0.01	0.06	4	0	0
Sweet, milk. See Candy.																							
Chow mein, canned, chicken without noodles	250	1 c	95	6.5	0.3	18	45	85	45	725	420	1.2	0.3	1.3	150	0.05	0.10	1.0	0.4	1.2	10	1.6	15
Clams, canned, with liquid	100	3½ oz, ½ c	50	8.0	0.7	3	55	135	115	u	140	1.2	0	4.0	u	0.01	0.1	1.0	0.08	0.3	3	20	u
Cocoa, dry	5	1 tbsp	15	0.9	1.0	3	5	55	20	tr	80	0.3	0.2	0.6	tr	0.01	0.02	0.1	tr	tr	1	0	0
Coconut, dry, unsweetened	30	1 oz	180	2.0	17.5	6	5	50	u	u	160	u	0.2	0.9	0	0.02	0.01	0.2	0.01	0.06	u	0	0
Coffee, instant, regular dry powder	2.5	1 tbsp	3	tr	tr	1	4	10	10	2	80	0.01	0.02	0.1	0	0	0.01	0.08	0.02	u	u	0	0
Collards, boiled	70	½ c	20	2.0	0.4	4	110	30	30	35	170	0.5	0.2	0.4	3900	0.1	0.2	0.8	0.1	0.3	25	0	35
Cookies																							
Commercial assortment	35	4 cookies	170	1.5	7.0	25	10	55	5	125	25	0.2	0.05	0.2	30	0.01	0.02	0.1	0.02	0.1	1	0	0
Fig bar	55	4 cookies	200	2.0	3.0	40	45	35	15	140	110	0.6	0.1	0.6	60	0.02	0.04	0.2	0.05	0.2	2	0	tr
Oatmeal with raisins	50	4 cookies	235	3.0	8.0	40	10	55	u	85	190	0.6	0.06	1.5	30	0.06	0.04	0.3	u	u	2	u	tr

tr — trace amounts
u — unknown thought to be present
0 — Absent or below detection level

Nutritive Values of the Edible Part of Foods

Food	Weight g	Approximate Measure	Energy Kcal	Protein g	Fat g	Total Carbo-hydrate g	Minerals: Calcium mg	Phos-phorus mg	Mag-nesium mg	Sodium mg	Potas-sium mg	Zinc mg	Copper mg	Iron mg	Vitamins: Total Vitamin A Activity IU	Thia-min mg	Ribo-flavin mg	Niacin mg	Vitamin B-6 mg	Panto-thenic Acid mg	Folacin (free) mcg	Vitamin B-12 mcg	Vitamin C mg
Corn, sweet, yellow																							
Fresh or frozen, boiled	80	½ c	70	2.5	0.8	15	2	75	25	tr	135	0.3	0.08	0.5	350	0.09	0.08	1.0	0.2	0.3	2	0	6
Canned, whole kernel	80	½ c	70	2.0	0.6	16	4	40	15	195	80	0.3	0.05	0.4	300	0.02	0.04	0.8	0.2	0.2	2	0	4
Cream style	130	4 c	110	2.5	0.8	25	4	70	25	300	125	0.6	0.08	0.8	400	0.04	0.06	1.5	0.3	0.4	2	0	6
Corn fritter	35	1 fritter 2 in. × 1½ in.	130	2.5	8.0	14	20	55	u	165	45	u	u	0.6	150	0.06	0.07	0.6	u	u	u	u	tr
Corn syrup	20	1 tbsp	60	0	0	15	10	3	u	15	1	u	0.07	u	0	0	0	0	0	0	0	0	0
Cowpeas or *blackeye peas*																							
Immature	80	½ c	90	7.0	0.6	15	20	120	15	1	310	0.6	0.2	1.7	300	0.2	0.09	1.0	0.04	0.2	20	0	15
Mature, dry, cooked	125	½ c (1 oz dry wt)	95	6.5	0.4	17	20	120	u	10	285	2.0	0.2	1.6	10	0.2	0.05	0.5	0.07	0.3	20	0	u
Crabmeat	100	½ c, packed	100	18.0	2.0	0.6	45	185	u	u	90	4.5	1.0	0.8	2300	0.2	0.08	3.0	0.3	0.6	2	10	2
Crackers																							
Butter (e.g., Ritz)	15	5 round	75	1.1	3.0	11	25	40	u	180	20	u	0.03	0.1	30	tr	tr	0.1	u	u	u	0	0
Graham	15	1 cracker 5 in. × 2½ in.	55	1.0	1.0	10	5	20	5	95	55	0.2	0.03	0.2	0	0.01	0.03	0.2	0.01	0.08	4	0	0
Rye wafer (e.g., Rykrisp)	15	2 wafers	40	1.5	0.2	10	5	50	u	110	u	u	0.04	0.5	0	0.04	0.03	0.2	u	u	u	0	0
Saltines	10	4 each, 2 in. square	50	1.0	1.5	8	2	10	3	125	15	0.05	0.02	0.1	0	tr	tr	0.1	0.01	0.05	2	0	0
Cranberry jelly, or sauce, canned	35	⅛ c	50	tr	tr	13	2	1	u	tr	10	tr	u	tr	10	tr	tr	tr	0.01	u	u	0	tr
Cream																							
half-and-half	60	¼ c or 4 tbsp	80	2.0	7.0	3	65	55	8	25	80	0.3	0.07	tr	300	0.02	0.08	0.02	0.02	0.2	1	0.2	tr
Heavy whipping	60	¼ c; ½ c whipped volume	210	1.0	22.0	2	45	35	4	20	45	0.1	0.06	tr	850	0.01	0.08	0.02	0.01	0.2	0.6	0.1	tr
Light, for coffee	60	¼ c, 4 tbsp	120	2.0	12.0	2	60	50	5	25	75	0.2	0.06	tr	450	0.02	0.08	tr	0.02	0.2	0.6	0.1	tr
Sour	60	¼ c, 4 tbsp	130	1.5	11.0	2	60	50	5	25	80	0.2	0.06	tr	450	0.02	0.09	0.05	0.01	0.2	7	0.1	tr
Cream substitutes																							
Coffee whitener	3	1 tsp or packet	15	0.1	0.8	2	1	12	tr	5	20	0.02	u	tr	5	0	0	0	0	0	0	0	0
Whipped topping, frozen	10	2 tbsp	30	0.1	2.5	2	1	1	tr	2	2	tr	u	tr	80	0	0	0	0	0	0	0	0
Cucumber, raw, peeled	80	½ small	10	0.4	0.1	2	15	15	5	4	125	0.08	0.04	0.2	tr	0.02	0.03	0.2	0.03	0.2	10	0	8
Custard, baked	130	½ c	150	7.0	7.5	15	150	155	u	105	195	u	0.1	0.6	450	0.06	0.2	0.2	u	u	4	u	0
Dandelion greens, boiled	50	½ c	20	1.0	0.3	3	75	20	20	25	120	u	u	1.0	6100	0.07	0.08	u	u	u	u	0	10
Dasheen (Japanese taro), raw	100	1⅓ corms	100	2.0	0.2	25	30	60	u	5	515	u	u	1.0	20	0.1	0.04	1.1	u	u	u	0	4
Dates, dried	80	10, pitted	220	2.0	0.4	60	45	50	45	1	520	u	0.2	2.4	40	0.07	0.08	2.0	0.1	0.6	10	0	0
Doughnuts																							
Cake type	40	1 average	160	2.0	8.0	20	15	80	5	210	40	0.2	0.04	0.6	30	0.07	0.07	0.5	0.02	0.2	3	0	0
Yeast, raised	40	1 average	180	2.5	11.0	16	15	30	5	100	35	0.3	0.04	0.6	30	0.07	0.07	0.6	0.02	0.2	4	0	0
Eggnog	250	1 c	340	9.5	19.0	34	330	275	45	140	420	1.1	u	0.6	900	0.08	0.5	0.3	0.1	1.1	2	1.1	3
Eggs, chicken																							
Whole, raw or hard cooked	50	1 large	80	6.0	5.5	0.6	30	90	6	60	65	0.7	0.05	1.0	300	0.04	0.15	tr	0.06	0.9	25	0.6	0
white	33	1 white	15	3.5	tr	0.4	4	4	3	50	45	tr	0.01	tr	0	tr	0.09	tr	tr	0.07	1	0.02	0
yolk	17	1 yolk	65	3.0	5.0	tr	25	85	3	10	15	0.6	0.05	0.9	300	0.04	0.07	tr	0.05	0.9	25	0.6	0
Scrambled	140	2 eggs	190	12.0	14.0	30	95	195	15	310	170	1.4	0.07	1.9	600	0.07	0.30	0.1	0.1	1.8	50	1.3	tr
Eggplant, boiled	100	½ c diced	20	1.0	0.2	4	10	20	15	1	150	u	0.1	0.6	10	0.05	0.04	0.5	0.08	0.2	2	0	3
Enchiladas, beef																							
Frozen, commercial	200	7-oz portion	240	15.0	8.5	25	20	190	u	725	155	u	u	2.5	600	0.1	0.2	3.0	u	u	u	u	u
Home recipe	190	2 enchiladas	365	32.0	16.7	22	450	480	u	510	585	u	u	5	6000	0.1	0.4	6.0	0.8	0.7	10	2	10
Fats, shortening, solid	100	½ c	880	0	100.0	0	0	0	0	0	0	0	0	0	0	0	0	0	0	0	0	0	0
or oil	12	1 tbsp	110	0	12.0	0	0	0	0	0	0	0	0	0	0	0	0	0	0	0	0	0	0
Figs, fresh	100	2 medium	80	1.0	0.4	20	35	20	20	2	195	u	0.07	0.6	80	0.06	0.06	0.4	0.1	0.3	u	0	2
Dried	30	2 small	80	1.5	0.4	20	40	25	20	u	190	u	0.08	0.6	20	0.03	0.03	0.2	0.05	0.1	1	0	0
Fish																							
Cod, steak, sautéed	110	4 oz	180	30.0	6.0	0	30	285	30	115	420	0.9	0.2	1.0	200	0.08	0.1	3.0	0.3	0.3	10	0.9	0
Fish sticks, breaded	110	4 sticks	200	19.0	10.0	7	10	190	20	u	u	0.3	0.2	0.4	0	0.04	0.08	2.0	0.06	0.3	10	1.1	0
Haddock, fried	110	4 oz	180	22.0	7.0	6	45	270	30	195	385	1.1	0.2	1.3	u	0.04	0.08	3.5	0.2	0.1	5	1.4	2
Mackerel, sautéed	105	3 average	250	23.0	17.0	0	5	295	30	u	u	1.0	0.2	1.3	550	0.2	0.3	8.0	0.7	0.9	5	9.4	0
Salmon, steak, broiled	145	1 average 6 in. × 2 in.	230	35.0	9.0	0	u	630	60	150	565	2.4	1.2	1.5	200	0.2	0.08	12.5	1.0	1.9	6	5.8	0

canned, pink	110	½ c	160	23.0	6.0	0	215	315	30	425	395	1.0	0.3	0.9	80	0.04	0.2	9.0	0.3	0.6	10	7.6	0
red	110	½ c	190	22.0	10.0	0	285	380	30	575	380	1.0	0.3	1.3	250	0.04	0.2	8.0	0.3	0.6	10	7.6	0
Sardines																							
canned in oil	85	3 oz drained	170	20.5	9.0	0	370	425	35	700	500	2.4	0.03	2.4	200	0.03	0.2	4.5	0.2	0.7	10	8.5	0
Sole or flounder, fillet, baked	100	3 oz	200	30.0	8.0	0	25	345	30	235	585	1.0	0.07	1.4	u	0.07	0.08	2.5	0.2	0.8	10	1.2	2
Swordfish, broiled	100	3 oz	170	26.5	6.0	0	25	260	u	u	u	u	u	1.3	2000	0.04	0.05	10.5	u	0.2	u	1.0	0
Tuna, raw	100	½ c	135	27.5	3.0	0	5	175	30	35	180	0.5	0.5	1.3	50	0.02	0.05	6.6	0.9	0.5	3	3.0	7
canned in oil	100	½ c	200	28.0	8.0	0	10	230	25	u	u	1.0	0.1	1.9	80	0.05	0.1	12.0	0.4	0.3	8	2.2	0
in water	100	½ c	130	28.0	0.8	0	15	190	25	865	275	u	u	1.6	80	0.05	0.1	13.0	0.4	0.3	8	2.2	0
Flour, wheat																							
White, all purpose																							
unenriched	115	1 c	420	12.0	1.0	90	20	100	30	2	110	0.8	0.2	0.9	0	0.07	0.06	1.0	0.07	0.5	20	0	0
enriched	115	1 c	420	12.0	1.0	90	20	100	30	2	110	0.8	0.2	3.3	0	0.05	0.3	4.0	0.07	0.5	20	0	0
Whole-grain	120	1 c	400	16.0	2.5	85	50	445	135	4	445	2.9	0.6	4.0	0	0.7	0.1	5.0	0.4	1.3	35	0	0
French toast, frozen	65	1 slice	130	5.0	4.3	18	50	85	u	305	80	u	u	1.3	250	0.1	0.1	0.7	u	u	u	u	0
Frozen dinners																							
Chicken, fried, with potatoes, mixed vegetables	310	11-oz dinner	570	28.0	29.0	48	70	350	60	1075	350	3.0	0.4	3.2	1800	0.2	0.6	16.0	0.9	1.6	20	0.7	10
Meat loaf, with tomato sauce, potatoes, peas	310	11-oz dinner	410	25.0	21.0	30	60	365	60	1225	360	3.5	0.5	4.0	1300	0.3	0.4	5.5	0.7	0.9	20	1.1	10
Turkey with gravy, potatoes, peas	310	11-oz dinner	340	25.0	9.0	40	80	260	65	1200	530	3.0	0.4	3.3	400	0.2	0.3	7.0	0.8	1.8	30	0.6	10
Fruit cocktail	130	½ c	95	0.5	0.2	25	10	15	40	5	205	u	0.04	0.5	200	0.02	0.02	0.5	0.04	u	u	0	2
Gelatin, dry	8	1 tbsp or packet	30	7.0	0	0	u	u	2	1	u	u	0.1	u	0	0	0	0	0	0	0	0	0
Gelatin dessert, plain	120	½c	70	2.0	0	17	u	u	2	u	u	0.02	0.03	u	0	0	0	0	0	0	0	0	0
Grapefruit, raw	100	½ medium	40	0.5	0.1	10	15	15	12	1	130	0.1	0.04	0.4	80	0.04	0.02	0.2	0.03	0.03	8	0	35
Grapefruit juice, canned																							
Unsweetened	180	¾ c	75	0.9	0.2	18	15	25	22	2	300	u	0.02	0.7	20	0.06	0.04	0.4	0.02	0.2	15	0	65
Sweetened	180	¾ c	100	0.9	0.2	25	15	25	20	2	300	u	0.02	0.7	20	0.06	0.04	0.4	u	u	15	0	60
Grapes, raw																							
Slip-skin	100	20 grapes	45	0.8	0.8	10	10	10	10	2	105	0.17	0.1	0.2	80	0.02	0.02	0.2	0.08	0.08	4	0	2
Adherent skin	100	20 grapes	70	0.6	0.4	17	10	20	6	4	175	0.3	0.1	0.4	100	0.06	0.04	0.4	0.08	0.08	4	0	4
Grape juice	190	¾ c	120	0.4	tr	30	20	20	25	4	220	u	0.03	0.6	u	0.08	0.04	0.4	0.04	0.08	4	0	tr
Guacamole	120	½ c	140	2.1	12.8	7	15	40	u	165	565	u	0.3	0.7	550	0.10	0.2	1.6	0.4	0.9	30	0	35
Ham, baked	85	3 oz	250	18.0	19.0	0	10	145	15	635	200	3.4	0.3	2.2	0	0.4	0.2	3.0	0.3	0.3	1	0.4	0
Hominy grits. See Cereal, cooked.																							
Honey, strained	20	1 tbsp	65	0.1	0	17	1	1	1	1	10	0.02	0.03	0.1	0	tr	0.01	0.1	tr	0.04	0	0	tr
Ice cream, vanilla																							
Plain, 10% fat	65	½ c	135	2.5	7.0	15	90	70	10	60	130	0.7	0.02	0.05	300	0.02	0.2	0.05	0.03	0.3	1	0.3	0
Rich, 16% fat	75	½ c	175	2.0	12.0	16	75	60	8	50	110	0.6	0.02	0.05	450	0.02	0.15	0.05	0.03	0.03	1	0.3	0
Ice milk, vanilla	65	½ c	90	2.5	3.0	15	90	65	10	50	130	0.3	u	0.09	100	0.04	0.2	0.05	0.04	0.3	1	0.4	0
Ices, water, lime	95	½ c	120	0.4	tr	30	tr	tr	u	tr	3	u	u	tr	0	tr	tr	tr	0	0	0	0	0
Jams and jellies	20	1 tbsp	55	0.1	tr	14	4	2	1	2	20	0.1	0.02	0.2	tr	tr	0.01	tr	0.01	0.02	1	0	tr
Kale, boiled without stems	55	½ c	20	2.5	0.4	3	105	30	18	25	120	u	u	0.9	4600	0.06	0.1	0.9	0.2	0.6	25	0	50
Kidney, braised	100	3½ oz	250	33.0	12.0	0.8	20	240	20	250	320	2.4	0.1	13.0	1100	0.5	4.87	10.5	0.4	3.8	60	30	u
Kohlrabi, boiled	80	½ c, diced	20	1.5	0.1	4	25	35	30	5	215	u	u	0.2	15	0.05	0.02	0.2	0.1	0.5	u	0	35
Kumquat, raw	20	1 medium	10	0.2	tr	3	10	4	u	1	45	u	u	0.1	100	0.01	0.02	u	u	u	u	0	7
Lamb, choice grade																							
Chop, loin, broiled																							
lean and fat	95	1 average	340	21.0	28.0	0	10	165	15	50	235	u	0.1	1.2	u	0.1	0.2	5.0	0.3	0.5	1	2.0	0
lean only	65	1 average	120	18.0	5.0	0	10	140	15	45	205	3.0	0.1	1.3	u	0.1	0.2	4.0	0.2	0.4	1	1.4	0
Leg, roasted																							
lean only	85	3 oz	160	24.0	6.0	0	10	200	15	60	275	3.6	0.05	1.9	u	0.1	0.3	5.5	0.2	0.5	1	1.8	0
Shoulder, roasted																							
lean and fat	85	3 oz	280	18.5	23.0	0	10	145	15	45	205	u	0.1	1.0	u	0.1	0.2	4.0	0.2	0.5	1	1.8	0
Lard. see Fats.																							
Lasagna, frozen	225	8-oz serving	380	27.0	12.4	43	310	470	55	1100	740	1.4	u	5.6	1300	0.4	0.4	4.5	u	u	u	u	15
Lemon juice, fresh	15	1 tbsp	5	0.1	tr	1	1	2	1	tr	20	tr	0.01	tr	tr	tr	tr	tr	0.01	0.02	u	0	7
Lemonade, from frozen concentrate	250	1 c	110	0.1	tr	30	2	3	2	1	40	0.02	0.02	0.1	10	0.01	0.02	0.2	0.01	0.03	5	0	15
Lentils, dried, cooked	100	½ c	110	8.0	tr	19	25	120	20	u	250	1.0	0.3	2.1	20	0.07	0.06	0.6	u	u	6	0	0
Lettuce, raw																							
Head, solid (iceberg type)	90	⅙ head	10	0.8	0.1	3	20	20	10	10	160	0.4	0.08	0.5	300	0.05	0.05	0.3	0.05	0.2	30	0	5
Loose leaf, romaine, cos	55	1 c, chopped	10	0.7	0.2	2	35	15	10	5	145	0.2	0.05	0.8	1000	0.03	0.04	0.2	0.03	0.1	30	0	10
Liver																							
Beef, fried	85	3 oz	200	22.5	9.0	4	10	405	15	155	325	4.3	2.5	7.5	45,400	0.2	3.6	24.0	0.7	6.5	70	68.0	25
Calf, fried	85	3 oz	220	25.0	11.2	3	10	455	20	100	385	5.2	6.5	12.1	27,800	0.2	3.5	14.0	0.6	6.5	70	51.0	30
Chicken, simmered	70	½ c, chopped	120	18.5	3.0	2	10	110	u	40	105	2.4	0.2	6.0	8600	0.1	1.9	8.0	0.5	4.2	u	17.5	10

tr — trace amounts
u — unknown thought to be present
0 — Absent or below detection level

Nutritive Values of the Edible Part of Foods

Food	Weight g	Approximate Measure	Energy Kcal	Protein g	Fat g	Total Carbo-hydrate g	Minerals: Calcium mg	Phos-phorus mg	Mag-nesium mg	Sodium mg	Potas-sium mg	Zinc mg	Copper mg	Iron mg	Vitamins: Total Vitamin A Activity IU	Thia-min mg	Ribo-flavin mg	Niacin mg	Vitamin B-6 mg	Panto-thenic Acid mg	Folacin (free) mcg	Vitamin B-12 mcg	Vitamin C mg
Lobster, northern, cooked	95	⅔ c meat	90	18.0	1.5	0.3	65	185	20	205	175	2.1	1.6	0.8	u	0.1	0.07	u	u	1.4	8	0.5	u
Lychee nuts, raw	150	10 nuts	60	0.8	0.3	15	5	40	u	3	155	u	u	0.4	0	u	0.05	u	u	u	u	0	40
Macaroni and other pastas, cooked																							
Unenriched	130	1 c	190	6.5	0.7	40	15	85	25	1	105	0.6	0.03	0.7	0	0.03	0.03	0.5	0.03	0.2	5	0	0
Enriched	130	1 c	190	6.5	0.7	40	15	85	25	1	105	0.6	0.03	1.4	0	0.2	0.1	2.0	0.03	0.2	5	0	0
Mangos, raw	165	1 c, diced	110	1.0	0.7	30	15	20	30	10	310	0.8	0.2	0.7	7900	0.08	0.08	2.0	u	0.3	u	u	60
Margarine	5	1 tsp, 1 pat (90/lb)	35	tr	4	tr	1	1	tr	50	1	0.01	tr	0	160	0	0	0	0	0	0	0	0
Melons																							
Cantaloupe	160	½ melon or 1 c, cubed	50	1.0	0.2	12	20	25	20	20	400	0.1	0.06	0.6	5400	0.06	0.05	1.0	0.1	0.4	50	0	5
Honeydew	170	⅛ melon or 1 c, cubed	55	1.4	0.5	13	25	25	u	20	425	0.1	0.06	0.7	70	0.07	0.05	1.0	u	u	u	0	40
Watermelon	425	1/16 melon (2 lb with rind)	110	2.0	0.9	25	30	45	35	5	425	u	0.3	2.1	2500	0.1	0.1	0.9	0.3	1.2	8	0	30
Milk, cow																							
Whole, fluid	245	1 c	155	8.0	8.5	11	290	225	30	120	370	1.0	0.08	0.1	350	0.09	0.4	0.2	0.1	0.8	10	0.9	2
2%, low-fat	245	1 c	140	10.0	5.0	14	350	275	40	145	450	1.1	0.08	0.1	200	0.1	0.5	0.2	0.1	0.9	15	1.0	2
Skim, nonfat, or buttermilk	245	1 c	90	8.5	0.4	12	300	245	3	125	400	1.0	0.08	0.1	10	0.09	0.4	0.2	0.1	0.8	15	1.0	2
Chocolate, low-fat	250	1 c	180	8.0	5.0	26	285	255	30	150	420	1.0	u	0.6	200	0.1	0.4	0.3	0.1	0.7	10	0.8	2
Dried, instant																							
whole	30	¼ c	160	8.5	8.5	12	290	250	25	120	425	1.0	0.06	0.1	300	0.09	0.4	0.2	0.09	0.7	10	1.0	2
nonfat	35	¼ c	125	12.0	0.2	13	445	345	40	190	600	1.5	0.1	0.1	10	0.09	0.5	0.3	0.1	1.1	15	1.4	2
Evaporated	250	1 c	340	17.5	20.0	25	660	510	60	265	765	1.9	0.2	0.4	600	0.1	0.8	0.5	0.1	1.6	20	0.4	3
Condensed, sweetened	40	1 fl oz	120	3.0	3.5	20	105	95	10	50	140	0.4	0.08	0.1	100	0.03	0.2	0.1	0.02	0.3	4	0.2	tr
Milk, human, U.S.	30	1 fl oz	21	0.3	1.3	2.1	10	4	1	5	16	0.05	0.01	0.01	70	.004	0.01	0.1	0.003	0.07	2	0.02	2
Milkshakes, commercial	270	10 fl oz	320	11.0	7.0	50	365	340	30	300	600	0.5	0.04	0.3	300	0.08	0.5	0.4	0.1	1.0	15	0.6	tr
Molasses																							
Light	20	1 tbsp	50	0	0	13	35	10	9	3	185	u	u	0.9	0	0.01	0.01	tr	u	u	u	0	0
Medium	20	1 tbsp	50	0	0	12	60	15	16	5	215	0.9	03	1.2	0	u	0.02	0.2	0.04	0.07	2	0	0
Blackstrap	20	1tbsp	45	tr	0	11	135	15	52	20	585	u	u	3.2	0	0.02	0.04	0.4	u	u	u	0	0
Muffins																							
Bran	40	1 muffin	100	3.0	4.0	15	55	160	u	180	170	u	u	1.5	100	0.06	0.1	1.5	u	u	u	u	0
Cornmeal	40	1 muffin	130	3.0	4.0	19	40	70	20	190	55	u	u	0.7	100	0.08	0.09	0.6	u	u	u	u	0
Plain or blueberry	40	1 muffin	120	3.0	4.0	17	40	60	10	175	50	0.5	0.09	0.6	50	0.07	0.09	0.6	0.02	0.2	3	0.1	0
Mushrooms, raw	35	½ c, sliced	10	1.0	0.1	2	2	40	5	5	145	0.1	0.04	0.3	tr	0.04	0.2	1.5	0.04	0.8	7	0	1
Mustard greens, boiled	70	½ c	15	1.5	0.3	3	95	20	10	10	155	0.2	0.06	1.2	4100	0.06	0.1	0.4	0.09	0.1	u	0	35
Mustard, prepared, yellow	5	1 tsp	4	0.2	0.2	0.3	4	4	2	65	5	0.03	0.02	0.1	0	u	u	u	u	u	u	0	0
Noodles, egg, cooked																							
Unenriched	105	⅔ c	130	4.5	1.5	25	10	65	25	2	45	0.6	0.02	0.6	70	0.03	0.02	0.4	0.02	0.2	2	tr	0
Enriched	105	⅔ c	130	4.5	1.5	25	10	65	25	2	45	0.6	0.02	0.9	70	0.10	0.09	1.3	0.02	0.2	2	tr	0
Oils. See Fats.																							
Okra, boiled	105	10 pods	30	2.0	0.3	6	100	45	40	2	185	u	0.1	0.5	500	0.1	0.2	1.0	0.08	0.2	10	0	20
Olives																							
Green	25	5 large	20	0.2	2.5	0.2	10	4	5	465	10	0.02	0.09	0.3	60	u	u	u	0.01	0	3	0	0
Ripe	25	5 large	35	0.2	4.0	0.6	20	4	u	150	5	0.07	0.09	0.4	20	tr	tr	u	tr	tr	u	0	0
Onions																							
Green, raw, bulb and top	25	¼ c, chopped or 3 onions	10	0.4	tr	2	15	10	3	1	60	0.07	0.01	0.3	500	0.01	0.01	0.1	u	0.4	10	0	8
Mature, dry	85	½ c, chopped	30	1.5	0.1	7	25	30	10	10	135	0.3	0.1	0.4	35	0.02	0.04	0.2	0.1	0.1	8	0	8
raw	10	1 tbsp, ⅛ onion	4	0.2	tr	0.9	3	4	1	1	15	0.03	0.01	0.1	tr	tr	tr	tr	0.01	0.01	1	0	1
boiled	105	½ c, sliced	30	1.0	0.1	7	25	30	10	10	115	0.6	0.08	0.4	40	0.03	0.03	0.2	0.1	0.1	10	0	8
Oranges, raw	140	1 medium	80	1.8	0.1	18	60	30	30	1	270	0.3	0.09	0.6	280	0.14	0.06	0.6	0.08	0.4	45	0	85
Orange juice, fresh or frozen	185	¾ c	85	1.5	0.4	19	20	30	20	2	370	0.04	0.09	0.4	400	0.2	0.05	0.8	0.07	0.4	65	0	95
Oysters, raw																							
Eastern	120	6 oysters	80	10.0	2.0	4	115	170	40	90	145	90.0	4.0	6.6	350	0.2	0.2	3.0	0.6	0.3	u	21.6	u
Pacific	120	6 oysters	110	12.5	2.5	8	100	185	30	u	u	10.8	4.0	8.6	u	0.1	u	1.6	u	u	u	u	35
Pakchoy, raw	100	⅔ c	15	1.0	0.1	3	165	45	u	25	305	u	u	0.8	3000	0.05	0.1	0.8	u	u	u	0	25
Pancakes, plain	110	4, ea. 4-in. diam	245	7.5	10.0	35	230	280	15	610	170	0.9	0.06	1.2	300	0.2	0.2	0.8	0.4	0.8	10	u	0

Papaya, raw	225	½ fruit or 1 c, cubed	60	0.9	0.2	15	30	25	u	4	355	u	0.02	0.4	2700	0.06	0.06	0.4	u	0.5	u	0	85
Parsley, raw	5	1 tbsp, chopped	2	0.1	tr	0.3	5	2	2	2	25	u	0.02	0.2	300	tr	0.01	tr	0.01	0.02	2	0	6
Peaches, without skin																							
Raw, yellow	115	1 medium	40	0.6	0.1	10	10	20	12	1	200	0.2	0.06	0.5	1300	0.02	0.05	1.0	0.03	0.2	2	0	7
Canned, heavy syrup	150	2 halves and 3 tbsp juice	120	0.6	0.2	30	5	20	9	4	200	0.1	0.1	0.4	650	0.02	0.04	1.0	0.03	0.08	u	0	4
water pack	155	2 halves and 3 tbsp juice	50	0.6	0.2	12	5	20	9	4	210	u	0.08	0.4	700	0.02	0.04	1.0	u	u	u	0	4
Dried, unsulfured, uncooked	65	5 halves	170	2.0	0.4	45	30	75	30	10	620	u	u	3.9	2500	tr	0.1	3.5	0.06	u	u	0	10
Peanuts, roasted, salted	30	1 oz, 30 nuts	165	7.5	14.0	5	20	115	50	120	190	0.9	0.1	0.6	0	0.09	0.04	4.9	0.1	0.6	8	0	0
Peanut butter	15	1 tbsp	95	4.0	8.0	3	10	60	25	95	100	0.4	0.09	0.3	0	0.02	0.02	2.4	0.05	0.3	3	0	0
Pears																							
Raw, with skin	180	1, 3½ in. × 2½ in.	100	1.0	0.7	25	15	20	15	3	215	u	0.3	0.5	30	0.03	0.07	0.2	0.03	0.1	9	0	7
Canned syrup	150	2 halves and 3 tbsp juice	115	0.4	0.4	30	10	10	7	2	130	u	0.06	0.4	tr	0.02	0.04	0.2	0.02	0.3	9	0	2
water pack	155	2 halves and 3 tbsp juice	50	0.4	0.4	13	10	10	7	2	135	u	0.08	0.4	tr	0.02	0.04	0.2	u	u	u	0	2
Peas																							
Green, frozen, boiled	80	½ c	55	4.0	0.2	9	15	70	15	90	110	0.6	0.2	1.5	500	0.2	0.1	2.2	0.1	0.3	14	0	15
Canned, drained	85	½ c	75	4.0	0.4	14	20	65	10	200	80	0.7	0.1	1.6	500	0.08	0.05	0.7	0.04	0.1	5	0	7
Split, dry, cooked	100	½ c (1 oz, dry wt)	115	8.0	0.3	20	10	90	8	15	295	1.1	0.07	1.7	40	0.2	0.09	0.9	0.04	0.6	20	0	0
Peas and carrots, frozen, boiled	80	½ c	40	2.5	0.2	8	20	45	15	65	125	u	u	0.9	7400	0.2	0.05	1.0	0.08	0.2	u	0	6
Pecans	30	1 oz, 20 halves	200	2.5	20.0	4	20	80	40	tr	170	u	0.3	0.7	40	0.2	0.04	0.3	0.05	0.5	4	0	1
Peppers, hot (chili)																							
Green, canned sauce	15	1 tbsp	3	0.1	tr	1	1	2	u	u	u	u	u	0.1	100	tr	tr	0.1	u	u	u	0	10
Red, dry, chili powder	3	1 tsp	8	0.3	0.4	1	7	8	4	25	50	0.07	u	0.4	900	0.01	0.02	0.2	u	u	u	0	2
Peppers, sweet																							
Green, raw	75	½ c, chopped	15	0.9	0.1	4	5	15	15	10	155	0.2	0.07	0.5	300	0.06	0.06	0.4	0.2	0.2	5	0	95
Red, raw	90	1 medium	25	1.0	0.2	5	10	20	u	u	u	u	u	0.4	3300	0.06	0.06	0.4	u	0.2	20	0	150
Pickles, cucumber																							
Dill	135	1 large	15	0.9	0.3	3	35	30	1	1930	270	0.4	0.03	1.4	150	tr	0.03	tr	0.01	0.3	4	0	8
Sweet	35	1 medium	50	0.2	0.1	13	4	5	tr	u	u	0.05	0.07	0.4	30	tr	0.01	tr	tr	0.07	1	0	2
Relish, sweet	15	1 tbsp	20	0.1	0.1	5	3	2	u	105	u	0.01	0.05	0.1	u	0	0	0	u	u	0	0	tr
Pies																							
Apple, berry, rhubarb	160	⅙ of 9-in. pie	400	3.5	17.5	60	15	35	5	475	125	0.1	0.1	0.5	50	0.03	0.03	0.6	0.06	0.2	3	0	2
Cherry, peach	160	⅙ of 9-in. pie	410	4.0	18.0	60	20	40	u	480	165	0.06	0.1	0.5	700	0.03	0.03	0.8	u	u	u	0	tr
Cream, pudding type with meringue	150	⅙ of 9-in. pie	380	7.5	18.0	50	105	150	u	390	210	u	u	1.1	300	0.05	0.20	0.3	u	1.4	u	0	tr
Custard	150	⅙ of 9-in. pie	330	9.5	17.0	35	145	170	u	u	u	u	u	0.9	350	0.08	0.30	0.5	u	u	u	u	0
Lemon meringue	140	⅙ of 9-in. pie	360	5.0	14.5	55	20	70	u	395	70	u	u	0.7	250	0.04	0.10	0.3	u	u	3	u	4
Mince	160	⅙ of 9-in. pie	430	4.0	18.0	65	45	60	u	710	280	u	0.1	1.6	tr	0.10	0.06	0.6	u	u	u	u	2
Pecan	140	⅙ of 9-in. pie	580	7.0	31.5	70	65	140	u	305	170	u	u	3.9	200	0.20	0.10	0.4	u	u	u	u	tr
Pumpkin	150	⅙ of 9-in. pie	320	6.0	17.0	35	80	105	10	325	245	0.6	0.08	0.8	3800	0.05	0.20	0.8	0.06	0.8	5	u	tr
Sweet potato	150	⅙ of 9-in. pie	325	7.0	17.0	36	105	130	u	330	250	u	u	0.8	3800	0.08	0.20	0.5	u	u	u	u	6
Pineapple, diced or crushed																							
Raw	155	1 c	80	0.6	0.3	20	25	10	20	2	225	0.3	0.1	0.8	100	0.1	0.05	0.3	0.1	0.2	15	0	25
Canned, in heavy syrup	130	½ c solids and liquid	95	0.4	0.2	25	15	6	10	2	120	0.3	0.2	0.4	60	0.1	0.02	0.2	0.1	0.1	3	0	9
in juice	125	½ c solids and liquid	70	0.4	0.2	17	15	8	15	1	180	0.3	0.1	0.6	80	0.1	0.04	0.2	0.1	0.2	u	0	15
water pack	125	½ c solids and liquid	50	0.4	0.1	13	15	5	u	1	120	u	u	0.4	60	0.1	0.02	0.2	u	u	u	0	8
Pineapple juice vv9.8190		¾ c	105	0.8	0.6	25	30	15	20	2	280	u	0.1	0.6	100	0.1	0.04	0.4	0.2	0.2	u	0	15
Pinenuts, piñon	30	1 oz, 4 tbsp	180	3.5	17.0	6	3	170	u	u	u	u	u	1.5	10	0.4	0.07	1.3	u	u	u	u	tr
Pizza, cheese	65	⅛ of 14-in. pizza	150	8.0	6.5	18	145	125	20	455	85	0.8	0.2	0.7	400	0.04	0.1	0.7	u	u	u	u	5
Sausage	65	⅛ of 14-in. pizza	160	5.0	6.0	20	10	60	u	490	115	0.8	u	0.8	400	0.06	0.08	1.0	u	u	u	u	6
Plantain	265	1 banana 11 in. × 2 in.	310	3.0	1.0	82	20	80	u	15	1010	u	u	1.8	u	0.2	0.1	1.6	u	0.7	u	0	35
Plums, raw	70	1 medium	30	0.3	0.1	8	10	10	6	1	110	u	0.07	0.3	150	0.02	0.02	0.3	0.04	0.1	1	0	4
Canned, purple in heavy syrup	140	3 and 3 tbsp syrup	110	0.5	0.1	30	10	15	7	1	190	u	u	1.2	500	0.03	0.03	0.5	0.04	0.1	u	0	3
Popcorn with oil and salt	10	1 c	40	0.9	2.0	5	1	20	10	175	u	0.2	0.03	0.2	u	u	0.01	0.2	0.02	0.04	0	0	0
Pork																							
Chop, broiled																							
lean and fat	80	1 medium	300	19.5	24.5	0	10	210	15	45	215	u	u	2.7	0	0.8	0.2	4.5	0.3	0.5	3	0.4	0
lean only	50	1 medium	110	13.0	6.5	0	5	135	10	30	145	1.5	0.04	1.6	0	0.5	0.1	2.9	0.1	0.2	2	0.2	0
Loin, roasted																							
lean and fat	85	2½ in. × 2½ in. × ¼ in.	310	21.0	24.0	0	10	220	20	50	235	u	0.05	2.7	0	0.8	0.2	4.6	0.3	0.5	1	0.5	0
Spareribs, braised	90	yield from ½ lb, raw wt	400	18.5	35.0	0	15	220	u	65	300	u	u	4.7	0	0.8	0.4	6.1	u	u	u	0.6	0

tr — trace amounts
u — unknown thought to be present
0 — Absent or below detection level

Nutritive Values of the Edible Part of Foods

Food	Weight g	Approximate Measure	Energy Kcal	Protein g	Fat g	Total Carbohydrate g	Minerals: Calcium mg	Phosphorus mg	Magnesium mg	Sodium mg	Potassium mg	Zinc mg	Copper mg	Iron mg	Vitamins: Total Vitamin A Activity IU	Thiamin mg	Riboflavin mg	Niacin mg	Vitamin B-6 mg	Pantothenic Acid mg	Folacin (free) mcg	Vitamin B-12 mcg	Vitamin C mg
Potatoes																							
Baked	200	1 large	140	4.0	0.2	35	15	100	45	5	780	0.4	0.3	1.1	tr	0.2	0.07	2.7	0.5	0.8	20	0	30
Boiled, pared before cooking	135	1 medium	90	2.5	0.1	20	10	55	u	3	385	0.4	0.1	0.7	tr	0.1	0.05	1.6	0.5	0.8	15	0	20
French-fried																							
commercial	70	1 "order"	220	3.0	10.2	28	9	70	20	120	u	u	u	0.4	tr	0.1	0.04	2.4	0.2	u	5	0	9
frozen, reheated	100	20 strips	220	3.5	8.4	35	10	90	30	4	660	0.3	0.3	0.8	tr	0.1	0.02	2.6	0.2	0.5	10	0	20
Mashed with milk	100	½ c	100	2.0	4.5	13	25	50	15	350	260	0.1	0.1	0.4	200	0.08	0.05	1.0	0.1	0.2	10	0	10
Potato chips	20	10 chips, 2-in. diameter each	115	1.0	8.0	10	10	30	10	200	225	0.2	0.04	0.4	tr	0.04	0.01	1.0	0.04	0.1	2	0	3
Potato salad. See salads.																							
Pretzels	30	10, 3-ring pretzels	120	3.0	1.5	25	5	40	u	500	80	0.3	0.04	0.5	0	0.01	0.02	0.4	0.01	0.2	u	tr	0
Prunes, dried, raw	50	5	130	1.0	0.3	35	25	40	u	4	355	u	0.1	2.0	800	0.04	0.08	0.8	0.1	0.2	tr	0	2
Cooked without sugar	125	½ c	120	1.0	0.3	35	25	40	u	4	350	u	0.2	1.9	800	0.04	0.08	0.8	u	u	u	0	1
Prune juice, canned	190	¾ c	150	0.8	0.2	35	25	40	u	4	450	tr	0.04	2.0	800	0.02	0.02	0.8	u	u	u	u	4
Puddings																							
Almendrado	65	⅓ c and 2 tbsp sauce	100	2.7	4.3	14	35	50	u	35	50	u	u	0.3	250	0.02	0.08	0.03	0.02	0.3	8	0.4	tr
Apple Brown Betty	110	½ c	160	1.5	4.0	30	20	25	5	165	110	u	u	0.6	100	0.06	0.04	0.4	u	u	u	u	1
Capirotada	155	½ c	385	10.8	14.0	58	230	200	u	335	355	u	u	2.5	250	0.10	0.20	3.0	0.10	0.4	6	0.3	0
Chocolate, instant, packaged	130	½ c	160	5.0	3.0	30	185	120	u	160	170	u	u	0.4	150	0.04	0.20	0.2	u	u	u	u	0
Custard	130	½ c	150	7.0	7.5	15	150	155	u	105	195	u	u	0.6	450	0.06	0.2	0.2	u	u	4	u	tr
Rice with raisins	130	½ c	200	5.0	4.0	35	130	125	u	95	235	0.4	0.04	0.6	150	0.04	0.2	0.2	u	u	5	u	tr
Tapioca	80	½ c	110	4.0	4.0	14	85	90	u	130	110	u	0.04	0.4	250	0.04	0.2	0.1	u	u	2	u	0
Vanilla, home recipe	130	½ c	140	4.5	5.0	20	150	115	u	85	175	u	0.05	tr	200	0.04	0.2	0.2	u	u	u	u	0
Pumpkin, canned	245	1 c	80	2.5	0.7	19	60	65	30	5	560	u	0.3	1.0	15,700	0.07	0.1	1.5	0.1	1.0	4	0	10
Radishes, raw	45	4 large	7	0.4	tr	1	10	10	7	10	130	0.1	0.04	0.4	5	0.01	0.01	0.1	0.03	0.08	10	0	10
Raisins	35	¼ c	100	0.9	0.1	30	20	35	10	10	275	0.06	0.08	1.3	10	0.04	0.03	0.2	0.08	0.2	1	0	tr
Rhubarb, cooked with sugar	135	½ c	190	0.7	0.2	50	105	20	20	2	275	0.1	0.1	0.8	100	0.02	0.07	0.4	0.03	0.09	10	0	8
Rice cooked, salt added																							
Brown	130	⅔ c	160	3.5	0.8	35	15	95	40	370	90	0.8	0.1	0.7	0	0.1	0.03	1.8	0.2	0.5	10	0	0
White, enriched	135	⅔ c	150	3.0	0.1	35	15	85	10	515	40	0.5	0.07	1.2	0	0.2	0.01	1.4	0.05	0.3	1	0	0
Precooked, instant	110	⅔ c	120	2.5	tr	25	3	20	u	300	u	0.2	u	0.9	0	0.1	u	1.1	u	u	u	0	0
Rolls and Buns																							
Danish pastry	85	1, of 4-in. diameter	270	5.0	15.5	30	35	70	15	240	75	u	u	0.6	200	0.04	0.1	0.5	u	u	5	u	tr
Hamburger or frankfurter bun, enriched	40	1 average	120	3.5	2.0	20	30	35	10	200	40	0.2	0.08	0.8	tr	0.1	0.07	0.9	u	u	5	u	0
Hard rolls, enriched	50	1 large	160	5.0	1.5	30	25	45	15	315	50	0.6	u	1.2	tr	0.1	0.1	1.4	u	u	6	0	0
Plain pan rolls, white, enriched	30	1 small	85	2.5	1.5	15	20	25	10	140	25	0.4	u	0.5	tr	0.08	0.05	0.6	0.01	0.09	4	u	0
Rutabagas, boiled	85	½ c, cubed	30	0.8	0.1	7	50	25	12	4	140	u	u	0.2	500	0.05	0.05	0.7	0.08	0.1	u	0	20
Salads																							
Chef's (lettuce w/ham, cheese, dressing)	u	1 serving	285	13.0	24.0	3	150	185	u	u	u	u	u	2.2	1250	0.2	0.2	1.2	u	u	u	u	13
Potato, home recipe	125	½ c	120	3.5	3.5	20	40	80	u	650	400	0.3	u	0.8	150	0.1	0.09	1.4	u	u	u	u	14
Tuna fish	100	½ c	170	15.0	10.0	4	20	145	u	u	u	u	u	1.3	250	0.04	0.1	5.1	u	u	u	u	1
Salad dressings																							
Blue cheese	15	1 tbsp	75	0.7	8.0	1	10	10	u	165	5	0.04	u	tr	30	tr	0.02	tr	u	u	u	tr	tr
French, regular	15	1 tbsp	65	0.1	6.0	3	2	2	2	220	15	0.01	u	0.1	u	u	u	u	u	u	u	0	u
low-calorie	15	1 tbsp	15	0.1	0.7	3	2	2	u	125	15	u	u	0.1	u	u	u	u	u	u	u	0	u
Italian, regular	15	1 tbsp	85	tr	9.0	1.0	2	1	1	315	2	0.02	0.1	tr	tr	tr	tr	tr	0	0	0	0	0
low-calorie	15	1 tbsp	10	tr	0.7	0.4	tr	1	u	120	2	u	u	tr	tr	tr	tr	tr	0	0	0	0	0
Mayonnaise	15	1 tbsp	100	0.2	11.0	0.3	3	4	tr	85	5	0.02	0.04	0.1	40	tr	0.01	tr	u	0.02	0	0	0
Salad dressing	15	1 tbsp	65	0.2	6.5	2.0	2	4	tr	90	1	0.8	u	tr	30	tr	tr	tr	0	0.02	0	0	0
Thousand Island, or Louis-type	15	1 tbsp	80	0.1	8.0	2.5	2	3	u	110	20	0.02	u	0.1	50	tr	tr	tr	u	u	u	u	tr
Salmon. See Fish.																							
Sandwiches																							
Bacon, lettuce, tomato on white bread	150	1 average	280	7.0	15.5	30	55	90	u	u	u	u	u	1.5	850	0.2	0.1	1.5	u	u	u	u	15
Egg salad on white bread	140	1 average	280	10.5	12.5	30	70	155	u	u	u	u	u	2.4	600	0.2	0.02	1.0	u	u	u	u	2
Fish fillet, fried on bun	135	1 average	410	15.0	21.5	37	95	235	20	760	u	u	u	1.6	80	0.2	0.4	2.9	0.1	u	20	0.8	2

Ham and cheese on white bread	u	1 average	350	20.0	19.0	30	215	240	u	u	u	u	u	3.1	300	0.4	0.3	2.5	u	u	u	u	0
Hamburger on bun	95	1 regular	250	13.0	9.6	28	50	120	15	540	u	u	u	2.6	160	0.2	0.4	3.7	0.1	u	20	0.8	4
"Big Mac"	185	1 large	560	26.0	32.0	40	160	290	30	1060	u	u	u	3.8	200	0.8	0.6	6.5	0.2	u	30	1.5	5
Tuna salad on white bread	105	1 average	280	11.0	14.0	25	50	135	u	u	u	u	u	1.2	250	0.1	0.1	4.0	u	u	u	u	1
Sashimi. See Fish, tuna, raw.																							
Sardines. See Fish.																							
Sauces																							
Butterscotch	45	2 tbsp	200	0.5	7.0	35	40	25	u	u	u	u	u	1.4	300	tr	tr	tr	u	u	u	0	0
Cheese	40	2 tbsp	65	3.0	5.0	2	90	65	u	u	u	u	u	0.1	200	0.01	0.08	0.1	u	u	u	u	tr
Chocolate																							
thin syrup	40	2 tbsp	100	0.9	0.8	25	7	35	u	u	u	u	0.2	0.6	tr	0.01	0.03	0.2	u	u	u	0	0
fudge type	40	2 tbsp	125	2.0	5.0	20	50	60	u	35	105	u	u	0.5	60	0.02	0.08	0.2	u	u	u	tr	0
Custard	70	¼ c	85	3.5	4.0	10	80	80	u	u	u	u	u	0.4	250	0.04	0.2	0.1	u	u	u	u	tr
Hard sauce	20	2 tbsp	95	0.1	5.5	12	2	1	u	u	u	u	u	tr	250	tr	tr	tr	0	0	0	0	0
Hollandaise	50	¼ c scant	180	2.0	18.5	0.4	25	80	u	u	u	u	u	0.9	1000	0.03	0.04	tr	u	u	u	u	tr
Soy	35	2 tbsp	25	2.0	0.5	4	30	40	u	2665	135	u	u	1.7	0	0.01	0.09	0.1	u	u	u	0	0
Tartar	15	1 tbsp	75	0.2	8.0	0.6	3	4	u	100	10	u	u	0.1	30	tr	tr	tr	u	u	u	u	tr
Tomato catsup	15	1 tbsp	15	0.3	0.1	4	3	10	3	155	55	0.04	0.09	0.1	200	0.01	0.01	0.2	0.02	u	tr	0	2
White, medium	125	½ c	200	5.0	15.5	11	145	115	20	475	175	0.5	0.05	0.2	600	0.05	0.2	0.2	0.06	0.8	1	0.2	1
Sauerkraut, canned	120	½ c	20	1.0	0.2	5	40	20	u	880	165	1.0	0.1	0.6	60	0.04	0.04	0.2	0.2	0.1	u	0	16
Sausages																							
Bologna	30	1 slice, 4½ in. × ¼ in.	85	3.5	8.0	0.3	2	35	u	370	65	0.5	tr	0.5	0	0.05	0.06	0.7	0.03	u	1	u	0
Frankfurter (all-meat)	45	1 average	135	5.5	12.0	0.7	2	45	u	u	u	0.7	0.04	0.7	0	0.07	0.09	1.1	0.06	0.2	1	0.6	0
Liverwurst	30	1 oz	85	4.5	7.0	0.5	3	70	5	u	u	2.2	0.9	1.5	1800	0.06	0.4	1.6	0.06	0.8	6	4.2	tr
Luncheon meat, pork, cured	30	1 oz	85	4.5	7.0	0.4	3	30	u	350	65	u	0.02	0.6	0	0.09	0.06	0.9	u	0.2	1	u	0
Pork sausage, links	40	3 links	185	7.0	17.0	tr	3	60	5	375	105	0.2	0.06	0.9	0	0.3	0.1	1.5	0.07	0.3	1	0.2	0
Salami, dry	30	3 small slices	130	6.5	11.0	0.3	4	80	u	u	u	u	u	1.0	0	0.1	0.07	1.5	0.04	u	1	u	0
Vienna, canned	50	3 sausages	115	6.5	9.5	0.1	3	75	u	u	u	u	u	0.9	0	0.03	0.06	1.2	0.04	u	1	u	0
Scallops																							
Breaded, fried	95	3½ oz	180	17.0	8.0	10	u	u	u	u	u	u	0.1	u	0	u	u	u	u	0.1	15	u	0
Steamed	95	3½ oz	105	22.0	1.5	3	110	320	u	250	455	u	0.1	2.8	0	u	0.06	1.3	u	u	18	1.1	u
Sesame seeds, hulled	40	¼ c	220	7.0	20.0	7	40	220	7	u	u	u	0.6	0.9	0	0.07	0.05	2.0	u	u	25	0	0
Sherbet, orange	95	½ c	135	1.0	2.0	30	50	75	8	45	100	0.6	0.02	0.1	90	0.01	0.04	tr	0.01	tr	7	0.1	2
Shrimp, canned	85	3 oz	100	20.5	0.9	0.6	100	225	45	u	105	1.8	0.1	2.7	60	0.01	0.03	1.5	0.05	0.2	6	u	0
French-fried	85	3 oz	190	17.5	9.5	8	60	160	40	160	195	0.8	0.3	1.8	u	0.03	0.06	2.5	0.05	0.3	5	0.6	0
Soups																							
Albondiga (meatballs in tomato broth)	240	1 c with 4 meatballs	340	18.5	21.4	17	25	175	u	180	460	u	u	3.6	500	0.2	0.2	5.0	0.6	0.7	10	1.2	8
Bean, with pork	250	1 c	170	8.0	6.0	22	65	130	u	1010	395	u	u	2.3	650	0.1	0.08	1.0	u	u	u	u	3
Bouillon, broth, consomme	240	1 c	30	5.0	0	3	tr	30	u	780	130	u	0.02	0.5	tr	tr	0.02	1.0	u	u	u	u	0
Cream soups, canned,																							
diluted with water	240	1 c	65	2.5	1.5	10	25	40	u	985	120	u	u	0.7	300	0.05	0.1	0.7	u	u	u	u	u
diluted with milk	245	1 c	150	7.0	6.0	17	175	160	u	1070	300	u	u	0.7	500	0.07	0.3	0.7	u	u	10	u	tr
Chicken noodle, from dry mix	240	1 c	55	2.0	1.5	8	7	20	u	580	20	0.1	0.1	0.2	50	0.07	0.05	0.5	u	u	u	u	0
Clam chowder, Manhattan	245	1 c	80	2.0	2.5	12	35	45	u	940	185	1.4	u	1.0	900	0.02	0.02	1.0	u	u	8	u	u
Onion	240	1 c	35	1.5	1.0	6	10	10	u	690	60	0.07	u	0.2	tr	tr	tr	tr	u	u	u	u	2
Split pea	245	1 c	140	8.5	3.0	20	30	150	15	940	270	1.0	0.2	1.5	450	0.2	0.2	1.5	0.1	0.2	2	0.4	tr
Tomato	245	1 c	90	2.0	2.5	16	15	35	15	970	230	0.2	0.2	0.7	1000	0.05	0.05	1.0	0.05	0.2	5	0	10
Vegetable beef	245	1 c	80	5.0	2.0	10	10	50	25	1050	160	0.4	0.1	0.7	2700	0.05	0.05	1.0	0.07	0.2	5	u	u
Spaghetti																							
Canned, with tomato sauce and meatballs	210	1 can, 7½ oz	250	10.4	12.8	23	20	120	u	1035	375	u	0.3	2.2	1030	0.15	0.2	3.4	u	u	u	u	u
Home recipe, with tomato sauce																							
with cheese	250	1 c	260	9.0	9.0	35	80	135	30	955	410	0.2	0.3	2.3	1100	0.2	0.2	2.5	0.1	0.8	2	0.6	15
with meatballs	250	1 c	330	18.5	11.5	40	125	235	40	1010	665	3.5	0.4	3.7	1600	0.2	0.3	4.0	0.4	0.5	15	0.6	20
Spinach, fresh or frozen, boiled	90	½ c	20	2.5	0.2	3	90	40	60	50	300	0.5	0.1	2.0	7300	0.06	0.1	0.4	0.2	0.2	60	0	20
Sprouts, raw																							
Alfalfa	100	1 c, packed	40	5.0	0.6	5	30	u	u	u	u	1.0	u	1.4	u	0.1	0.2	1.5	u	u	u	0	15
Mung bean	100	1 c	35	4.0	0.2	7	20	65	u	5	235	0.9	u	1.4	20	0.1	0.1	0.8	u	u	u	0	20
Soybean	100	1 c	50	6.5	1.5	6	50	70	u	u	u	1.6	u	1.1	80	0.2	0.2	0.8	u	u	u	0	15
Squash																							
Summer, boiled	90	½ c	10	0.8	0.1	3	20	20	15	1	125	0.2	0.07	0.4	350	0.04	0.07	0.7	0.2	0.1	2	0	9
Winter																							
baked	100	½ c	65	2.0	0.4	15	30	50	17	1	470	u	u	0.8	430	0.05	0.1	0.7	0.09	0.3	u	0	15
boiled	120	½ c	45	1.5	0.4	10	25	40	17	1	315	u	u	0.6	4300	0.05	0.1	0.5	0.1	0.3	u	0	10

tr — trace amounts
u — unknown thought to be present
0 — Absent or below detection level

Nutritive Values of the Edible Part of Foods

Food	Weight g	Approximate Measure	Energy Kcal	Protein g	Fat g	Total Carbohydrate g	Minerals: Calcium mg	Phosphorus mg	Magnesium mg	Sodium mg	Potassium mg	Zinc mg	Copper mg	Iron mg	Vitamins: Total Vitamin A Activity IU	Thiamin mg	Riboflavin mg	Niacin mg	Vitamin B-6 mg	Pantothenic Acid mg	Folacin (free) mcg	Vitamin B-12 mcg	Vitamin C mg
Strawberries																							
Fresh	100	⅔ c chole	35	0.7	0.5	8	20	20	12	1	165	0.08	u	1.0	60	0.03	0.07	0.6	0.06	0.3	15	0	60
Frozen, sweetened	170	⅔ c	160	0.7	0.3	40	20	25	14	2	180	u	u	1.0	50	0.03	0.1	0.9	0.07	0.2	15	0	95
Sugar																							
Brown	220	1 c, packed	820	0	0	210	185	40	u	65	765	u	0.7	7.5	0	0.02	0.07	0.4	u	u	u	0	0
White																							
granulated	200	1 c	770	0	0	200	0	0	0	2	5	0.1	0.04	0.2	0	0	0	0	0	0	0	0	0
	4	1 tsp	15	0	0	4	0	0	0	tr	tr	tr	tr	tr	0	0	0	0	0	0	0	0	0
powdered	8	1 tbsp	30	0	0	8	0	0	0	tr	tr	tr	tr	tr	0	0	0	0	0	0	0	0	0
Sunflower seeds, hulled	36	¼ c	200	8.5	17.0	7	45	305	13	10	335	u	0.6	2.6	20	0.7	0.08	2.0	0.4	0.5	u	0	0
Sweet potatoes																							
Baked in skin	145	1 potato, 5 in. × 2 in.	160	2.5	0.6	35	45	65	45	15	340	1.0	0.2	1.0	9200	0.1	0.08	0.8	0.05	1.0	10	0	25
Boiled in skin	130	½ c mashed	150	2.0	0.5	35	40	60	u	15	620	u	0.2	0.9	9200	0.1	0.08	0.8	0.3	1.0	9	0	20
Candied	105	½ medium	180	1.5	3.5	35	40	45	u	45	200	u	0.06	0.9	6600	0.06	0.04	0.4	u	u	7	0	10
Syrup, maple-flavored, artificial	20	1 tbsp	50	0	0	13	20	2	u	2	35	tr	0.08	0.2	0	0	0	0	0	0	0	0	0
Tacos, beef	80	1 taco	160	11.0	8.5	9	135	160	u	200	210	u	u	2.0	530	0.07	0.1	2.3	0.3	0.3	25	0.7	3
Tamales, canned	100	3½ oz	140	4.5	7.0	14	20	40	10	665	u	0.9	0.05	1.2	u	u	u	u	u	u	u	u	u
Home recipe, chicken	130	2 tamales	275	8.3	23.7	8	100	60	u	60	90	u	u	0.9	2800	0.05	0.1	2.7	0.2	0.3	1	0.1	7
Tea, instant	1	½ tsp	3	0	0	1	tr	u	4	u	45	u	u	tr	0	0	tr	tr	u	u	u	0	0
Tofu, soybean curd	120	1 piece, 2½ in. × 2¾ in. × 1 in.	85	9.5	5.0	3	155	150	130	10	50	u	u	2.3	0	0.07	0.04	0.1	u	u	u	0	0
Tomatoes, raw	135	1 medium	25	1.5	0.2	6	15	35	20	4	300	0.3	0.1	0.6	1100	0.07	0.05	0.9	0.1	0.4	25	0	30
Canned	120	½ c	25	1.0	0.2	5	5	25	15	155	260	0.2	0.2	0.6	1100	0.06	0.04	0.8	0.1	0.3	10	0	20
Tomato juice, canned	180	¾ c	35	1.5	0.2	8	15	35	20	365	415	u	0.1	1.6	1500	0.09	0.05	1.5	0.3	0.4	18	0	30
Tomato paste	130	½ c	110	4.5	0.5	25	35	90	25	50	1120	u	0.9	4.6	4300	0.3	0.2	4.0	0.5	0.6	25	0	65
Tongue, beef, braised	100	3½ oz	250	21.5	17.0	0.4	5	120	16	60	165	u	0.07	2.2	0	0.05	0.3	3.5	0.1	2.0	u	u	0
Tortillas																							
Corn, lime-treated	30	1, of 6-in. diameter	65	1.5	0.6	14	60	40	30	u	u	0.03	0.06	0.9	tr	0.04	0.02	0.3	0.02	0.03	tr	0	0
White flour	30	1, of 6-in. diameter	110	3.0	1.0	20	4	50	15	250	30	u	u	1.0	0	0.08	0.04	0.5	0.02	0.03	5	0	0
Tostada with beans and small portion of cheese	210	1 tostada	335	11.6	17.6	35	195	245	u	350	425	u	u	3.2	1650	0.3	0.2	1.3	0.2	0.4	10	0.2	10
Tuna. See Fish.																							
Turkey, roasted																							
Light meat	85	2 slices, each 4 in. × 2 in. × ¼ in.	150	28.0	3.5	0	7	200	20	70	350	1.8	0.2	1.0	u	0.04	0.1	9.5	0.3	0.5	3	0.4	0
Dark meat	85	4 slices, each 2½ in. × 1½ in. × ¼ in.	170	25.5	7.0	0	7	200	20	85	340	3.7	0.2	2.0	u	0.03	0.2	3.5	0.3	1.0	7	0.4	0
Turnips, boiled	80	½ c, cubed	20	0.6	0.2	4	25	20	10	25	145	0.07	0.03	0.3	tr	0.03	0.04	0.2	0.06	0.08	u	0	15
Turnip greens, boiled	70	½ c	15	1.5	0.2	3	135	25	20	u	u	u	u	0.8	4600	0.1	0.2	0.4	0.7	0.1	u	0	50
Veal cutlet, broiled	85	3 oz	180	23.0	9.5	0	10	195	20	55	260	4.1	0.04	2.7	0	0.06	0.2	4.5	0.3	0.8	15	1.6	0
Vinegar cider	15	1 tbsp	2	tr	0	1	1	1	u	tr	15	0.02	0.01	0.1	0	0	0	0	0	0	0	0	0
Waffles																							
Made from mix	75	1, of 7-in. diameter	210	6.5	8.0	25	180	260	20	515	145	u	u	1.0	200	0.1	0.2	0.7	u	0.5	u	u	0
Frozen	45	2 sections	120	3.0	4.0	16	130	195	u	340	u	u	u	0.5	u	0.04	0.05	0.5	u	u	u	u	0
Walnuts, English	100	1 c halves	650	15.0	64.0	16	100	380	135	2	450	2.8	0.9	3.1	30	0.3	0.1	0.9	0.7	0.9	45[16]	0	2
	15	2 tbsp, chopped	100	2.5	10.0	3	15	60	20	tr	70	0.4	0.1	0.4	10	0.06	0.02	0.2	0.1	0.1	5[16]	0	tr
Watercress, raw	35	10 sprigs	5	0.8	0.1	1	55	20	5	20	100	u	0.03	0.6	1700	0.03	0.06	0.3	0.04	0.1	70	0	30
Wheat bran, crude	30	1 oz	60	4.5	1.0	17	35	355	135	3	315	2.7	0.4	4.2	0	0.2	0.1	6.0	0.2	0.1	u	0	0
Wheat germ, raw	30	1 oz	100	7.5	3.0	13	20	315	90	tr	230	1.7	0.7	2.6	u	0.6	0.2	1.0	0.3	0.9	80	0	0
Toasted	30	1 oz	120	9.0	3.5	15	15	[illegible]	90	tr	285	1.7	0.7	2.5	50	0.5	0.2	1.5	0.3	0.4	u	0	0
Wine, dessert (18.8%)	105	3½ fl oz	140	0.1	0	8	10	[illegible]	5	4	75	0.1	0.08	0.4	u	0.01	0.02	0.2	0.04	0	0	0	0
Table (12.2%)	100	3½ fl oz	85	0.1	0	4	10	[illegible]	10	5	95	0.1	[illegible]	0.4	u	tr	0.01	0.1	0.04	0	0	0	0
Yeast																							
Dry, active	5	1 tbsp	20	2.5	0.1	3	3	[illegible]	3	4	140	u	0.2	1.1	tr	0.2	0.4	2.5	0.1	0.6	7	0	0
Brewer's, debittered	5	1 tbsp	25	3.0	0.1	3	15	140	10	10	150	u	u	1.4	tr	1.2	0.3	3.0	0.1	0.6	9	0	0
Yogurt																							
Low-fat																							
plain	230	8 fl oz carton	145	12.0	3.5	16	415	325	40	160	530	2.0	u	0.2	150	0.1	0.5	0.3	0.1	1.3	25	1.3	2
fruit, sweetened	230	8 fl oz carton	225	9.0	2.6	42	315	245	30	120	400	1.5	u	0.1	110	0.08	0.4	0.2	0.1	1.0	20	1.0	1
Regular																							
plain	230	8 fl oz carton	140	8.0	7.5	11	275	215	25	105	350	1.3	u	0.1	280	0.07	0.3	0.2	0.1	0.9	20	0.8	2

tr — trace amounts
u — unknown thought to be present
0 — Absent or below detection level